The Faber Book of Drink, Drinkers and Drinking

In the same series

THE FABER BOOK OF ANECDOTES
THE FABER BOOK OF APHORISMS
THE FABER BOOK OF CRICKET
THE FABER BOOK OF DIARIES
THE FABER BOOK OF FEVERS AND FRETS
THE FABER BOOK OF GAY SHORT FICTION
THE FABER BOOK OF LETTERS
THE FABER BOOK OF MADNESS
THE FABER BOOK OF REPORTAGE
THE FABER BOOK OF THE SEA
THE FABER BOOK OF SEDUCTIONS
THE FABER BOOK OF SOCCER
THE FABER BOOK OF TALES OF THE SEA
THE FABER BOOK OF THE TURF

The Faber Book of

DRINK, DRINKERS AND DRINKING

Simon Rae

faber and faber
LONDON · BOSTON

First published in 1991
by Faber and Faber Limited
3 Queen Square London WC1N 3AU

Photoset by Parker Typesetting Service, Leicester
Printed in England by Clays Ltd, St Ives plc

A CIP record for this book is available from the
British Library

ISBN 0-571-16229-0

In memory of my father, Alec Rae (1915–1989)
Bookseller and Keeper of the Booze-Bag

R.T.C. LIBRARY
LETTERKENNY

Contents

Editor's Preface

DRINKS

Punch *Larousse Gastronomique* 3
He Set Down the Empty Glass *George Orwell* 3
Port *Evelyn Waugh* 4
The Thread of Gold Cordial Flowed from the Bottle *Osip Mandelstam* 5
Queen Victoria's Tipple *Kingsley Amis* 5
Wine and Milk *Roland Barthes* 6
Wine Tasting *Evelyn Waugh* 9
First Thoughts on Wine *Kingsley Amis* 11
Mavrodaphne *Henry Miller* 11
A Good Sherris-Sack *William Shakespeare* 12
Look Out for the Police *Thomas Mann* 13
Elizabeth Taylor Dries Out *Truman Capote* 15
Champagne *Raymond Carver* 16
Pomagne *Blake Morrison* 19
Utilitarianism *Kingsley Amis* 20
Guid Ale Keeps the Heart Aboon *Robert Burns* 21
Local Brew *Garrison Keillor* 21
Lees *John Philips* 24
Great Things *Thomas Hardy* 25
A Real Drink *Stephen Potter* 25
A Drink with Something in It *Ogden Nash* 26
A Glass of Gin *Punch* 27
Ontology *Hermann Melville* 28
A Favour *Patrick Branwell Brontë* 28

Mouth Organ *J.-K. Huysmans* 28
Whiskey *Dr Guthrie* 30
Poor Stuff *James Boswell* 31
Blue Blazer *Jerry Thomas* 32
Bottles *Malcolm Lowry* 32
Real Absinthe *Ernest Hemingway* 33

HALF SEAS OVER

Dionysus *Ezra Pound* 37
Bacchus *John Milton* 41
Noah *François Rabelais* 42
Uncovered Within His Tent *Genesis* 42
Well, Maybe *Julian Barnes* 43

PHILOSOPHIES

A Drinking Song *W. B. Yeats* 47
Upon His Drinking a Bowl *John Wilmot, Earl of Rochester* 47
The Rolling English Road *G. K. Chesterton* 48
Hock and Soda Water *Lord Byron* 49
On the Need of Drinking *Charles Cotton* 50
Head and Bottle *Edward Thomas* 50
Water of Life *Macedonius* 51
Do You Want To Live Forever, Pig? *Strato* 51
Terence, This Is Stupid Stuff *A. E. Housman* 52
To a Nightingale *John Keats* 54
A Drunken Man's Praise of Sobriety *W. B. Yeats* 56
Wine Is Life *Petronius* 57
Tipple *Arthur Hugh Clough* 58
Epigram *Thomas Love Peacock* 58
The Discourse of the Drinkers *François Rabelais* 58
The Rubáiyát of Omar Khayyám *Edward Fitzgerald* 60

Why Time Spins Fast *Robert Browning* 63
The Flaw in Paganism *Dorothy Parker* 65
Credo *Charles Baudelaire* 65
A Sussex Drinking Song *Hilaire Belloc* 65
The Expense of Spirits *Wendy Cope* 66
The Toper's Rant *John Clare* 67
Drinking Song *Kingsley Amis* 68
The Whole Problem of Drinking *Patrick Hamilton* 69
On the Pleasures of Drink *Bertolt Brecht* 71
Instead *Jeffrey Bernard* 71

DRINKERS

Passing The Wine-Seller's *Wang Chi* 75
A Pint of Plain *Flann O'Brien* 75
Plague on't *Richard Brinsley Sheridan* 79
Mrs Gamp *Charles Dickens* 82
The Pig Woman *Ben Jonson* 84
Drunk *Martin Amis* 86
On the Courthouse Steps *Nelson Algren* 87
Communion Wine *Graham Greene* 91
I Have Conquered It *Jack London* 93
Bender *Henry Miller* 93
Molten Ruby *The Temperance Handbook* 95
Captain Hunter *Kingsley Amis* 95
The Brandy Glass *Louis MacNeice* 99
The Third Degree of Drink *William Shakespeare* 99
A Goodly Regimen *Samuel Pepys* 100
I Am Not Drunk *William Shakespeare* 103
Porson (Classical Scholar) *Lord Byron* 105
A Greek Professor's Ruin *The Temperance Handbook* 106
Mrs Botham *Martin Amis* 108

A Stiff Drink *William Dalrymple* 108
Daily Dose *George Melly* 109
Weak Stuff *James Boswell* 109
Achilles Heel *Dr James Currie* 110
News from Newstead Abbey *Lord Byron* 113
Squire Headlong *Thomas Love Peacock* 113
A Drunk Man Looks at the Thistle *Hugh MacDiarmid* 115
Hogmanay *Norman MacCaig* 118
Essentials *Jean Rhys* 119
Mead *Marco Polo* 122
A Wise Custom *Laurence Sterne* 123
Dull Intervals of Peace *Edward Gibbon* 123
German Drinkers *Samuel Taylor Coleridge* 124
Back in Beer-Territory *Patrick Leigh Fermor* 124
Stephano Remembers *James Simmons* 129
By Royal Command *Henry Fielding* 130
Under-Age Drinking at the Adelphi Hotel in Edinburgh – 1963
John Whitworth 131
The Card-Players *Philip Larkin* 131
Homecoming *Derek Mahon* 132
Tube *Dmitri Shostakovich* 133
Willie Brew'd a Peck o' Maut *Robert Burns* 134
Walking To Inveruplan *Norman MacCaig* 135
Nineties *Alan Jenkins* 136
Civilized Drinking, Civilized Chat *Fergus Pickering* 137
Chain Reaction *Tom Dardis* 137
Banish All the World *William Shakespeare* 138
The Drinker *Robert Lowell* 139
Valentine *Samuel Taylor Coleridge* 140
Dick Straightup *Ted Hughes* 141
Outback Male *Bruce Chatwin* 143
Uptown *Allen Ginsburg* 145

Atrocities *Siegfried Sassoon* 145
Casualty *Seamus Heaney* 146
Livings *Philip Larkin* 149
Drunks *John Berryman* 150
To Delmore Schwartz *Robert Lowell* 151
Hall of Fame *Mick Imlah* 152
'To Speak of Woe That Is in Marriage' *Robert Lowell* 154

CHILDREN

My Papa's Waltz *Theodore Roethke* 157
The Birth of Paul, and Another Battle *D. H. Lawrence* 157
Suspenders *Raymond Carver* 162
The Outing: A Story *Dylan Thomas* 163
First Drink *Jack London* 171
Aversion Therapy *Anne Brontë* 177
Come Home, Father *Henry Clay Work* 178
What's for My Dinner? *James Joyce* 179

INNS, PUBS AND TAVERNS

A Capital Tavern *James Boswell* 185
At Some Lone Alehouse *Matthew Arnold* 185
A Trampwoman's Tragedy *Thomas Hardy* 186
The Potwell Inn *H. G. Wells* 190
Ye Olde *Edward Thomas* 191
The Major *T. E. B. Clarke* 191
The Average Pub *George Orwell* 192
The Moon under Water *George Orwell* 194
Arrers *Richard Boston* 197
Darts Night *Simon Rae* 198
Inns *George Crabbe* 199
Villers *Alexander Pope* 201

The Village Inn *John Betjeman* 202
Good Mine Host *Ben Jonson* 204
McCabe *Richard Boston* 206
A Roach of the Taverns *Don Marquis* 209
Lord Landlord *Johannes Prinz* 212
The Maypole *Charles Dickens* 213

BARS AND CAFÉS

The Commodore Hotel Bar *Thomas Friedman* 221
Cocktail Hour *P. J. O'Rorke* 223
Two Young Men, 23 to 24 Years Old *C. P. Cavafy* 224
1 September, 1939 *W. H. Auden* 225
Cruising *Edmund White* 229
At Six O'Clock *John Berryman* 230
The Terminal Bar *Derek Mahon* 230

CELEBRATIONS

Prayer for Patroclus *Christopher Logue* 235
Water into Wine *St John* 236
Royal Wedding *Christopher Hibbert* 236
Divorce *Joseph Wechsberg* 238
Fleadh Cheoil *Pearse Hutchinson* 239
Enlisted by Bacchus *Horace* 242
A Reading *Walter Duranty* 242
Gargantua's Grief *François Rabelais* 244
Wake *Spike Milligan* 246

PARTIES

Etiquette *Aristophanes* 251
Dinner with Trimalcio *Petronius* 253

Who Goes There? *Lord Byron* 255
Unmasked *Patrick Leigh Fermor* 256
A Merrymaking in Question *Thomas Hardy* 259
A Party on Lundy *Evelyn Waugh* 259
Wet, Beige Morning *Dylan Thomas* 260
Vers de Société *Philip Larkin* 261
Read Us Your Play *John Updike* 262
The Select Party *Gavin Ewart* 271
Party Politics *Philip Larkin* 272

TROUBLE

A Light Fantastic Round *John Milton* 276
A Bet *Leo Tolstoy* 277
A Bear *Penelope Fitzgerald* 283
Night Club *Louis MacNeice* 286
Dangerfield *J. P. Donleavy* 286
Suck Hour *Thomas Pynchon* 289
Frogs *John Steinbeck* 290
About Coronation Ale *Graham Swift* 299
Bedlam Gates *Charles Dickens* 305

EFFECTS

Blotto Motto *Homer* 313
Intoxication *Sigmund Freud* 313
Now and Then *Robert Burns* 313
Three Things *William Shakespeare* 314
Brewer's Droop *Aristotle* 315
Wine as a Picklock *James Boswell* 315
In Vino Veritas? *Henry Fielding* 316
In the Drink *William Shakespeare* 316
Rotten Honey *William Golding* 321

Plunder *Edward Gibbon* 325
Prompting *Horace* 326
Seeing Double *Aristotle* 326
And so to Bed *Kingsley Amis* 326
Drink Me *William Faulkner* 328
To William Godwin *Samuel Taylor Coleridge* 328
To Robert Southey *Samuel Taylor Coleridge* 329
My First Dissipation *Charles Dickens* 331
Proof Reading *Henry Miller* 333
Behind Bars *Victor Hugo* 334
Dutch Courage *P. G. Wodehouse* 334
Chronic *Charles Dickens* 341

SIDE-EFFECTS

The Hellenistic Period *Hedylos* 351
Sow's Ear *Henry Fielding* 353
Drinking Song *Adrian Henri* 353
Franglais *Liz Lochhead* 353
Oozing Confidence *Martin Amis* 355
Rough Seas *Craig Raine* 356
Was it the Cockles? *Lord Byron* 358
It Was the Excitement *Evelyn Waugh* 359
It Was the Salmon *Charles Dickens* 359
It Was the Mixture *Evelyn Waugh* 361
Small Tudor Windows *Philip Larkin* 362
The Orifice of the Throat *Flann O'Brien* 363
Farewell to Paris *Henry Miller* 364
Unlucky for Some *Alan Sillitoe* 366
Observing the Decencies *Diana Athill* 367
Bedroom Farce *Geoffrey Chaucer* 371
7 Eccles Street *James Joyce* 371
Brook Green, Hammersmith *Rudyard Kipling* 381

AFTER-EFFECTS

All At Sea *Ezra Pound* 389
The Drunken Swine *Charles Cotton* 390
Alive Again *Kingsley Amis* 390
I Am Ill *William Golding* 391
Darkness At Noon *James Boswell* 392
The Morning After *Martin Amis* 394
Blah Blah Blah *Michael Frayn* 395
Spellbound *Homer* 403
You Were Perfectly Fine *Dorothy Parker* 407
The Skip *James Fenton* 407
If Grant Had Been Drinking at Appomattox *James Thurber* 410
TLS *John Berryman* 413
The Hangover *Kingsley Amis* 413
Tissue-Restorer *P. G. Wodehouse* 418

ILL-EFFECTS

All His Own Work? *Kingsley Amis* 423
An Eye for an Eye *Homer* 425
Trappists Silence Broken in Shoot-Out as Monks Defend
Monastery Wine *The Guardian* 427
The Wine of Astonishment *Psalms* 428
Desire of Wine *John Milton* 428
As Lords *John Milton* 428
Wine *Raymond Carver* 428
Erred Through Wine *Isaiah* 430
Opiates of the People *Frederick Engels* 430
Miracle *Raymond Carver* 431
Amid the Horrors *Robert Burns* 431
Past All Surgery *William Shakespeare* 435
Pure Genius *Daily Telegraph* 437

ADMONITIONS

Wine Hath Destroyed Many *Ecclesiasticus* 441
It Is Not for Kings *Proverbs* 441
Stanzas from *The Church-Porch* *George Herbert* 442
The Art of Getting Drunk *James Boswell* 443
Take My Advice *Nelson Algren* 443

RESOLUTIONS

Beer Only *Malcolm Lowry* 447
Giving Up *Martin Amis* 448
Bad Practice *James Boswell* 449

ROCK BOTTOM

Brief Reality *Jean Rhys* 455
The Black Man *Sergei Essenin* 459
Committed *John Berryman* 460
Bottle *Charles Jackson* 460
Small Hours *F. Scott Fitzgerald* 461
The Fell of Dark *Charles Jackson* 461
Why? *William Faulkner* 462
Terminal *F. Scott Fitzgerald* 462
Step One *John Berryman* 462
Pulley *Arthur and Barbara Gelb* 464
Bellevue And Back *Agnes Boulton* 464
Ecce Homo *Feodor Dostoevsky* 468
A Green Song *Wendy Cope* 469
Rough Stuff *John Healy* 470
Haven *Peter Reading* 471
Sneaking a Shit *John Healy* 471
Fuel *Peter Reading* 473

PRO AND CON

Legacy *Louis MacNeice* 477
Because Thou Art Virtuous *William Shakespeare* 477
Benevolence *James Boswell* 479
Bob Polter *W. S. Gilbert* 481
The Road that Leads from Competence and Peace *William Cowper* 485
Resources *John Milton* 486
Little Song *Bertolt Brecht* 487
Your Good Elf *Martin Amis* 488

ABSTINENCE AND TEMPERANCE

The Hissing Urn *William Cowper* 491
Pleasure versus Happiness *James Boswell* 491
Cumberland Water Authority *William Wordsworth* 491
His Fare-well to Sack *Robert Herrick* 492
Pulse Rate *The Temperance Handbook* 493
Death by Alcohol Is Murder *The Temperance Handbook* 494
The Brick Lane Branch *Charles Dickens* 495

LIQUOR AND THE LAW

How His Cold Was Cured *Thomas Hardy* 505
A Smuggler's Song *Rudyard Kipling* 509
Bootlegging in Slobodka *Anton Chekhov* 510
Gulag *Irina Ratushinskaya* 511
Prohibition *John Asbury* 512
Organized Crime *John Asbury* 517
Disorganized Crime *Saul Bellow* 519
A Raid *Eliot Ness* 521
Home Brew *William Faulkner* 522

Jake *John Asbury* 523
Good Time Charley's *Damon Runyon* 525
Abe North *F. Scott Fitzgerald* 525
Moonshine *Mary McCarthy* 526
No Good Liquor *Carson McCullers* 527

LAST ORDERS

Kerouac *Barry Miles* 531
Sonnet for Dick *Kit Wright* 531
Last Orders *Ciaran Carson* 532
Flood *D. H. Lawrence* 532
One Drunkard the Less *Emile Zola* 535
Over and Out *John O'Hara* 536
Sonnet: The Last Things *Gavin Ewart* 538
End of the Road *John Braine* 539
Epitaphs *Ezra Pound* 540
Finis *Isaiah* 540

Acknowledgements 542
Index 547

Editor's Preface

When I began thinking about this anthology some three years ago, I drew up a list of names and titles which convinced me there would be sufficient material. As I actually started reading for the book, I realized there was enough for any number of anthologies. Once you start looking, drink, drinkers and drinking crop up in the most astonishing variety of places, and this selection can have no claims to be definitive. However, as the section headings should indicate, I have made my choices with a view to providing a fully rounded portrait of our favourite drug, with as much space given to the ugly sides of alcohol as to its celebratory or hilarious aspects.

The anthology has been an enormous pleasure to compile. From the start the project attracted a widespread and generous interest. I was constantly asked, 'Have you thought of X?' or 'Are you going to put Y in?' My pockets bulged with scribbled-on backs of envelopes as my horizons were extended to include much that I would otherwise have overlooked.

Those whose suggestions have born fruit in the following pages are: Mike Adams, Mark Bland, Richard Boston, John Caperon, Lucy Carolan, Wendy Cope, Oliver Cyriax, Tony Lurcock, Michael McGregor, Felix Pryor, Christopher Reid, Susan Roberts, Ritchie Robertson, Nick Shave, John Whitworth, David Wilson and Robert Woof.

I am also happy to acknowledge a debt to Tom Dardis, from whose provocative study of four American alcoholic writers, *The Thirsty Muse*, I have lifted a clutch of striking quotations.

Special thanks are due to: Sue Fry, who tackled the onerous task of clearing permissions with her customary cheerfulness and efficiency; my mother, Jill Rae, who came to share a paper-littered flat over Christmas, and, in addition to keeping morale high generally, gave invaluable help with last-minute photocopying and card-indexing; and Jill Grey, who appointed herself my researcher for the crucial stages of the book's development. Boundlessly enthusiastic and highly efficient, Jill was also a constant source of ideas and suggestions. Without her the anthology would not have been completed on time; nor would its scope have been so wide.

Finally, I would like to thank Craig Raine for his energetic support and great editorial stamina, Malcolm Ward, my tireless copy-editor, Alexa Stace for her meticulous proof-reading, and my two desk-editors, Helen Gray and Mary Hill.

A NOTE ON THE TEXT

The contents of the anthology have been drawn from a wide variety of sources, most readily accessible in paperback. Deciding on the amount of detail to give each entry on the page has not been easy. Perhaps inconsistently, the titles of collections of short stories have been given but not the titles of collections from which poems have been taken. (This information will however be found in the Acknowledgements at the back of the book for work still in copyright.) Where a complete work – poetry or prose – is included I have of course used the author's own title, but I have taken the liberty of inventing titles for the excerpts which make up the majority of items. *McCabe* was written specially for the anthology by Richard Boston, to whom I owe particular thanks.

Simon Rae

DRINKS

Punch

PUNCH – A drink said to have originated among English sailors, and which, about 1552, consisted of a simple mixture of cane spirit and sugar, heated.

On 25 October 1599, Sir Edward Kennel, commander-in-chief of the English navy, offered to his ships' companies a monster punch which he had prepared in a vast marble basin. For his concoction he used 80 casks of brandy, 9 of water, 25,000 large limes, 80 pints of lemon juice, 13 quintals (1,300 pounds) of Lisbon sugar, 5 pounds of nutmeg and 300 biscuits, plus a great cask of Malaga.

A platform had been constructed over the basin to shelter it from the rain, and the serving was done by a ship's boy who sailed on this sea of punch in a rosewood boat. To serve the 6,000 guests one ship's boy had to be replaced by another several times, each one finding himself intoxicated by the fumes from the lake of alcohol at the end of a quarter of an hour.

Larousse Gastronomique

He Set Down the Empty Glass

O'Brien took the decanter by the neck and filled up the glasses with a dark-red liquid. It aroused in Winston dim memories of something seen long ago on a wall or a hoarding – a vast bottle composed of electric lights which seemed to move up and down and pour its contents into a glass. Seen from the top the stuff looked almost black, but in the decanter it gleamed like a ruby. It had a sour-sweet smell. He saw Julia pick up her glass and sniff at it with frank curiosity.

'It is called wine,' said O'Brien with a faint smile. 'You will have read about it in books, no doubt. Not much of it gets to the Outer Party, I am afraid.' His face grew solemn again, and he raised his glass: 'I think it is fitting that we should begin by drinking a health. To our Leader: To Emmanuel Goldstein.'

Winston took up his glass with a certain eagerness. Wine was a thing he had read and dreamed about. Like the glass paperweight or Mr Charrington's half-remembered rhymes, it belonged to the vanished, romantic past, the olden time as he liked to call it in his secret thoughts. For some reason he had always thought of wine as having an intensely sweet taste, like that of blackberry jam and an immediate intoxicating effect. Actually, when he came to swallow it, the stuff was distinctly disappointing. The truth was that after years of gin-drinking he could barely taste it. He set down the empty glass.

George Orwell, *Nineteen Eighty-four*

Port

Port is the wine proper to the heavy drinker, and it may be admitted that whereas champagne, claret, burgundy and hock are all entirely beneficial and indeed, in a well-ordered constitution, essential to the digestion of food, port, and the very finest port at that, can be slightly deleterious. Its charm insidiously invites excess, and excess of port, though not in itself harmful, sometimes discloses latent infirmities. The heavy port drinker must be prepared to make some sacrifice of personal beauty and agility. Its martyrs are usually well content with the bargain and in consolation it may be remarked that a red nose never lost a friend worth holding and that by universal testimony the sharpest attacks of gout are preceded by a period of peculiar mental lucidity . . . Port is not for the very young, the vain and the active. It is the comfort of age and the companion of the scholar and the philosopher. The particular qualities of British university scholarship – its alternations of mellow appreciation and acid criticism – may be plausibly derived from the habits of our Senior Common Rooms.

Evelyn Waugh *Wine in Peace and War*

The Thread of Gold Cordial Flowed from the Bottle

I said the grape vines live on like an antique battle,
with gnarled cavalry tangling in curving waves.
Here in stone-starred Tauris is an art of Hellas: here, rusted,
are the noble ranks of the golden acres.

Osip Mandelstam, trans. Clarence Brown & W. S. Merwin

Queen Victoria's Tipple

½ tumbler red wine
Scotch

I have it on the authority of Colm Brogan that the Great Queen was 'violently opposed to teetotalism, consenting to have one cleric promoted to a deanery only if he promised to stop advocating the pernicious heresy', and that the above was her dinner-table drink, 'a concoction that startled Gladstone' – as I can well believe.

The original recipe calls for claret, but anything better than the merely tolerable will be wasted. The quantity of Scotch is up to you, but I recommend stopping a good deal short of the top of the tumbler. Worth trying once.

Scholars will visualize, pouring in the whisky, the hand of John Brown, the Queen's Highland servant, confidant and possibly more besides; and I for one, if I listen carefully, can hear him muttering, 'Och, Your Majesty, dinna mak' yoursel' unweel wi' a' yon parleyvoo moothwash – ha'e a wee dram o' guid malt forbye.' Or words to that effect.

Kingsley Amis *Amis on Drink*

Wine and Milk

Wine is felt by the French nation to be a possession which is its very own, just like its three hundred and sixty types of cheese and its culture. It is a totem-drink, corresponding to the milk of the Dutch cow or the tea ceremonially taken by the British Royal Family. Bachelard has already given the 'substantial psychoanalysis' of this fluid, at the end of his essay on the reveries on the theme of the will, and shown that wine is the sap of the sun and the earth, that its basic state is not the moist but the dry, and that on such grounds the substance which is most contrary to it is water.

Actually, like all resilient totems, wine supports a varied mythology which does not trouble about contradictions. This galvanic substance is always considered, for instance, as the most efficient of thirst-quenchers, or at least this serves as the major alibi for its consumption ('It's thirsty weather'). In its red form, it has blood, the dense and vital fluid, as a very old hypostasis. This is because in fact its humoral form matters little; it is above all a converting substance, capable of reversing situations and states, and of extracting from objects their opposites – for instance, making a weak man strong or a silent one talkative. Hence its old alchemical heredity, its philosophical power to transmute and create *ex nihilo*.

Being essentially a function whose terms can change, wine has at its disposal apparently plastic powers: it can serve as an alibi to dream as well as reality, it depends on the users of the myth. For the worker, wine means enabling him to do his task with demiurgic ease ('heart for the work'). For the intellectual, wine has the reverse function: the local white wine or the beaujolais of the writer is meant to cut him off from the all too expected environment of cocktails and expensive drinks (the only ones which snobbishness leads one to offer him). Wine will deliver him from myths, will remove some of his intellectualism, will make him the equal of the proletarian; through wine, the intellectual comes nearer to a natural virility, and believes he can thus escape the curse that a century and a half of romanticism still brings to bear on the purely cerebral (it is well known that one of the myths peculiar to the modern intellectual is the obsession to 'have it where it matters').

But what is characteristic of France is that the converting power of wine is never openly presented as an end. Other countries drink to get drunk, and this is accepted by everyone; in France, drunkenness is a consequence, never an intention. A drink is felt as the spinning out of a pleasure, not as the necessary cause of an effect which is sought: wine is not only a philtre, it is also the leisurely act of drinking. The *gesture* has here a decorative value, and the power of wine is never separated from its modes of existence (unlike whisky, for example, which is drunk for its type of drunkenness – the most agreeable, with the least painful after-effects – which one gulps down repeatedly, and the drinking of which is reduced to a causal act).

All this is well known and has been said a thousand times in folklore, proverbs, conversations and Literature. But this very universality implies a kind of conformism: to believe in wine is a coercive collective act. A Frenchman who kept this myth at arm's length would expose himself to minor but definite problems of integration, the first of which, precisely, would be that of having to explain his attitude. The universality principle fully applies here, inasmuch as society calls anyone who does not believe in wine by *names* such as sick, disabled or depraved: it does not *comprehend* him (in both senses, intellectual and spatial, of the word). Conversely, an award of good integration is given to whoever is a practising wine-drinker: knowing *how* to drink is a national technique which serves to qualify the Frenchman, to demonstrate at once his performance, his control and his sociability. Wine gives thus a foundation for a collective morality, within which everything is redeemed: true, excesses, misfortunes and crimes are possible with wine, but never viciousness, treachery or baseness; the evil it can generate is in the nature of fate and therefore escapes penalization, it evokes the theatre rather than a basic temperament.

Wine is a part of society because it provides a basis not only for a morality but also for an environment; it is an ornament in the slightest ceremonials of French daily life, from the snack (plonk and camembert) to the feast, from the conversation at the local café to the speech at a formal dinner. It exalts all climates of whatever kind: in cold weather, it is associated with all the myths of becoming warm, and at the height of summer, with all the images of shade, with all things cool and sparkling. There is no situation involving some physical constraint (temperature, hunger, boredom, compulsion, disorientation) which does not give rise to dreams of wine. Combined as a basic substance with other alimentary figures, it can cover all the aspects of space and time for the Frenchman. As soon as one gets to know someone's daily life fairly well, the absence of wine gives a sense of shock, like something exotic: M. Coty, having allowed himself to be photographed, at the beginning of his seven years' presidency, sitting at home before a table on which a bottle of beer seemed to replace, by an extraordinary exception, the familiar litre of red wine, the whole nation was in a flutter; it was as intolerable as having a bachelor king. Wine is here a part of the reason of state.

Bachelard was probably right in seeing water as the opposite of wine: mythically, this is true; sociologically, today at least, less so; economic and historical circumstances have given this part to milk. The latter is now the true anti-wine: and not only because of M. Mendès-France's popularizing efforts (which had a purposely mythological look as when he used to drink milk during his speeches in the Chamber, as Popeye eats spinach), but also because in the basic morphology of substances milk is the opposite of fire by all the denseness of its molecules, by the creamy, and therefore soothing, nature of its spreading. Wine is mutilating, surgical, it transmutes and delivers; milk is cosmetic, it joins, covers, restores. Moreover, its purity, associated with the innocence of the child, is a token of strength, of a strength which is not revulsive, not congestive, but calm, white, lucid, the equal of reality. Some American films, in which the hero, strong and uncompromising, did not shrink from having a glass of milk before drawing his avenging Colt, have paved the way for this new Parsifalian myth. A strange mixture of milk and pomegranate, originating in America, is to this day sometimes drunk in Paris, among gangsters and hoodlums. But milk remains an exotic substance; it is wine which is part of the nation.

The mythology of wine can in fact help us to understand the

usual ambiguity of our daily life. For it is true that wine is a good and fine substance, but it is no less true that its production is deeply involved in French capitalism, whether it is that of the private distillers or that of the big settlers in Algeria who impose on the Muslims, on the very land of which they have been dispossessed, a crop of which they have no need, while they lack even bread. There are thus very engaging myths which are however not innocent. And the characteristic of our current alienation is precisely that wine cannot be an unalloyedly blissful substance, except if we wrongfully forget that it is also the product of an expropriation.

Roland Barthes *Mythologies*, trans. Annette Lavers

Wine Tasting

One day we went down to the cellars with Wilcox and saw the empty bays which had once held a vast store of wine; one transept only was used now; there the bins were well stocked, some of them with vintages fifty years old.

'There's been nothing added since his Lordship went abroad,' said Wilcox. 'A lot of the old wine wants drinking up. We ought to have laid down the eighteens and twenties. I've had several letters about it from the wine merchants, but her Ladyship says to ask Lord Brideshead, and he says to ask his Lordship, and his Lordship says to ask the lawyers. That's how we get low. There's enough here for ten years at the rate it's going, but how shall we be then?'

Wilcox welcomed our interest; we had bottles brought up from every bin, and it was during those tranquil evenings with Sebastian that I first made a serious acquaintance with wine and sowed the seed of that rich harvest which was to be my stay in many barren years. We would sit, he and I, in the Painted Parlour with three bottles open on the table and three glasses before each of us; Sebastian had found a book on wine-tasting, and we followed its instructions in detail. We warmed the glass slightly at a candle, filled it a third high, swirled the wine round, nursed it in our hands, held it to the light, breathed it, sipped it, filled our mouths with it, and rolled it over the tongue, ringing it on the palate like a coin on a counter, tilted our heads back and let it trickle down the throat. Then we talked of it and nibbled Bath Oliver biscuits, and passed on to another wine; then back to the first, then on to another, until all three were in circulation and the order of glasses got confused, and we fell out over which was which, and we passed the glasses to and fro between us until there were six glasses, some of them with mixed wines in them which we had filled from the wrong bottle, till we were obliged to start again with three clean glasses each, and the bottles were empty and our praise of them wilder and more exotic.

'. . . It is a little, shy wine like a gazelle.'

'Like a leprechaun.'

'Dappled, in a tapestry meadow.'

'Like a flute by still water.'

'. . . And this is a wise old wine.'

'A prophet in a cave.'

'. . . And this is a necklace of pearls on a white neck.'

'Like a swan.'

'Like the last unicorn.'

And we would leave the golden candlelight of the dining-room for the starlight outside and sit on the edge of the fountain, cooling our hands in the water and listening drunkenly to its splash and gurgle over the rocks.

'Ought we to be drunk *every* night?' Sebastian asked one morning.

'Yes, I think so.'

'I think so too.'

Evelyn Waugh *Brideshead Revisited*

First Thoughts on Wine

'Deep colour and big shaggy nose. Rather a jumbly, untidy sort of wine, with fruitiness shooting off one way, firmness another and body pushing about underneath. It will be as comfortable and as comforting as the 1961 Nuits-St-Georges once it has pulled its ends in and settled down.'

That genuine extract from a wine journal is the sort of thing that gets the stuff a bad name with a lot of people who would enjoy wine if they could face trying it seriously . . .

Kingsley Amis *Amis on Drink*

Mavrodaphne

Alexandros was beckoning to me. Lunch was ready. I saw that he had set the table for me alone. I insisted that he set a place for himself. I had difficulty persuading him to do so. I had to put my arm round him, point to the sky, sweep the horizon, include everything in one large gesture before I could induce him to consent to share the meal with me. He opened a bottle of black wine, a heady, molten wine that situated us immediately in the centre of the universe with a few olives, some ham and cheese. Alexandros was begging me to stay a few days. He got out the guest book to show me when the last visitor had arrived. The last visitor was a drunken American apparently who had thought it a good joke to sign the Duke of Windsor's name to the register, adding 'Oolala, what a night!' I glanced quickly over the signatures and discovered to my astonishment the name of an old friend of mine. I couldn't believe my eyes. I felt like crossing it out. I asked Alexandros if many Americans came to Phaestos. He said yes and from the glow in his eyes I gathered that they left liberal tips. I gathered that they liked the wine too.

I believe the wine was called *mavrodaphne*. If not it should have been because it is a beautiful black word and describes the wine perfectly. It slips down like molten glass, firing the veins with a heavy red fluid which expands the heart and the mind. One is heavy and light at the same time; one feels as nimble as the antelope and yet powerless to move. The tongue comes unloosed from its mooring, the palate thickens pleasurably, the hands describe thick, loose gestures such as one would love to obtain with a fat, soft pencil. One would like to depict everything in sanguine or Pompeian red with splashes of charcoal and lamp black. Objects become enlarged and blurred, the colours more true and vivid, as they do for the myopic person when he removes his glasses. But above all it makes the heart glow.

I sat and talked with Alexandros in the deaf and dumb language of the heart. In a few minutes I would have to go. I was not unhappy about it; there are experiences so wonderful, so unique, that the thought of prolonging them seems like the basest form of ingratitude. If I were not to go now then I should stay forever, turn my back on the world, renounce everything.

Henry Miller *The Colossus of Maroussi*

A Good Sherris-Sack

(*Exeunt all but Falstaff.*)

FALSTAFF: I would you had but the wit: 'twere better than your dukedom. Good faith, this same young sober-blooded boy doth not love me, nor a man cannot make him laugh: but that's no marvel, he drinks no wine. There's never any of these demure boys come to any proof: for thin drink doth so overcool their blood, and making many fish-meals, that they fall into a kind of male green-sickness: and then, when they marry, they get wenches. They are generally fools, and cowards; which some of us should be too, but for inflammation. A good sherris-sack hath a two-fold operation in it: it ascends me into the brain, dries me there all the foolish, and dull, and crudy vapours, which environ it: makes it apprehensive, quick, forgetive, full of nimble, fiery, and delectable shapes: which delivered o'er to the voice, the tongue, which is the birth, becomes excellent wit. The second property of your excellent sherris is, the warming of the blood: which before (cold, and settled) left the liver white, and pale; which is the badge of pusillanimity, and cowardice: but the sherris warms it, and makes it course from the inwards, to the parts extreme: it illumineth the face, which (as a beacon) gives warning to all the rest of this little kingdom, man, to arm: and then the vital commoners, and inland petty spirits, muster me all to their captain, the heart; who great, and puff'd up with this retinue, doth any deed of courage: and this valour comes of sherris. So that skill in the weapon is nothing, without sack (for that sets it a-work): and learning, a mere hoard of gold, kept by a devil, till sack commences it, and sets it in act, and use. Hereof comes it, that Prince Harry is valiant: for the cold blood he did naturally inherit of his father, he hath, like lean, sterile, and bare land, manured, husbanded, and till'd with excellent endeavour of drinking good, and good store of fertile sherris, that he is become very hot, and valiant. If I had a thousand sons, the first humane principle I would teach them, should be to forswear thin potations, and to addict themselves to sack.

William Shakespeare *Henry IV Part 2*

Look Out for the Police

My poor father owned the firm of Engelbert Krull, makers of the now discontinued brand of champagne *Loreley extra cuvée*. Their cellars lay on the bank of the Rhine not far from the landing, and often as a boy I used to linger in the cool vaults, wandering pensively along the stone-paved passages that led back and forth between the high shelves, examining the array of bottles, which lay on their sides in slanting rows. 'There you lie,' I thought to myself (though of course at that time I could not give such apt expression to my thoughts), 'there you lie in the subterranean twilight, and within you the bubbling golden sap is clearing and maturing, the sap that will enliven so many hearts and awaken a brighter gleam in so many eyes! Now you look plain and unpromising, but one day you will rise to the upper world magnificently adorned, to take your place at feasts, at weddings, to send your corks popping to the ceilings of private dining-rooms and evoke intoxication, irresponsibility, and desire in the hearts of men.' So, or approximately so, spoke the boy; and this much at least was true, the firm of Engelbert Krull paid unusual attention to the outside of their bottles, those final adornments that are technically known as the coiffure. The compressed corks were secured with silver wire and gilt cords fastened with purplish-red wax; there was, moreover, an impressive round seal – such as one sees on ecclesiastical bulls and old state documents – suspended from a gold cord; the necks of the bottles were liberally wrapped in gleaming silver foil, and their swelling bellies bore a flaring red label with gold flourishes round the edges. This label had been designed for the firm by my godfather Schimmelpreester and bore a number of coats of arms and stars, my father's monogram, the brand name, *Loreley extra cuvée*, all in gold letters, and a female figure, arrayed only in bangles and necklaces, sitting with legs crossed on top of a rock, her arm raised in the act of combing her flowing hair. Unfortunately it appears that the quality of the wine was not entirely commensurate with the splendour of its coiffure. 'Krull,' I have heard my godfather Schimmelpreester say to my father, 'with all due respect to you, your champagne ought to be forbidden by law. Last week I let myself be talked into drinking half a bottle, and my system hasn't recovered from the shock yet. What sort of vinegar goes into that brew? And do you use petroleum or fusel oil to doctor it with? The stuff's simply poison. Look out for the police!' At this my poor father would be embarrassed, for he was a gentle man and unable to hold his own against harsh criticism.

'It's easy enough for you to laugh, Schimmelpreester,' he would reply, gently stroking his belly with his fingertips in his usual fashion, 'but I have to keep the price down because there is so much prejudice against the domestic product – in short, I give the public something to increase its confidence. Besides, competition is so fierce, my friend, I'm hardly able to go on.' Thus my father.

Thomas Mann *Confessions of Felix Krull, Confidence Man*,
trans. Denver Lindley

Elizabeth Taylor Dries Out

She was very lively, though one could see she had undergone a massive ordeal. She was whiter by far than the hospital's bedsheets; her eyes, without make-up, seemed bruised and swollen, like a weeping child's. What she was recovering from was a form of pneumonia. 'My chest and lungs were filled with a sort of thick black fire. They had to cut a hole in my throat to drain out the fire. You see,' she said, pointing at a wound in her throat that was stopped with a small rubber plug. 'If I pull this out my voice disappears,' and she pulled it out, and indeed her voice did disappear, an effect which made me nervous, which made her merry.

She was laughing, but I didn't hear her laughter until she had reinserted the plug. 'This is the second time in my life that I felt – that I *knew* – I was dying. Or maybe the third. But this was the most real. It was like riding on a rough ocean. Then slipping over the edge of the horizon. With the roar of the ocean in my head. Which I suppose was really the noise of my trying to breathe. No,' she said, answering a question, 'I wasn't afraid. I didn't have time to be. I was too busy fighting. I didn't want to go over that horizon. And I never will. I'm not the type.'

Perhaps not; not like Marilyn Monroe and Judy Garland, both of whom had yearned to go over the horizon, some darker rainbow, and before succeeding, had attempted the voyage innumerable times. And yet there was some common thread between these three, Taylor, Monroe, Garland – I knew the last two fairly well, and yes, there *was* something. An emotional extremism, a dangerously greater need to be loved than to love, the hotheaded willingness of an incompetent gambler to throw good money after bad.

'Would you like some champagne?' she said, indicating a bottle of Dom Perignon cooling in a bucket beside the bed. 'I'm not supposed to have any. But – that. I mean when you've been through what I've been through. . . .' She laughed, and once more uncorked the throat incision, sending her laughter into soundless oblivion.

I opened the champagne, and filled two ugly white plastic hospital glasses.

She sighed. 'Hmm, that's good. I really like only champagne. The trouble is, it gives you permanently bad breath. Tell me, have you ever thought you were dying?'

Truman Capote *Portrait of Elizabeth Taylor*

Champagne

He no longer had any appetite for literary work, and hadn't for a long time. In fact, he had very nearly failed to complete *The Cherry Orchard* the year before. Writing that play was the hardest thing he'd ever done in his life. Towards the end, he was able to manage only six or seven lines a day. 'I've started losing heart,' he wrote Olga. 'I feel I'm finished as a writer, and every sentence strikes me as worthless and of no use whatever.' But he didn't stop. He finished his play in October 1903. It was the last thing he ever wrote, except for letters and a few entries in his notebook.

A little after midnight on 2 July 1904, Olga sent someone to fetch Dr Schwöhrer. It was an emergency: Chekhov was delirious. Two young Russians on holiday happened to have the adjacent room, and Olga hurried next door to explain what was happening. One of the youths was in his bed asleep, but the other was still awake, smoking and reading. He left the hotel at a run to find Dr Schwöhrer. 'I can still hear the sound of the gravel under his shoes in the silence of that stifling July night,' Olga wrote later on in her memoirs. Chekhov was hallucinating, talking about sailors, and there were snatches of something about the Japanese. 'You don't put ice on an empty stomach,' he said when she tried to place an ice pack on his chest.

Dr Schwöhrer arrived and unpacked his bag, all the while keeping his gaze fastened on Chekhov, who lay gasping in the bed. The sick man's pupils were dilated and his temples glistened with sweat. Dr Schwöhrer's face didn't register anything. He was not an emotional man, but he knew Chekhov's end was near. Still, he was a doctor, sworn to do his utmost, and Chekhov held on to life, however tenuously. Dr Schwöhrer prepared a hypodermic and administered an injection of camphor, something that was supposed to speed up the heart. But the injection didn't help – nothing, of course, could have helped. Nevertheless, the doctor made known to Olga his intention of sending for oxygen. Suddenly, Chekhov roused himself, became lucid, and said quietly, 'What's the use? Before it arrives I'll be a corpse.'

Dr Schwöhrer pulled on his big moustache and stared at Chekhov. The writer's cheeks were sunken and grey, his complexion waxen; his breath was raspy. Dr Schwöhrer knew the time could be reckoned in minutes. Without a word, without conferring with Olga, he went over to an alcove where there was a telephone on the wall. He read the instructions for using the device. If he activated it by holding his finger on a button and turning a handle on the side of the phone, he could reach the lower regions of the hotel – the kitchen. He picked up the receiver, held it to his ear, and did as the instructions told him. When someone finally answered, Dr Schwöhrer ordered a bottle of the hotel's best champagne. 'How many glasses?' he was asked. 'Three glasses!' the doctor shouted into the mouthpiece. 'And hurry, do you hear?' It was one of those rare moments of inspiration that can easily enough be overlooked later on, because the action is so entirely appropriate it seems inevitable.

The champagne was brought to the door by a tired-looking young man whose blond hair was standing up. The trousers of his uniform were wrinkled, the creases gone, and in his haste he'd missed a loop while buttoning his jacket. His appearance was that of someone who'd been resting (slumped in a chair, say, dozing a little), when off in the distance the phone had clamoured in the early-morning hours – great God in Heaven! – and the next thing he knew he was being shaken awake by a superior and told to deliver a bottle of Moët to Room 211. 'And hurry, do you hear?'

The young man entered the room carrying a silver ice bucket with the champagne in it and a silver tray with three cut-crystal glasses. He found a place on the table for the bucket and glasses, all the while craning his neck, trying to see into the other room, where someone panted ferociously for breath. It was a dreadful, harrowing sound, and the young man lowered his chin into his collar and turned away as the ratchety breathing worsened. Forgetting himself, he stared out the open window towards the darkened city. Then this big imposing man with a thick moustache pressed some coins into his hand – a large tip, by the feel of it – and suddenly the young man saw the door open. He took some steps and found himself on the landing, where he opened his hand and looked at the coins in amazement.

Methodically, the way he did everything, the doctor went about the business of working the cork out of the bottle. He did it in such a way as to minimize, as much as possible, the festive explosion. He poured three glasses and, out of habit, pushed the cork back into the neck of the bottle. He then took the glasses of champagne over to the bed. Olga momentarily released her grip on Chekhov's hand – a hand, she said later, that burned her fingers. She arranged another pillow behind his head. Then she put the cool glass of champagne against Chekhov's palm and made sure his fingers closed around the stem. They exchanged looks – Chekhov, Olga, Dr Schwöhrer. They didn't touch glasses. There was no toast. What on earth was there to drink to? To death? Chekhov summoned his remaining strength and said, 'It's been so long since I've had champagne.' He brought the glass to his lips and drank. In a minute or two Olga took the empty glass from his hand and set it on the nightstand. Then Chekhov turned on to his side. He closed his eyes and sighed. A minute later, his breathing stopped.

Dr Schwöhrer picked up Chekhov's hand from the bed-sheet. He held his fingers to Chekhov's wrist and drew a gold watch from his vest pocket, opening the lid of the watch as he did so. The second hand on the watch moved slowly, very slowly. He let it move around the face of the watch three times while he waited for signs of a pulse. It was three o'clock in the morning and still sultry in the room. Badenweiler was in the grip of its worst heat wave in years. All the windows in both rooms stood open, but there was no sign of a breeze. A large, black-winged moth flew through a window and banged wildly against the electric lamp. Dr Schwöhrer let go of Chekhov's wrist. 'It's over,' he said. He closed the lid of his watch and returned it to his vest pocket.

At once Olga dried her eyes and set about composing herself. She thanked the doctor for coming. He asked if she wanted some medication – laudanum, perhaps, or a few drops of valerian. She shook her head. She did have one request, though: before the authorities were notified and the newspapers found out, before the time came when Chekhov was no longer in her keeping, she wanted to be alone with him for a while. Could the doctor help with this? Could he withhold, for a while anyway, news of what had just occurred?

Dr Schwöhrer stroked his moustache with the back of a finger. Why not? After all, what difference would it make to anyone whether this matter became known now or a few hours from now? The only detail that remained was to fill out a death certificate, and this could be done at his office later in the morning, after he'd slept a few hours. Dr Schwöhrer nodded his agreement and prepared to leave. He murmured a few words of condolence. Olga inclined her head. 'An honour,' Dr Schwöhrer said. He picked up his bag and left the room and, for that matter, history.

It was at this moment that the cork popped out of the champagne bottle; foam spilled down on to the table. Olga went back to Chekhov's bedside. She sat on a footstool, holding his hand, from time to time stroking his face. 'There were no human voices, no everyday sounds,' she wrote. 'There was only beauty, peace, and the grandeur of death.'

Raymond Carver 'Errand' *Elephant and Other Stories*

Pomagne

'Be careful not to spill it when it pops.
He'd bloody crucify me if he caught us.'

We had taken months to get to this,
our first kiss a meeting of stalagmite

and stalactite. The slow drip of courtship:
her friend June interceding with letters,

the intimate struggle each Friday
under the Plaza's girder of light.

But here we were at last, drinking Pomagne
in her parent's double bed, Christmas Eve

and the last advent-calendar door.
'Did you hear the gate click?' 'No, did you?'

Blake Morrison

Utilitarianism

Sandra sat on Bowen's lap, though not at his suggestion. He soon began thinking about beer. He wanted a pint of English beer, but not because of its nationality or anything like that. Although Portuguese beer tasted much less of bone-handled knives than other continental beers, it still wasn't as nice as English beer. He thought of the time when Barbara, after a bad night with Sandra, had accused him at two hundred words a minute of pretending to like beer because he thought it was working-class, British, lower-middle-class, Welsh, anti-foreign, anti-upper-class, anti-London, anti-intellectual, British and proletarian. He had replied more slowly that she was mistaken if she thought he would deny himself large gins-and-tonic or magnums of sparkling red Burgundy just because nasty people liked them too. (How he thrilled to both the idea and the name of sparkling red Burgundy. Other entities had this same strange double appeal: rhythm and blues, dinotherium, deposit account. Little article there?) He had added to Barbara that beer was cheaper while still sharing with gin and Burgundy the property of making him drunk. This last factor had received insufficient acclaim. He thought to himself now that if ever he went into the brewing business his posters would have written across the top 'Bowen's Beer', and then underneath that in the middle a picture of Mrs Knowles drinking a lot of it and falling about, and then across the bottom in bold or salient lettering the words '*Makes You Drunk*'.

Kingsley Amis *I Like It Here*

Guid Ale Keeps the Heart Aboon

O gude ale comes and gude ale goes;
Gude ale gars me sell my hose,
Sell my hose, and pawn my shoon –
Gude ale keeps my heart aboon!

I had sax owsen in a pleugh,
And they drew a' weel eneugh:
I sell'd them a' just ane by ane –
Gude ale keeps the heart aboon!

Gude ale hauds me bare and busy,
Gars me moop wi' the servant hizzie,
Stand i' the stool when I hae done –
Gude ale keeps the heart aboon!

Robert Burns

Local Brew

Saint Wendell's beer, brewed by the Dimmers family at the old Dimmers Brewery in nearby Saint Wendell's for five generations, since their ancestor evaded the selective-service system of the Prince of Prussia and fled to the New World. He also skipped out on some debts in the process and broke the hearts of three young women who had the impression they would become Mrs Dimmers as soon as he paid his debts and finished military service. The young rounder came to Minnesota and became rich and distinguished making beer. He thought at first of calling it Dimmers beer but listened to good advice and called it Saint Wendell's. For as long as anyone remembers, men in the little taverns around Mist County

Aboon, high; *owsen*, oxen; *ane*, one; *gars*, forces me to; *hauds*, keeps; *moop*, meddle; *hizzie*, hussy; *stool*, repentance or cutty stool.

have said, 'Gimme a Wendy,' and some bartenders don't ask, they just give you a Wendy, and if you say, 'I didn't ask for that,' they say, 'Where'd you say you were from?'

'I don't believe I said.'

'Good. I don't want to know.'

Wendy's is the beer a man drinks because it is the best. It's made from the deep wellwater from the town of Saint Wendell's, there's no water like it. People from all over the world have said so: it's good water. Saint Wendell's has a municipal faucet, and people drive up with a trunk full of plastic bottles and get a month's supply. A Frenchman came and got two gallons and took it home. This is true. French customs wasn't going to let him take it through, but then they tasted it and said 'Ahhhhh,' and those men were French, and the French make great water themselves. Wendy's is made from it, using an old German recipe, by people who have worked for Dimmers Brewery so long they don't remember if they were hired or if they took a vow. The old brick brewery was supposed to resemble a Bavarian castle, but when it was built, in 1879, bricklayers had beer rights: there was two-fisted day-long drinking on the job. When the layers got on high scaffolding, it made them dizzy. So the building starts out to be a castle and rises royally for two stories and then it quits and becomes a sort of barn. The bricks for the towers were used to make a brick road because the layers felt more comfortable on their hands and knees. The brick road is a hundred feet wide for about seventy-five feet and then it's seventy-five feet wide for one hundred feet and then it becomes a path.

You think of this as you sit in an old dim bar and drink a Wendy, and you think of how the beer wagons kept rolling in Saint Wendell's through Prohibition. They trained the horses to make the deliveries, and these smart Percherons memorized complicated beer routes – stop here, skip two houses, stop there – and when they stopped, a guy ran out of the house and grabbed his beer. The horses didn't make change but they did everything else, but of course if a horse got on the sauce himself, he might get mixed up, but usually they did the job and if the sheriff came, all he found was a wagon and a horse with red eyes and bad breath.

A man thinks of the Dimmerses' history when he drinks a Wendy, especially the first Dimmers, who ran away from responsibility, shirked his duty to his country, reneged on his debts, seduced women and lied to them – but, hey, who's perfect? Those are the very sins a man goes into a tavern to contemplate committing.

You think of history while sitting in a bar unchanged in your lifetime, and you feel peaceable: the long mirror, the neon beer signs, the old oak back bar with glass doors and columns and dark figures (angels or trolls) at the top, brooding, and below them the Minnesota Twins scoreboard (that's what they're brooding about) and the old Swancrest radio, the fancy cut glasses in the cabinet for drinks nobody knows how to make, drinks with swizzle sticks – they don't use those here. Wally's nephew tended bar once and put ice and sweet vermouth in Mr Berge's whiskey and said, 'Here, try this.' Mr Berge didn't see the swizzle stick, though it had a big fleur-de-lis on the end. When Mr Berge removed the fleur-de-lis from his left nostril, he bled a little, but he was peaceable. He only said, 'Sonny, don't do that again unless you tell me , and then don't do it anyway. Gosh, it hurts.'

In Minneapolis, you go to any hotel or shopping mall and find an English pub or a Western saloon or small-town tavern with a name like BILLY BOB'S, but the antiques come from the antique factory and the concept was developed by a design team – the city is full of new places made to look old, but those aren't the same as a joint where people have sat for fifty years, and all of them people you know. It's the difference between a lie and the truth. It's not true that Wendy's is the best beer in the world, actually it's not that good. And it gives me terrible gas. The fact that we can sit and say it's the best and defend it against superior brews is one more reason why it *is* the best, and maybe the gas helps us do that.

Garrison Keillor 'A Glass of Wendy' *Leaving Home*

Lees

He'll tread the circling Path 'till dewy Eve,
From early Day-spring, pleas'd to find his Age
Declining, not unusual to his Lord.
Some, when the Press, by utmost Vigour screw'd,
Has drain'd the pulpous Mass, regale their Swine
With the dry Refuse; thou, more wise shalt steep
Thy Husks in Water, and again employ
The pondrous Engine. Water will imbibe
The small Remains of Spirit, and acquire
A vinous Flavour; this the Peasants blith
Will quaff, and whistle, as thy tinkling Team
They drive, and sing of *Fusca's* radiant Eyes,
Pleas'd with the medly Draught. Nor shalt thou now
Reject the *Apple-Cheese*, tho' quite exhaust;
Ev'n now 'twill cherish, and improve the Roots
Of sickly Plants; new Vigor hence convey'd
Will yield an Harvest of unusual Growth.
Such Profit springs from Husks discreetly us'd!

John Philips *Cyder* Book II

Great Things

Sweet cyder is a great thing,
A great thing to me,
Spinning down to Weymouth town
By Ridgway thirstily,
And maid and mistress summoning
Who tend the hostelry:
O cyder is a great thing,
A great thing to me!

The dance it is a great thing,
 A great thing to me,
With candles lit and partners fit
 For night-long revelry;
And going home when day-dawning
 Peeps pale upon the lea:
O dancing is a great thing,
 A great thing to me!

Love is, yea, a great thing,
 A great thing to me,
When, having drawn across the lawn
 In darkness silently,
A figure flits like one a-wing
 Out from the nearest tree:
O love is, yes, a great thing,
 A great thing to me!

Will these be always great things,
 Great things to me? . . .
Let it befall that One will call,
 'Soul, I have need of thee:'
What then? Joy-jaunts, impassioned flings,
 Love, and its ecstasy,
Will always have been great things,
 Great things to me!

Thomas Hardy

A Real Drink

But if in real difficulties, remember that there are moments when the pickaxe is a more useful instrument than the most delicate surgeon's forceps. And I shall always remember Odoreida thrusting aside sixteen founder members of the Wine and Food Society with a 'Well, let's have a real drink,' and throwing together a mixture which left them breathless.

'Pop-skull, they called it in Nevada,'* he said, and poured two parts of vodka into one of sherry and three of rum, adding a slice cut from the disc of a sunflower.

*A basic subdivision of Winemanship is the US hard-drink gambit and the question of its counters. The US gambit is to be amused when anybody orders sherry, and to flock round and watch it being drunk, particularly in a club at six o'clock. It is an exaggeration to say that they expect the drinker to bring out knitting or start reading *Old Mother Goose*, but they are interested.

Nevertheless, the deliberate drinking of sherry will wear many US men down, particularly, of course, if it is mixed with a rather pi-faced lecture on the American 'inability to enjoy wine' and a richly exaggerated account of one's own national habits with drink, making your audience really believe that every typical British family serves a different wine at a different temperature with every course.

A wholly different counter to the US, icy hard-drink gambit, based on our management of religious men, is to go one better. Serve drinks yourself so cold that they are frozen to the glass and have to be filed out and chewed. Let your Martinis be mixed in a much stronger proportion of gin to vermouth than six to one, in fact, some counter-US experts pour vermouth into the glass and then pour it out again, lightly mopping the sides with their handkerchiefs, and then fill the glass with what is, of course, neat gin. Another ploy is to invent some 'little drink' or name of a drink which 'everybody is drinking in Nevada' (all Americans admire the suggestion that you have been to Nevada). Call it not 'Frozen Larynx' or 'Surgeon's Knife', which is 1937–8, but Martini, mixing two absolute disparates as in the Odoreida Iceberg described above. Then peck at it and say, 'Oh for a real Martini – a big Martini, one you can pull over your head like a jersey' (phrase of US Lifeman 46, reported to me in April 1952 by USI).

Stephen Potter *One-Upmanship*

A Drink with Something in It

There is something about a Martini,
A tingle remarkably pleasant;
A yellow, a mellow Martini;
I wish that I had one at present.
There is something about a Martini,
Ere the dining and dancing begin,
And to tell you the truth,
It is not the vermouth –
I think that perhaps it's the gin.

Ogden Nash

A Glass of Gin

Gin! Gin! A glass of Gin! What magnified monsters encircle therein! Ragged and stained with filth and mud, Some plague-spotted, and some with blood, Shapes of misery, shame and sin! Figures that make us loathe and tremble, Creatures scarce human, that more resemble Broods of diabolical kin, Ghoul and Vampire, Demon and din. Gin! Gin! A Glass of Gin! THE DRAM OF SATAN! The LIQUOR OF SIN! Distilled from the fell Alembic of hell. Guilt and Death, his own brother and twin! That man might fall Still lower than all The meanest creatures with scale and fin. Gin! Gin! A Glass of Gin! When darkly adversity's days set in, And friends and peers, Of earlier years, No longer can trace, A familiar face, Because, poor rat! He has no cravat; A seedy coat, and a hole in that! No sole to his shoe, and no brim to his hat; No gloves, no vest – Either second or best; No credit, no cash, No cold mutton to hash. No bread – nor even potatoes to mash; Till weary of life, Its worry and strife, Black visions are rife, Of a razor or knife! Gin! Gin! A Glass of Gin! Oh! then its tremendous temptations begin. To take alas! To the fatal Glass – And happy the wretch that it does not win, To change the black hue, of his ruin to blue, While Angels sorrow and Demons grin, To see him plunge into the Palace of Gin

The World's Temperance Reciter *Punch* 1843

Ontology

Have ready a bottle of brandy, because I always feel like drinking that heroic drink when we talk ontological heroics together.

Herman Melville to Nathaniel Hawthorne, 29 June 1851

A Favour

Dear John,

I shall feel very much obliged to you if you can contrive to get me Five pence worth of Gin in a proper measure.

Should it be speedily got I could perhaps take it from you or Billy at the lane top, or, what would be quite as well, sent out for, to you.

I anxiously ask the favour because I know the good it will do me.

Punctually at Half-past Nine in the morning you will be paid the 5d. out of a shilling given me then. – Yours, P. B. B.

Patrick Branwell Brontë to John Brown, 1848

Mouth Organ

He shut the window again. This quick change, straight from the torrid heat of the room to the biting cold of midwinter had taken his breath away; and curling up beside the fire again, it occurred to him that a drop of spirits would be the best thing to warm him up.

He made his way to the dining-room, where there was a cupboard built into one of the walls containing a row of little barrels, resting side-by-side on tiny sandalwood stands and each broached at the bottom with a silver spigot.

This collection of liqueur casks he called his mouth organ.

A rod could be connected to all the spigots, enabling them to be turned by one and the same movement, so that once the apparatus was in position it was only necessary to press a button concealed in the wainscoting to open all the conduits simultaneously and so fill with liqueur the minute cups underneath the taps.

The organ was then open. The stops labelled 'flute', 'horn', and 'vox angelica' were pulled out, ready for use. Des Esseintes would drink a drop here, another there, playing internal symphonies to himself, and providing his palate with sensations analogous to those which music dispenses to the ear.

Indeed, each and every liqueur, in his opinion, corresponded in taste with the sound of a particular instrument. Dry curaçao, for instance, was like the clarinet with its piercing, velvety note; kümmel like the oboe with its sonorous, nasal timbre; crème de menthe and anisette like the flute, at once sweet and tart, soft and shrill. Then to complete the orchestra there was kirsch, blowing a wild trumpet blast; gin and whisky raising the roof of the mouth with the blare of their cornets and trombones; marc-brandy matching the tubas with its deafening din; while peals of thunder came from the cymbal and the bass drum, which arak and mastic were banging and beating with all their might.

He considered that this analogy could be pushed still further and that string quartets might play under the palatal arch, with the violin represented by an old brandy, choice and heady, biting and delicate; with the viola simulated by rum, which was stronger, heavier, and quieter; with vespetro as poignant, drawn-out, sad, and tender as a violoncello; and with the double-bass a fine old bitter, full-bodied, solid, and dark. One might even form a quintet, if this were thought desirable, by adding a fifth instrument, the harp, imitated to near perfection by the vibrant savour, the clear, sharp, silvery note of dry cumin.

The similarity did not end there, for the music of liqueurs had its own scheme of interrelated tones; thus, to quote only one example, Benedictine represents, so to speak, the minor key corresponding to the major key of those alcohols which wine-merchants' scores indicate by the name of green Chartreuse.

Once these principles had been established, and thanks to a series of erudite experiments, he had been able to perform upon his tongue silent melodies and mute funeral marches; to hear inside his mouth crème-de-menthe solos and rum-and-vespetro duets.

He even succeeded in transferring specific pieces of music to his palate, following the composer step by step, rendering his intentions, his effects, his shades of expression, by mixing or contrasting related liqueurs, by subtle approximations and cunning combinations.

At other times he would compose melodies of his own, executing pastorals with the sweet blackcurrant liqueur that filled his throat with the warbling song of a nightingale; or with the delicious cacaochouva that hummed sugary bergerets like the *Romances of Estelle* and the *'Ah! vous dirai-je, maman'* of olden days.

But tonight Des Esseintes had no wish to listen to the taste of music; he confined himself to removing one note from the keyboard of his organ, carrying off a tiny cup which he had filled with genuine Irish whiskey.

He settled down in his armchair again and slowly sipped this fermented spirit of oats and barley, a pungent odour of creosote spreading through his mouth.

J. K. Huysmans *Against Nature*, trans. Robert Baldick

Whiskey

'Whiskey. – There is nothing like whiskey in this world for preserving a man when he is dead; but it is one of the worst things in the world for preserving a man when he is living. If you want to keep a dead man, put him in whiskey – if you want to kill a living man, put the whiskey into him. It was a capital thing for preserving the dead admiral when they put him into a rum puncheon; but it was a bad thing for the sailors when they tapped the cask and drank the liquor, till they had left the admiral, as he had never left his ship, high and dry.'

Dr Guthrie *The Temperance Handbook*

Poor Stuff

Wednesday, 7 April 1779. I dined with him at Sir Joshua Reynolds's. I have not marked what company was there. Johnson harangued upon the qualities of different liquors; and spoke with great contempt of claret, as so weak, that 'a man would be drowned by it before it made him drunk.' He was persuaded to drink one glass of it, that he might judge, not from recollection which might be dim, but from immediate sensation. He shook his head, and said, 'Poor stuff! No, Sir, claret is the liquor for boys; port, for men; but he who aspires to be a hero (smiling,) must drink brandy. In the first place, the flavour of brandy is most grateful to the palate; and then brandy will do soonest for a man what drinking *can* do for him. There are, indeed, few who are able to drink brandy. That is a power rather to be wished for than attained. And yet, (proceeded he,) as in all pleasure hope is a considerable part, I know not but fruition comes too quick by brandy. Florence wine I think the worst; it is wine only to the eye; it is wine neither while you are drinking it, nor after you have drunk it; it neither pleases the taste, nor exhilarates the spirits.' I reminded him how heartily he and I used to drink wine together, when we were first acquainted; and how I used to have a head-ache after sitting up with him. He did not like to have this recalled, or, perhaps, thinking that I boasted improperly, resolved to have a witty stroke at me: 'Nay, Sir, it was not the *wine* that made your head ache, but the *sense* that I put into it.' BOSWELL. 'What, Sir! will sense make the head ache?' JOHNSON. 'Yes, Sir, (with a smile,) when it is not used to it.' – No man who has a true relish of pleasantry could be offended at this: especially if Johnson in a long intimacy had given him repeated proofs of his regard and good estimation. I used to say, that as he had given me a thousand pounds in praise, he had a good right now and then to take a guinea from me.

James Boswell *Life of Johnson*

Blue Blazer

The inventor of this drink was formerly principal bartender at the Metropolitan Hotel, New York, and the Planter's House, St Louis. 'He was the greatest drink mixer of his age', Herbert Asbury.

Use two large silver-plated mugs, with handles.

One wineglass of scotch whiskey. One wineglass boiling water..

Put the whiskey and the boiling water in one mug, ignite the liquid with fire, and while blazing mix both ingredients by pouring them four or five times from one mug to the other. If well done this will have the appearance of a continued stream of liquid fire.

Sweeten with one tablespoon of pulverized white sugar, and serve in a small bar tumbler, with a piece of lemon peel.

The *Blue Blazer* does not have a very euphonious or classic name, but it tastes better to the palate than it sounds to the ear. A beholder gazing for the first time upon an experienced artist compounding this beverage, would naturally come to the conclusion that it was a nectar for Pluto rather than Bacchus. The novice in mixing this beverage should be careful not to scald himself. To become proficient in throwing the liquid from one mug to the other, it will be necessary to practise for some time with cold water.

Jerry Thomas *The Bon Vivant's Guide, or How to Mix Drinks*

Bottles

The Consul dropped his eyes at last. How many bottles since then? In how many glasses, how many bottles had he hidden himself, since then alone? Suddenly he saw them, the bottles of aguardiente, of anis, of jerez, of Highland Queen, the glasses, a babel of glasses – towering, like the smoke from the train that day – built to the sky, then falling, the glasses toppling and crashing, falling downhill from the Generalife Gardens, the bottles breaking, bottles of Oporto, tinto, blanco, bottles of Pernod, Oxygénée, absinthe, bottles smashing, bottles cast aside, falling with a thud on the ground in parks, under benches, beds, cinema seats, hidden in drawers at Consulates, bottles of Calvados dropped and broken, or bursting into smithereens, tossed into garbage heaps, flung into the sea, the Mediterranean, the Caspian, the Caribbean, bottles floating in the ocean, dead Scotchmen on the Atlantic highlands – and now he saw them, smelt them, all from the very beginning – bottles, bottles, bottles, and glasses, glasses, glasses, of bitter, of Dubonnet, of Falstaff, Rye, Johnny Walker, Vieux Whisky, *blanc* Canadien, the apéritifs, the digestifs, the demis, the dobles, the *noch ein* Herr Obers, the *et glas* Araks, the *tusen taks*, the bottles, the bottles, the beautiful bottles of tequila, and the gourds, gourds, gourds, the millions of gourds of beautiful mescal . . . The Consul sat very still. His conscience sounded muffled with the roar of water. It whacked and whined round the wooden frame-house with the spasmodic breeze, massed, with the thunderclouds over the trees, seen through the windows, its factions. How indeed could he hope to find himself to begin again when, somewhere, perhaps, in one of those lost or broken bottles, in one of those glasses, lay, for ever, the solitary clue to his identity? How could he go back and look now, scrabble among the broken glass, under the eternal bars, under the oceans?

Malcolm Lowry *Under the Volcano*

Real Absinthe

Robert Jordan pushed the cup toward him. It was a milky yellow now with the water and he hoped the gipsy would not take more than a swallow. There was very little left and one cup of it took the place of the evening papers, of all the old evenings in cafés, of all chestnut trees that would be in bloom now in this month, of the great slow horses of the outer boulevards, of bookshops, of kiosks, and of galleries, of the Parc Montsouris, of the Stade Buffalo, and of the Butte Chaumont, of the Guaranty Trust Company and the Ile de la Cité, of Foyot's old hotel, and of being able to read and relax in the evening; of all the things he had enjoyed and forgotten and that came back to him when he tasted that opaque, bitter, tongue-numbing, brain-warming, stomach-warming, idea-changing liquid alchemy.

The gipsy made a face and handed the cup back. 'It smells of anis but it is bitter as gall,' he said. 'It is better to be sick than have that medicine.'

'That's the wormwood,' Robert Jordan told him. 'In this, the real absinthe, there is wormwood. It's supposed to rot your brain out but I don't believe it. It only changes the ideas. You should pour water into it very slowly, a few drops at a time. But I poured it into the water.'

'What are you saying?' Pablo said angrily, feeling the mockery.

'Explaining the medicine,' Robert Jordan told him and grinned. 'I bought it in Madrid. It was the last bottle and it's lasted me three weeks.' He took a big swallow of it and felt it coasting over his tongue in delicate anaesthesia. He looked at Pablo and grinned again.

'How's business?' he asked.

Ernest Hemingway *For Whom the Bell Tolls*

HALF SEAS OVER

Dionysus

Hang it all, Robert Browning,
there can be but the one 'Sordello'.
But Sordello, and my Sordello?
Lo Sordels si fo di Mantovana.
So-shu churned in the sea.
Seal sports in the spray-whited circles of cliff-wash,
Sleek head, daughter of Lir,
eyes of Picasso
Under black fur-hood, lithe daughter of Ocean;
And the wave runs in the beach-groove:
'Eleanor, ἑλέναυς and ἑλέπτολις!'
And poor old Homer blind, blind, as a bat,
Ear, ear for the sea-surge, murmur of old men's voices:
'Let her go back to the ships,
Back among Grecian faces, lest evil come on our own,
Evil and further evil, and a curse cursed on our children,
Moves, yes she moves like a goddess
And has the face of a god
and the voice of Schoeney's daughters,
And doom goes with her in walking,
Let her go back to the ships,
back among Grecian voices.'
That by the beach-run, Tyro,
Twisted arms of the sea-god,
Lithe sinews of water, gripping her, cross-hold,
And the blue-gray glass of the wave tents them,
Glare azure of water, cold-welter, close cover.
Quiet sun-tawny sand-stretch,
The gulls broad out their wings,
nipping between the splay feathers;
Snipe come for their bath,
bend out their wing-joints,
Spread wet wings to the sun-film,

And by Scios,
        to left of the Naxos passage,
Naviform rock overgrown,
        algæ cling to its edge,
There is a wine-red glow in the shallows,
        a tin flash in the sun-dazzle.

The ship landed in Scios,
        men wanting spring-water,
And by the rock-pool a young boy loggy with vine-must,
        'To Naxos? Yes, we'll take you to Naxos,
Cum' along lad.' 'Not that way!'
'Aye, that way is Naxos.'
        And I said: 'It's a straight ship.'
And an ex-convict out of Italy
        knocked me into the fore-stays,
(He was wanted for manslaughter in Tuscany)
        And the whole twenty against me,
Mad for a little slave money.
        And they took her out of Scios
And off her course . . .
        And the boy came to, again, with the racket,
And looked out over the bows,
        and to eastward, and to the Naxos passage.
God sleight then, god-sleight:
        Ship stock fast in sea-swirl,
Ivy upon the oars, King Pentheus,
        grapes with no seed but sea-foam,
Ivy in scupper-hole.
Aye, I Acœtes, stood there,
        and the god stood by me,
Water cutting under the keel,
Sea-break from stern forrards,
        wake running off from the bow,
And where was gunwale, there now was vine-trunk,
And tenthril where cordage had been,
        grape-leaves on the rowlocks,

Heavy vine on the oarshafts,
And, out of nothing, a breathing,
        hot breath on my ankles,
Beasts like shadows in glass,
        a furred tail upon nothingness.
Lynx-purr, and heathery smell of beasts,
        where tar smell had been,
Sniff and pad-foot of beasts,
        eye-glitter out of black air.
The sky overshot, dry, with no tempest,
Sniff and pad-foot of beasts,
        fur brushing my knee-skin,
Rustle of airy sheaths,
        dry forms in the *æther*.
And the ship like a keel in ship-yard,
        slung like an ox in smith's sling,
Ribs stuck fast in the ways,
        grape-cluster over pin-rack,
        void air taking pelt.
Lifeless air become sinewed,
        feline leisure of panthers,
Leopards sniffing the grape shoots by scupper-hole,
Crouched panthers by fore-hatch,
And the sea blue-deep about us,
        green-ruddy in shadows,
And Lyæus: 'From now, Acœtes, my altars,
Fearing no bondage,
        Fearing no cat of the wood,
Safe with my lynxes,
        feeding grapes to my leopards,
Olibanum is my incense,
        the vines grow in my homage.'
The back-swell now smooth in the rudder-chains,
Black snout of a porpoise
        where Lycabs had been,
Fish-scales on the oarsmen.
        And I worship.

I have seen what I have seen.
        When they brought the boy I said:
'He has a god in him,
        though I do not know which god.'
And they kicked me into the fore-stays.
I have seen what I have seen:
        Medon's face like the face of a dory,
Arms shrunk into fins. And you, Pentheus,
Had as well listen to Tiresias, and to Cadmus,
        or your luck will go out of you.
Fish-scales over groin muscles,
        lynx-purr amid sea . . .
And of a later year,
        pale in the wine-red algæ,
If you will lean over the rock,
        the coral face under wave-tinge,
Rose-paleness under water-shift,
        Ileuthyeria, fair Dafne of sea-bords,
The swimmer's arms turned to branches,
Who will say in what year,
        fleeing what band of tritons,
The smooth brows, seen, and half seen,
        now ivory stillness.
So-shu churned in the sea, So-shu also,
        using the long moon for a churn-stick . . .
Lithe turning of water,
        sinews of Poseidon,
Black azure and hyaline,
        glass wave over Tyro,
Close cover, unstillness,
        bright welter of wave-cords,
Then quiet water,
        quiet in the buff sands,
Sea-fowl stretching wing-joints,
        splashing in rock-hollows and sand-hollows
In the wave-runs by the half-dune;
Glass-glint of wave in the tide-rips against sunlight,

pallor of Hesperus,
Grey peak of the wave,
wave, colour of grape's pulp,

Olive grey in the near,
far, smoke grey of the rock-slide,
Salmon-pink wings of the fish-hawk
cast grey shadows in water,
The tower like a one-eyed great goose
cranes up out of the olive-grove,

And we have heard the fauns chiding Proteus
in the smell of hay under the olive-trees.
And the frogs singing against the fauns
in the half-light.
And . . .

Ezra Pound *Canto* II

Bacchus

Bacchus, that first from out the purple grape
Crushed the sweet poison of misusèd wine,
After the Tuscan mariners transformed,
Coasting the Tyrrhene shore, as the winds listed,
On Circe's island fell. (Who knows not Circe,
The daughter of the Sun? whose charmèd cup
Whoever tasted, lost his upright shape,
And downward fell into a groveling swine.)
This nymph that gazed upon his clust'ring locks,
With ivy berries wreathed, and his blithe youth,
Had by him, ere he parted thence, a son
Much like his father, but his mother more,
Whom therefore she brought up and Comus named;
Who, ripe and frolic of his full-grown age,
Roving the Celtic and Iberian fields,

At last betakes him to this ominous wood,
And, in thick shelter of black shades imbow'red,
Excels his mother at her mighty art,
Off'ring to every weary traveller
His orient liquor in a crystal glass,
To quench the drouth of Phoebus, which as they taste
(For most do taste through fond intemperate thirst),
Soon as the potion works, their human count'nance,
Th' express resemblance of the gods, is changed
Into some brutish form of wolf, or bear,
Or ounce, or tiger, hog, or bearded goat,
All other parts remaining as they were;
And they, so perfect is their misery,
Not once perceive their foul disfigurement,
But boast themselves more comely than before
And all their friends, and native home forget
To roll with pleasure in a sensual sty.

John Milton *Comus*

Noah

Noah, that holy man, to whom we are so much beholding, bound, and obliged, for that he planted to us the vine, from whence we have that nectarian, delicious, precious, heavenly, joyful, and deific liquor, which they call *piot* or *tiplage*, was deceived in the drinking of it, for he was ignorant of the great virtue and power thereof.

François Rabelais *Gargantua and Pantagruel*,
trans. Sir Robert Urquhart

Uncovered Within His Tent

And Noah began to be an husbandman, and he planted a vineyard: and he drank of the wine, and was drunken; and he was uncovered within his tent.

And Ham, the father of Canaan, saw the nakedness of his father, and told his two brethren without.

And Shem and Japheth took a garment and laid it upon both their shoulders, and went backward, and covered the nakedness of their father: and their faces were backward, and they saw not their father's nakedness.

And Noah awoke from his wine, and knew what his younger son had done unto him.

And he said, Cursed be Canaan; a servant of servants shall he be unto his brethren.

And he said, Blessed be the Lord God of Shem; and Canaan shall be his servant.

God shall enlarge Japheth, and he shall dwell in the tents of Shem; and Canaan shall be his servant.

And Noah lived after the flood three hundred and fifty years.

And all the days of Noah were nine hundred and fifty years: and he died.

Genesis 9: 20–29

Well, Maybe

Take the story of Noah's nakedness – you remember? It happened after the Landing. Noah, not surprisingly, was even more pleased with himself than before – he'd saved the human race, he'd ensured the success of his dynasty, he'd been given a formal covenant by God – and he decided to take things easy in the last three hundred and fifty years of his life. He founded a village (which you call Arghuri) on the lower slopes of the mountain, and spent his days dreaming up new decorations and honours for himself: Holy Knight of the Tempest, Grand Commander of the Squalls, and so on. Your sacred text informs you that on his estate he planted a vineyard. Ha! Even the least subtle mind can decode that particular euphemism: he was drunk all the time. One night, after a particularly hard session, he'd just finished undressing when he collapsed on the bedroom floor – not an unusual occurrence. Ham and his brothers happened to be passing his 'tent' (they still used the old sentimental desert word to describe their palaces) and called in to check that their alcoholic father hadn't done himself any harm. Ham went into the bedroom and . . . well, a naked man of six hundred and fifty odd years lying in a drunken stupor is not a pretty sight. Ham did the decent, the filial thing: he got his brothers to cover their father up. As a sign of respect – though even at that time the custom was passing out of use – Shem and the one beginning with J entered their father's chamber backwards, and managed to get him into bed without letting their gaze fall on those organs of generation which mysteriously incite your species to shame. A pious and honourable deed all round, you might think. And how did Noah react when he awoke with one of those knifing new-wine hangovers? He cursed the son who had found him and decreed that all Ham's children should become servants to the family of the two brothers who had entered his room arse-first. Where is the sense in that? I can guess your explanation: his sense of judgment was affected by drink, and we should offer pity not censure. Well, maybe. But I would just mention this: *we* knew him on the Ark.

He was a large man, Noah – about the size of a gorilla, although there the resemblance ends. The flotilla's captain – he promoted himself to Admiral halfway through the Voyage – was an ugly old thing, both graceless in movement and indifferent to personal hygiene. He didn't even have the skill to grow his own hair except around his face; for the rest of his covering he relied on the skins of other species. Put him side by side with the gorilla and you will easily discern the superior creation: the one with graceful movement, superior strength and an instinct for delousing. On the Ark we puzzled ceaselessly at the riddle of how God came to choose man as His protégé ahead of the more obvious candidates. He would have found most other species a lot more loyal. If He'd plumped for the gorilla, I doubt there'd have been half so much disobedience – probably no need to have had the Flood in the first place.

Julian Barnes *A History of the World in 10½ Chapters*

PHILOSOPHIES

A Drinking Song

Wine comes in at the mouth
And love comes in at the eye;
That's all we shall know for truth
Before we grow old and die.
I lift the glass to my mouth,
I look at you, and I sigh.

W. B. Yeats

Upon his Drinking a Bowl

Vulcan contrive me such a Cup,
  As *Nestor* us'd of old;
Shew all thy skill to trim it up,
  Damask it round with *Gold*.

Make it so large, that fill'd with *Sack*,
  Up to the swelling brim,
Vast Toasts, on the delicious *Lake*,
  Like *Ships* at *Sea* may swim.

Engrave no *Battail* on his Cheek,
  With *War*, I've nought to do;
I'm none of those that took *Mastrich*,
  Nor *Yarmouth Leager* knew.

Let it no name of *Planets* tell,
  Fixt *Stars*, or *Constellations*;
For I am not Sir *Sydrophell*,
  Nor none of his *Relations*.

But carve thereon a spreading *Vine*,
Then add Two lovely *Boys*;
Their Limbs in Amorous folds intwine,
The *Type* of future joys.

Cupid, and *Bacchus*, my Saints are,
May drink, and Love, still reign,
With *Wine*, I wash away my cares,
And then to *Cunt* again.

John Wilmot, Earl of Rochester

The Rolling English Road

Before the Roman came to Rye or out to Severn strode,
The rolling English drunkard made the rolling English road.
A reeling road, a rolling road, that rambles round the shire,
And after him the parson ran, the sexton and the squire;
A merry road, a mazy road, and such as we did tread
The night we went to Birmingham by way of Beachy Head.

I knew no harm of Bonaparte and plenty of the Squire,
And for to fight the Frenchman I did not much desire;
But I did bash their baggonets because they came arrayed
To straighten out the crooked road an English drunkard made,
Where you and I went down the lane with ale-mugs in our hands,
The night we went to Glastonbury by way of Goodwin Sands.

His sins they were forgiven him; or why do flowers run
Behind him; and the hedges all strengthening in the sun?
The wild thing went from left to right and knew not which was which,
But the wild rose was above him when they found him in the ditch.
God pardon us, nor harden us; we did not see so clear
The night we went to Bannockburn by way of Brighton Pier.

My friends, we will not go again or ape an ancient rage,
Or stretch the folly of our youth to be the shame of age,
But walk with clearer eyes and ears this path that wandereth,
And see undrugged in evening light the decent inn of death;
For there is good news yet to hear and fine things to be seen
Before we go to Paradise by way of Kensal Green.

G. K. Chesterton

Hock and Soda Water

Few things surpass old wine; and they may preach
  Who please – the more because they preach in vain.
Let us have wine and woman, mirth and laughter,
Sermons and soda water the day after.

Man being reasonable must get drunk;
  The best of life is but intoxication.
Glory, the grape, love, gold, in these are sunk
  The hopes of all men and of every nation;
Without their sap, how branchless were the trunk
  Of life's strange tree, so fruitful on occasion.
But to return. Get very drunk, and when
You wake with headache, you shall see what then.

Ring for your valet, bid him quickly bring
  Some hock and soda water. Then you'll know
A pleasure worthy Xerxes, the great king;
  For not the blest sherbet, sublimed with snow,
Nor the first sparkle of the desert spring,
  Nor Burgundy in all its sunset glow,
After long travel, ennui, love, or slaughter,
Vie with that draught of hock and soda water.

Lord Byron *Don Juan* Canto II

Εἰς τὸ δεῖν πίνειν
(On the Need of Drinking)

Paraphrased from Anacreon

The earth with swallowing drunken showers
  Reels a perpetual round,
And with their healths the trees and flowers
  Again drink up the ground.

The sea, of liquor spuing full,
  The ambient air doth sup,
And thirsty Phoebus at a pull
  Quaffs off the ocean's cup.

When stagg'ring to a resting place,
  His bus'ness being done,
The moon, with her pale platter face,
  Comes and drinks up the sun.

Since elements and planets then
  Drink an eternal round,
'Tis much more proper sure for men
  Have better liquor found.

Why may not I then, tell me pray,
Drink and be drunk as well as they?

Charles Cotton

Head and Bottle

The downs will lose the sun, white alyssum
Lose the bees' hum;
But head and bottle tilted back in the cart
Will never part

Till I am cold as midnight and all my hours
Are beeless flowers.
He neither sees, nor hears, nor smells, nor thinks,
But only drinks,
Quiet in the yard where tree trunks do not lie
More quietly.

Edward Thomas

Water of Life

Interfering quacks, they said
To cut the scotch or drop down dead.
I did, and spent the week in bed.
But that was then, and now I'm well
The lot of them can go to hell.
My best physician's Doctor Bell.

Macedonius *The Greek Anthology*, 11.61,
trans. Fergus Pickering

Do You Want to Live for Ever, Pig?

Drink and fuck, my little chuck,
Do it till we're out of luck,
Screw and booze and booze and screw,
Lose a few and draw a few,
Exercising arms and cocks
Till they screw us in the box,
Alcohol and tit and bum
To the crematorium.

Strato *The Greek Anthology* 11.19,
trans. Fergus Pickering

Terence, This Is Stupid Stuff

'Terence, this is stupid stuff:
You eat your victuals fast enough;
There can't be much amiss, 'tis clear,
To see the rate you drink your beer.
But oh, good Lord, the verse you make,
It gives a chap the belly-ache.
The cow, the old cow, she is dead;
It sleeps well, the horned head:
We poor lads, 'tis our turn now
To hear such tunes as killed the cow.
Pretty friendship 'tis to rhyme
Your friends to death before their time
Moping melancholy mad:
Come, pipe a tune to dance, to, lad.'

Why, if 'tis dancing you would be,
There's brisker pipes than poetry.
Say, for what were hop-yards meant,
Or why was Burton built on Trent?
Oh many a peer of England brews
Livelier liquor than the Muse,
And malt does more than Milton can
To justify God's ways to man.
Ale, man, ale's the stuff to drink
For fellows whom it hurts to think:
Look into the pewter pot
To see the world as the world's not.
And faith, 'tis pleasant till 'tis past:
The mischief is that 'twill not last.

Oh I have been to Ludlow fair
And left my necktie God knows where,
And carried half-way home, or near,
Pints and quarts of Ludlow beer:

Then the world seemed none so bad,
And I myself a sterling lad;
And down in lovely muck I've lain,
Happy till I woke again.
Then I saw the morning sky:
Heigho, the tale was all a lie;
The world, it was the old world yet,
I was I, my things were wet,
And nothing now remained to do
But begin the game anew.

Therefore, since the world has still,
Much good, but much less good than ill,
And the sun and moon endure
Luck's a chance, but trouble's sure,
I'd face it as a wise man would,
And train for ill and not for good.
'Tis true, the stuff I bring for sale
Is not so brisk a brew as ale:
Out of a stem that scored the hand
I wrung it in a weary land.
But take it: if the smack is sour,
The better for the embittered hour;
It should do good to heart and head
When your soul is in my soul's stead;
And I will friend you, if I may,
In the dark and cloudy day.

There was a king reigned in the East:
There, when kings will sit to feast,
They get their fill before they think
With poisoned meat and poisoned drink.
He gathered all that springs to birth
From the many-venomed earth;
First a little, thence to more,
He sampled all her killing store;
And easy, smiling, seasoned sound,

Sate the king when healths went round.
They put arsenic in his meat
And stared aghast to watch him eat;
They poured strychnine in his cup
And shook to see him drink it up:
They shook, they stared as white's their shirt:
Them it was their poison hurt.
– I tell the tale that I heard told.
Mithridates, he died old.

A. E. Housman

To a Nightingale

My heart aches, and a drowsy numbness pains
  My sense, as though of hemlock I had drunk,
Or emptied some dull opiate to the drains
  One minute past, and Lethe-wards had sunk:
'Tis not through envy of thy happy lot,
  But being too happy in thy happiness, –
    That thou, light-wingèd Dryad of the trees,
        In some melodious plot
  Of beechen green, and shadows numberless,
    Singest of summer in full-throated ease.

O for a draught of vintage, that hath been
  Cooled a long age in the deep-delvèd earth,
Tasting of Flora and the country-green,
  Dance, and Provençal song, and sun-burnt mirth!
O for a beaker full of the warm South,
  Full of the true, the blushful Hippocrene,
    With beaded bubbles winking at the brim,
        And purple-stainèd mouth;
  That I might drink, and leave the world unseen,
    And with thee fade away into the forest dim:

Fade far away, dissolve, and quite forget
  What thou among the leaves hast never known,
The weariness, the fever, and the fret
  Here, where men sit and hear each other groan;
Where palsy shakes a few, sad, last grey hairs,
  Where youth grows pale, and spectre-thin, and dies;
    Where but to think is to be full of sorrow
      And leaden-eyed despairs;
  Where beauty cannot keep her lustrous eyes,
    Or new Love pine at them beyond to-morrow.

Away! away! for I will fly to thee,
  Not charioted by Bacchus and his pards,
But on the viewless wings of Poesy,
  Though the dull brain perplexes and retards:
Already with thee! tender is the night,
  And haply the Queen-Moon is on her throne,
    Clustered around by all her starry Fays;
      But here there is no light,
  Save what from heaven is with the breezes blown
    Through verdurous glooms and winding mossy ways

I cannot see what flowers are at my feet,
  Nor what soft incense hangs upon the boughs,
But, in embalmèd darkness, guess each sweet
  Wherewith the seasonable month endows
The grass, the thicket, and the fruit-tree wild;
  White hawthorn, and the pastoral eglantine;
    Fast-fading violets covered up in leaves;
      And mid-May's eldest child,
  The coming musk-rose, full of dewy wine,
    The murmurous haunt of flies on summer eves.

Darkling I listen; and for many a time
  I have been half in love with easeful Death,
Called him soft names in many a musèd rhyme,
  To take into the air my quiet breath;

Now more than ever seems it rich to die,
To cease upon the midnight with no pain,
While thou art pouring forth thy soul abroad
In such an ecstasy!
Still wouldst thou sing, and I have ears in vain –
To thy high requiem become a sod.

Thou wast not born for death, immortal Bird!
No hungry generations tread thee down;
The voice I hear this passing night was heard
In ancient days by emperor and clown:
Perhaps the self-same song that found a path
Through the sad heart of Ruth, when, sick for home,
She stood in tears amid the alien corn;
The same that oft-times hath
Charmed magic casements, opening on the foam
Of perilous seas, in faery lands forlorn.

Forlorn! the very word is like a bell
To toll me back from thee to my sole self.
Adieu! the fancy cannot cheat so well
As she is famed to do, deceiving elf.
Adieu! adieu! thy plaintive anthem fades
Past the near meadows, over the still stream,
Up the hill-side; and now 'tis buried deep
In the next valley-glades:
Was it a vision, or a waking dream?
Fled is that music: – do I wake or sleep?

John Keats

A Drunken Man's Praise of Sobriety

Come swish around, my pretty punk,
And keep me dancing still
That I may stay a sober man

Although I drink my fill.

Sobriety is a jewel
That I do much adore;
And therefore keep me dancing
Though drunkards lie and snore.
O mind your feet, O mind your feet,
Keep dancing like a wave,
And under every dancer
A dead man in his grave.
No ups and downs, my pretty,
A mermaid, not a punk;
A drunkard is a dead man,
And all dead men are drunk.

W. B. Yeats

Wine Is Life

Carefully sealed wine bottles were immediately brought, their necks labelled:

FALERNIAN
CONSUL OPIMIUS
ONE HUNDRED YEARS OLD

While we were examining the labels, Trimalchio clapped his hands and said with a sigh:

'Wine has a longer life than us poor folks. So let's wet our whistles. Wine is life. I'm giving you real Opimian. I didn't put out such good stuff yesterday, though the company was much better class.'

Naturally we drank and missed no opportunity of admiring his elegant hospitality. In the middle of this a slave brought in a silver skeleton, put together in such a way that its joints and backbone could be pulled out and twisted in all directions. After he had flung it about on the table once or twice, its flexible joints falling into various postures, Trimalchio recited:

'O woe, woe, man is only a dot:
Hell drags us off and that is the lot;
So let us live a little space,
At least while we can feed our face.'

Petronius *The Satyricon*, trans. J. P. Sullivan

Tipple

We sit at our tables and tipple champagne;
Ere one bottle goes, comes another again;
The waiters they skip and they scuttle about,
And the landlord attends us so civilly out.
  So pleasant it is to have money, heigh ho!
  So pleasant it is to have money.

Arthur Hugh Clough *Dipsychus*

Epigram

Not drunk is he who from the floor
Can rise alone and still drink more;
But drunk is he, who prostrate lies,
Without the power to drink or rise.

Thomas Love Peacock *The Misfortunes of Elphin*

The Discourse of the Drinkers

Then did they fall upon the chat of victuals and some belly furniture to be snatched at in the very same place. Which purpose was no sooner mentioned, but forthwith began flagons to go, gammons to trot, goblets to fly, great bowls to ting, glasses to ring. Draw, reach, fill, mix, give it me without water. So my friend, so, whip me off this glass neatly, bring me hither some claret, a full weeping glass till it run over. A cessation and truce with thirst. Ha, thou false fever, wilt thou not be gone? By my figgins, god-mother, I cannot as yet enter in the humour of being merry, nor drink so currently as I would. You have catch'd a cold, gammer? Yes, forsooth, sir. By the belly of Sanct Buff, let us talk of our drink: I never drink but at my hours, like the Pope's mule. And I never drink but in my breviary, like a fair father guardian. Which was first, thirst or drinking? Thirst, for who in the time of innocence would have drunk without being athirst? Nay, sir, it was drinking; for *privatio præsupponit habitum*. I am learned, you see: *Fæcundi calices quem non fecere disertum?* We poor innocents drink but too much without thirst. Not I truly, who am a sinner, for I never drink without thirst, either present or future. To prevent it, as you know, I drink for the thirst to come. I drink eternally. This is to me an eternity of drinking, and drinking of eternity. Let us sing, let us drink, and tune up our roundelays. Where is my funnel? What, it seems I do not drink but by an attorney? Do you wet yourselves to dry, or do you dry to wet you? Pish, I understand not the rhetoric (theoric I should say), but I help myself somewhat by the practice. *Baste!* enough! I sup, I wet, I humect, I moisten my gullet, I drink, and all for fear of dying. Drink always and you shall never die. If I drink not, I am a ground dry, gravelled and spent. I am stark dead without drink, and my soul ready to fly into some marsh amongst frogs: the soul never dwells in a dry place, drought kills it. O you butlers, creators of new forms, make me of no drinker a drinker, a perenity and everlastingness of sprinkling, and bedewing me through these my parched and sinewy bowels. He drinks in vain that feels not the pleasure of it. This entereth into my veins, the pissing tool and urinal vessels shall have nothing of it. I would willingly wash the tripes of the calf, which I apparelled this morning. I have pretty well now ballasted my stomach, and stuffed my paunch. If the papers of my bonds and bills could drink as well as I do, my creditors would not want for wine when they come to see me, or, when they are to make any formal exhibition of their rights to what of me they can demand. This hand of yours spoils your nose. O how many other such will enter here before this go out! What, drink so shallow? It is enough to break both girds and pettrel. This is called a cup of dissimulation, or flaggonal hypocrisy.

What difference is there between a bottle and a flagon? Great difference; for the bottle is stopped and shut up with a stoppel, but the flagon with a vice. Bravely and well played upon the words! Our fathers drank lustily, and emptied their cans. Well cacked, well sung! Come, let us drink: will you send nothing to the river? Here is one going to wash the tripes. I drink no more than a sponge. I drink like a Templar Knight. And I, *tanquam aponsus*. And I, *sicut terra sine aqua*. Give me a synonymon for a gammon of bacon. It is the compulsory of drinkers: it is a pully. By a pully-rope wine is let down into the cellar and by a gammon into the stomach. Hey! now boys, hither, some drink, some drink. There is no trouble in it. *Respice personam, pone pro duos, bus non est in usu*. If I could get up as well as I can swallow down, I had been long ere now very high in the air.

Thus became Tom Tosspot rich; thus went in the tailor's stitch. Thus did Bacchus conquer Inde; thus Philosophy, Melinde. A little rain allays a great deal of wind; long tippling breaks the thunder. But, if there came such liquor from my ballock, would you not willingly thereafter suck the udder whence it issued?

François Rabelais *Gargantua and Pantagruel*,
trans. Sir Thomas Urquhart

The Rubáiyát of Omar Khayyám

I

AWAKE! for Morning in the Bowl of Night
Has flung the Stone that puts the Stars to Flight:
And Lo! the Hunter of the East has caught
The Sultán's Turret in a Noose of Light.

II

Dreaming when Dawn's Left Hand was in the Sky
I heard a Voice within the Tavern cry,
'Awake, my Little ones, and fill the Cup
'Before Life's Liquor in its Cup be dry.'

III

And, as the Cock crew, those who stood before
The Tavern shouted – Open then the Door!
'You know how little while we have to stay,
'And, once departed, may return no more.'

VII

Come, fill the Cup, and in the Fire of Spring
The Winter Garment of Repentance fling:
The Bird of Time has but a little way
to fly – and Lo! the Bird is on the Wing.

XI

Here with a Loaf of Bread beneath the Bough,
A Flask of Wine, a book of Verse – and Thou
Beside me singing in the Wilderness –
And Wilderness is Paradise enow.

XX

Ah, my Belovéd, fill the Cup that clears
TO-DAY of past Regrets and future Fears –
To-morrow – Why, To-morrow I may be
Myself with Yesterday's Sev'n Thousand Years.

XXI

Lo! some we loved, the loveliest and best
That Time and Fate of all their Vintage prest,
Have drunk their Cup a Round or two before,
And one by one crept silently to Rest.

XXII

And we, that now make merry in the Room
They left, and Summer dresses in new Bloom,
Ourselves must we beneath the Couch of Earth
Descend, ourselves to make a Couch – for whom?

XXIII

Ah, make the most of what we yet may spend,
Before we too into the Dust descend;
Dust into Dust, and under Dust, to lie
Sans Wine, sans Song, sans Singer, and – sans End!

XXIV

Alike for those who for TODAY prepare,
And those that after a TO-MORROW stare,
A Muezzin from the Tower of Darkness cries
'Fools! your Reward is neither Here nor There!'

XXXIV

Then to this earthen Bowl did I adjourn
My Lip the secret Well of Life to learn:
And Lip to Lip it murmur'd – 'While you live
'Drink! – for once dead you never shall return.'

XXXV

I think the Vessel, that with fugitive
Articulation answer'd, once did live,
And merry-make; and the cold Lip I kiss'd
How many Kisses might it take – and give!

XXXVI

For in the Market-place, one Dusk of Day,
I watch'd the Potter thumping his wet Clay:
And with its all obliterated Tongue
It murmur'd – 'Gently, Brother, gently, pray!'

XXXVII

Ah! fill the Cup: – what boots it to repeat
How Time is slipping underneath our Feet:
Unborn TO-MORROW and dead YESTERDAY,
Why fret about them if TO-DAY be sweet!

LI

The Moving Finger writes; and, having writ,
Moves on: nor all thy Piety nor Wit
  Shall lure it back to cancel half a Line,
Nor all thy Tears wash out a Word of it.

Edward Fitzgerald

Why Time Spins Fast

XXVI

  Ay, note that Potter's wheel,
  That metaphor! and feel
Why time spins fast, why passive lies our clay, –
  Thou, to whom fools propound,
  When the wine makes its round,
'Since life fleets, all is change; the Past gone, seize today!'

XXVII

  Fool! All that is, at all,
  Lasts ever, past recall;
Earth changes, but thy soul and God stand sure:
  What entered into thee,
  That was, is, and shall be:
Time's wheel runs back or stops: Potter and clay endure.

XXVIII

  He fixed thee'mid this dance
  Of plastic circumstance,
This Present, thou, forsooth, wouldst fain arrest:
  Machinery just meant
  To give thy soul its bent,
Try thee and turn thee forth, sufficiently impressed.

XXIX

What though the earlier grooves
Which ran the laughing loves
Around thy base, no longer pause and press?
What though, about thy rim,
Skull-things in order grim
Grow out, in graver mood, obey the sterner stress?

XXX

Look not thou down but up!
To uses of a cup,
The festal board, lamp's flash and trumpet's peal,
The new wine's foaming flow,
The Master's lips a-glow!
Thou, heaven's consummate cup, what need'st thou with earth's wheel?

XXXI

But I need, now as then,
Thee, God, who mouldest men;
And since, not even while the whirl was worst,
Did I, – to the wheel of life
With shapes and colours rife,
Bound dizzily, – mistake my end, to slake Thy thirst:

XXXII

So, take and use Thy work:
Amend what flaws may lurk,
What strain o' the stuff, what warpings past the aim!
My times be in Thy hand!
Perfect the cup as planned!
Let age approve of youth, and death complete the same!

Robert Browning *Rabbi Ben Ezra*

The Flaw in Paganism

Drink and dance and laugh and lie,
  Love, the reeling midnight through.
For tomorrow we shall die!
  (But, alas, we never do.)

Dorothy Parker

Credo

Be always drunken. Nothing else matters: that is the only question. If you would not feel the horrible burden of Time weighing on your shoulders and crushing you to the earth, be drunken continually.

Drunken with what? With wine, with poetry, or with virtue, as you will. But be drunken.

And if sometimes, on the stairs of a palace, or on the green side of a ditch, or in the dreary solitude of your own room, you should awaken and the drunkeness be half or wholly slipped away from you, ask of the wind, or of the wave, or of the star, or of the bird, or of the clock, of whatever flies, or sighs, or rocks, or sings, or speaks, ask what hour it is; and the wind, wave, star, bird, clock, will answer you: 'It is the hour to be drunken! Be drunken, if you would not be martyred slaves of Time; be drunken continually! With wine, with poetry, or with virtue, as you will.'

Charles Baudelaire *Credo*, trans. Arthur Symons

A Sussex Drinking Song

On Sussex hills where I was bred,
When lanes in autumn rains are red,
When Arun tumbles in his bed,
  And busy great gusts go by;

When branch is bare in Burton Glen
And Bury Hill is a whitening, then,
I drink strong ale with gentlemen;
Which nobody can deny, deny,
Deny, deny, deny, deny,
Which nobody can deny!

In half-November off I go,
To push my face against the snow,
And watch the winds wherever they blow
Because my heart is high:
Till I settle me down in Steyning to sing
Of the women I met in my wandering,
And of all that I mean to do in the spring
Which nobody can deny, deny,
Deny, deny, deny, deny,
Which nobody can deny!

Then times be rude and weather be rough,
And ways be foul and fortune tough,
We are of the stout South Country stuff,
That never can have good ale enough,
And do this chorus cry!
From Crowboro' Top to Ditchling Down,
From Hurstpierpoint to Arundel town,
The girls are plump and the ale is brown:
Which nobody can deny, deny,
Deny, deny, deny, deny!
If he does he tells a lie!

Hilaire Belloc

The Expense of Spirits

The expense of spirits is a crying shame,
So is the cost of wine. What bard today
Can live like old Khayyám? It's not the same –

A loaf and Thou and Tesco's Beaujolais.
I had this bird called Sharon, fond of gin –
Could knock back six or seven. At the price
I paid a high wage for each hour of sin
And that is why I only had her twice.
Then here was Tracy, who drank rum and Coke,
So beautiful I didn't mind at first.
But love grows colder. Now some other bloke
Is subsidizing Tracy and her thirst.
I need a woman, honest and sincere,
Who'll come across on half a pint of beer.

Wendy Cope *Strugnell's Sonnets*

The Toper's Rant

Give me an old crone of a fellow
  Who loves to drink ale in a horn,
And sing racy songs when he's mellow,
  Which topers sung ere he was born.
For such a friend fate shall be thankèd,
  And, line but our pockets with brass,
We'd sooner suck ale through a blanket
  Than thimbles of wine from a glass.

Away with your proud thimble-glasses
  Of wine foreign nations supply,
A toper ne'er drinks to the lasses
  O'er a draught scarce enough for a fly.
Club me with the hedger and ditcher
  Or beggar that makes his own horn,
To join o'er an old gallon pitcher
  Foaming o'er with the essence of corn.

I care not with whom I get tipsy
  Or where with brown stout I regale,

I'll weather the storm with a gipsy
   If he be a lover of ale.
I'll weather the toughest storm weary
   Altho' I get wet to the skin,
For my outside I never need fear me
   While warm with real stingo within.

We'll sit till the bushes are dropping
   Like the spout of a watering pan,
And till the cag's drained there's no stopping,
   We'll keep up the ring to a man.
We'll sit till Dame Nature is feeling
   The breath of our stingo so warm,
And bushes and trees begin reeling
   In our eyes like to ships in a storm.

We'll start it three hours before seven,
   When larks wake the morning to dance,
And we'll stand it till night's black eleven,
   When witches ride over to France;
And we'll sit it in spite of the weather
   Till we tumble dead drunk on the plain,
When the morning shall find us together,
   All willing to stand it again.

John Clare

Drinking Song

Look at old Morrison!
Isn't he wonderful?
Fit as a fiddle
   And tight as a tick;
Seventy-seven
And spouting his stories –
Just listen a minute
   And laugh yourself sick.

Same with the other chaps:
Bloody good company,
Never let anyone
  Drink on his own;
Out of your parish
Or widowed or derelict –
Once you're in here
  You're no longer alone.

Different for Weatherby,
Struck with incontinence,
Mute in his wheelchair
  And ready to go;
Different for Hooper,
Put back on the oxygen,
Breathing, but breathing
  Uncommonly slow.

Did what we could, of course,
While there was anything;
Best to remember 'em
  Not as they are,
But as they used to be,
Chattering, chaffing and . . .
You go and eat
  And I'll stay in the bar.

Kingsley Amis

The Whole Problem of Drinking

They began to talk about the firm, and about the theatre, and the more they talked the more friendly they became and the more pleased George looked. Soon the time came to order more drinks and it became clear to Johnnie that they were all going to get drunk.

He came to this conclusion with a certain amount of gloom, as he always did nowadays, but he realized philosophically that on this occasion it was more or less a practical necessity. His friend George was in a state of happiness he could not spoil: the girl, previously hostile, had become mellow and friendly, and he himself was elated and talkative. So, at a given moment, he resigned himself to the joys of alcohol, wisely telling himself that if there was to be a hateful and repentant morning after the night before, he would at least see that the pleasure of the night before was not marred by the hatefulness of repentance – so that the night before and the morning after, the one in its pleasure, and the other in its pain, might from the true perspective of a long-distance view in time seem to cancel each other out. It was largely a question of time, and Johnnie always thought that if you could only have your morning after first, and your night before afterwards, the whole problem of drinking, and indeed of excess and sin in life generally, would be simplified or solved.

Patrick Hamilton *Hangover Square*

On The Pleasures of Drink

[1]

In the greenish hugger-mugger
With his bottle sits a bugger
Swigging schnapps. (Swigging schnapps.)
With his bottle sits a bugger near collapse.
(Near collapse.)

[2]

Look, chaste Josef though dumbfounded
By great mounds of flesh surrounded
Sits content. (Sits content.)
Sucks his fingers which are chaste and innocent.
(Innocent.)

[3]

Seven stars can taste too bitter.
Gentle plucking on the zither
Puts that right. (Puts that right.)
Seven songs and seven litres, you show fight.
(You show fight.)

[4]

Linsel Klopps walked straight and steady
Now feels freer as instead he
Walks askew. (Walks askew.)
And, oh swan, to you already thanks are due.
(Thanks are due.)

Bertolt Brecht, trans. Edith Anderson,
Lee Bremer, John Cullen *et al*

Instead

Try substituting the word 'women' for the word 'drinking' in the AA questionnaire. Are women affecting your peace of mind? Are women making your home life unhappy? Do you show a marked moodiness since women? Are women disturbing the harmony of your life? Have women changed your personality? Do you crave a woman at a definite time daily? Do you require a woman next morning? Do you prefer a woman alone? Have women made you irritable? Yes, yes, yes, and again yes.

Jeffrey Bernard *Spectator*, 4 October 1986

DRINKERS

Passing the Wine-Seller's

In these days I am ever befuddled with wine,
But it is not for nourishing my nature and soul.
When I see that all men are drunk,
How can I bear to be the only one sober?

Wang Chi, trans. Robert Kotewall & Norman L. Smith

A Pint of Plain

Biographical reminiscence, part the first: It was only a few months before composing the foregoing that I had my first experience of intoxicating beverages and their strange intestinal chemistry. I was walking through the Stephen's Green on a summer evening and conducting a conversation with a man called Kelly, then a student, hitherto a member of the farming class and now a private in the armed forces of the King. He was addicted to unclean expressions in ordinary conversation and spat continually, always fouling the flowerbeds on his way through the Green with a mucous deposit dislodged with a low grunting from the interior of his windpipe. In some respects he was a coarse man but he was lacking in malice or ill-humour. He purported to be a medical student but he had failed at least once to satisfy a body of examiners charged with regulating admission to the faculty. He suggested that we should drink a number of *jars* or pints of plain porter in Grogan's public house. I derived considerable pleasure from the casual quality of his suggestion and observed that it would probably do us no harm, thus expressing my whole-hearted concurrence by a figure of speech.

Name of figure of speech: Litotes (or Meiosis).

He turned to me with a facetious wry expression and showed me a penny and a sixpence in his rough hand.

I'm thirsty, he said. I have sevenpence. Therefore I buy a pint.

I immediately recognized this as an intimation that I should pay for my own porter.

The conclusion of your syllogism, I said lightly, is fallacious, being based on licensed premises.

Licensed premises is right, he replied, spitting heavily. I saw that my witticism was unperceived and quietly replaced it in the treasury of my mind.

We sat in Grogan's with our faded overcoats finely disarrayed on easy chairs in the mullioned snug. I gave a shilling and two pennies to a civil man who brought us in return two glasses of black porter, imperial pint measure. I adjusted the glasses to the front of each of us and reflected on the solemnity of the occasion. It was my first taste of porter. Innumerable persons with whom I had conversed had represented to me that spirituous liquors and intoxicants generally had an adverse effect on the senses and the body and that those who became addicted to stimulants in youth were unhappy throughout their lives and met with death at the end by a drunkard's fall, expiring ingloriously at the stair-bottom in a welter of blood and puke. Indian tonic-waters had been proposed to me by an aged lay-brother as an incomparable specific for thirst. The importance of the subject had been impressed upon me in a schoolbook which I read at the age of twelve.

Extract from Literary Reader, the Higher Class, by the Irish Christian Brothers: And in the flowers that wreathe the sparkling bowl, fell adders hiss and poisonous serpents roll – Prior. What is alcohol? All medical authorities tell us it is a double poison – an irritant and a narcotic poison. As an irritant it excites the brain, quickens the action of the heart, produces intoxication and leads to degeneration of the tissues. As a narcotic, it chiefly affects the nervous system; blunts the sensibility of the brain, spinal cord and nerves; and, when taken in sufficient quantity, produces death. When alcohol is taken into the system, an extra amount of work is thrown on various organs, particularly the lungs. The lungs, being overtaxed, become degenerated, and this is why so many inebriates suffer from a peculiar form of consumption called alcoholic phthisis – many, many cases of which are, alas, to be found in our hospitals, where the unhappy victims await the slow but sure march of an early death. It is a well-established fact that alcohol not only does not give strength but lessens it. It relaxes the muscles or instruments of motion and consequently their power decreases. This muscular depression is often followed by complete paralysis of the body, drink having unstrung the whole nervous system, which, when so unstrung leaves the body like a ship without sails or ropes – an unmovable or unmanagable thing. Alcohol may have its uses in the medical world, to which it should be relegated; but once a man becomes its victim, it is a terrible and a merciless master, and he finds himself in that dreadful state when all will-power is gone and he becomes a helpless imbecile, tortured at times by remorse and despair. Conclusion of the foregoing.

On the other hand, young men of my acquaintance who were in the habit of voluntarily placing themselves under the influence of alcohol had often surprised me with a recital of their strange adventures. The mind may be impaired by alcohol, I mused, but withal it may be pleasantly impaired. Personal experience appeared to me to be the only satisfactory means to the resolution of my doubts. Knowing it was my first one, I quietly fingered the butt of my glass before I raised it. Lightly I subjected myself to an inward interrogation.

Nature of interrogation: Who are my future cronies, where our mad carousals? What neat repast shall feast us light and choice of Attic taste with wine whence we may rise to hear the lute well touched or artful voice warble immortal notes or Tuscan air? What mad pursuit? What pipes and timbrels? What wild ecstasy?

Here's to your health, said Kelly.

Good luck, I said.

The porter was sour to the palate, but viscid, potent. Kelly made a long noise as if releasing air from his interior.

I looked at him from the corner of my eye and said:

You can't beat a good pint.

He leaned over and put his face close to me in an earnest manner.

Do you know what I am going to tell you, he said with his wry mouth, a pint of plain is your only man.

Notwithstanding this eulogy, I soon found that the mass of plain porter bears an unsatisfactory relation to its toxic content and I became subsequently addicted to brown stout in bottle, a drink which still remains the one that I prefer the most despite the painful and blinding fits of vomiting which a plurality of bottles has often induced in me.

I proceeded home one evening in October after leaving a gallon of half-digested porter on the floor of a public-house in Parnell Street and put myself with considerable difficulty into bed, where I remained for three days on the pretence of a chill. I was compelled to secrete my suit beneath the mattress because it was offensive to at least two of the senses and bore an explanation of my illness contrary to that already advanced.

The two senses referred to: Vision, smell.

On the evening of the third day, a friend of mine, Brinsley, was admitted to my chamber. He bore miscellaneous books and papers. I complained on the subject of my health and ascertained from him that the weather was inimical to the well-being of invalids. . . . He remarked that there was a queer smell in the room.

Description of my friend: Thin, dark-haired, hesitant; an intellectual Meath-man; given to close-knit epigrammatic talk; weak-chested, pale.

I opened wide my windpipe and made a coarse noise unassociated with the usages of gentlemen.

I feel very bad, I said.

By God you're the queer bloody man, he said.

I was down in Parnell Street, I said with the Shader Ward, the two of us drinking pints. Well, whatever happened to me, I started to puke and I puked till the eyes nearly left my head. I made a right haimes of my suit. I puked till I puked air.

Is that the way of it? said Brinsley.

Look at here, I said.

I arose in my bed, my body on the prop of an elbow.

I was talking to the Shader, I said, talking about God and one thing and another, and suddenly I felt something inside me like a man trying to get out of my stomach. The next minute my head was in the grip of the Shader's hand and I was letting it out in great style. O Lord save us. . . .

Here Brinsley interposed a laugh.

I thought my stomach was on the floor, I said. Take it easy, says the Shader, you'll be better when you get that off. Better? How I got home at all I couldn't tell you.

Well you did get home, said Brinsley.

I withdrew my elbow and fell back again as if exhausted by my effort. My talk had been forced, couched in the accent of the lower or working-classes. Under the cover of the bed-clothes I poked idly with a pencil at my navel. Brinsley was at the window giving chuckles out.

Nature of chuckles: Quiet, private, averted.

Flann O'Brien *At Swim-Two-Birds*

Plague on't They Won't Drink

CHARLES – CARELESS – *etc. etc. at a Table with Wine etc.*

CHARLES: 'Fore heaven, 'tis true – there's the great Degeneracy of the age – many of our acquaintance have Taste, spirit, and Politeness – but plague on't they won't drink.

CARELESS: It is so indeed Charles – they give into all the Substantial Luxuries of the Table – and abstain from nothing but wine and wit –

CHARLES: O certainly Society suffers by it intolerably – for now instead of the social spirit of Raillery that used to mantle over a glass of bright Burgundy their conversation is become just like the Spa water they drink which has all the Pertness and flatulence of Champaine without its Spirit or Flavour –

1ST GENT: But what are they to do who love Play better than wine?

CARELESS: True – there's Harry diets himself – for Gaming and is now under a Hazard – Regimen –

CHARLES: Then He'll have the worst of it – what you wouldn't train a horse for the course by keeping him from corn – for my Part egad I am now – never so successful as when I am a little – merry – let me throw on a Bottle of Champaine and I never lose – at least I never feel my losses which is exactly the same thing.

2ND GENT: Aye – that I believe.

CHARLES: And then what man can pretend to be a Believer in Love who is an abjuror of Wine – tis the Test by which the Lover knows his own Heart, fill a dozen Bumpers to a dozen Beauties – and she that floats at top is the Maid that has bewitch'd you –

CARELESS: Now then Charles – be honest and give us your real favorite –

CHARLES: Why I have withheld her only in compassion to you – if I toast her you must give a round of her Peers which is impossible! on earth!

CARELESS: O then we'll find some canonized Vestals or heathen Goddess that will do I warrant –

CHARLES: Here then – Bumpers – you Rogues – Bumpers! – Maria – Maria – [*drink*]

1ST GENT: Maria who?

CHARLES: O damn the Surname! 'tis too formal to be register'd in Love's Calendar – out now Sir Toby Bumper beware – we must have Beauty superlative.

CARELESS: Nay never Study Sir Toby – we'll Stand to The toast – tho' your mistress should want an Eye – and you know you have a song will excuse you –

SIR TOBY: Egad so I have – and I'll give him the Song instead of the Lady –

Song and Chorus

Here's to the maiden of Bashful fifteen
Here's to the Widow of Fifty

Here's to the flaunting, Extravagant Quean,
And here's to the House Wife that's thrifty.
Let the toast pass –
Drink to the Lass –
I'll warrant She'll prove an Excuse for the Glass!

2d.

Here's to the Charmer whose Dimples we Prize!
Now to the Maid who has none Sir;
Here's to the Girl with a pair of blue Eyes,
– And Here's to the Nymph with but one Sir!
Let the Toast pass etc.

3d.

Here's to the Maid with a Bosom of Snow,
Now to her that's as brown as a berry:
Here's to the Wife with a face full of Woe,
And now for the Damsel that's Merry.
Let the Toast pass etc.

4th.

For let 'Em be Clumsy or let 'Em be Slim
Young or Ancient, I care not a Feather:
– So fill a Pint Bumper Quite up to the Brim
– And let us E'en toast 'Em together!
Let the Toast pass etc.

ALL: – Bravo. Bravo!

(*Enter* TRIP *and Whispers* CHARLES.)

CHARLES: Gentlemen you must excuse me a little – Careless take the Chair will you?

CARELESS: Nay prithee Charles – what now – this is one of your Peerless Beauties I suppose – has dropt in by chance.

CHARLES: No – Faith – to tell you the Truth 'tis a Jew – and a broker who are come – by appointment.

CARELESS: O damn it let's have the Jew in –

1ST GENT: Aye and the Broker too by all means –

2ND GENT: Yes yes the Jew and the Broker.

CHARLES: Egad with all my Heart – Trip – bid the Gentlemen walk in – tho' there's one of them a Stranger I can tell you –

CARELESS: Charles – let us Give them some Generous Burgundy – and perhaps they'll grow conscientious.

CHARLES: O Hang 'em – no – wine does but draw forth a man's natural qualities and to make them drink would only be to whet their Knavery –

Richard Brinsley Sheridan *The School for Scandal*

Mrs Gamp

She was a fat old woman, this Mrs Gamp, with a husky voice and a moist eye, which she had a remarkable power of turning up, and only showing the white of it. Having very little neck, it cost her some trouble to look over herself, if one may say so, at those to whom she talked. She wore a very rusty black gown, rather the worse for snuff, and a shawl and bonnet to correspond. In these dilapidated articles of dress she had, on principle, arrayed herself, time out of mind, on such occasions as the present; for this at once expressed a decent amount of veneration for the deceased, and invited the next of kin to present her with a fresher suit of weeds: an appeal so frequently successful, that the very fetch and ghost of Mrs Gamp, bonnet and all, might be seen hanging up, any hour in the day, in at least a dozen of the second-hand clothes shops about Holborn. The face of Mrs Gamp – the nose in particular – was somewhat red and swollen, and it was difficult to enjoy her society without becoming conscious of a smell of spirits. Like most persons who have attained to great eminence in their profession, she took to hers very kindly: insomuch that, setting aside her natural predilections as a woman, she went to a lying-in or a laying-out with equal zest and relish.

'Ah!' repeated Mrs Gamp; for it was always a safe sentiment in cases of mourning. 'Ah dear! When Gamp was summoned to his long home, and I see him a-lying in Guy's Hospital with a penny-piece on each eye, and his wooden leg under his left arm, I thought I should have fainted away. But I bore up.'

If certain whispers current in the Kingsgate Street circles had any truth in them, she had indeed borne up surprisingly; and had exerted such uncommon fortitude as to dispose of Mr Gamp's remains for the benefit of science. But it should be added, in fairness, that this had happened twenty years before; and that Mr and Mrs Gamp had long been separated on the ground of incompatibility of temper in their drink.

'You have become indifferent since then, I suppose?' said Mr Pecksniff. 'Use is second nature, Mrs Gamp.'

'You may well say second natur, sir,' returned that lady. 'One's first ways is to find sich things a trial to the feelings, and so is one's lasting custom. If it wasn't for the nerve a little sip of liquor gives me (I never was able to do more than taste it), I never could go through with what I sometimes has to do. "Mrs Harris," I says, at the very last case as ever I acted in, which it was but a young person, "Mrs Harris," I says, "leave the bottle on the chimley-piece, and don't ask me to take none, but let me put my lips to it when I am so dispoged, and then I will do what I'm engaged to do, according to the best of my ability." "Mrs Gamp," she says, in answer, "if ever there was a sober creetur to be got at eighteen pence a day for working people, and three and six for gentlefolks – night watching,"' said Mrs Gamp, with emphasis, '"being a extra charge – you are that inwallable person." "Mrs Harris," I says to her, "don't name the charge, for if I could afford to lay all my feller creeturs out for nothink, I would gladly do it, sich is the love I bears 'em. But what I always says to them as has the management of matters, Mrs Harris:"' here she kept her eye on Mr Pecksniff: '"be they gents or be they ladies, is, don't ask me whether I won't take none, or whether I will, but leave the bottle on the chimley-piece, and let me put my lips to it when I am so dispoged."'

Charles Dickens *Martin Chuzzlewit*

The Pig Woman

(*Enter* URSULA *from her booth.*)

URSULA: Fie upon't! Who would wear out their youth and prime thus in roasting of pigs, that had any cooler vocation? Hell's a kind of cold cellar to't, a very fine vault, o' my conscience! What Mooncalf!

MOONCALF (*within*): Here, Mistress.

NIGHTINGALE: How, now, Urs'la? In a heat, in a heat?

URSULA (*to* MOONCALF): My chair, you false faucet you; and my morning's draught, quickly, a bottle of ale to quench me, rascal. – I am all fire and fat, Nightingale; I shall e'en melt away to the first woman, a rib again, I am afraid. I do water the ground in knots as I go, like a great garden-pot; you may follow me by the S's I make.

NIGHTINGALE: Alas, good Urs; was 'Zekiel here this morning?

URSULA: 'Zekiel? what 'Zekiel?

NIGHTINGALE: 'Zekiel Edgworth, the civil cutpurse; you know him well enough – he that talks bawdy to you still. I call him my secretary.

URSULA: He promised to be here this morning, I remember.

NIGHTINGALE: When he comes, bid him stay. I'll be back again presently.

URSULA: Best take your morning's dew in your belly, Nightingale.

(MOONCALF *brings in the chair.*)

Come, sir, set it here. Did not I bid you should get this chair let out o' the sides for me, that my hips might play? You'll never think of anything till your dame be rump-galled. 'Tis well, changeling; because it can take in your grasshopper's thighs, you care for no more. Now you look as you had been i' the corner o' the booth, fleaing your breech with a candle's end, and set fire o' the Fair. Fill, stot, fill.

OVERDO (*aside*): This pig-woman do I know, and I will put her in for my second enormity. She hath been before me, punk, pinnace, and bawd, any time these two and twenty years, upon record i' the Pie-powders.

URSULA: Fill again, you unlucky vermin.

MOONCALF: Pray you be not angry, mistress; I'll ha' it widened anon.

URSULA: No, no, I shall e'en dwindle away to't, ere the Fair be done, you think, now you ha' heated me! A poor vexed thing I am. I feel myself dropping already, as fast as I can; two stone o' suet a day is my proportion. I can but hold life and soul together with this (here's to you, Nightingale) and a whiff of tobacco, at most. Where's my pipe now? Not filled? Thou arrant incubee!

NIGHTINGALE: Nay, Urs'la, thou'lt gall between the tongue and the teeth with fretting, now.

URSULA: How can I hope that ever he'll discharge his place of trust – tapster, a man of reckoning under me – that remembers nothing I say to him?

(*Exit* NIGHTINGALE.)

But look to't, sirrah, you were best; threepence a pipeful I will ha' made of all my whole half-pound of tobacco, and a quarter of a pound of colts-foot mixed with it too, to eke it out. I that have dealt so long in the fire will not be to seek in smoke, now. Then, six and twenty shillings a barrel I will advance o' my beer, and fifty shillings a hundred o' my bottle-ale; I ha' told you the ways how to raise it. Froth your cans well i' the filling, at length, rogue, and jog your bottles o' the buttock, sirrah, then skink out the first glass, ever, and drink with all companies, though you be sure to be drunk; you'll misreckon the better, and be less ashamed on't. But your true trick, rascal, must be ever busy, and mis-take away the bottles and cans in haste before they be half drunk off, and never hear anybody call (if they should chance to mark you) till you ha' brought fresh, and be able to forswear 'em. Give me a drink of ale.

Ben Johnson *Bartholomew Fair*

Faucet, tap for drawing liquor out of a barrel; *secretary*, a confidant; *changeling*, stupid or ugly child left by fairies in exchange for an attractive one; *stot*, a stupid, clumsy person; *pinnace*, go-between or whore; *incubee*, incubus – possibly here the offspring of a human being and an evil spirit; *colts-foot*, a herb used to adulterate tobacco; *be to seek*, be at a loss; *advance*, raise; *skink*, pour.

Drunk

'What happened to you?' I asked the telephone. I was all prepared to be big about it.

'... I didn't show up.'

'Yes, so I seem to recall.' I waited. 'Why didn't you?'

'No point. I tried to cancel on the telephone but you weren't listening.'

I waited. 'I waited,' I said.

Martina sighed. 'You were drunk. You know, it's quite a lot to ask, to spend a whole evening with someone who's drunk.'

... I had always known the truth of this, of course. Drunks know the truth of this. But usually people are considerate enough not to bring it up. The truth is very tactless. That's the trouble with these non-alcoholics – you never know what they're going to say next. Yes, a rum type, the sober: unpredictable, blinkered and selective. But we cope with them as best we can.

'Meet me tonight. I won't be drunk, I promise. Look, I'm really sorry about last night.'

'Last night?'

'Yeah. Things got a little out of hand.'

'Last night?'

'Yeah. I don't know what came over me.'

'It wasn't last night. It was the night before. Call me at eight. I'll be able to tell. If you're drunk then I'll just hang up.

Then she just hung up.

Now I'd felt some queasy queries posed my way as I climbed out of bed, and undressed slowly before the window's span, sensing huge chemical betrayals and wicked overlappings up there in the spilled sky. I had even said to myself, Christ, it's another of those inner eclipse deals – but then Felix appeared with my breakfast, and wished me good morning, and all seemed well. Apart, that is, from the food. My omelette looked docile enough on the plate, yet it soon took on strange powers of life.

I buzzed down to Felix and summoned him to Room 101.

'Now look, kid,' I said, pretty stern. 'Why did you let me oversleep like that yesterday? You're supposed to look out for me. Time is money. God damn it, Felix, I'm a busy man.'

'Huh?' said Felix, tipping his head. 'Man, you weren't even *here* yesterday. I thought you gone away for the weekend or something. You got in last night. Late.'

'Drunk?'

'Drunk?' And here he began his smile. 'Downstairs they don't agree but me I think it was the best yet. You had a party hat on your head. Your whole face was covered in lipstick. *Drunk?* They ain't got a word for where you were at. You gone and beat yourself up with that bottle. You were – you were just dead.'

This was a real bitch, no error. I could remember nothing to speak of about last night, yesterday, or the night before. Worse, I could remember nothing at all about *Animal Farm*.

Martin Amis *Money*

On the Courthouse Steps

Some of the folk of that little town offered the widower no greeting at all. He was too unpredictable. He would take one man's jibes without offence and get his back up at another's 'Howdy, friend.' In a town where nearly everyone danced, swore and gambled, the only fun Fitz had left was getting his back up.

He was against modern dancing, modern dress, swearing, gambling, cigarettes and sin. He preached that the long drought of 1930 was God's way of putting an end to such things. But as the drought went on and on and never a drop of rain he reversed himself and said it must be the pope's doing.

He was also said to be against fornication. But then it was said he was against corn whiskey too.

Saturday nights he pulled an ancient black frock coat over his patches; a coat with a pocket under the slit of the tail to hold the little brown bottle he called his 'Kill-Devil'. Getting stiff on the courthouse steps while denouncing the Roman Catholic clergy was a feat which regularly attracted scoffers and true believers alike, the believers as barefoot as the scoffers. For drunk as a dog or broke as a beggar, Fitz could spout religion like a hog in a bucket of slops.

Sometimes a girl would stand a moment among the men, pretending interest in The Word. But hunger has a scent more dry than love's and she would move along wishing she were in Dallas.

For many in Arroyo the Lord's Day was Saturday; but every night of the week was the Lord's to Fitz.

'"And when they wanted wine"' – he put down a mocker who wanted to know what caused the bulge on his hip – '"the mother of Jesus saith unto him, 'Give them wine.'" Satan didn't claim Jesus' mother 'count of wine, ah reckon he won't claim me 'count of a half-pint of busthead.'

'What cause folk to git dispatched to Hellfire then?' a believer demanded to know right now.

'You don't git "*dispatched*" to Hellfire,' Fitz assured him – 'You're born right *in* it. Gawd got a fence clean a-*round* Hell. So a sinner cain't git out! Sinner caint dig underneath! Too deep! Sinner caint crawl between! Caint climb over! It's ee-o-lectrified!'

'How'd *you* git out?' the mocker asked softly. He was astride the barrel of the town howitzer, his face and figure shadowed like a cannoneer's who has lost both battle and cause.

'Ah *clumb*,' Fitz explained, and clumb right into his theme – 'Ah clumb the lowest strand 'cause that's the strand of LOVE. Ah clumb the second strand 'cause that's the MERCY strand. Ah clumb the third because ah been LONGSUFFERIN'!' –

' – thought you said that fence was ee-o-lectrified,' the cannoneer reminded him, but Fitz was climbing too hard to hear – 'Ah clumb clean ovah the topmost one of HIS MOST PRECIOUS BLOOD! Brothers! Sisters! Step on the strand of LOVE! Step on the strand of MERCY! Step on the LONGSUFFERING strand and get ready – to cross the strand of THE BLOOD!'

'You know, I was thinking along those lines myself,' the cannoneer commented, and spat. Yet Fitz paid him no heed.

'I know some of you boys come a mighty far way in hope I'd save you for the Heavenly Home,' he acknowledged. 'That *was* my pure intent. But now that I see your actual faces I've had a change of mind. Boys, I'm woeful sorry, but the Lord just don't want a bunch of dirt-eating buggers walking the Streets of Gold. The Lord don't mind sinners – but he just can't stand rats. And I'll be god*damned* if *I'll* take the responsibility!' – and openly took a defiant swig of his half-pint.

Both sceptics and hopers cheered at that – the old man was warming up. 'You tell 'em, Preacher! Drink 'er down! Don't you play whore to no man!'

Fitz smacked his lips, rewound his dirty bandanna about his bottle and replaced it in the hidden pocket.

'*Now* tell us about Temptation, Father,' the man on the cannon asked, trying to get Fitz pointed at the pope.

'I'll tell you this much about Temptation, Byron Linkhorn,' the old man answered directly – 'there are so-called Christians right in this gathering tonight who voted for the pope in '28. Do you think the Lord caint remember two year?'

Fitz could forgive a man for using marijuana, but not for voting for Al Smith. Others who had voted for the pope in '28 stood silent, letting Byron take the full brunt of their guilt. It was Byron who had ruined everyone's chance for the New Jerusalem, that silence implied. Now no one could go.

'Tell the *rest* of us how to be saved, Preacher,' one hypocrite pleaded.

'Or the time you fell in the cesspool,' Byron stayed in there.

Fitz was hell on the pope, but Byron was hell on Fitz.

'The Lord *does* work in mysterious ways, that's certain sure,' the old man found his text – 'for example, the pitiful critter atop the county property happen to be my son.'

'Here come the part *I* come for,' somebody dug his naked toes in the earth with anticipated pleasure – 'Here's where thet busthead starts *really* taken holt.'

' – a critter not long for this world,' Fitz gave hope to all creation – 'the Lord giveth, the Lord taketh away – and the sooner he taketh away that particular civet, the air hereabouts will be considerable fitter for humans. His lungs is gone, his mind is weak, his heart is dry as an autumn leaf. The brickle thread of his life is ready to snap. I envy him his trials is about to cease!'

The man on the cannon tried to reply, but was trapped by a

cough so racking that every face turned to his own. He was good as dead, those cold looks told, yet not one cared a tear.

Pressing a bandanna to his lips, Byron dismounted cautiously. His father's cracked voice, with a dozen others as cracked, joined in a hymn familiar to all. That rose, contented in all its discords, in a chorus above all argument.

O lovely appearance of death
No sight upon earth is so fair;
Not all the gay pageants that breathe
Can with a dead body compare –

and pursued him down every step of the street hawking bloodily all the way.

They had come to see someone lose. That it should be the same doomed fool week after week gave a flip to their satisfaction. Saturday night after Saturday night, it was always Byron to be singled out. Between his cough, the crowd and his father, he always lost. What was it in him they had to disprove? What was it that mere repetition added?

Byron was one whose beginnings had been more brave than most – that was what needed disproving.

For how Fitz leaped then – literally *leaped* – clapping his hands above his head and barking triumphantly –

'Just as I am though tossed about
With many a conflict many a doubt
Fighting and fears within, without
O lamb of God, I come! I come!
Just as I am! Just as I am! –

– in the name of Jesus, now come as you are!' – and would skip down the steps, his sermon done, to take anyone's bottle and everyone's praise, mocking or sincere.

'Keeps your boots on, Preacher! Come just as you are!'

Fitz would be weaving a bit. Yet behind his shrouded glance a gleeful victory glinted. The Lord would forgive one who had defended His ark so well.

'Preacher,' one told him, 'you just done my heart good tonight. You plumb restored me. Next week I'm bringen the younguns, they need restorin' too. The old woman is beyond restoren. She aint been the same since the time she got throwed by the Power.'

'You never should have picked her up,' Fitz recalled an occasion when one of his listeners had passed out – 'You should have left her right there where Jesus flang her. How's she feeling?'

'Better, thank you kindly. We got a bit of a job for you any time you're of a mind to run out our way.'

That was all right with Fitz. If Protestant privies lined both sides of the road to the City of Pure Gold, by God he'd shovel his way to Salvation. But before he'd take money from papist rapists he'd go the other route. He was playing the whore to no man.

He was a Witness for Jehovah and saw the Holy See engaged in an international conspiracy against the Anglo-Saxon race in general and the Linkhorns in particular.

Papists Rapists! – that's who it was who kept cheating!

Nelson Algren *A Walk on the Wild Side*

Communion Wine

It took no time at all for the police to be gone – they took with them two or three chickens, a turkey and the man called Miguel. The priest said aloud, 'I did my best.' He went on, 'It's *your* job – to give me up. What do you expect me to do? It's my job not to be caught.'

One of the men said, 'That's all right, father. Only will you be careful . . . to see that you don't leave any wine behind . . . like you did at Concepción?'

Another said, 'It's no good staying, father. They'll get you in the end. They won't forget your face again. Better go north, to the mountains. Over the border.'

'It's a fine state over the border,' a woman said. 'They've still got churches there. Nobody can go in them of course – but they are there. Why, I've heard that there are priests too in the towns. A cousin of mine went over the mountains to Las Casas once and heard Mass – in a house, with a proper altar, and priest all dressed up like in the old days. You'd be happy there, father.'

The priest followed Maria to the hut. The bottle of brandy lay on the table; he touched it with his fingers – there wasn't much left. He said, 'My case, Maria? Where's my case?'

'It's too dangerous to carry that around any more,' Maria said.

'How else can I take the wine?'

'There isn't any wine.'

'What do you mean?'

She said, 'I'm not going to bring trouble on you and everyone else. I've broken the bottle. Even if it brings a curse . . .'

He said gently and sadly, 'You mustn't be superstitious. That was simply – wine. There's nothing sacred in wine. Only it's hard to get hold of here. That's why I kept a store of it in Concepión. But they've found that.'

'Now perhaps you'll go – go away altogether. You're no good any more to anyone,' she said fiercely. 'Don't you understand, father? We don't want you any more.'

'Oh yes,' he said. 'I understand. But it's not what you want – or I want . . .'

She said savagely, 'I know about things. I went to school. I'm not like these others – ignorant. I know you're a bad priest. That time we were together – that wasn't all you've done. I've heard things, I can tell you. Do you think God wants you to stay and die – a whisky priest like you?' He stood patiently in front of her, as he had stood in front of the lieutenant, listening. He hadn't known she was capable of all this thought. She said, 'Suppose you die. You'll be a martyr, won't you? What kind of a martyr do you think you'll be? It's enough to make people mock.'

That had never occurred to him – that anybody would consider him a martyr. He said, 'It's difficult. Very difficult. I'll think about it. I wouldn't want the Church to be mocked . . .'

'Think about it over the border then . . .'

'Well . . .'

She said, 'When you-know-what happened, I was proud. I thought the good days would come back. It's not everyone who's a priest's woman. And the child . . . I thought you could do a lot for her. But you might as well be a thief for all the good . . .'

He said vaguely, 'There've been a lot of good thieves.'

'For God's sake take this brandy and go.'

Graham Greene *The Power and the Glory*

I Have Conquered It

This physical loathing for alcohol I have never got over. But I have conquered it. To this day I conquer it every time I take a drink. The palate never ceases to rebel, and the palate can be trusted to know what is good for the body. But men do not drink for the effect alcohol produces on the body. What they drink for is the brain-effect; and if it must come through the body, so much the worse for the body.

Jack London *John Barleycorn*

Bender

Standing at the Dôme bar is Marlowe, soused to the ears. He's been on a bender, as he calls it, for the last five days. That means a continuous drunk, a peregrination from one bar to another, day and night without interruption, and finally a layoff at the American Hospital. Marlowe's bony emaciated face is nothing but a skull perforated by two deep sockets in which there are buried a pair of dead clams. His back is covered with sawdust – he has just had a little snooze in the water closet. In his coat pocket are the proofs for the next issue of his review, he was on his way to the printer with the proofs, it seems, when someone inveigled him to have a drink. He talks about it as though it happened months ago. He takes out the proofs and spreads them over the bar; they are full of coffee stains and dried spittle. He tries to read a poem which he had written in Greek, but the proofs are undecipherable. Then he decides to deliver a speech, in French, but the *gérant* puts a stop to it. Marlowe is piqued: his one ambition is to talk a French which even the *garçon* will understand. Of Old French he is a master; of the surrealists he has made excellent translations; but to say a simple thing like 'get the hell out of here, you old prick!' – that is beyond him. Nobody understands Marlowe's French, not even the whores. For that matter, it's difficult enough to understand his English when he's under the weather. He blabbers and spits like a confirmed stutterer . . . no sequence to his phrases. '*You pay!*' that's one thing he manages to get out clearly.

Henry Miller *Tropic of Cancer*

Molten Ruby

William Pitt. – We find, from a recently published life of Matthews, comedian, by Mrs Matthews, that he had a great desire to see the celebrated William Pitt, but could not gratify it for some time: at length, his wish was gratified by his early friend General Phipps inviting him to his house, on the occasion of the great statesman dining there. Mr Matthews only arrived in time to witness the following extraordinary and humbling exhibition: – 'It was not without a sensation somewhat approaching to awe, that the actor followed the servant who ushered him into the dining-room, where the party still remained, though nearly midnight. As he entered, he was startled by a crash of something breaking, followed by a suppressed titter, and he found the table in great disorder, the guests silent, the General and the candles burning blue – the new guest looked a little blue at the constrained, nay, vexed manner with which his heretofore warm and cordial host received him, and who, without a word of welcome, pointed to the chair just placed for him by the servant. My husband's eye glanced from face to face, in the fear that he was too late to behold the only one he came to see, and having hastily scanned each countenance, his quick eye being familiar with Gilray's and other likenesses of the prime minister, could not fail to recognize, though in a haze, in the sharp features of the long slim personage, seated at the top of the table, the political guiding star of Britain, the great son of the great Chatham, the dignified statesman, the observed of all observers – undisturbed by the entrance of the new guest – gravely and even thoughtfully employed in collecting the wine-glasses within his reach, and piling them one upon another, as high as they could balance, and then with the fragments of the dessert pelting them down in pieces, (the crash and suppressed mirth heard by my husband at his *entré* being occasioned by the destruction of the first batch,) and not till all the glasses upon the table were, in auctioneer's phrase, showed up, did the mighty perpetrator think of desisting. He then rose with something like an effort, and with a silent bow to his host, not very steadily withdrew, accompanied by two of the gentlemen present. The much-annoyed General then explained to my husband that the scene he had just witnessed of the self-diversion of his illustrious guest was not unfrequently the result of his having suffered too much of the 'molten ruby' to pass his lips, as on the present occasion, when he taxed his hospitable entertainers in the manner described. This was the only time my husband saw this great man, who died, I believe, shortly afterwards.' – *Anecdotes of Actors, by Mrs Matthews.*

The Temperance Handbook

Captain Hunter

The three officers entered a long airy room with sunlight beating through the windows. More light was reflected from the glossy walls and from the glass of the many pictures hanging on these. Down the middle ran a trestle table that bore dozens of vases of flowers and plants in pots. Thick streamers of greenery curled down from wire baskets attached to the ceiling.

A figure sitting up in bed at the far end of the room raised an arm and the visitors approached. On either side, also in bed, were men reading, men apparently asleep, men lying down but not asleep. One man was looking carefully round the room, as if for the first time, while another man in white trousers and tee-shirt watched him as carefully from a nearby chair. Yet another man, with irregular patches of grey hair on a grey scalp, got up from a bench by the window and moved away, keeping track of the arrivals out of the corner of his eye.

The man who was putting the Army to so much trouble seemed very much at home. He was lying back against advantageously arranged pillows within reach of various comforts: non-glossy illustrated magazines, paperback novels on the covers of which well-developed girls cringed or sneered, a comparatively hardback work on how to win at poker, a couple of newspapers folded so as to reveal half-completed crossword puzzles, a tin jug containing a cloudy greyish fluid, packets of French cigarettes and an open box of chocolates. Captain Hunter, a thin pale man of twenty-eight with a thin black moustache, smiled and extended his hand.

'Hullo, boys,' he said, and offered cigarettes which Ayscue and Churchill accepted. 'I'm afraid I can't give you a light. You're not allowed to have matches and stuff in here because you might start burning the place down. Almost certainly would, in fact. Oh, thank you, James. Is that parcel for me? What's in it?'

'A cake,' said Ayscue. 'But don't go cutting it now.'

'My dear Willie, I couldn't if I wanted to. No knives like no matches. But the nice nurse comes on at six and he might see his way to lending me one.'

'Well, mind he isn't about when you start slicing.'

'What . . . ? I suppose there's a file and a rope-ladder in it.'

'Not exactly.' Naidu spoke with some disapproval. 'A different mode of escape.'

'You don't mean . . . ?'

'Yes,' said Churchill. 'Three quarter-bottles of White Horse. Corporal Beavis baked the thing up in the Mess kitchen. Sorry we could't get any more in.'

'Quite enough for a man in my condition. Thank you all most awfully.'

'How is your condition, Max?' asked Ayscue.

'Oh, splendid. Dr Best is very pleased with me. He says he's been able to explain to me just why I got myself into the state I did and so

I shouldn't have any more trouble. He's letting me out on probation next Wednesday.'

Churchill said diffidently, 'What was the explanation he gave you? If you want to talk about it, of course.'

'I haven't the remotest notion, dear boy. I'm only telling you what he says he's done. He likes doing all the talking himself. It must come from being supposed to ask so many questions. I just let him get on with it.'

'It's bound to be a difficult task, giving it up,' said Naidu. 'But you can rely on us three to give you all the support and encouragement in the world.'

'Whatever is possessing you, Moti? Nobody said anything about giving it up. Any fool can give it up. I'm going to do something much more worthwhile than that – ditching alcoholism and taking up very heavy drinking. Talking of drinking, I'll have to watch that Scotch. Too much at one go and I'll start acting sober, and that'd be suspicious. You see, these pills they give you, when they really get hold of you you start acting pissed all the time. That's how they know when you're taking a turn for the better.'

'You're not acting pissed,' said Churchill.

'I'd like to think I've always known how to hold my liquor.'

'You weren't holding it too well the night we brought you here.'

'No gentleman can or should be always a gentleman. Some get more ungentlemanly than others, though. You see that white-haired old buffer down by the door? Last Saturday he was let out on a week's probation. Very early indeed on Tuesday morning they carted him back in, pissed. The "they" included a small detachment of police as well as a crying wife. There was no end of a to-do, I can assure you. I haven't heard such language since that last Sergeants' Mess party. At lunch-time today he fell out of bed. What do you think of that? Just try to imagine how he must have attacked the stuff to be still pissed after four and a half days. And he only had two days and a bit to fill his tanks. You know, I can't help finding that rather disturbing? It seems to flout some basic law. Oh, if you can't manage another cake by say Monday, do you think you could send me a book about drinks, cocktail recipes or what-not? There's a lot to be said for pornography in the absence of the real thing. Ask anybody.'

'You'd better be careful with those empties,' said Ayscue.

'Oh, no problem. I shall just heave them out of the loo window. There's a sort of cairn of broken bottles in the bushes by that corner. I found it on one of my rambles through the extensive grounds when, disinclined to trudge all the way back indoors for the purpose, I was looking for a place to pee. That wasn't all I found, either. In a brief circuit of fifty yards or so I came across no fewer than three very amorous couples, and that was without trying to come across them. Quite the contrary. I was virtually threading my way. I get the impression everybody's at it all the time. It's no more than you'd expect in an environment like this.'

Churchill ground out his cigarette. 'Not everybody, surely.'

'I was speaking figuratively. Not everybody, no. I question whether the catatonics do much in that way, and no doubt the senility wards have a stainless record. Dr Best took me round them the other afternoon. Nothing personal about it – it's a standard trip, all part of the service. I was expecting him to take the opportunity to deliver a little lecture on the perils of self-abuse, but for once he let things speak for themselves.'

When none of the three said anything, Hunter went on, 'I had our old buddy Brian Leonard round here a couple of days ago. He'd really come to keep Fawkes up to the mark, he told me, but having come so far he saw nothing against walking the few extra yards to my bedside. He wasn't entirely happy, he said. He seemed to think that a dipsomaniac in charge of the administration of a secret-weapons training unit represented some kind of danger to security. I did what I could to reassure him. I pointed out that if the worst threat of that sort came from the odd dipsomaniac then he hadn't much to worry about. He agreed with that, and said that anyway he was satisfied I didn't know enough to be a menace.'

Kingsley Amis *The Anti-Death League*

The Brandy Glass

Only let it form within his hands once more –
The moment cradled like a brandy glass.
Sitting alone in the empty dining hall . . .
From the chandeliers the snow begins to fall
Piling around carafes and table legs
And chokes the passage of the revolving door.
The last diner, like a ventriloquist's doll
Left by his master, gazes before him, begs:
'Only let it form within my hands once more.'

Louis MacNeice

The Third Degree of Drink

(*Exit* MALVOLIO.)

OLIVIA: Now you see, sir, how your fooling grows old, and people dislike it.

FESTE: Thou hast spoke for us, madonna, as if thy eldest son should be a fool, whose skull Jove cram with brains, for – here he comes –
(*Enter* SIR TOBY.)
one of thy kin has a most weak *pia mater*.

OLIVIA: By mine honour, half-drunk. What is he at the gate, cousin?

SIR TOBY: A gentleman.

OLIVIA: A gentleman? What gentleman?

SIR TOBY: 'Tis a gentleman here. (*He belches.*) A plague o' these pickle herring! (*To* FESTE.) How now, sot?

FESTE: Good Sir Toby.

OLIVIA: Cousin, cousin, how have you come so early by this lethargy?

SIR TOBY: Lechery? I defy lechery. There's one at the gate.

OLIVIA: Ay, marry, what is he?

SIR TOBY: Let him be the devil an he will, I care not. Give me faith, say I. Well, it's all one. (*Exit.*)

OLIVIA: What's a drunken man like, fool?

FESTE: Like a drowned man, a fool, and a madman – one draught above heat makes him a fool, the second mads him, and a third drowns him.

OLIVIA: Go thou and seek the coroner, and let him sit o' my coz, for he's in the third degree of drink, he's drowned. Go look after him.

FESTE: He is but mad yet, madonna, and the fool shall look to the madman. (*Exit.*)

William Shakespeare *Twelfth Night*

A Goodly Regimen

1 April 1661. This day my wayting at the Privy Seale comes in again.

Up earely among my workmen. So to the office and went home to dinner with Sir W. Batten. And after that to the Goate taverne by Charing-cross to meet Dr Castle, where he and I drank a pint of wine and talked about Privy Seale business. Then to the Privy Seale Office and there find Mr Moore, but no business yet. Then to White-fryers and there saw part of *Rule a Wife and Have a Wife** – which I never saw before, but do not like it.

So to my father; and there finding a discontent between my father and mother about the mayde (which my father likes and my mother dislikes), I stayed till 10 at night, persuading my mother to understand herself; and that in some high words – which I was sorry for, but she is grown, poor woman, very froward. So leaving them in the same discontent, I went away home – it being a brave moone-shine, and to bed.

*A comedy by John Fletcher, acted in 1624, and published in 1640; despite Pepys's verdict, one of Fletcher's most popular plays during the seventeenth century.

2 *April*. Among my workmen earely. And then along with my wife and Pall to my father's by coach, there to have them lie a while till my house be done. I found my mother alone, weeping upon the last night's quarrel. And so left her and took my wife to Charing-cross and there left her to see her mother, who is not well. So I into St James parke, where I saw the Duke of Yorke playing at *Peslemesle** – the first time that I ever saw that sport.

Then to my Lord's, where I dined with my Lady; and after we had dined, in comes my Lord and Ned Pickering hungry, and there was not a bit of meat left in the house, the servants having eat up all – at which my Lord was very angry – and at last got something dressed. Then to Privy Seale and signed some things.

So to Whyte-fryers and saw *The Little thiefe*, which is a very merry and pretty play – and the little boy doth very well.†

Then to my father's, where I find my mother and my wife in a very good moode; and so left them and went home.

Then to the Dolphin to Sir W. Batten and Pen and other company; among others, Mr Delabar – where strange how these men, who at other times are all wise men, do now in their drink betwitt and reproach one another with their former conditions and their actions as to public concernments, till I was shamed to see it.

But parted all friends at 12 at night, after drinking a great deal of wine. So home and alone to bed.

3 *April*. Up among my workmen – my head akeing all day from last night's debauch. To the office all the morning; and at noon dined with Sir W. Batten and Pen, who would needs have me drink two good draughts of Sack today, to cure me of last night's disease – which I thought strange, but I think find it true.

Then home with my workmen all the afternoon. At night into the garden to play on my flagilette, it being Mooneshine – where I stayed a good while; and so home and to bed. . . .

*Pell-mell; forerunner of croquet; introduced under Charles I.

†*The night walker, or The little thief* was a comedy by John Fletcher written c. 1611, revised by James Shirley in 1633, and published in 1640. Now acted at the S. Ct, Whitefriars. The heroine, Alathe, carried out some comic deceptions disguised as a boy. A boy may in fact have played the part.

5 November 1661. At the office all the morning. At noon came my brother Tom and Mr Armiger to dine with me; and did, and we were very merry. After dinner and having drunk a great deal of wine, I went away, seeming to go about business with Sir W. Pen to my Lady Battens (Sir W. being at Chatham); and there sat a good while and then went away (before I went, I called at home to see whether they were gone, and find them there and Armiger inviting my wife to go to a play; and like a fool would be courting her, but he is an asse; and lays out money with Tom, otherwise I should not think him worthy half this respect I show him) to the Dolphin, where he and I and Captain Cocke sat late and drank much, seeing the boys in the street fling their Crackers – this day being keeped all the day very stricktly in the City. At last broke up and called at my Lady Battens again; and would have gone to Cards, but Sir W. Penn was so fuddled that we could not woo him to play; and therefore we parted, and I home and to bed.

6 November. Going forth this morning, I met Mr Davenport and a friend of his, one Mr Furbisher, to drink their morning draught with me; and I did give it them in good wine and anchoves, and pickled oysters; and took them to the Sun in fishstreete and there did give them a barrel of good ones and a great deal of wine, and sent for Mr W. Bernard (Sir Robts. son, a grocer thereabouts) and were very merry; and cost me a good deal of money. And at noon left them, with my head full of wine; and being invited by a note from Luellin that came to my hand this morning in bed, I went to Nick. Osborne's at the Victualling Office and there saw his wife, who he hath lately married, a good sober woman and new-come to their house. We had a good dish or two of marrowbones and another of neats tongs to dinner; and that being done, I bid them adieu and hastened to White-hall (calling Mr Moore by the way) to my Lord Privy Seale, who will at last force the Clerkes to bring in a table of their Fees, which they have so long denied. But I do not joyne with them and so he is very respectful to me: so he desires me to bring in one which I observe in taking of Fees, which I will speedily do. So back again and endeavoured to speak with Tom. Trice (who I fear is haching some mischief); but could not, which vexed me; and so I went home and sat late with pleasure at my lute; and so to bed.

Samuel Pepys *Diary*

I am Not Drunk

(*Enter* CASSIO *with* MONTANO *and* GENTLEMEN, *and servants with wine.*)

CASSIO: 'Fore God, they have given me a rouse already.

MONTANO: Good faith, a little one; not past a pint, as I am a soldier.

IAGO: Some wine, ho! (*Sings.*)

And let me the canakin clink, clink;
And let me the canakin clink;
  A soldier's a man
  O, man's life's but a span;
Why, then, let a soldier drink.

Some wine, boys.

CASSIO: 'Fore God, an excellent song.

IAGO: I learned it in England, where indeed they are most potent in potting. Your Dane, your German, and your swag-bellied Hollander – drink, ho! – are nothing to your English.

CASSIO: Is your Englishman so expert in his drinking?

IAGO: Why, he drinks you with facility your Dane dead drunk; he sweats not to overthrow your Almaine; he gives your Hollander a vomit, ere the next pottle can be filled.

CASSIO: To the health of our General!

MONTANO: I am for it, Lieutenant; and I'll do you justice.

IAGO: O, sweet England! (*Sings.*)

King Stephen was and-a worthy peer,
  His breeches cost him but a crown;
He held them sixpence all too dear;

With that he called the tailor lown.
He was a wight of high renown,
And thou art but of low degree;
'Tis pride that pulls the country down;
Then take thine auld cloak about thee.

Some wine, ho!

CASSIO: 'Fore God, this is a more exquisite song than the other.

IAGO: Will you hear't again?

CASSIO: No, for I hold him to be unworthy of his place that does those things. Well, God's above all; and there be souls must be saved, and there be souls must not be saved.

IAGO: It's true, good Lieutenant.

CASSIO: For mine own part – no offence to the General, nor any man of quality – I hope to be saved.

IAGO: And so do I too, Lieutenant.

CASSIO: Ay, but, by your leave, not before me. The Lieutenant is to be saved before the Ancient. Let's have no more of this; let's to our affairs. God forgive us our sins. Gentlemen, let's look to our business. Do not think, gentlemen, I am drunk: this is my Ancient, this is my right hand, and this is my left. I am not drunk now: I can stand well enough and I speak well enough.

GENTLEMEN: Excellent well.

CASSIO: Why, very well; you must not think then that I am drunk. (*Exit.*)

William Shakespeare *Othello*

Porson (Classical Scholar)

I remember to have seen Porson at Cambridge, in the Hall of our College, and in private parties, but not frequently; and I never can recollect him except as drunk or brutal, and generally both: I mean in an evening, for in the hall he dined at the Dean's table, and I at the Vice-master's, so that I was not near him; and he then and there appeared sober in his demeanour, nor did I ever hear of excess or outrage on his part in public, – Commons, college, or Chapel; but I have seen him in a private party of undergraduates, many of them freshmen and strangers – take up a poker to one of them, and heard him use language as blackguard as his action. I have seen Sheridan drunk, too, with all the world; but his intoxication was that of Bachus, and Porson's that of Silenus. Of all the disgusting brutes, sulky, abusive, and intolerable, Porson was the most bestial, as far as the few times I saw him went, which were only at William Bankes's (the Nubian Discoverer's) rooms. I saw him once go away in a rage because nobody knew the name of the 'Cobbler of Messina', insulting their ignorance with the most vulgar terms of reprobation. He was tolerated in this state amongst the young men for his talents – as the Turks think a Madman inspired, and bear with him. He used to recite, or rather vomit, pages of all languages, and could hiccup Greek like a Helot; and certainly Sparta never shocked her children with a grosser exhibition than this man's intoxication.

Lord Byron *Letters and Journals*

A Greek Professor's Ruin

Early in the year 1806, Professor Porson's stupendous memory began to fail, which was the first indication of his breaking up. Later in the year, he had symptoms of intermitting fever; and in the autumn he complained of being out of order, and feeling as if he had the ague. On the morning of the 19th of September, he left the Old Jewry to call on his brother-in-law, Mr Perry, in the Strand, and reached his house about half-past one. His friend was from home, and Porson proceeded along the Strand towards Charing-Cross, and had reached the corner of Northumberland-street when he was seized with a fit of apoplexy, which deprived him of speech, and rendered him motionless. A crowd gathered round him; and as he remained senseless, and nothing was found upon him to indicate where he resided, he was conveyed to St Martin's Workhouse, St Martin's-lane, where medical aid was immediately given, and he was partially restored to consciousness. How afflicting to think of this wreck of a man of rare genius, struck down in the public street through his own depraved appetite, his love of drink; and the person whom the sons of learning at the universities regarded as the finest classical scholar of the age, lying unknown and unclaimed, and carried to the common receptacle of poverty and misfortune! As he still remained unable to speak, the authorities sent to the *British Press* newspaper an advertisement, which appeared next morning, describing him as 'a tall man, apparently about five-and-forty years of age, dressed in a blue coat and black breeches, and having in his pocket a gold watch, a trifling quantity of silver, and a memorandum-book, the leaves of which were chiefly filled with Greek lines written in pencil, and partly effaced, two or three lines of Latin, and an algebraical calculation; the Greek extracts being principally from eminent medical works.' This advertisement met the eye of Mr Savage, the under-librarian at the London Institution, who, knowing that Porson had not slept at home on the preceding night, concluded that the professor was the person described in the newspaper. It proved to be correct. Porson was conveyed to his home, and died in a few days, in the very prime of life, having destroyed his constitution by a frightful course of intemperance. Horne Tooke used to say, as Mr Maltby tells us, that 'Porson would drink ink rather than not drink at all. Indeed,' adds Mr Maltby, 'he would drink anything. He was sitting with a gentleman after dinner, in the chambers of a mutual friend, a Templar, who was then ill and confined to bed. A servant came into the room, sent thither by his master, for a bottle of embrocation which was on the chimney-piece. 'I drank it an hour ago,' said Porson. When Hoppner, the painter, was residing in a cottage a few miles from London, Porson, one afternoon, unexpectedly arrived there. Hoppner said that he could not offer him dinner, as Mrs Hoppner had gone to town, and had carried with her the key of the closet, which contained the wine. Porson, however, declared that he would be content with a mutton-chop and beer from the next alehouse; and accordingly stayed to dine. During the evening, Porson said, 'I am quite certain that Mrs Hoppner keeps some nice bottle for her private drinking in her own bedroom; so pray try if you can lay your hands on it.' His host assured him that Mrs Hoppner had no such secret store; but Porson insisting that a search should be made, a bottle was at last discovered in the lady's apartment, to the surprise of Hoppner and the joy of Porson, who soon finished its contents, pronouncing it to be the best gin he had tasted for a long time. Next day Hoppner, somewhat out of temper, informed his wife that Porson had drunk every drop of her concealed dram. 'Drunk every drop of it!' cried she, 'my God! it was spirits of wine for the lamp!'

The Temperance Handbook

Mrs Botham

'Moderation,' said Mrs Botham. 'Temperance. Calmness. Reserve. Not being drunk all the time. *That's* what sobriety means, Mary! And if you lose your sobriety you lose everything. I admit it, oh, I admit it, Mary! Shoe-polish, shampoo, Pledge, Brobat, Right-Guard, Radox, Sanflush, Harpic . . .'

Martin Amis *Other People*

A Stiff Drink

Prinsep was an engineer who worked in the Calcutta Mint and became interested in oriental culture through his study of ancient Indian coins. He is remembered today largely for his work in translating two forgotten Indian scripts: Gupta Brahmi and Ashoka Brahmi, the script of the rock edicts. At the time, however, he was at least equally famous for his rust-proof treatment for steam boats and his design for the Calcutta Ice House, a project in which he co-operated with an alcoholic named James Pattle, my great-great-great grandfather. The Ice House was Calcutta's first experiment in refrigeration, and the day the first cargo of ice arrived from America a public holiday was declared. 'All business was suspended until noon. ... Everybody invited everybody to dinner to taste claret and beer cooled by the American importation.' Pattle served 'tip-top champagne'.

Despite this public-spirited act both men came to sticky ends. Prinsep fell ill from overwork trying to translate the Ashoka Brahmi and after four years, having finally cracked its secrets, he developed 'an affectation of the brain'. By the time he was bundled aboard the *Hertfordshire* his 'mind was addled'. He reached England, but never recovered his sanity 'lingering a year until relieved of his sufferings' in 1840. His old partner, James Pattle, fared no better. 'The biggest liar in India', as he was known (with justice; one of his claims was to have rowed across the Atlantic in a hen coop), drank himself to death, and was put in a cask of rum to preserve him during the voyage back to England. His wife had the cask placed outside her bedroom door. In the middle of the night there was a violent explosion, and when the widow rushed out into the passage she found the container had burst and her husband was stuck half in, half out of the barrel. 'The shock sent her off her head then and there, poor thing, and she died raving. ...' But the worst was yet to come. The cask was nailed down and put on board ship. Sometime after the boat had set off, the sailors guessed that the cask was full of liquor, bored a hole into the side of it and began to get drunk. The rum continued to run out, caught fire and set the ship ablaze. While the drunken sailors were trying to extinguish the flames, the ship ran on to a rock and blew up. So it was that Pattle was cremated rather than buried in England, as he had wished.

William Dalrymple *In Xanadu*

Daily Dose

I'm very fond of alcohol, but I drink a minute amount compared with what I did at one period in my life, when I drank at least a bottle of brandy a night plus gins and things during the day.

Now I'll have a dry sherry around noon, maybe a glass of wine at lunch and then in the evening I'll have two or three gin and tonics and half a bottle of wine and probably a couple of brandies, which for me is practically being teetotal.

George Melly *The Times*, 10 May 1990

Weak Stuff

Thursday, 23 September 1773. We set out this morning on our way to Talisker, in Ulinish's boat, having taken leave of him and his family. Mr Donald M'Queen still favoured us with his company, for which we were much obliged to him. As we sailed along Dr Johnson got into one of his fits of railing at the Scots. He owned that they had been a very learned nation for a hundred years, from about 1550 to 1650; but that they afforded the only instance of a people among whom the arts of civil life did not advance in proportion with learning; that they had hardly any trade, any money, or any elegance, before the Union; that it was strange that, with all the advantages possessed by other nations, they had not any of those conveniences and embellishments which are the fruit of industry, till they came in contact with a civilized people. 'We have taught you, (said he,) and we'll do the same in time to all barbarous nations, – to the Cherokees, – and at last to the Ouran-Outangs;' laughing with as much glee as if Monboddo had been present. – BOSWELL. 'We had wine before the Union.' – JOHNSON. 'No, sir; you had some weak stuff, the refuse of France, which would not make you drunk.' – BOSWELL. 'I assure you, sir, there was a great deal of drunkenness.' – JOHNSON. 'No, sir; there were people who died of dropsies, which they contracted in trying to get drunk.'

James Boswell *A Tour of the Western Isles and Hebrides*

Achilles' Heel

Still however he cultivated the society of persons of taste and of respectability, and in their company could impose on himself the restraints of temperance and decorum. Nor was his muse dormant. In the four years which he lived in Dumfries, he produced many of his beautiful lyrics, though it does not appear that he attempted any poems of considerable length. During this time he made several excursions into the neighbouring country, of one of which, through Galloway, an account is preserved in a letter of Mr Syme, written soon after, which, as it gives an animated picture of him by a correct and masterly hand, we shall present to the reader.

'I got Burns a grey Highland shelty to ride on. We dined the first day, 27th July, 1793, at Glendenwynes of Parton; a beautiful situation on the banks of the Dee. In the evening we walked out and ascended a gentle eminence, from which we had as fine a view of Alpine scenery as can well be imagined. A delightful soft evening showed all its wilder as well as its grander graces. Immediately opposite, and within a mile of us, we saw Airds, a charming romantic place, where dwelt Low, the author of *Mary weep no more for me*. This was classical ground for Burns. He viewed "the highest hill, which rises o'er the source of Dee;" and would have staid till the "passing spirit" had appeared, had we not resolved to reach Kenmore that night. We arrived as Mr and Mrs Gordon were sitting down to supper.

'Here is a genuine baron's seat. The castle, an old building, stands on a large natural moat. In front the river Ken winds for several miles through the most fertile and beautiful *holm*; till it expands into a lake twelve miles long, the banks of which on the south present a fine and soft landscape of green knolls, natural wood, and here and there, a grey rock. On the north the aspect is great, wild, and, I may say, tremendous. In short, I can scarcely conceive a scene more terribly romantic than the castle of Kenmore. Burns thinks so highly of it, that he meditates a description of it in poetry. Indeed I believe he has begun the work. We spent three days with Mr Gordon, whose polished hospitality is of an original and endearing kind. Mrs Gordon's lapdog *Echo* was dead. She would have an epitaph for him. Several had been made. Burns was asked for one. This was setting Hercules to his distaff. He disliked the subject, but to please the lady, he would try. Here is what he produced.

In wood and wild ye warbling throng,
 Your heavy loss deplore;
Now half-extinct your powers of song,
 Sweet Echo is no more.

'We left Kenmore, and went to Gatehouse. I took him the moor-road, where savage and desolate regions extended wide around. The sky was sympathetic with the wretchedness of the soil; it became louring and dark. The hollow winds sighed, the lightnings gleamed, the thunder rolled. The poet enjoyed the awful scene – he spoke not a word, but seemed rapt in meditation. In a little while the rain began to fall; it poured in floods upon us. For three hours did the wild elements *rumble their belly-full* upon our defenceless heads. *Oh, oh! 'twas foul.* We got utterly wet, and to revenge ourselves Burns insisted at Gatehouse, on our getting utterly drunk.

'From Gatehouse we went next day to Kirkudbright, through a fine country. But here I must tell you that Burns had got a pair of *jemmy* boots for the journey, which had been thoroughly wet, and which had been dried in such a manner, that it was not possible to get them on again. The brawny poet tried force, and tore them to shreds. A whiffling vexation of this sort is more trying to the temper than a serious calamity. We were going to Saint Mary's Isle, the seat of the Earl of Selkirk, and the forlorn Burns was discomfited at the thought of his ruined boots. A sick stomach, and a head-ache, lent their aid, and the man of verse was quite *accablé*. I attempted to reason with him. Mercy on us how he did fume and rage! Nothing could re-instate him in temper. I tried various expedients, and at last hit on one that succeeded. I shewed him the house of ****, across the bay of Wigton. Against ****, with whom he was offended, he expectorated his spleen, and regained a most agreeble temper. He was in a most epigrammatic humour indeed! He afterwards fell on humbler game. There is one ****** whom he does not love. He had a passing blow at him.

When ******, deceased, to the devil went down,
'Twas nothing would serve him but Satan's own crown:
Thy fool's head, quoth Satan, that crown shall wear never,
I grant thou'rt as wicked, but not quite so clever.

'Well, I am to bring you to Kirkudbright along with our poet without boots. I carried the torn ruins across my saddle in spite of his fulminations, and in contempt of appearances; and what is more, Lord Selkirk carried them in his coach to Dumfries. He insisted they were worth mending.'

Dr James Currie *Life of Burns*

News from Newstead Abbey

My dear Ly. M[elbourn]e – The whole party are here – and now to my narrative. – But first I must tell you that I am rather unwell owing to a folly of last night – About midnight after deep and drowsy potations I took it into my head to empty my *skull cup* which holds rather better than a bottle of Claret at *one draught* – and nearly died the death of Alexander – which I shall be content to do when I have achieved his conquests – I had just sense enough left to feel that I was not fit to join the ladies – & went to bed – where my Valet tells me that I was first convulsed & afterwards so motionless that he thought 'Good Night to Marmion.' – I don't know how I came to do so very silly a thing – but I believe my guests were boasting – & 'company villainous company hath been the spoil of me' I detest drinking in general – & beg your pardon for this excess – I *can't* do so any more.

Lord Byron to Lady Melbourne, 17 October 1813

Squire Headlong

SQUIRE HEADLONG (*taking the skull*): *Memento mori.* Come, a bumper of Burgundy.

MR NIGHTSHADE: A very classical application, Squire Headlong. The Romans were in the practice of adhibiting skulls at their banquets, and sometimes little skeletons of silver, as a silent admonition to the guests to enjoy life while it lasted.

THE REVEREND DOCTOR GASTER: Sound doctrine, Mr Nightshade.

MR ESCOT: I question its soundness. The use of vinous spirit has a tremendous influence in the deterioration of the human race.

MR FOSTER: I fear, indeed, it operates as a considerable check to the progress of the species towards moral and intellectual perfection. Yet many great men have been of opinion that it exalts the imagination, fires the genius, accelerates the flow of ideas, and imparts to dispositions naturally cold and deliberative that enthusiastic sublimation which is the source of greatness and energy.

MR NIGHTSHADE: *Laudibus arguitur vini vinosus Homerus.**

MR JENKISON: I conceived the use of wine to be always pernicious in excess, but often useful in moderation: it certainly kills some, but it saves the lives of others: I find that an occasional glass, taken with judgment and caution, has a very salutary effect in maintaining that equilibrium of the system, which it is always my aim to preserve; and this calm and temperate use of wine was, no doubt, what Homer meant to inculcate, when he said: *Παρ δε δεπας οινοιο, πιειν ὀτε ϑυμος ανωγοι*†

SQUIRE HEADLONG: Good. Pass the bottle. (*Un morne silence*). Sir Christopher does not seem to have raised our spirits. Chromatic, favour us with a specimen of your vocal powers. Something in point.

*Homer is proved to have been a lover of wine by the praises he bestows upon it.
†A cup of wine at hand, to drink as inclination prompts.

MR CHROMATIC, without further preface, immediately struck up the following

SONG

In his last binn SIR PETER lies,
  Who knew not what it was to frown:
Death took him mellow, by surprise,
  And in his cellar stopped him down.
Through all our land we could not boast
  A knight more gay, more prompt than he,
To rise and fill a bumper toast.
  And pass it round with THREE TIMES THREE.

None better knew the feast to sway,
  Or keep Mirth's boat in better trim;
For Nature had but little clay
  Like that of which she moulded him.
The meanest guest that graced his board
  Was there the freest of the free,
His bumper toast when PETER poured,
  And passed it round with THREE TIMES THREE.

He kept at true good humour's mark
  The social flow of pleasure's tide:
He never made a brow look dark,
  Nor caused a tear, but when he died.
No sorrow round his tomb should dwell:
  More pleased his gay old ghost would be,
For funeral song, and passing bell,
  To hear no sound but THREE TIMES THREE.

(*Hammering of knuckles and glasses and shouts of bravo!*)

Thomas Love Peacock *Headlong Hall*

A Drunk Man Looks at the Thistle

Sic transit gloria Scotiae – a' the floo'ers
O' the Forest are wede awa'. (A blin' bird's nest
Is aiblins biggin' in the thistle tho'? . . .
And better blin' if'ts brood is like the rest!)

You canna gang to a Burns supper even
Wi'oot some wizened scrunt o' a knock-knee
Chinee turns roon to say, "Him Haggis – velly goot!"
And ten to wan the piper is a Cockney.

No' wan in fifty kens a wurd Burns wrote
But misapplied is a'body's property,
And gin there was his like alive the day
They'd be the last a kennin' haund to gi'e –

Croose London Scotties wi' their braw shirt fronts
And a' their fancy freen's, rejoicin'
That similah gatherings in Timbuctoo,
Bagdad – and Hell, nae doot – are voicin'

Burns' sentiments o' universal love,
In pidgin English or in wild-fowl Scots,
And toastin' ane wha's nocht to them but an
Excuse for faitherin' Genius wi' *their* thochts.

A' *they've* to say was aften said afore
A lad was born in Kyle to blaw aboot.
What unco fate mak's *him* the dumpin'-grun'
For a' the sloppy rubbish they jaw oot?

aiblins, perhaps; *biggin'*, building; *gang*, go; *scrunt*, person whose growth is stunted or emaciated.

Mair nonsense has been uttered in his name
Than in ony's barrin' liberty and Christ.
If this keeps spreedin' as the drink declines,
Syne turns to tea, wae's me for the *Zeitgeist*!

Rabbie, wad'st thou wert here – the warld hath need,
And Scotland mair sae, o' the likes o' thee!
The whisky that aince moved your lyre's become
A laxative for a' loquacity.

O gin they'd stegh their guts and haud their wheesht
I'd thole it, for 'a man's a man,' I ken,
But though the feck ha'e plenty o' the 'a' that,'
They're nocht but zoologically men.

I'm haverin', Rabbie, but ye understaun'
It gets my dander up to see your star
A bauble in Babel, banged like a saxpence
Twixt Burbank's Baedeker and Bleistein's cigar.

There's nane sae ignorant but think they can
Expatiate on *you*, if on nae ither.
The sumphs ha'e ta'en you at your wurd, and, fegs!
The foziest o' them claims to be a – Brither!

Syne 'Here's the cheenge' – the star o' Rabbie Burns.
Sma' cheenge, 'Twinkle, Twinkle.' The memory slips
As G. K. Chesterton heaves up to gi'e
'The Immortal Memory' in a huge eclipse,

wan, one; *kens*, knows; *a'body's*, everyone's; *gin*, if; *the day*, today; *kennin'*, understanding; *croose*, self-important; *braw*, grand; *freen's*, friends; *ane*, one; *wha's*, who's; *nocht*, nothing; *blaw*, boast; *mair*, more; *unco*, strange; *wae's*, woe's, *sae*, so; *stegh*, stuff; *haud their wheest*, be quiet; *thole*, bear, endure; *feck*, majority; *haverin'*, rambling; *dander*, temper; *nae ither*, no other; *sumphs*, blockheads; *fegs* faith!, strewth!; *foziest*, spongiest, stupidest; *cheenge,* change; *sma'*, small; *gi'e*, give (a toast to);

Or somebody else as famous if less fat.
You left the like in Embro in a scunner
To booze wi' thieveless cronies sic as me.
I'se warrant you'd shy clear o' a' the hunner

Odd Burns Clubs tae, or ninety-nine o' them,
And haud your birthday in a different kip
Whaur your name isna ta'en in vain – as Christ
Gied a' Jerusalem's Pharisees the slip

– Christ wha'd ha'e been Chief Rabbi gin he'd lik't! –
Wi' publicans and sinners to forgether,
But, losh! the publicans noo are Pharisees,
And I'm no' shair o' maist the sinners either.

But that's aside the point! I've got fair waun'ert.
It's no' that I'm sae fou' as juist deid dune,
And dinna ken as muckle's whaur I am
Or hoo I've come to sprawl here 'neth the mune.

That's it! It isna me that's fou' at a',
But the fu' mune, the doited jade, that's led
Me fer agley, or 'mogrified the warld.
– For a' I ken I'm safe in my ain bed.

Jean! Jean! Gin *she*'s no' here it's no *oor* bed,
Or else I'm dreamin' deep and canna wauken.
But it's a fell queer dream if this is no'
A real hillside – and thae things thistles and bracken!

Hugh MacDiarmid *A Drunk Man Looks at the Thistle*

Embro, Edinburgh; *scunner*, (fit of) disgust; *thieveless*, profligate; *sic*, such; *I'se*, I'll; *haud*, hold; *kip*, brothel (and cf. 'play the kip', play truant); *maist*, most (of), *fair waun'ert*, quite confused; *fu'*, full; *doited*, confused (as in dotage); *fer agley*, far astray; *ain*, own; *fell*, extremely; *thae*, those.

Hogmanay

Murdo gave the cock meal
damped with whisky. It stood
on tiptoe, crowed eight times
and fell flat on its beak.

Later, Murdo, after the fifth verse
of *The Isle of Mull*,
fell, glass in hand,
flat on his back – doing in six hours
what the cock had done
in two minutes.

I was there. And now I see
the cock crowing with Murdo's face
and Murdo's wings flapping
as down he went.

It was a long way home.

Norman MacCaig

Essentials

Usually, in the interval between my afternoon sleep and my night sleep I went for a walk, turned up the Boulevard Arago, walked to a certain spot and turned back. And one evening I was walking along with my hands in the pockets of my coat and my head down. This was the time when I got in the habit of walking with my head down. ... I was walking along in a dream, a haze, when a man came up and spoke to me.

This is unhoped-for. It's also quite unwanted. What I really want to do is to go for my usual walk, get a bottle of wine on tick and go back to the hotel to sleep. However, it has happened, and there you are. Life is curious when it is reduced to its essentials.

Well, we go into the Café Buffalo. Will I have a little apéritif? I certainly will. Two Pernods arrive.

I start thinking about food. Choucroute, for instance – you ought to be able to get choucroute garnie here. Lovely sausage, lovely potato, lovely, lovely cabbage. ... My mouth starts watering violently. I drink half the glass of Pernod in order to swallow convenablement. And then I feel like a goddess. It might have made me sick, but it has done the other thing.

The orchestra was playing *L'Arlésienne*, I remember so well. I've just got to hear that music now, any time, and I'm back in the Café Buffalo, sitting by that man. And the music going heavily. And he's talking away about a friend who is so rich that he has his photograph on the bands of his cigars. A mad conversation.

'One day,' he says, 'I too will be so rich that I shall have my photo on the bands of the cigars I offer to my friends. That is my ambition.'

Will I have another little Pernod? I certainly will have another little Pernod. (Food? I don't want any food now. I want more of this feeling – fire and wings.)

There we are, jabbering away as if we had known each other for years. He reads me a letter that he has just had from a girl.

What's the matter with it? It seems to me a letter any man ought to be proud to have. All about frissons and spasms and unquestionable réussites. (Chéri, chéri, rappelles-tu que. ...) A testimonial, that letter is.

But the snag is at the end, as usual. The girl wants a new pair of shoes and she is asking for three hundred francs to buy them. Chéri, you will remember the unforgettable hours we passed together and not refuse me when I tell you that my shoes are quite worn out. I am ashamed to go into the street. The valet de chambre knows that there are large holes in both my shoes. Really, I am ashamed to be so poor. I stay all the time in my room. And so, chéri, etcetera, etcetera, etcetera. ...

He is chewing and chewing over this letter. 'I don't believe it,' he says. 'It's all a lie, it's a snare, it's a trap. This girl, you understand, is a liar. What she wants is three hundred francs to give to her maquereau. Will I give her three hundred francs for her maquereau? No. I won't. I will not.... All the same,' he says, 'I can't bear to think of that poor little one with holes in her shoes. That can't be amusing, walking about with your feet on the ground.'

'No, it isn't amusing,' I say. 'Especially on a rainy day.'

'Well, what do you think? Do you think this letter can be genuine? What do you think?'

Every word has been chewed over by the time we have finished our second drink.

'Besides,' he says, 'even if it is genuine, I mustn't send the money at once. That would never do. If she thought she had only to ask, to have – that would never do. No, no, I must keep her waiting.'

Chew, chew, chew....

'No. I think she's lying.'

All the time he is staring at me, sizing me up. He has his hand on my knee under the table.

He is not a Parisian. He lives in Lille. He is staying at a friend's flat, he says, and it's a very nice flat. Will I come along there and have a little porto? ... Well, why not?

What does this man look like? I don't remember. I don't think I ever looked at him. I remember that he had very small hands and that he wore a ring with a blue stone in it.

We got out into the street. And, of course, vlung – first breath of fresh air and I'm so drunk I can't walk.

'Hé là,' he says. 'What's the matter? Have you been dancing too much?'

'All you young women,' he says, 'dance too much. Mad for pleasure, all the young people.... Ah, what will happen to this after-war generation? I ask myself. What will happen? Mad for pleasure.... But we'll take a taxi.'

We cross the road unsteadily and stand under a sickly town-tree waiting to signal a taxi. I start to giggle. He runs his hand up and down my arm.

I say: 'Do you know what's really the matter with me? I'm hungry. I've had hardly anything to eat for three weeks.'

'Comment?' he says, snatching his hand. 'What's this you're relating?'

'C'est vrai,' I say, giggling still more loudly. 'It's quite true. I've had nothing to eat for three weeks.' (Exaggerating, as usual.)

At this moment a taxi draws up. Without a word he gets into it, bangs the door and drives off, leaving me standing there on the pavement.

And did I mind? Not at all, not at all. If you think I minded, then you've never lived like that, plunged in a dream, when all the faces are masks and only the trees are alive and you can almost see the strings that are pulling the puppets. Close-up of human nature – isn't it worth something?

I expect that man thought Fate was conspiring against him – what with his girl's shoes and me wanting food. But there you are, if you're determined to get people on the cheap, you shouldn't be so surprised when they pitch you their own little story of misery sometimes.

Jean Rhys *Good Morning, Midnight*

Mead

Let me tell you of one of their customs. They make an excellent wine out of honey and panic, which is called mead; and with this they hold great drinking-bouts in the following fashion. They form numerous clubs of men and women, especially nobles and magnates, ranging from thirty to fifty persons – husbands and wives and children. Each club elects its own king or captain and makes its own statutes, so that anyone who makes an unseemly remark or does something contrary to statute is punished by the imposition of a fine. There are men equivalent to tavern-keepers who have stocks of this mead for sale. The clubs resort to these taverns and spend a whole day in drinking. They call these drinking bouts *stravitza*. In the evening the tavern-keepers make a reckoning of the mead they have drawn, and everyone pays the share allotted to him, and to his wife and children if they are present.

While they are engaged in these *stravitza*, they borrow money on the security of their children from merchants who come from Khazaria, Sudak, and other neighbouring countries, and then spend it on drink, and so they sell their own children. During these all-day bouts the ladies do not withdraw to relieve themselves, but their handmaids contrive to give them relief unobserved, when need arises, with the aid of large sponges. Let me tell you something that happened on one occasion. A man and his wife were going home in the evening after one of these bouts, when the wife paused to relieve herself. The cold was so fierce that the hairs of her thighs froze on to the grass, so that she could not move for the pain and cried aloud. Her husband reeling drunk and distressed at her plight, stopped down and began to breathe over her, hoping to melt the ice by the warmth of his breath. But, while he breathed, the moisture of his breath congealed and so the hairs of his beard froze together with his wife's and he too was stuck there unable to move for pain. Before they could budge from the spot, other helpers had to come and break the ice.

Marco Polo *The Travels*, trans. R. E. Latham

A Wise Custom

The ancient Goths of Germany, who (the learned Cluverius is positive) were first seated in the country between the Vistula and the Oder, and who afterwards incorporated the Herculi, the Bugians, and some other Vandallic clans to 'em, – had all of them a wise custom of debating every thing of importance to their state, twice; that is, – once drunk, and once sober: – Drunk – that their councils might not want vigour; – and sober – that they might not want discretion.

Laurence Sterne *Tristram Shandy*

Dull Intervals of Peace

In the dull intervals of peace, these barbarians were immoderately addicted to deep gaming and excessive drinking; both of which, by different means, the one by inflaming their passions, the other by extinguishing their reason, alike relieved them from the pain of thinking. They gloried in passing whole days and nights at table; and the blood of friends and relations often stained their numerous and drunken assemblies. Their debts of honour (for in that light they have transmitted to us those of play) they discharged with the most romantic fidelity. The desperate gamester, who had staked his person and liberty on a last throw of the dice, patiently submitted to the decision of fortune, and suffered himself to be bound, chastised, and sold into remote slavery, by his weaker but more lucky antagonist.

Edward Gibbon *The History of the Decline and Fall of the Roman Empire*

German Drinkers

After the Concert Hamilton, a Cambridge man, took me, as his Guest, to the Saturday Club – where *what is called* the first Class of Students meet & sup once a week – Here were all the nobility, & three Englishmen, Hamilton, Brown, & Kennet. – Such an Evening I never passed before – roaring, kissing, embracing, fighting, smashing bottles & glasses against the wall, singing – in short, such a scene of uproar I never witnessed before, no, not even at Cambridge. – I drank nothing – but all, except two of the Englishmen, were drunk – & the party broke up a little after one o/clock in the morning. I thought of what I had been at Cambridge, & of what I was – of the wild & bacchanalian Sympathy with which I had *formerly* joined similar Parties, & of my total inability now to do aught *but meditate* – & the feeling of the deep alteration in my moral Being gave the scene a melancholy interest to me! – There were two Customs which I had never seen before – the one they call *smollets* [Schmollis], & consists in two men drinking a glass of wine under each other's arm, & then kissing & embracing each other – after which they always say *Thou* to each other. The other custom was this – when all were drunk & all the Bottles smashed, they brought a huge Sword, sung a Song round it, then each fixed his Hat on the sword, Hat over Hat, still singing – & then all kissed & embraced each other, still singing. – This Kissing is a most loathsome Business – & the English are known to have such an aversion to it, that it is never expected of them. –

Samuel Taylor Coleridge to Mrs Coleridge, March 1799

Back in Beer-Territory

I was back in beer-territory. Half-way up the vaulted stairs a groaning Brownshirt, propped against the wall on a swastika'd arm, was unloosing, in a staunchless gush down the steps, the intake of hours. Love's labour lost. Each new storey radiated great halls given over to ingestion. In one chamber a table of SA men were grinding out *Lore, Lore, Lore,* scanning the slow beat with the butts of their mugs, then running the syllables in double time, like the carriages of an express: '*UND – KOMMT – DER – FRÜHLingindastal! GRÜSS – MIR – DIE – LORenocheinmal*'. But it was certain civilian figures seated at meat that drew the glance and held it.

One must travel east for a hundred and eighty miles from the Upper Rhine and seventy north from the Alpine watershed to form an idea of the transformation that beer, in collusion with almost nonstop eating – meals within meals dovetailing so closely during the hours of waking that there is hardly an interprandial moment – can wreak on the human frame. Intestine strife and the truceless clash of intake and digestion wrecks many German tempers, twists brows into scowls and breaks out in harsh words and deeds.

The trunks of these feasting burghers were as wide as casks. The spread of their buttocks over the oak benches was not far short of a yard. They branched at the loins into thighs as thick as the torsos of ten-year-olds and arms on the same scale strained like bolsters at the confining serge. Chin and chest formed a single column, and each close-packed nape was creased with its three deceptive smiles. Every bristle had been cropped and shaven from their knobbly scalps. Except when five o'clock veiled them with shadow, surfaces as polished as ostriches' eggs reflected the lamplight. The frizzy hair of their wives was wrenched up from scarlet necks and pinned under slides and then hatted with green Bavarian trilbys and round one pair of elephantine shoulders a little fox stole was clasped. The youngest of this group, resembling a matinée idol under some cruel spell, was the bulkiest. Under tumbling blond curls his china blue eyes protruded from cheeks that might have been blown up with a bicycle pump, and cherry lips laid bare the sort of teeth that make children squeal. There was nothing bleary or stunned about their eyes. The setting may have reduced their size, but it keyed their glances to a sharper focus. Hands like bundles of sausages flew nimbly, packing in forkload on forkload of ham, salami, frankfurter, krenwurst and blutwurst and stone tankards were lifted for long swallows of liquid which sprang out again instantaneously on cheek and brow. They might have been competing with stop-watches, and their voices, only partly gagged by the cheekfuls of good things they were grinding down, grew louder while their unmodulated laughter jarred the air in frequent claps. Pumpernickel and aniseed rolls and bretzels bridged all the slack moments but supplies always came through before a true lull threatened. Huge oval dishes, laden with schweinebraten, potatoes, sauerkraut, red cabbage and dumplings were laid in front of each diner. They were followed by colossal joints of meat – unclassifiable helpings which, when they were picked clean, shone on the scoured chargers like calves' pelvises or the bones of elephants. Waitresses with the build of weight-lifters and all-in wrestlers whirled this provender along and features dripped and glittered like faces at an ogre's banquet. But all too soon the table was an empty bone-yard once more, sound faltered, a look of bereavement clouded those small eyes and there was a brief hint of sorrow in the air. But succour was always at hand; beldames barged to the rescue at full gallop with new clutches of mugs and fresh plate-loads of consumer goods; and the damp Laestrygonian brows unpuckered again in a happy renewal of clamour and intake.

I strayed by mistake into a room full of SS officers, Gruppen and Sturmbannführers, black from their lightning-flash-collars to the forest of tall boots underneath the table. The window embrasure was piled high with their skull-and-crossbones caps. I still hadn't found the part of this Bastille I was seeking, but at last a noise like the rush of a river guided me downstairs again to my journey's end.

The vaults of the great chamber faded into infinity through blue strata of smoke. Hobnails grated, mugs clashed and the combined smell of beer and bodies and old clothes and farmyards sprang at the newcomer. I squeezed in at a table full of peasants, and was soon lifting one of those masskrugs to my lips. It was heavier than a brace of iron dumb-bells, but the blond beer inside was cool and marvellous, a brooding, cylindrical litre of Teutonic myth. This was the fuel that had turned the berserk feeders upstairs into Zeppelins and floated them so far from heart's desire. The gunmetal-coloured cylinders were stamped with a blue HB conjoined under the Bavarian crown, like the foundry-mark on cannon. The tables, in my mind's eye, were becoming batteries where each gunner served a silent and recoil-less piece of ordnance which, trained on himself, pounded away in steady siege. *Mass*-gunfire! Here and there on the tables, with their heads in puddles of beer, isolated bombardiers had been mown down in their emplacements. The vaults reverberated with the thunder of a creeping barrage. There must have been over a thousand pieces engaged! – Big Berthas, Krupp's pale brood, battery on battery crashing at random or in salvoes as hands adjusted the elevation and traverse and then tightened on the stone trigger-guard. Supported by comrades, the walking wounded reeled through the battle smoke and a fresh gunner leaped into each place as it fell empty.

My own gun had fired its last shot, and I wanted to change to a darker-hued explosive. A new *Mass* was soon banged down on the board. In harmony with its colour, it struck a darker note at once, a long Wagnerian chord of black-letter semibreves: *Nacht und Nebel!* Rolling Bavarian acres formed in the inscape of the mind, fanning out in vistas of poles planted pyramidally with the hops gadding over them heavy with poppy-sombre flowers.

The peasants and farmers and the Munich artisans that filled the tables were much nicer than the civic swallowers overhead. Compared to the trim, drilled figures of the few soldiers there, the Storm Troopers looked like brown-paper parcels badly tied with string. There was even a sailor with two black silk streamers falling over his collar from the back of his cap, round the front of which, in gold letters, was written *Unterseeboot.* What was this Hanseatic submariner doing here, so far inland from Kiel and the Baltic? My tablemates were from the country, big, horny-handed men, with a wife or two among them. Some of the older men wore green and grey loden jackets with bone buttons and badgers' brushes or blackcocks' feathers in the back of their hatbands. The bone mouthpieces of long cherrywood pipes were lost in their whiskers and on their glazed china bowls, painted castles and pine-glades and chamois glowed cheerfully while shag-smoke poured through the perforations of their metal lids. Some of them, gnarled and mummified, puffed at cheroots through which straws were threaded to make them draw better. They gave me one and I added a choking tribute to the enveloping cloud. The accent had changed again, and I could only grasp the meaning of the simplest sentences. Many words were docked of their final consonants; '*Bursch*' – 'a chap' – for instance, became 'bua'; 'A' was rolled over into 'O', 'Ö' became 'E', and every O and U seemed to have a final A appended, turning it into a disyllable. All this set up a universal moo-ing note, wildly distorted by resonance and echo; for these millions of vowels, prolonged and bent into boomerangs, sailed ricochetting up through the fog to swell the tidal thunder. This echoing and fluid feeling, the bouncing of sounds and syllables and the hogsheads of pungent liquid that sloshed about the tables and blotted the sawdust underfoot, must have been responsible for the name of this enormous hall. It was called the *Schwemme*, or horse-pond. The hollowness of those tall mugs augmented the volume of noise like the amphorae which the Greeks embedded in masonry to add resonance to their chants. My own note, as the mug emptied, was sliding down to middle C.

Mammoth columns were rooted in the flagstones and the sawdust. Arches flew in broad hoops from capital to capital; crossing in diagonals, they groined the barrel-vaults that hung dimly above in the smoke. The place should have been lit by pine-torches in stanchions. It was beginning to change, turning now, under my clouding glance, into the scenery for some terrible Germanic saga, where snow vanished under the breath of dragons whose red-hot blood thawed sword-blades like icicles. It was a place for battle-axes and bloodshed and the last pages of the *Nibelungenlied* when the capital of Hunland is in flames and everybody in the castle is hacked to bits. Things grew quickly darker and more fluid; the echo, the splash, the boom and the roar of fast currents sunk this beer-hall under the Rhine-bed; it became a cavern full of more dragons, misshapen guardians of gross treasure; or the fearful abode, perhaps, where Beowulf, after tearing the Grendel's arm out of its socket, tracked him over the snow by the bloodstains and, reaching the mere's edge, dived in to swim many fathoms down and slay his loathsome water-hag of a mother in darkening spirals of gore.

Or so it seemed, when the third mug arrived.

Patrick Leigh Fermor *A Time of Gifts*

Stephano Remembers

We broke out of our dream into a clearing
and there were all our masters still sneering.
My head bowed, I made jokes and turned away,
living over and over that strange day.

The ship struck before morning. Half past four,
on a huge hogshead of claret I swept ashore
like an evangelist aboard his god:
his will was mine, I laughed and kissed the rod,
and would have walked that foreign countryside
blind drunk, contentedly till my god died;
but finding Trinculo made it a holiday;
two Neapolitans had got away,
and that shipload of scheming toffs we hated
was drowned. Never to be humiliated
again, 'I will no more to sea,' I sang.
Down white empty beaches my voice rang,
and that dear monster, half fish and half man,
went on his knees to me. Oh, Caliban,
you thought I'd take your twisted master's life;
but a drunk butler's slower with a knife
than your fine courtiers, your dukes, your kings.
We were distracted by too many things . . .
the wine, the jokes, the music, fancy gowns.
We were no good as murderers, we were clowns.

James Simmons

By Royal Command

KING: Let nothing but a Face of Joy appear;
The Man who frowns this Day, shall lose his Head,
That he may have no Face to frown again.
Smile, *Dollalolla*; – Ha! what wrinkled Sorrow
Sits, like some *Mother Demdike,* * on thy Brow?
Whence flow those Tears fast down thy blubber'd Cheeks,
Like a swoln Gutter, gushing through the Streets?
QUEEN: Excess of Joy, I've heard Folks say,
Gives Tears, as often as Excess of Grief.
KING: If it be so, let all Men cry for Joy,
'Till my whole Court be drowned with their Tears;
Nay, 'till they overflow my utmost Land,
And leave me nothing but the Sea to rule.
DOODLE: My Liege! I've a Petition –
KING: Petition me no Petitions, Sir, to-day;
Let other Hours be set apart for Bus'ness.
To-day it is our Pleasure to be drunk,
And this our Queen shall be as drunk as Us.
QUEEN: If the capacious Goblet overflow
With *Arrack-Punch*† – 'fore *George*! I'll see it out;
Of *Rum*, or *Brandy*, I'll not taste a Drop.
KING: Tho' *Rack*, in *Punch*, Eight Shillings be a Quart,
And *Rum* and *Brandy* be no more than Six,
Rather than quarrel, you shall have your Will.
(*Trumpets.*)
But, ha! the Warrior comes; *Tom Thumb* approaches;
The welcome Hero, Giant-killing Lad,
Preserver of my Kingdom, is arrived.

Henry Fielding *Tom Thumb*

*Mother Demdike: A notorious witch of the early seventeenth century.
†*Arrack-Punch*: An oriental term for various fermented juices, originally of the date.

Under-Age Drinking at the Adelphi Hotel in Edinburgh – 1963

Snug in that austere Lounge in the Old Town,
  New-shaved and after-shaved, two Beatlecuts
Over two bottles of Newcastle Brown,
  Two shortie-coats, two ties in Windsor knots
On wide-striped shirts with button-collars, trousers
  The twelve-inch-bottom, charcoal-grey ballcrushers,
And Chelsea Boots with shiny chisel toes, as
  Exquisite as the Tsars of All the Russias,

Home on a brace of out-of-town wee hairies,
  Bumming the chat, relaxed and debonair,
'Two o' these, Jimmie, and two Bloody Maries.'
  'Fancy our chances, pal?' 'We're well in there.'
Prop up the bar and plan out the attack:

Kiss on the doorstep and a long walk back.

John Whitworth

The Card-Players

Jan van Hogspeuw staggers to the door
And pisses at the dark. Outside, the rain
Courses in cart-ruts down the deep mud lane.
Inside, Dirk Dogstoerd pours himself some more,
And holds a cinder to his clay with tongs,
Belching out smoke. Old Prijck snores with the gale,
His skull face firelit; someone behind drinks ale,
And opens mussels, and croaks scraps of songs
Towards the ham-hung rafters about love.
Dirk deals the cards. Wet century-wide trees

Clash in surrounding starlessness above
This lamplit cave, where Jan turns back and farts,
Gobs at the grate, and hits the queen of hearts.

Rain, wind and fire! The secret, bestial peace!

Philip Larkin

Homecoming

Has bath and shave,
clean shirt etcetera,
full of potatoes,
rested, yet
badly distraught
by six-hour flight
(Boston to Dublin)
drunk all night
with crashing bore
from Houston, Tex.,
who spoke at length
on guns and sex.
Bus into town
and, sad to say,
no change from when
he went away
two years ago.
Goes into bar,
affixes gaze
on evening star.
Skies change but not
souls change. Behold
this is the way
the world grows old.
Scientists, birds,
we cannot start

at this late date
with a pure heart,
or having seen
the pictures plain
be ever innocent again.

Derek Mahon

Tube

You could say that I'm a student of Glazunov's. In my day Glazunov taught only chamber music at the Conservatoire and naturally I studied with him. He had his own style of teaching which must have looked bizarre to a stranger.

We went to his office on the first floor. Bulky Glazunov sat at his desk and we played. He never interrupted. We finished the piece (perhaps it was a Schubert Trio) and he muttered quietly. Glazunov muttered to himself, without rising from his desk, quietly and briefly. It was hard to tell exactly what he was saying and most of the time we didn't know.

The trouble was that I was at the piano and my friends were next to me. Glazunov remained at his desk, that is, at a considerable distance from us. He never stood up or came closer, and he spoke so softly. It seemed wrong to ask him to repeat himself and it also seemed wrong to move closer to him. It was a strange situation.

So we would repeat the work from beginning to end, guessing at changes. There was never any objection to our initiative. After the repeat performance Glazunov gave another speech, even softer and even shorter, after which we left.

At first I was extremely put out by this method of instruction, and particularly surprised by the fact that Glazunov never left his desk and came over to us, not even to glance once at the music. But with time I worked out the secret of his strange behaviour.

This is what I noticed. During the lessons Glazunov sometimes leaned over with a grunt toward his large director's desk, remained in that position for some time, and then straightened out with some difficulty.

Interested, I increased my observations of our beloved director's actions and came to this conclusion: Glazunov really did resemble a large baby, as so many people liked to say. Because a baby is always reaching for a nipple and so was Glazunov. But there was an essential difference. And the difference was that first of all Glazunov used a special tube instead of a nipple, a rubber tube if my observations were correct, and secondly, instead of milk, he was sipping alcohol.

These are not my conjectures, these are facts that I determined and confirmed through repeated observations. Without this fortification, Glazunov was incapable of giving the lesson. That's why he never rose from his desk and that's why his instructions to the class grew more indistinct and shorter.

Dimitri Shostakovich *Testimony*, trans. Antonina W. Bouis

Willie Brew'd a Peck o' Maut

O Willie brew'd a peck o' maut,
And Rob and Allan cam to see;
Three blyther hearts, that lee lang night,
Ye wad na found in Christendie.

We are na fou, we're nae that fou,
But just a drappie in our e'e;
The cock may craw, the day may daw,
And ay we'll taste the barley bree.

Here are we met, three merry boys,
Three merry boys I trow are we;
And mony a night we've merry been,
And mony mae we hope to be!

It is the moon, I ken her horn,
That's blinkin in the lift sae hie;
She shines sae bright to wyle us hame,
But by my sooth she'll wait a wee!

Wha first shall rise to gang awa,
  A cuckold, coward loun is he!
Wha first beside his chair shall fa',
  He is the king amang us three!

Robert Burns

Walking to Inveruplan

Glowing with answers in the aromatic dark,
I walk, so wise,
Under the final problem of lit skies.

I reach the bridge, where the road turns north to Stoer,
And there perch me
Under the final problem of a tree.

I'm in my Li Po mood. I've half a mind
To sit and drink
Until the moon, that's just arisen, should sink.

The whisky's good, it constellates. How wise
Can a man be,
I think, inside that final problem, me.

If you are short of answers, I've got them all
As clear as day . . .
I blink at the moon and put the bottle away

And then walk on (for there are miles to go
And friends to meet)
Above the final problem of my feet.

Norman MacCaig

Maut, malt; *lee lang*, live long; *fou*, drunk; *drappie*, drop; *e'e*, eye; *bree*, brew; *mony may*, many more; *lift*, sky; *hie*, high; *wyle*, entice; *wee*, bit; *loun*, fellow; *fa'*, fall.

Nineties

Remember nights you breezed in to the Café Royal
for gins and absinthes with the poetry crowd,
poured wine and *bons mots* down Lydias and Giselles?
Then tottered back, weeks later, muzzy, to your rooms
through a Nocturne by Whistler, turned up wicks on lamps
and penned a few impressions in tetrameter, with rhymes?
(You favoured ABBA.) The girls were all gazelles;
London was a gaslit heaven, a *flower that, at last*
like Dante's rose, opens to the moonlight, soft
as a yielding breast when whalebone is unlaced –
Good, that. Morning, and the pile of envelopes and stamps,
a hock-and-seltzer, then: *My dear Symons/Dowson/Gosse* . . .
(They're all dead, stupid: gone where everyone goes,
the scribblers and the muses, ash in a slow sift.
Who writes letters now? Get down the Cow & Crud
with Mick and Kevin, for a pint of something *real*.)

Alan Jenkins

Civilized Drinking, Civilized Chat

(*Imitation of Horace, Odes I.27*)

Calm down, you rugger-bugger sons-of-bitches:
A beer-glass sandwich and a dozen stitches
Suits spit-and-sawdust on the Celtic Fringe,
But I know better ways to have a binge.

Here, the right side of Watford, balls of Malt
Are more than just the prelude to assault.
Let's make acquaintance with this pint of Scotch
And ease the trousers out another notch

Not rip our bloody belts off. Ten-year-old
Laphroaig is the sweetest nectar ever sold.
Let's savour it like Christian men. Our chat
Shall be of sex, for everyone likes that,

And Love, ah careless Love, and Jacko's brother,
Who's never had to pay to get the other.
Now someone's got him by the short and curlies
He'll have to tell us who the lucky girl is.

Lucky is right, and it would be a pity
For any slag to bag a boy so pretty.
Your secret's safe with us in these four walls.
What lovely lady's itching for your balls

Now you're in love? . . . WHO? That's not even funny.
Those Northern girls do anything for money
And, as for her, she's into crack and speed.
Take it from me, she's just what you don't need.

Fergus Pickering

Chain Reaction

Hemingway appeared to have a special talent for drinking, despite occasional signs that all was not as benign as it might appear. In 1928 he suffered the first of his long series of self-inflicted accidents – the one involving his pulling the wrong chain in the hall toilet of his apartment, thereby bringing down the entire heavy glass skylight. The wound left a scar on his forehead that he carried for the rest of his life.

Tom Dardis *The Thirsty Muse*

Banish All the World

PRINCE HAL: Well, here I am set.

FALSTAFF: And here I stand. Judge, my masters.

PRINCE HAL: (*as* KING): Now, Harry, whence come you?

FALSTAFF: (*as* HAL): My noble lord, from Eastcheap.

PRINCE HAL: (*as* KING): The complaints I hear of thee are grievous.

FALSTAFF: (*as* HAL): 'Sblood, my lord, they are false!
Nay, I'll tickle ye for a young prince, i'faith.

PRINCE HAL: (*as* KING): Swearest thou, ungracious boy? Henceforth ne'er look on me. Thou art violently carried away from grace. There is a devil haunts thee in the likeness of an old fat man, a tun of man is thy companion. Why dost thou converse with that trunk of humours, that bolting-hutch of beastliness, that swollen parcel of dropsies, that huge bombard of sack, that stuffed cloak-bag of guts, that roasted Manningtree ox with the pudding in his belly, that reverend Vice, that grey Iniquity, that Father Ruffian, that Vanity in years? Wherein is he good, but to taste sack and drink it? Wherein neat and cleanly, but to carve a capon and eat it? Wherein cunning, but in craft? Wherein crafty, but in villainy? Wherein villainous, but in all things? Wherein worthy, but in nothing?

FALSTAFF: (*as* HAL): I would your grace would take me with you. Whom means your grace?

PRINCE HAL: (*as* KING): That villainous abominable misleader of youth, Falstaff, that old white-bearded Satan.

FALSTAFF: (*as* HAL): My lord, the man I know.

PRINCE HAL: (*as* KING): I know thou dost.

FALSTAFF: (*as* HAL): But to say I know more harm in him than in my self were to say more than I know. That he is old, the more the pity, his white hairs do witness it, but that he is, saving your reverence, a whoremaster, that I utterly deny. If sack and sugar be a fault, God help the wicked! If to be old and merry be a sin, then many an old host that I know is damned. If to be fat be to be hated, then Pharoah's lean kine are to be loved. No, my good lord! Banish Peto, banish Bardolph, banish Poins –

but for sweet Jack Falstaff, kind Jack Falstaff, true Jack Falstaff, valiant Jack Falstaff – and therefore more valiant, being as he is old Jack Falstaff – banish not him thy Harry's company, banish not him thy Harry's company. Banish plump Jack, and banish all the world.

PRINCE HAL: I do, I will.

William Shakespeare *Henry IV Part 1*

The Drinker

The man is killing time – there's nothing else.
No help now from the fifth of Bourbon
chucked helter-skelter into the river,
even its cork sucked under.

Stubbed before-breakfast cigarettes
burn bull's-eyes on the bedside table;
a plastic tumbler of alka seltzer
champagnes in the bathroom.

No help from his body, the whale's
warm-hearted blubber, foundering down
leagues of ocean, gasping whiteness.
The barbed hooks fester. The lines snap tight.

When he looks for neighbors, their names blur in the window,
his distracted eye sees only glass sky.
His despair has the galvanized color
of the mop and water in the galvanized bucket.

Once she was close to him
as water to the dead metal.

He looks at her engagements inked on her calendar.
A list of indictments.
At the numbers in her thumbed black telephone book.
A quiver full of arrows.

Her absence hisses like steam,
the pipes sing . . .
even corroded metal somehow functions.
He snores in his iron lung,

and hears the voice of Eve,
beseeching freedom from the Garden's
perfect and ponderous bubble. No voice
outsings the serpent's flawed, euphoric hiss.

The cheese wilts in the rat-trap,
the milk turns to junket in the cornflakes bowl,
car keys and razor blades
shine in an ashtray.

Is he killing time? Out on the street,
two cops on horseback clop through the April rain
to check the parking meter violations –
their oilskins yellow as forsythia.

Robert Lowell

Valentine

If I could draw, I would have sent a pretty heart stuck through with arrows, with some such sweet posy underneath it as this –

The rose is red, the violet blue,
The pink is sweet – and so are you.

But as the Gods have not made me a drawer (of anything but corks) you must accept the will for the deed.

P.S. I add a postscript on purpose to communicate a joke to you. A party of us had been drinking wine together, and three or four freshmen were most deplorably intoxicated – (I have too great a respect for delicacy to say Drunk). As we were returning homewards two of them fell into the gutter (or kennel.) We ran to assist one of them – who very generously stuttered out, as he lay sprawling in the mud – Nnn no nn no! – ssave my ffrfrfriend there – nnever mind me – *I* can swim.

Samuel Taylor Coleridge to Anne Evans, 14 February 1792

Dick Straightup

Past eighty, but never in eighty years –
Eighty winters on the windy ridge
Of England – has he buttoned his shirt or his jacket.
He sits in the bar-room seat he has been
Polishing with his backside sixty-odd years
Where nobody else sits. White is his head,
But his cheek high, hale as when he emptied
Every Saturday the twelve-pint tankard at a tilt,
Swallowed the whole serving of thirty eggs,
And banged the big bass drum for Heptonstall –
With a hundred other great works, still talked of.
Age has stiffened him, but not dazed or bent,
The blue eye has come clear of time:
At a single pint, now, his memory sips slowly,
His belly strong as a tree bole.

He survives among hills, nourished by stone and height.
The dust of Achilles and Cuchulain
Itches in the palms of scholars; thin clerks exercise
In their bed-sitters at midnight, and the meat salesman can
Loft fully four hundred pounds. But this one,
With no more application than sitting,
And drinking, and singing, fell in the sleet, late,
Dammed the pouring gutter; and slept there; and, throughout
A night searched by shouts and lamps, froze,
Grew to the road with welts of ice. He was chipped out at dawn
Warm as a pie and snoring.

The gossip of men younger by forty years –
Loud in his company since he no longer says much –
Empties, refills and empties their glasses.
Or their strenuous silence places the dominoes
(That are old as the house) into patterns
Gone with the game; the darts that glint to the dartboard
Pin no remarkable instant. The young men sitting
Taste their beer as by imitation,
Borrow their words as by impertinence
Because he sits there so full of legend and life
Quiet as a man alone.

He lives with sixty and seventy years ago,
And of everything he knows three quarters is in the grave,
Or tumbled down, or vanished. To be understood
His words must tug up the bottom-most stones of this village,
This clutter of blackstone gulleys, peeping curtains,
And a graveyard bigger and deeper than the village
That sways in the tide of wind and rain some fifty
Miles off the Irish sea.
The lamp above the pub-door
Wept yellow when he went out and the street
Of spinning darkness roared like a machine
As the wind applied itself. His upright walk,
His strong back, I commemorate now,
And his white blown head going out between a sky and an earth
That were bundled into placeless blackness, the one
Company of his mind.

Obit.

Now, you are strong as the earth you have entered.

This is a birthplace picture. Green into blue
The hills run deep and limpid. The weasel's
Berry-eyed red lock-head, gripping the dream
That holds good, goes lost in the heaved calm

Of the earth you have entered.

Ted Hughes

Outback Male

I had had to change buses in Katherine, on my way down to Alice from the Kimberleys.

It was lunchtime. The pub was full of truckies and construction workers, drinking beer and eating pasties. Most of them were wearing the standard uniform of the Outback male: desert boots, 'navvy' singlets to show off their tattoos, yellow hardhats and 'stubbies', which are green, tight-fitting, zipless shorts. And the first thing you saw, pushing past the frosted glass door, was a continuous row of hairy red legs and bottle-green buttocks.

Katherine is a stopover for tourists who come to see its famous Gorge. The Gorge was designated a National Park, but some Land Rights lawyers found a flaw in the legal documents and were claiming it back for the blacks. There was a lot of ill-feeling in the town.

I went to the men's room and, in the passage, a black whore pressed her nipples against my shirt and said, 'You want me, darling?'

'No.'

In the time I took to piss, she had already attached herself to a stringy little man on a bar-stool. He had bulging veins on his forearm, and a Park Warden's badge on his shirt.

'Nah!' he sneered. 'Yer dirty Gin! You couldn't excite me. I got me missus. But if you sat on the bar here, and spread your legs apart, I'd probably stick a bottle up yer.'

I took my drink and went to the far end of the room. I got talking to a Spaniard. He was short, bald and sweaty, and his voice was high-pitched and hysterical. He was the town baker. A few feet away from us, two Aboriginals were starting, very slowly, to fight.

The older Aboriginal had a crinkled forehead and a crimson shirt open to the navel. The other was a scrawny boy in skin-tight orange pants. The man was drunker than the boy, and could scarcely stand. He supported himself by propping his elbows on his stool. The boy was shrieking blue murder and frothing from the side of his mouth.

The baker dug me in the ribs. 'I come from Salamanca,' he screeched. 'Is like a bullfight, no?'

Someone else shouted, 'The Boongs are fighting,' although they weren't fighting – yet. But the drinkers, jeering and cheering, began shifting down the bar to get a look.

Gently, almost with a caress, the Aboriginal man tipped the boy's glass from his hand, and it fell and shattered on the floor. The boy stooped, picked up the broken base and held it like a dagger in his palm.

The truckie on the next stool poured out the contents of his own glass, smashed its rim against the lip of the counter, and shoved it in the older man's hand. 'Go on,' he said, encouragingly. 'Give it 'im.'

The boy lunged forward with his glass, but the man parried him with a flick of the wrist. Both had drawn blood.

'Olé!' shouted the Spanish baker, his face contorted into a grimace. 'Olé! Olé! Olé!'

The bouncer vaulted over the bar and dragged the two Aboriginals outside on to the sidewalk, across the tarmac, to an island in the highway where they lay, side by side, bleeding beneath the pink oleanders while the road-trains from Darwin rumbled by.

I walked away but the Spaniard followed me.

'They are best friends,' he said. 'No?'

Bruce Chatwin *The Song Lines*

Uptown

Yellow-lit Budweiser signs over oaken bars,
'I've seen everything' – the bartender handing me change of $10,
I stared at him amiably eyes thru an obvious Adamic beard –
with Montana musicians homeless in Manhattan, teen age
curly hair themselves – we sat at the antique booth & gossiped,
Madame Grady's literary salon a curious value in New York –
'If I had my way I'd cut off your hair and send you to Vietnam' –
'Bless you then' I replied to a hatted thin citizen hurrying to the
   barroom door
upon wet dark Amsterdam Avenue decades later –
'And if I couldn't do that I'd cut your throat' he snarled farewell,
and 'Bless you sir' I added as he went to his fate in the rain,
   dapper Irishman.

Allen Ginsberg

Atrocities

You told me, in your drunken-boasting mood,
How once you butchered prisoners. That was good!
I'm sure you felt no pity while they stood
Patient and cowed and scared, as prisoners should.

How did you do them in? Come, don't be shy:
You know I love to hear how Germans die,
Downstairs in dug-outs. 'Camerad!' they cry;
Then squeal like stoats when bombs begin to fly.

. . .

And you? I know your record. You went sick
When orders looked unwholesome; then, with trick
And lie, you wangled home. And here you are,
Still talking big and boozing in a bar.

Siegfried Sassoon

Casualty

[I]

He would drink by himself
And raise a weathered thumb
Towards the high shelf,
Calling another rum
And blackcurrant, without
Having to raise his voice,
Or order a quick stout
By a lifting of the eyes
And a discreet dumb-show
Of pulling off the top;
At closing time would go
In waders and peaked cap
Into the showery dark,
A dole-kept breadwinner
But a natural for work.
I loved his whole manner,
Sure-footed but too sly,
His deadpan sidling tact,
His fisherman's quick eye
And turned observant back.

Incomprehensible
To him, my other life.
Sometimes, on his high stool,
Too busy with his knife
At a tobacco plug

And not meeting my eye,
In the pause after a slug
He mentioned poetry.
We would be on our own
And, always politic
And shy of condescension,
I would manage by some trick
To switch the talk to eels
Or lore of the horse and cart
Or the Provisionals.

But my tentative art
His turned back watches too:
He was blown to bits
Out drinking in a curfew
Others obeyed, three nights
After they shot dead
The thirteen men in Derry.
PARAS THIRTEEN, the walls said,
BOGSIDE NIL. That Wednesday
Everybody held
His breath and trembled.

[2]

It was a day of cold
Raw silence, wind-blown
Surplice and soutane:
Rained-on, flower-laden
Coffin after coffin
Seemed to float from the door
Of the packed cathedral
Like blossoms on slow water.
The common funeral
Unrolled its swaddling band,
Lapping, tightening
Till we were braced and bound
Like brothers in a ring.

But he would not be held
At home by his own crowd
Whatever threats were phoned,
Whatever black flags waved.
I see him as he turned
In that bombed offending place,
Remorse fused with terror
In his still knowable face,
His cornered outfaced stare
Blinding in the flash.

He had gone miles away
For he drank like a fish
Nightly, naturally
Swimming towards the lure
Of warm lit-up places,
The blurred mesh and murmur
Drifting among glasses
In the gregarious smoke.
How culpable was he
That last night when he broke
Our tribe's complicity?
'Now you're supposed to be
An educated man,'
I hear him say. 'Puzzle me
The right answer to that one.'

[3]

I missed his funeral,
Those quiet walkers
And sideways talkers
Shoaling out of his lane
To the respectable
Purring of the hearse . . .
They move in equal pace
With the habitual
Slow consolation

Of a dawdling engine,
The line lifted, hand
Over fist, cold sunshine
On the water, the land
Banked under fog: that morning
I was taken in his boat,
The screw purling, turning
Indolent fathoms white,
I tasted freedom with him.
To get out early, haul
Steadily off the bottom,
Dispraise the catch, and smile
As you find a rhythm
Working you, slow mile by mile,
Into your proper haunt
Somewhere, well out, beyond . . .

Dawn-sniffing revenant,
Plodder through midnight rain,
Question me again.

Seamus Heaney

Livings

Tonight we dine without the Master
(Nocturnal vapours do not please);
The port goes round so much the faster,
Topics are raised with no less ease –
Which advowson looks the fairest,
What the wood from Snape will fetch,
Names for *pudendum mulieris*,
Why is Judas like Jack Ketch?

The candleflames grow thin, then broaden:
Our butler Starveling piles the logs
And sets behind the screen a jordan
(Quicker than going to the bogs).
The wine heats temper and complexion:
Oath-enforced assertions fly
On rheumy fevers, resurrection,
Regicide and rabbit pie.

The fields around are cold and muddy,
The cobbled streets close by are still,
A sizar shivers at his study,
The kitchen cat has made a kill;
The bells discuss the hour's gradations,
Dusty shelves hold prayers and proofs:
Above, Chaldean constellations
Sparkle over crowded roofs.

Philip Larkin

Drunks

One night in Albany
on a geology field-trip, in a corridor
upstairs of our hotel
I found McGovern on his hands & knees

heading for his lost room after a bet
which upright I had won.
I read everybody, borrowing their books from Mark,
it took me quite a while to get to Yeats.

I wondered every day about suicide.
Once at South Kent – maybe in the Third Form? –
I lay down on the tracks before a train
& had to be hauled off, the Headmaster was furious.

Once at a New Year's party at Mark Van Doren's
to which I took my Jane & H
cautioning them to behave themselves
the place was crawling with celebrities

poor H got stuck in an upstairs bedroom
with the blonde young wife of a famous critic
a wheel at one of the book clubs
who turned out to have nothing on under her gown

sprawled out half-drunk across her hostess's bed
moaning 'Put it in! Put it in!'
He was terrified
I passed out & was put in that same bed.

John Berryman

To Delmore Schwartz

(Cambridge 1946)

We couldn't even keep the furnace lit!
Even when we had disconnected it,
the antiquated
refrigerator gurgled mustard gas
through your mustard-yellow house,
and spoiled our long maneuvered visit
from T. S. Eliot's brother, Henry Ware. . . .

Your stuffed duck craned toward Harvard from my trunk:
its bill was a black whistle, and its brow
was high and thinner than a baby's thumb;
its webs were tough as toenails on its bough.
It was your first kill; you had rushed it home,
pickled in a tin wastebasket of rum –
it looked through us, as if it'd died dead drunk.
You must have propped its eyelids with a nail,

and yet it lived with us and met our stare,
Rabelaisian, lubricious, drugged. And there,
perched on my trunk and typing-table,
it cooled our universal
Angst a moment, Delmore. We drank and eyed
the chicken-hearted shadows of the world.
Underseas fellows, nobly mad,
we talked away our friends. 'Let Joyce and Freud,
the Masters of Joy,
be our guests here,' you said. The room was filled
with cigarette smoke circling the paranoid,
inert gaze of Coleridge, back
from Malta – his eyes lost in flesh, lips baked and black.
Your tiger kitten, *Oranges,*
cartwheeled for joy in a ball of snarls.
You said:
'*We poets in our youth begin in sadness;*
thereof in the end come despondency and madness;
Stalin has had two cerebral hemorrhages!'
The Charles
River was turning silver. In the ebb-
light of morning, we stuck
the duck
-'s web-
foot, like a candle, in a quart of gin we'd killed.

Robert Lowell

Hall of Fame

It seemed that from the beer-tent I escaped
Down some profound depression, where they kept

Silent the damaged and the down-and-out.
A sergeant rang the bell for them to eat,

That being the hour appointed; but the failures
Who shuffled from the darkness on all fours

Had burned away their appetite for solids
And only a couple accepted watery salads

To sip at on their disinfected bunks.
These were the veterans of such bloody banquets

Eternal headaches hurt them, and still hurt;
'Hey soldier!' I called at one I seemed to hate

Who was sitting helpless in his vest and pants
Over a tray of flat insipid pints:

'Didn't I see you when you were so pissed
On the road here, that a mug of whisky passed

Straight back out of your nostrils as you drank?
Tell me, how did a soldier get that drunk?

And how did you fare later?' Out of luck
He shed his numbered shorts and made me look

At something that I wished I had not seen,
The ruined arse-hole, flapping, crudely sewn,

Through which he spoke: 'After the rout – I lost,
I think, or won – came either first or last –

'They bore me up, oblivious to my wound,
On eager shoulders; but before they could be warned,

'With a loud noise, the crap larruped down my leg.
Now every Christmas I raise half a lager

'To absent friends; and absent is the word,
For nobody loves me in the Drinking Ward

'Or brings me chocolates or forget-me-nots . . .'
So moaning he withdrew; the last three notes

Blew like reveille from their fading source.

Mick Imlah

'To Speak of Woe That Is in Marriage'

'It is the future generation that presses into being by means of these exuberant feelings and supersensible soap bubbles of ours.'

SCHOPENHAUER

'The hot night makes us keep our bedroom windows open.
Our magnolia blossoms. Life begins to happen.
My hopped up husband drops his home disputes,
and hits the streets to cruise for prostitutes,
free-lancing out along the razor's edge.
This screwball might kill his wife, then take the pledge.
Oh the monotonous meanness of his lust.
It's the injustice . . . he is so unjust –
whiskey-blind, swaggering home at five.
My only thought is how to keep alive.
What makes him tick? Each night now I tie
ten dollars and his car key to my thigh. . . .
Gored by the climacteric of his want,
he stalls above me like an elephant.'

Robert Lowell

CHILDREN

My Papa's Waltz

The whiskey on your breath
Could make a small boy dizzy;
But I hung on like death:
Such waltzing was not easy.

We romped until the pans
Slid from the kitchen shelf;
My mother's countenance
Could not unfrown itself.

The hand that held my wrist
Was battered on one knuckle;
At every step you missed
My right ear scraped a buckle.

You beat time on my head
With a palm caked hard by dirt,
Then waltzed me off to bed
Still clinging to your shirt.

Theodore Roethke

The Birth of Paul, and Another Battle

A wave of hot love went over her to the infant. She held it close to her face and breast. With all her force, with all her soul she would make up to it for having brought it into the world unloved. She would love it all the more now it was here; carry it in her love. Its clear, knowing eyes gave her pain and fear. Did it know all about her? When it lay under her heart, had it been listening then? Was there a reproach in the look? She felt the marrow melt in her bones, with fear and pain.

Once more she was aware of the sun lying red on the rim of the hill opposite. She suddenly held up the child in her hands.

'Look!' she said. 'Look, my pretty!'

She thrust the infant forward to the crimson, throbbing sun, almost with relief. She saw him lift his little fist. Then she put him into her bosom again, ashamed of her impulse to give him back again whence he came.

'If he lives,' she thought to herself, 'what will become of him – what will he be?'

Her heart was anxious.

'I will call him "Paul",' she said suddenly; she knew not why.

After a while she went home. A fine shadow was flung over the deep green meadow, darkening all.

As she expected, she found the house empty. But Morel was home by ten o'clock, and that day, at least, ended peacefully.

Walter Morel was, at this time, exceedingly irritable. His work seemed to exhaust him. When he came home he did not speak civilly to anybody. If the fire were rather low he bullied about that; he grumbled about his dinner; if the children made a chatter he shouted at them in a way that made their mother's blood boil, and made them hate him.

On the Friday, he was not home by eleven o'clock. The baby was unwell, and was restless, crying if he were put down. Mrs Morel, tired to death, and still weak, was scarcely under control.

'I wish the nuisance would come,' she said wearily to herself.

The child at last sank down to sleep in her arms. She was too tired to carry him to the cradle.

'But I'll say nothing, whatever time he comes,' she said. 'It only works me up: I won't say anything. But I know if he does anything it'll make my blood boil,' she added to herself.

She sighed, hearing him coming, as if it were something she could not bear. He, taking his revenge, was nearly drunk. She kept her head bent over the child as he entered, not wishing to see him. But it went through her like a flash of hot fire when, in passing, he lurched against the dresser, setting the tins rattling, and clutched at the white pot knobs for support. He hung up his hat and coat, then returned, stood glowering from a distance at her, as she sat bowed over the child.

'Is there nothing to eat in the house?' he asked, insolently, as if to a servant. In certain stages of his intoxication he affected the clipped, mincing speech of the towns. Mrs Morel hated him most in this condition.

'You know what there is in the house,' she said, so coldly it sounded impersonal.

He stood and glared at her without moving a muscle.

'I asked a civil question, and I expect a civil answer,' he said affectedly.

'And you got it,' she said, still ignoring him.

He glowered again. Then he came unsteadily forward. He leaned on the table with one hand, and with the other jerked at the table drawer to get a knife to cut bread. The drawer stuck because he pulled sideways. In a temper he dragged it, so that it flew out bodily, and spoons, forks, knives, a hundred metallic things, splashed with a clatter and a clang upon the brick floor. The baby gave a little convulsed start.

'What are you doing, clumsy, drunken fool?' the mother cried.

'Then tha should get the flamin' thing thysen. Tha should get up, like other women have to, an' wait on a man.'

'Wait on you – wait on you?' she cried. 'Yes, I see myself.'

'Yis, an' I'll learn thee tha's got to. Wait on *me*, yes, tha sh'lt wait on me –'

'Never, milord. I'd wait on a dog at the door first.'

'What – what?'

He was trying to fit in the drawer. At her last speech he turned round. His face was crimson, his eyes bloodshot. He stared at her one silent second in threat.

'P-h!' she went quickly, in contempt.

He jerked at the drawer in his excitement. It fell, cut sharply on his shin, and on the reflex he flung it at her.

One of the corners caught her brow as the shallow drawer crashed into the fireplace. She swayed, almost fell stunned from her chair. To her very soul she was sick; she clasped the child tightly to her bosom. A few moments elapsed; then, with an effort, she brought herself to. The baby was crying plaintively. Her left brow was bleeding rather profusely. As she glanced down at the child, her brain reeling, some drops of blood soaked into its white shawl; but the baby was at least not hurt. She balanced her head to keep equilibrium, so that the blood ran into her eye.

Walter Morel remained as he had stood, leaning on the table with one hand, looking blank. When he was sufficiently sure of his balance, he went across to her, swayed, caught hold of the back of her rocking-chair, almost tipping her out; then, leaning forward over her, and swaying as he spoke, he said, in a tone of wondering concern:

'Did it catch thee?'

He swayed again, as if he would pitch on to the child. With the catastrophe he had lost all balance.

'Go away,' she said, struggling to keep her presence of mind.

He hiccoughed. 'Let's – let's look at it,' he said, hiccoughing again.

'Go away!' she cried.

'Lemme – lemme look at it, lass.'

She smelled him of drink, felt the unequal pull of his swaying grasp on the back of her rocking-chair.

'Go away,' she said, and weakly she pushed him off.

He stood, uncertain in balance, gazing upon her. Summoning all her strength she rose, the baby on one arm. By a cruel effort of will, moving as if in sleep, she went across to the scullery, where she bathed her eye for a minute in cold water; but she was too dizzy. Afraid lest she should swoon, she returned to her rocking-chair, trembling in every fibre. By instinct, she kept the baby clasped.

Morel, bothered, had succeeded in pushing the drawer back into its cavity, and was on his knees, groping, with numb paws, for the scattered spoons.

Her brow was still bleeding. Presently Morel got up and came craning his neck towards her.

'What has it done to thee, lass?' he asked, in a very wretched, humble tone.

'You can see what it's done,' she answered.

He stood, bending forward, supported on his hands, which grasped his legs just above the knee. He peered to look at the wound. She drew away from the thrust of his face with its great moustache, averting her own face as much as possible. As he looked at her, who was cold and impassive as stone, with mouth shut tight, he sickened with feebleness and hopelessness of spirit. He was turning drearily away, when he saw a drop of blood fall from the averted wound into the baby's fragile, glistening hair. Fascinated he watched the heavy dark drop hang in the glistening cloud, and pull down the gossamer. Another drop fell. It would soak through to the baby's scalp. He watched, fascinated, feeling it soak in; then, finally, his manhood broke.

'What of this child?' was all his wife said to him. But her low, intense tones brought his head lower. She softened: 'Get me some wadding out of the middle drawer,' she said.

He stumbled away very obediently, presently returning with a pad, which she singed before the fire, then put on her forehead, as she sat with the baby on her lap.

'Now that clean pit-scarf.'

Again he rummaged and fumbled in the drawer, returning presently with a red, narrow scarf. She took it, and with trembling fingers proceeded to bind it round her head.

'Let me tie it for thee,' he said humbly.

'I can do it myself,' she replied. When it was done she went upstairs, telling him to rake the fire and lock the door.

In the morning Mrs Morel said:

'I knocked against the latch of the coal-place, when I was getting a raker in the dark, because the candle blew out.' Her two small children looked up at her with wide, dismayed eyes. They said nothing, but their parted lips seemed to express the unconscious tragedy they felt.

D. H. Lawrence *Sons and Lovers*

Suspenders

Mom said I didn't have a belt that fit and
I was going to have to wear suspenders to school
next day. Nobody wore suspenders to second grade,
or any other grade for that matter. She said,
You'll wear them or else I'll use them on you. I don't
want any more trouble. My dad said something then. He
was in the bed that took up most of the room in the cabin
where we lived. He asked if we would be quiet and settle this
in the morning. Didn't he have to go in early to work in
the morning? He asked if I'd bring him
a glass of water. It's all that whiskey he drank, Mom said. He's
dehydrated.

I went to the sink and, I don't know why, brought him
a glass of soapy dishwater. He drank it and said, That sure
tasted funny, son. Where'd this water come from?
Out of the sink, I said.
I thought you loved your dad, Mom said.
I do, I do, I said, and went over to the sink and dipped a glass
into the soapy water and drank off two glasses just
to show them. I love Dad, I said.
Still, I thought I was going to be sick then and there. Mom said,
I'd be ashamed of myself if I was you. I can't believe you'd
do your dad that way. And, by God, you're going to wear those
suspenders tomorrow, or else. I'll snatch you bald-headed if you
give me any trouble in the morning. I don't want to wear
suspenders,
I said. You're going to wear suspenders, she said. And with that
she took the suspenders and began to whip me around the bare legs
while I danced in the room and cried. My dad
yelled at us to stop, for God's sake, stop. His head was killing him,
and he was sick at his stomach from soapy dishwater
besides. That's thanks to this one, Mom said. It was then somebody
began to pound on the wall of the cabin next to ours. At first it

sounded like it was a fist – *boom-boom-boom* – and then
whoever it was switched to a mop or a broom
handle. For Christ's sake, go to bed over there! somebody yelled.
Knock if off! And we did. We turned out the lights and
got into our beds and became quiet. The quiet that comes to a house
where nobody can sleep.

Raymond Carver

The Outing: A Story

If you can call it a story. There's no real beginning or end and there's very little in the middle. It is all about a day's outing, by charabanc, to Porthcawl, which, of course, the charabanc never reached, and it happened when I was so high and much nicer.

I was staying at the time with my uncle and his wife. Although she was my aunt, I never thought of her as anything but the wife of my uncle, partly because he was so big and trumpeting and red-hairy and used to fill every inch of the hot little house like an old buffalo squeezed into an airing cupboard, and partly because she was so small and silk and quick and made no noise at all as she whisked about on padded paws, dusting the china dogs, feeding the buffalo, setting the mousetraps that never caught her; and once she sleaked out of the room, to squeak in a nook or nibble in the hayloft, you forgot she had ever been there.

But there he was, always, a steaming hulk of an uncle, his braces straining like hawsers, crammed behind the counter of the tiny shop at the front of the house, and breathing like a brass band; or guzzling and blustery in the kitchen over his gutsy supper, too big for everything except the great black boats of his boots. As he ate, the house grew smaller; he billowed out over the furniture, the loud check meadow of his waistcoat littered, as though after a picnic, with cigarette ends, peelings, cabbage stalks, birds' bones, gravy; and the forest fire of his hair crackled among the hooked hams from the ceiling. She was so small she could hit him only if she stood on a chair, and every Saturday night at half past ten he would lift her up, under his arm, on to a chair in the kitchen so that she could hit him on the head with whatever was handy, which was always a china dog. On Sundays, and when pickled, he sang high tenor, and had won many cups.

The first I heard of the annual outing was when I was sitting one evening on a bag of rice behind the counter, under one of my uncle's stomachs, reading an advertisement for sheep-dip, which was all there was to read. The shop was full of my uncle, and when Mr Benjamin Franklyn, Mr Weazley, Noah Bowen, and Will Sentry came in, I thought it would burst. It was like all being together in a drawer that smelt of cheese and turps, and twist tobacco and sweet biscuits and snuff and waistcoat. Mr Benjamin Franklyn said that he had collected enough money for the charabanc and twenty cases of pale ale and a pound apiece over that he would distribute among the members of the outing when they first stopped for refreshment, and he was about sick and tired, he said, of being followed by Will Sentry.

'All day long, wherever I go,' he said, 'he's after me like a collie with one eye. I got a shadow of my own *and* a dog. I don't need no Tom, Dick, or Harry pursuing me with his dirty muffler on.'

Will Sentry blushed, and said: 'It's only oily. I got a bicycle.'

'A man has no privacy at all,' Mr Franklyn went on.

'I tell you he sticks so close I'm afraid to go out the back in case I sit in his lap. It's a wonder to me,' he said, 'he don't follow me into bed at night.'

'Wife won't let,' Will Sentry said.

And that started Mr Franklyn off again, and they tried to soothe him down by saying: 'Don't you mind Will Sentry' . . . 'No harm in old Will' . . . 'He's only keeping an eye on the money, Benjie.'

'Aren't I honest?' asked Mr Franklyn in surprise.

There was no answer for some time, then Noah Bowen said: 'You know what the committee is. Ever since Bob the Fiddle they don't feel safe with a new treasurer.'

'Do you think *I*'m going to drink the outing funds, like Bob the Fiddle did?' said Mr Franklyn.

'You *might*,' said my uncle slowly.

'I resign,' said Mr Franklyn.

'Not with our money you won't,' Will Sentry said.

'Who put dynamite in the salmon pool?' said Mr Weazley, but nobody took any notice of him. And, after a time, they all began to play cards in the thickening dusk of the hot, cheesy shop, and my uncle blew and bugled whenever he won, and Mr Weazley grumbled like a dredger, and I fell to sleep on the gravy-scented mountain meadow of uncle's waistcoat.

On Sunday evening, after Bethesda, Mr Franklyn walked into the kitchen where my uncle and I were eating sardines with spoons from the tin because it was Sunday and his wife would not let us play draughts.

She was somewhere in the kitchen, too. Perhaps she was inside the grandmother clock, hanging from the weights and breathing. Then, a second later, the door opened again and Will Sentry edged into the room, twiddling his hard, round hat. He and Mr Franklyn sat down on the settee, stiff and moth-balled and black in their chapel and funeral suits.

'I brought the list,' said Mr Franklyn. 'Every member fully paid. You ask Will Sentry.'

My uncle put on his spectacles, wiped his whiskery mouth with a handkerchief big as a Union Jack, laid down his spoon of sardines, took Mr Franklyn's list of names, removed the spectacles so that he could read, and then ticked the names off one by one.

'Enoch Davies. Aye. He's good with his fists. You never know. Little Gerwain. Very melodious bass. Mr Cadwalladwr. That's right. He can tell opening time better than my watch. Mr Weazley. Of course. He's been to Paris. Pity he suffers so much in the charabanc. Stopped us nine times last year between the Beehive and the Red Dragon. Noah Bowen, ah, very peaceable. He's got a tongue like a turtle-dove. Never a argument with Noah Bowen. Jenkins Loughor. Keep him off economics. It cost us a plate-glass window. And ten pints for the Sergeant. Mr Jarvis. Very tidy.'

'He tried to put a pig in the charra,' Will Sentry said.

'Live and let live,' said my uncle.

Will Sentry blushed.

'Sinbad the Sailor's Arms. Got to keep in with him. Old O. Jones.'

'Why old O. Jones?' said Will Sentry.

'Old O. Jones always goes,' said my uncle.

I looked down at the kitchen table. The tin of sardines was gone. By Gee, I said to myself, Uncle's wife is quick as a flash.

'Cuthbert Johnny Fortnight. Now there's a card,' said my uncle.

'He whistles after women,' Will Sentry said.

'So do you,' said Mr Benjamin Franklyn, 'in your mind.'

My uncle at last approved the whole list, pausing only to say, when he came across one name: 'If we weren't a Christian community, we'd chuck that Bob the Fiddle in the sea.'

'We can do that in Porthcawl,' said Mr Franklyn, and soon after that he went, Will Sentry no more than an inch behind him, their Sunday-bright boots squeaking on the kitchen cobbles.

And then, suddenly, there was my uncle's wife standing in front of the dresser, with a china dog in one hand. By Gee, I said to myself again, did you ever see such a woman, if that's what she is. The lamps were not lit yet in the kitchen and she stood in a wood of shadows, with the plates on the dresser behind her shining – like pink-and-white eyes.

'If you go on that outing on Saturday, Mr Thomas,' she said to my uncle in her small, silk voice, 'I'm going home to my mother's.'

Holy Mo, I thought, she's got a mother. Now that's one old bald mouse of a hundred and five I won't be wanting to meet in a dark lane.

'It's me or the outing, Mr Thomas.'

I would have made my choice at once, but it was almost half a minute before my uncle said: 'Well, then, Sarah, it's the outing, my love.' He lifted her up, under his arm, on to a chair in the kitchen, and she hit him on the head with the china dog. Then he lifted her down again, and then I said good night.

For the rest of the week my uncle's wife whisked quiet and quick round the house with her darting duster, my uncle blew and bugled and swole, and I kept myself busy all the time being up to no good. And then at breakfast time on Saturday morning, the morning of the outing, I found a note on the kitchen table. It said: 'There's some eggs in the pantry. Take your boots off before you go to bed.' My uncle's wife had gone, as quick as a flash.

When my uncle saw the note, he tugged out the flag of his handkerchief and blew such a hubbub of trumpets that the plates on the dresser shook. 'It's the same every year,' he said. And then he looked at me. 'But this year it's different. *You*'ll have to come on the outing, too, and what the members will say I dare not think.'

The charabanc drew up outside, and when the members of the outing saw my uncle and me squeeze out of the shop together, both of us cat-licked and brushed in our Sunday best, they snarled like a zoo.

'Are you bringing a *boy*?' asked Mr Benjamin Franklyn as we climbed into the charabanc. He looked at me with horror.

'Boys is nasty,' said Mr Weazley.

'He hasn't paid his contributions,' Will Sentry said.

'No room for boys. Boys get sick in charabancs.'

'So do you, Enoch Davies,' said my uncle.

'Might as well bring *women*.'

The way they said it, women were worse than boys.

'Better than bringing grandfathers.'

'Grandfathers is nasty too,' said Mr Weazley.

'What can we do with him when we stop for refreshments?'

'I'm a grandfather,' said Mr Weazley.

'Twenty-six minutes to opening time,' shouted an old man in a panama hat, not looking at a watch. They forgot me at once.

'Good old Mr Cadwalladwr,' they cried, and the charabanc started off down the village street.

A few cold women stood at their doorways, grimly watching us go. A very small boy waved good-bye, and his mother boxed his ears. It was a beautiful August morning.

We were out of the village, and over the bridge, and up the hill towards Steeplehat Wood when Mr Franklyn, with his list of names in his hand, called out loud: 'Where's old O. Jones?'

'Where's old O?'

'We've left old O behind.'

'Can't go without old O.'

And though Mr Weazley hissed all the way, we turned and drove back to the village, where, outside the Prince of Wales, old O. Jones was waiting patiently and alone with a canvas bag.

'I didn't want to come at all,' old O. Jones said as they hoisted him into the charabanc and clapped him on the back and pushed him on a seat and stuck a bottle in his hand, 'but I always go.' And over the bridge and up the hill and under the deep green wood and along the dusty road we wove, slow cows and ducks flying by, until 'Stop the bus!' Mr Weazley cried. 'I left my teeth on the mantelpiece.'

'Never you mind,' they said, 'you're not going to bite nobody,' and they gave him a bottle with a straw.

'I might want to smile,' he said.

'Not you,' they said.

'What's the time, Mr Cadwalladwr?'

'Twelve minutes to go,' shouted back the old man in the panama, and they all began to curse him.

The charabanc pulled up outside the Mountain Sheep, a small, unhappy public-house with a thatched roof like a wig with ringworm. From a flagpole by the Gents fluttered the flag of Siam. I knew it was the flag of Siam because of cigarette cards. The landlord stood at the door to welcome us, simpering like a wolf. He was a long, lean, black-fanged man with a greased love-curl and pouncing eyes. 'What a beautiful August day!' he said, and touched his love-curl with a claw. That was the way he must have welcomed the Mountain Sheep before he ate it, I said to myself. The members rushed out, bleating, and into the bar.

'You keep an eye on the charra,' my uncle said; 'see nobody steals it now.'

'There's nobody to steal it,' I said, 'except some cows,' but my uncle was gustily blowing his bugle in the bar.

I looked at the cows opposite, and they looked at me. There was nothing else for us to do. Forty-five minutes passed, like a very slow cloud. The sun shone down on the lonely road, the lost, unwanted boy, and the lake-eyed cows. In the dark bar they were so happy they were breaking glasses. A Shoni-Onion Breton man, with a beret and a necklace of onions, bicycled down the road and stopped at the door.

'Quelle un grand matin, monsieur,' I said.

'There's French, boy bach!' he said.

I followed him down the passage, and peered into the bar. I could hardly recognize the members of the outing. They had all changed colour. Beetroot, rhubarb, and puce, they hollered and rollicked in that dark, damp hole like enormous ancient bad boys, and my uncle surged in the middle, all red whiskers and bellies. On the floor was broken glass and Mr Weazley.

'Drinks all round,' cried Bob the Fiddle, a small, absconding man with bright blue eyes and a plump smile.

'Who's been robbing the orphans?'

'Who sold his little babby to the gyppoes?'

'Trust old Bob, he'll let you down.'

'You will have your little joke,' said Bob the Fiddle, smiling like a razor, 'but I forgive you, boys.'

Out of the fug and babel I heard: 'Come out and fight.'

'No, not now, later.'

'No, now when I'm in a temper.'

'Look at Will Sentry, he's proper snobbled.'

'Look at his wilful feet.'

'Look at Mr Weazley lording it on the floor.'

Mr Weazley got up, hissing like a gander. 'That boy pushed me down deliberate,' he said, pointing to me at the door, and I slunk away down the passage and out to the mild, good cows. Time clouded over, the cows wondered, I threw a stone at them and they wandered, wondering, away. Then out blew my uncle, ballooning, and one by one the members lumbered after him in a grizzle. They had drunk the Mountain Sheep dry. Mr Weazley had won a string of onions that the Shoni-Onion man raffled in the bar. 'What's the good of onions if you left your teeth on the mantelpiece?' he said. And when I looked through the back window of the thundering charabanc, I saw the pub grow smaller in the distance. And the flag of Siam, from the flagpole by the Gents, fluttered now at half mast.

The Blue Bull, the Dragon, the Star of Wales, the Twll in the Wall, the Sour Grapes, the Shepherd's Arms, the Bells of Aberdovey: I had nothing to do in the whole, wild August world but remember the names where the outing stopped and keep an eye on the charabanc. And whenever it passed a public-house, Mr Weazley would cough like a billygoat and cry: 'Stop the bus, I'm dying of breath!' And back we would all have to go.

Closing time meant nothing to the members of that outing. Behind locked doors, they hymned and rumpused all the beautiful afternoon. And, when a policeman entered the Druid's Tap by the back door, and found them all choral with beer, 'Sssh!' said Noah Bowen, 'the pub is shut.'

'Where do you come from?' he said in his buttoned, blue voice.

They told him.

'I got a auntie there,' the policeman said. And very soon he was singing 'Asleep in the Deep.'

Off we drove again at last, the charabanc bouncing with tenors and flagons, and came to a river that rushed along among willows.

'Water!' they shouted.

'Porthcawl!' sang my uncle.

'Where's the donkeys?' said Mr Weazley.

And out they lurched, to paddle and whoop in the cool, white, winding water. Mr Franklyn, trying to polka on the slippery stones, fell in twice. 'Nothing is simple,' he said with dignity as he oozed up the bank.

'It's cold!' they cried.

'It's lovely!'

'It's smooth as a moth's nose!'

'It's *better* than Porthcawl!'

And dusk came down warm and gentle on thirty wild, wet, pickled, splashing men without a care in the world at the end of the world in the west of Wales.

And, 'Who goes there?' called Will Sentry to a wild duck flying.

They stopped at the Hermit's Nest for a rum to keep out the cold. 'I played for Aberavon in 1898,' said a stranger to Enoch Davies.'

'Liar,' said Enoch Davies.

'I can show you photos,' said the stranger.

'Forged,' said Enoch Davies.

'And I'll show you my cap at home.'

'Stolen.'

'I got friends to prove it,' the stranger said in fury.

'Bribed,' said Enoch Davies.

On the way home, through the simmering moon-splashed dark,

old O. Jones began to cook his supper on a primus stove in the middle of the charabanc. Mr Weazley coughed himself blue in the smoke. 'Stop the bus,' he cried, 'I'm dying of breath!' We all climbed down into the moonlight. There was not a public-house in sight. So they carried out the remaining cases, and the primus stove, and old O. Jones himself, and took them into a field, and sat down in a circle in the field and drank and sang while old O. Jones cooked sausage and mash and the moon flew above us. And there I drifted to sleep against my uncle's mountainous waistcoat, and, as I slept, 'Who goes there?' called out Will Sentry to the flying moon.

Dylan Thomas *A Prospect of the Sea*

First Drink

The Italian rancho was a bachelor establishment. Our visit was hailed with delight. The red wine was poured in tumblers for all, and the long dining-room was partly cleared for dancing. And the young fellows drank and danced with the girls to the strains of an accordion. To me that music was divine. I had never heard anything so glorious. The young Italian who furnished it would even get up and dance, his arms around his girl, playing the accordion behind her back. All of which was very wonderful for me, who did not dance, but who sat at a table and gazed wide-eyed at the amazingness of life. I was only a little lad, and there was so much of life for me to learn. As the time passed, the Irish lads began helping themselves to the wine, and jollity and high spirits reigned. I noted that some of them staggered and fell down in the dances, and that one had gone to sleep in a corner. Also, some of the girls were complaining, and wanting to leave, and others of the girls were titteringly complacent, willing for anything to happen.

When our Italian hosts had offered me wine in a general sort of way, I had declined. My beer experience had been enough for me, and I had no inclination to traffic further in the stuff, or in anything related to it. Unfortunately, one young Italian, Peter, an impish soul, seeing me sitting solitary, stirred by a whim of the moment, half-filled a tumbler with wine and passed it to me. He was sitting across the table from me. I declined. His face grew stern, and he insistently proffered the wine. And then terror descended upon me – a terror which I must explain.

My mother had theories. First, she steadfastly maintained that brunettes and all the tribe of dark-eyed humans were deceitful. Needless to say, my mother was a blonde. Next, she was convinced that the dark-eyed Latin races were profoundly sensitive, profoundly treacherous, and profoundly murderous. Again and again, drinking in the strangeness and the fearsomeness of the world from her lips, I had heard her state that if one offended an Italian, no matter how slightly and unintentionally, he was certain to retaliate by stabbing one in the back. That was her particular phrase – 'stab you in the back.'

Now, although I had been eager to see Black Matt kill Tom Morrisey that morning, I did not care to furnish to the dancers the spectacle of a knife sticking in *my* back. I had not yet learned to distinguish between facts and theories. My faith was implicit in my mother's exposition of the Italian character. Besides, I had some glimmering inkling of the sacredness of hospitality. Here was a treacherous, sensitive, murderous Italian, offering me hospitality. I had been taught to believe that if I offended him he would strike at me with a knife precisely as a horse kicked out when one got too close to its heels and worried it. Then, too, this Italian, Peter, had those terrible black eyes I had heard my mother talk about. They were eyes different from the eyes I knew, from the blues and greys and hazels of my own family, from the pale and genial blues of the Irish. Perhaps Peter had had a few drinks. At any rate, his eyes were brilliantly black and sparkling with devilry. They were the mysterious, the unknown, and who was I, a seven-year-old, to analyse them and know their prankishness? In them I visioned sudden death, and I declined the wine half-heartedly. The expression in his eyes changed. They grew stern and imperious as he shoved the tumbler of wine closer.

What could I do? I have faced real death since in my life, but never have I known the fear of death as I knew it then. I put the glass to my lips, and Peter's eyes relented. I knew he would not kill me just then. That was a relief. But the wine was not. It was cheap, new wine, bitter and sour, made of the leavings and scrapings of the vineyards and the vats, and it tasted far worse than beer. There is only one way to take medicine, and that is to take it. And that is the way I took that wine. I threw my head back and gulped it down. I had to gulp again and hold the poison down, for poison it was to my child's tissues and membranes.

Looking back now, I can realize that Peter was astounded. He half-filled a second tumbler and shoved it across the table. Frozen with fear, in despair at the fate which had befallen me, I gulped the second glass down like the first. This was too much for Peter. He must share the infant prodigy he had discovered. He called Dominick, a young moustached Italian, to see the sight. This time it was a full tumbler that was given me. One will do anything to live. I gripped myself, mastered the qualms that rose in my throat, and downed the stuff.

Dominick had never seen an infant of such heroic calibre. Twice again he refilled the tumbler, each time to the brim, and watched it disappear down my throat. By this time my exploits were attracting attention. Middle-aged Italian labourers, old-country peasants who did not talk English, and who could not dance with the Irish girls, surrounded me. They were swarthy and wild looking; they wore belts and red shirts; and I knew they carried knives; and they ringed me around like a pirate chorus. And Peter and Dominick made me show off for them.

Had I lacked imagination, had I been stupid, had I been stubbornly mulish in having my own way, I should never have got in this pickle. And the lads and lassies were dancing, and there was no one to save me from my fate. How much I drank I do not know. My memory of it is of an age-long suffering of fear in the midst of a murderous crew, and of an infinite number of glasses of red wine passing across the bare boards of a wine-drenched table and going down my burning throat. Bad as the wine was, a knife in the back was worse, and I must survive at any cost.

Looking back with the drinker's knowledge, I know now why I did not collapse stupefied upon the table. As I have said, I was frozen, I was paralysed, with fear. The only movement I made was to convey that never-ending procession of glasses to my lips. I was a poised and motionless receptacle for all that quantity of wine. It lay inert in my fear-inert stomach. I was too frightened, even, for my stomach to turn. So all that Italian crew looked on and marvelled at the infant phenomenon that downed wine with the *sang-froid* of an automaton. It is not in the spirit of braggadocio that I dare to assert they had never seen anything like it.

The time came to go. The tipsy antics of the lads had led a majority of the soberer-minded lassies to compel a departure. I found myself, at the door, beside my little maiden. She had not had my experience, so she was sober. She was fascinated by the titubations of the lads who strove to walk beside their girls, and began to mimic them. I thought this a great game, and I, too, began to stagger tipsily. But she had no wine to stir up, while my movements quickly set the fumes rising to my head. Even at the start, I was more realistic than she. In several minutes I was astonishing myself. I saw one lad, after reeling half a dozen steps, pause at the side of the road, gravely peer into the ditch, and gravely, and after apparent deep thought, fall into it. To me this was excruciatingly funny. I staggered to the edge of the ditch, fully intending to stop on the edge. I came to myself, in the ditch, in process of being hauled out by several anxious-faced girls.

I didn't care to play at being drunk any more. There was no more fun in me. My eyes were beginning to swim, and with wide-open mouth I panted for air. A girl led me by the hand on either side, but my legs were leaden. The alcohol I had drunk was striking my heart and brain like a club. Had I been a weakling of a child, I am confident that it would have killed me. As it was, I know I was nearer death than any of the scared girls dreamed. I could hear them bickering among themselves as to whose fault it was; some were weeping – for themselves, for me, and for the disgraceful way their lads had behaved. But I was not interested. I was suffocating, and I wanted air. To move was agony. It made me pant harder. Yet those girls persisted in making me walk, and it was four miles home. Four miles! I remember my swimming eyes saw a small bridge across the road an infinite distance away. In fact, it was not a hundred feet distant. When I reached it, I sank down and lay on my back panting. The girls tried to lift me, but I was helpless and suffocating. Their cries of alarm brought Larry, a drunken youth of seventeen, who proceeded to resuscitate me by jumping on my chest. Dimly I remember this, and the squalling of the girls as they struggled with him and dragged him away. And then I knew nothing, though I learned afterward that Larry wound up under the bridge and spent the night there.

When I came to, it was dark. I had been carried unconscious for four miles and been put to bed. I was a sick child, and, despite the terrible strain on my heart and tissues, I continually relapsed into the madness of delirium. All the contents of the terrible and horrible in my child's mind spilled out. The most frightful visions were realities to me. I saw murders committed, and I was pursued by murderers. I screamed and raved and fought. My sufferings were prodigious. Emerging from such delirium, I would hear my mother's voice: 'But the child's brain. He will lose his reason.' And sinking back into delirium, I would take the idea with me and be immured in madhouses, and be beaten by keepers, and surrounded by screeching lunatics.

One thing that had strongly impressed my young mind was the talk of my elders about the dens of iniquity in San Francisco's Chinatown. In my delirium I wandered deep beneath the ground through a thousand of these dens, and behind locked doors of iron I suffered and died a thousand deaths. And when I would come upon my father, seated at table in these subterranean crypts, gambling with Chinese for great stakes of gold, all my outrage gave vent in the vilest cursing. I would rise in bed, struggling against the detaining hands, and curse my father till the rafters rang. All the inconceivable filth a child running at large in a primitive countryside may hear men utter was mine; and though I had never dared utter such oaths, they now poured from me, at the top of my lungs, as I cursed my father sitting there underground and gambling with long-haired, long-nailed Chinamen.

It is a wonder that I did not burst my heart or brain that night. A seven-year-old child's arteries and nerve-centres are scarcely fitted to endure the terrific paroxysms that convulsed me. No one slept in the thin, frame farm-house that night when John Barleycorn had his will of me. And Larry, under the bridge, had no delirium like mine. I am confident that his sleep was stupefied and dreamless, and that he awoke next day merely to heaviness and moroseness, and that if he lives today he does not remember that night, so passing was it as an incident. But my brain was seared for ever by that experience. Writing now, thirty years afterward, every vision is as distinct, as sharp-cut, every pain as vital and terrible, as on that night.

I was sick for days afterward, and I needed none of my mother's injunctions to avoid John Barleycorn in the future. My mother had been dreadfully shocked. She held that I had done wrong, very wrong, and that I had gone contrary to all her teaching. And how was I, who was never allowed to talk back, who lacked the very words with which to express my psychology – how was I to tell my mother that it was her teaching that was directly responsible for my drunkenness? Had it not been for her theories about dark eyes and Italian character, I should never have wet my lips with the sour, bitter wine. And not until man-grown did I tell her the true inwardness of that disgraceful affair.

In those after days of sickness, I was confused on some points, and very clear on others. I felt guilty of sin, yet smarted with a sense of injustice. It had not been my fault, yet I had done wrong. But very clear was my resolution never to touch liquor again. No mad dog was ever more afraid of water than was I of alcohol.

Yet the point I am making is that this experience, terrible as it was, could not in the end deter me from forming John Barleycorn's cheek-by-jowl acquaintance. All about me, even then, were the forces moving me toward him. In the first place, barring my mother, ever extreme in her views, it seemed to me all the grown-ups looked upon the affair with tolerant eyes. It was a joke, something funny that had happened. There was no shame attached. Even the lads and lassies giggled and snickered over their part in the affair, narrating with gusto how Larry had jumped on my chest and slept under the bridge, how So-and-So had slept out in the sandhills that night, and what had happened to the other lad who fell in the ditch. As I say, so far as I could see, there was no shame anywhere. It had been something ticklishly, devilishly fine – a bright and gorgeous episode in the monotony of life and labour on that bleak, fog-girt coast.

The Irish ranchers twitted me good-naturedly on my exploit, and patted me on the back until I felt that I had done something heroic. Peter and Dominick and the other Italians were proud of my drinking prowess. The face of morality was not set against drinking. Besides, everybody drank. There was not a teetotaler in the community. Even the teacher of our little country school, a greying man of fifty, gave us vacations on the occasions when he wrestled with John Barleycorn and was thrown. Thus there was no spiritual deterrence. My loathing for alcohol was purely physiological. I didn't like the damned stuff.

Jack London *John Barleycorn*

Aversion Therapy

I had much trouble at first in breaking him off those evil habits his father had taught him to acquire, but already that difficulty is nearly vanquished now: bad language seldom defiles his mouth, and I have succeeded in giving him an absolute disgust of all intoxicating liquors, which I hope not even his father or his father's friends will be able to overcome. He was inordinately fond of them for so young a creature, and, remembering my unfortunate father as well as his, I dreaded the consequences of such taste. But if I had stinted him in his usual quantity of wine, or forbidden him to taste it altogether, that would only have increased his partiality for it, and made him regard it as a greater treat than ever. I therefore gave him quite as much as his father was accustomed to allow him – as much, indeed, as he desired to have, but into every glass I surreptitiously introduced a small quantity of tartar-emetic – just enough to produce inevitable nausea and depression without positive sickness. Finding such disagreeable consequences invariably to result from this indulgence, he soon grew weary of it, but the more he shrank from the daily treat, the more I pressed it upon him, till his reluctance was strengthened to perfect abhorrence. When he was thoroughly disgusted with every kind of wine, I allowed him, at his own request, to try brandy and water, and then gin and water; for the little toper was familiar with them all, and I was determined that all should be equally hateful to him. This I have now effected; and since he declares that the taste, the smell, the sight of any one of them is sufficient to make him sick, I have given up teasing him about them, except now and then as objects of terror in cases of misbehaviour: 'Arthur, if you're not a good boy I shall give you a glass of wine,' or, 'Now, Arthur, if you say that again you shall have some brandy and water,' is as good as any other threat; and, once or twice, when he was sick, I have obliged the poor child to swallow a little wine and water without the tartar-emetic, by way of medicine; and this practice I intend to continue for some time to come; not that I think it of any real service in a physical sense, but because I am determined to enlist all the powers of association in my service: I wish this aversion to be so deeply grounded in his nature that nothing in after life may be able to overcome it.

Anne Brontë *The Tenant of Wildfell Hall*

Come Home, Father

Father, dear father, come home with me now!
  The clock in the steeple strikes one;
You promis'd, dear father, that you would come home,
  As soon as your day's work was done.
Our fire has gone out, our house is all dark,
  And mother's been watching since tea,
With poor brother Benny so sick in her arms,
  And no one to help her but me.
Come home, come home, come home,
Please father, dear father, come home.

Hear the sweet voice of the child,
Which the night-winds repeat as they roam!
Oh! who could resist this most plaintive of pray'rs,
'Please father, dear father, come home.'

Father, dear father, come home with me now!
  The clock in the steeple strikes two;
The night has grown colder, and Benny is worse,
  But he has been calling for you.
Indeed he is worse – Ma says he will die
  Perhaps before morning shall dawn,
And this is the message she sent me to bring,
  'Come quickly or he will be gone.'
Come home, come home, come home,
Please father, dear father, come home.

Hear the sweet voice of the child, etc.

Father, dear father, come home with me now!
  The clock in the steeple strikes three;
The house is so lonely, the hours are so long
  For poor weeping mother and me.
Yes, we are alone – poor Benny is dead,
  And gone with the angels of light,
And these were the very last words that he said,
  'I want to kiss Papa goodnight.'
Come home, come home, come home,
Please father, dear father, come home.

Hear the sweet voice of the child, etc.

Henry Clay Work

What's for My Dinner?

A very sullen-faced man stood at the corner of O'Connell Bridge waiting for the little Sandymount tram to take him home. He was full of smouldering anger and revengefulness. He felt humiliated and discontented; he did not even feel drunk; and he had only twopence in his pocket. He cursed everything. He had done for himself in the office, pawned his watch, spent all his money; and he had not even got drunk. He began to feel thirsty again and he longed to be back again in the hot, reeking public-house. He had lost his reputation as a strong man, having been defeated twice by a mere boy. His heart swelled with fury and, when he thought of the woman in the big hat who had brushed against him and said *Pardon!* his fury nearly choked him.

His tram let him down at Shelbourne Road and he steered his great body along in the shadow of the wall of the barracks. He loathed returning to his home. When he went in by the side-door he found the kitchen empty and the kitchen fire nearly out. He bawled upstairs:

'Ada! Ada!'

His wife was a little sharp-faced woman who bullied her husband when he was sober and was bullied by him when he was drunk. They had five children. A little boy came running down the stairs.

'Who is that?' said the man, peering through the darkness.

'Me, pa.'

'Who are you? Charlie?'

'No, pa. Tom.'

'Where's your mother?'

'She's out at the chapel.'

'That's right . . . Did she think of leaving any dinner for me?'

'Yes, pa. I – '

'Light the lamp. What do you mean by having the place in darkness? Are the other children in bed?'

The man sat down heavily on one of the chairs while the little boy lit the lamp. He began to mimic his son's flat accent, saying half to himself: '*At the chapel. At the chapel, if you please!*' When the lamp was lit he banged his fist on the table and shouted:

'What's for my dinner?'

'I'm going . . . to cook it, pa,' said the little boy.

The man jumped up furiously and pointed to the fire.

'On that fire! You let the fire out! By God, I'll teach you to do that again!'

He took a step to the door and seized the walking-stick which was standing behind it.

'I'll teach you to let the fire out!' he said, rolling up his sleeve in order to give his arm free play.

The little boy cried '*O, pa!*' and ran whimpering round the table, but the man followed him and caught him by the coat. The little boy looked about him wildly but, seeing no way of escape, fell upon his knees.

'Now, you'll let the fire out the next time!' said the man, striking at him vigorously with the stick. 'Take that, you little whelp!'

The boy uttered a squeal of pain as the stick cut his thigh. He clasped his hands together in the air and his voice shook with fright.

'O, pa!' he cried. 'Don't beat me, pa! And I'll . . . I'll say a *Hail Mary* for you . . . I'll say a *Hail Mary* for you, pa, if you don't beat me . . . I'll say a *Hail Mary* . . .'

James Joyce 'Counterparts' *Dubliners*

INNS, PUBS AND TAVERNS

A Capital Tavern

We dined at an excellent inn at Chapel-house, where he expatiated on the felicity of England in its taverns and inns, and triumphed over the French for not having, in any perfection, the tavern life. 'There is no private house, (said he,) in which people can enjoy themselves so well, as at a capital tavern. Let there be ever so great plenty of good things, ever so much grandeur, ever so much elegance, ever so much desire that every body should be easy; in the nature of things it cannot be: there must always be some degree of care and anxiety. The master of the house is anxious to entertain his guests; the guests are anxious to be agreeable to him: and no man, but a very impudent dog indeed, can as freely command what is in another man's house, as if it were his own. Whereas, at a tavern, there is a general freedom from anxiety. You are sure you are welcome: and the more noise you make, the more trouble you give, the more good things you call for, the welcomer you are. No servants will attend you with the alacrity which waiters do, who are incited by the prospect of an immediate reward in proportion as they please. No, Sir; there is nothing which has yet been contrived by man, by which so much happiness is produced as by a good tavern or inn.'

James Boswell *Life of Johnson*

At Some Lone Alehouse

But rumours hung about the country-side,
That the lost Scholar long was seen to stray,
Seen by rare glimpses, pensive and tongue-tied,
In hat of antique shape, and cloak of grey,
The same the gipsies wore.
Shepherds had met him on the Hurst in spring;
At some lone alehouse in the Berkshire moors,

On the warm ingle-bench, the smock-frocked boors
Had found him seated at their entering,

But, 'mid their drink and clatter, he would fly . . .

Matthew Arnold 'The Scholar-Gipsy'

A Trampwoman's Tragedy

(*182–*)

[I]

From Wynyard's Gap the livelong day,
The livelong day,
We beat afoot the northward way
We had travelled times before.
The sun-blaze burning on our backs,
Our shoulders sticking to our packs,
By fosseway, fields, and turnpike tracks
We skirted sad Sedge-Moor.

[II]

Full twenty miles we jaunted on,
We jaunted on, –
My fancy-man, and jeering John,
And Mother Lee, and I.
And, as the sun drew down to west,
We climbed the toilsome Poldon crest,
And saw, of landskip sights the best,
The inn that beamed thereby.

[III]

For months we had padded side by side,
Ay, side by side
Through the Great Forest, Blackmoor wide,
And where the Parret ran.

We'd faced the gusts on Mendip ridge,
Had crossed the Yeo unhelped by bridge,
Been stung by every Marshwood midge,
    I and my fancy-man.

[IV]

Lone inns we loved, my man and I,
    My man and I;
'King's Stag', 'Windwhistle' high and dry,
    'The Horse' on Hintock Green,
The cosy house at Wynyard's Gap,
'The Hut' renowned on Bredy Knap,
And many another wayside tap
    Where folk might sit unseen.

[V]

Now as we trudged – O deadly day,
    O deadly day! –
I teased my fancy-man in play
    And wanton idleness.
I walked alongside jeering John,
I laid his hand my waist upon;
I would not bend my glances on
    My lover's dark distress.

[VI]

Thus Poldon top at last we won,
    At last we won,
And gained the inn at sink of sun
    Far-famed as 'Marshal's Elm'.
Beneath us figured tor and lea,
From Mendip to the western sea –
I doubt if finer sight there be
    Within this royal realm.

[VII]

Inside the settle all a-row –
All four a-row
We sat, I next to John, to show
That he had wooed and won.
And then he took me on his knee,
And swore it was his turn to be
My favoured mate, and Mother Lee
Passed to my former one.

[VIII]

Then in a voice I had never heard,
I had never heard,
My only Love to me: 'One word,
My lady, if you please!
Whose is the child you are like to bear? –
His? After all my months o' care?'
God knows 'twas not! But, O despair!
I nodded – still to tease.

[IX]

Then up he sprung, and with his knife –
And with his knife
He let out jeering Johnny's life,
Yes; there, at set of sun.
The slant ray through the window nigh
Gilded John's blood and glazing eye,
Ere scarcely Mother Lee and I
Knew that the deed was done.

[X]

The taverns tell the gloomy tale,
The gloomy tale,
How that at Ivel-chester jail
My Love, my sweetheart swung;
Though stained till now by no misdeed
Save one horse ta'en in time o' need;

(Blue Jimmy stole right many a steed
    Ere his last fling he flung.)

[XI]

Thereaft I walked the world alone,
        Alone, alone!
On his death-day I gave my groan
    And dropt his dead-born child.
'Twas nigh the jail, beneath a tree,
None tending me; for Mother Lee
Had died at Glaston, leaving me
    Unfriended on the wild.

[XII]

And in the night as I lay weak,
        As I lay weak,
The leaves a-falling on my cheek,
    The red moon low declined –
The ghost of him I'd die to kiss
Rose up and said: 'Ah, tell me this!
Was the child mine, or was it his?
    Speak, that I rest may find!'

[XIII]

O doubt not but I told him then,
        I told him then,
That I had kept me from all men
    Since we joined lips and swore.
Whereat he smiled, and thinned away
As the wind stirred to call up day . . .
– 'Tis past! And here alone I stray
    Haunting the Western Moor.

NOTES: 'Windwhistle' (Stanza IV). The highness and dryness of Windwhistle Inn was impressed upon the writer two or three years ago, when, after climbing on a hot afternoon to the beautiful spot near which it stands and entering the inn for tea, he was informed by the landlady that none could be had, unless he would fetch water from a valley half a mile off, the house containing not a drop, owing to its situation.

However, a tantalizing row of full barrels behind her back testified to a wetness of a certain sort, which was not at that time desired.

'Marshal's Elm' (Stanza VI), so picturesquely situated, is no longer an inn, though the house, or part of it, still remains. It used to exhibit a fine old swinging sign.

'Blue Jimmy' (Stanza X) was a notorious horse-stealer of Wessex in those days, who appropriated more than a hundred horses before he was caught, among others one belonging to a neighbour of the writer's grandfather. He was hanged at the now demolished Ivelchester or Ilchester jail above mentioned – that building formerly of so many sinister associations in the minds of the local peasantry, and the continual haunt of fever, which at last led to its condemnation.

Its site is now an innocent-looking green meadow.

April 1902

Thomas Hardy

The Potwell Inn

The nearer he came to the place the more he liked it. The windows on the ground floor were long and low, and they had pleasing red blinds. The green tables outside were agreeably ringed with memories of former drinks, and an extensive grape vine spread level branches across the whole front of the place. Against the wall was a broken oar, two boathooks, and the stained and faded red cushions of a pleasure boat. One went up three steps to the glass-panelled door and peeped into a broad, low room with a bar and a beer engine, behind which were many bright and helpful-looking bottles against mirrors, and great and little pewter measures, and bottles fastened in brass wire upside down, with their corks replaced by taps, and a white china cask labelled 'Shrub', and cigar boxes, and boxes of cigarettes, and a couple of Toby jugs and a beautifully coloured hunting scene framed and glazed, showing the most elegant people taking Piper's Cherry Brandy, and cards such as the law requires about the dilution of spirits and the illegality of bringing children into bars, and satirical verses about swearing and asking for credit, and three very bright, red-cheeked wax apples and a round-shaped clock.

H. G. Wells *The History of Mr Polly*

Ye Olde

At the inland end of this river valley is an antique red-tiled large village or small town, a perfect group of human dwellings, as inevitable as the Downs, dominated by a mound and on it a windmill in ruin; mothered by a church at the river's edge. Under the sign of 'Ye Olde ——' is a room newly wainscoted in shining matchboard. Its altar – its little red sideboard – is symmetrically decorated by tiers and rows of lemonade, cherry cider and ginger ale bottles, many-coloured, and in the midst of these two syphons of soda-water. The doorways and windows are draped in white muslin, the hearth filled by a crinkled blue paper fan; the mantelpiece supports a dozen small vases. The oilcloth is new and odorous and bright. There are pink geraniums in salmon-coloured bowls on the table; a canary in a suspended cage; and on the walls a picture of a girl teasing a dog with a toy mouse.

Edward Thomas *The South Country*

The Major

Another regular who commands much veneration is the Major. An elderly gentleman with a white moustache of rakish sweep, he is to be found in all but the meanest pubs. He may not be a major by official rank, or even a sergeant-major; indeed, he may never have served in the army at all. It matters not in Publand. So long as he has the requisite military bearing, a loud, authoritative voice and a few military habits – such as coming smartly to attention on entering the bar and saluting the company with a shouldered umbrella – his title is assured.

The major is the aristocrat of the place; because of that his friends are treated with especial respect. And he appears to have an enormous circle of friends. He is never able to remain in the bar more than a few minutes at a time, for although he may be the centre of the largest group there, you may be sure that other fellahs are awaiting him in other places at this same moment. Always the Major is popping out to keep an appointment, or popping in 'just for a very quick one' – he drinks whisky, of course – and to discover if a message has been left for him. The Major and his friends communicate to a tremendous extent by means of messages deposited with the barmaid.

If you desire to be accepted from the start in a strange pub – and who does not? – you can put the Major to very good use. After ordering your drink, glance quickly round the room, then lean over the counter and inquire: 'Major been in today?' It always works. Usually you will be told that 'he left a matter of five minutes ago,' in which case you ask: 'Did he leave a message for me? Spirket is the name.' (I am assuming, of course, that it is.) By the time you have disclaimed messages for Mr Stokes, Mr Wainwright and Steve your purpose will be accomplished. Call again next session and it will be, 'Good evening, Mr Spirket,' accompanied by a smile that you might not have earned in a dozen visits but for the Major's unwitting help.

T. E. B. Clarke *What's Yours?*

The Average Pub

It is a pity that this large and careful survey could not have had a short appendix indicating what effect the war has had on our drinking habits. It seems to have been compiled just before the war, and even in that short period of time beer has doubled in price and been heavily diluted.

Writing at a time when 'mild' was still fivepence a pint (between 1936 and 1941 rearmament only raised it by a penny), the Mass Observers found that in 'Worktown' the regular pub-goer was putting away, on average, between fifteen and twenty pints a week. This sounds a good deal, but it is unquestionable that in the past seventy years the annual consumption of beer per head has decreased by nearly two thirds, and it is the Mass Observers' conclusion that 'the pub as a cultural institution is at present declining'. This happens not merely because of persecution by

Nonconformist town councils, nor even primarily because of the increased price of drink, but because the whole trend of the age is away from creative communal amusements and towards solitary mechanical ones. The pub, with its elaborate social ritual, its animated conversations and – at any rate in the North of England – its songs and week-end comedians, is gradually replaced by the passive, drug-like pleasures of the cinema and the radio. This is only a cause for rejoicing if one believes, as a few Temperance fanatics still do, that people go to pubs to get drunk. The Mass Observers, however, have no difficulty in showing that there was extraordinarily little drunkenness in the period they were studying: for every five thousand hours that the average pub stays open, only one of its clients is drunk and disorderly.

Working on the more old-fashioned provincial pubs where the various bars are still separate rooms and not, as in London, merely one long counter separated by partitions, the authors of this book have unearthed much curious information. In a short review it is impossible to dilate on the complex social code that differentiates the saloon bar from the public bar, or on the delicate ritual that centres round treating, or the cultural implications of the trend towards bottled beer, or the rivalry between church and pub and the consequent guilt-feelings associated with drinking; but the average reader is likely to find Chapters V, VI, and VII the most interesting. At least one of the Observers seems to have taken the extreme step of being initiated into the Buffaloes, about which there are some surprising revelations. A questionnaire issued through the local press, asking people why they drank beer, elicited from more than half the answer that they drank it for their health – probably an echo of the brewers' advertisements which talk of beer as though it were a kind of medicine. There were some who answered more frankly, however: 'A middle-aged man of about forty of labouring type says "What the bloody hell dost tha tak it for?" I said for my health; he said "Th'art a – liar." I paid for him a gill.'

And one woman answered the questionnaire thus:

'My reason is, because I always liked to see my grandmother having a drink of beer at night. She did seem to enjoy it, and she could pick up a dry crust of bread and cheese, and it seemed like a feast. She said if you have a drink of beer you will live to be one hundred, she died at ninety-two. I shall never refuse a drink of beer. There is no bad ale, so Grandma said.'

This little piece of prose, which impresses itself upon the memory like a poem, would in itself be a sufficient justification for beer, if indeed it needed justifying.

George Orwell, Review of Mass Observation's *The Pub and the People*. *Listener*, 21 January 1943

The Moon under Water

My favourite public house, the Moon under Water, is only two minutes from a bus stop, but it is on a side-street, and drunks and rowdies never seem to find their way there, even on Saturday nights.

Its clientele, though fairly large, consists mostly of 'regulars' who occupy the same chair every evening and go there for conversation as much as for the beer.

If you are asked why you favour a particular public house, it would seem natural to put the beer first, but the thing that most appeals to me about the Moon under Water is what people call its 'atmosphere'.

To begin with, its whole architecture and fittings are uncompromisingly Victorian. It has no glass-topped tables or other modern miseries, and, on the other hand, no sham roof-beams, inglenooks or plastic panels masquerading as oak. The grained woodwork, the ornamental mirrors behind the bar, the cast-iron fireplaces, the florid ceiling stained dark yellow by tobacco-smoke, the stuffed bull's head over the mantelpiece – everything has the solid comfortable ugliness of the nineteenth century.

In winter there is generally a good fire burning in at least two of the bars, and the Victorian lay-out of the place gives one plenty of elbow-room. There is a public bar, a saloon bar, a ladies' bar, a bottle-and-jug for those who are too bashful to buy their supper beer publicly, and upstairs, a dining-room.

Games are only played in the public, so that in the other bars you can walk about without constantly ducking to avoid flying darts.

In the Moon under Water it is always quiet enough to talk. The house possesses neither a radio nor a piano, and even on Christmas Eve and such occasions the singing that happens is of a decorous kind.

The barmaids know most of their customers by name, and take a personal interest in everyone. They are all middle-aged women – two of them have their hair dyed in quite surprising shades – and they call everyone 'dear', irrespective of age or sex. ('Dear', not 'Ducky': pubs where the barmaid calls you 'Ducky' always have a disagreeable raffish atmosphere.)

Unlike most pubs, the Moon under Water sells tobacco as well as cigarettes, and it also sells aspirins and stamps, and is obliging about letting you use the telephone.

You cannot get dinner at the Moon under Water, but there is always the snack counter where you can get liver-sausage sandwiches, mussels (a speciality of the house), cheese, pickles and those large biscuits with caraway seeds in them which only seem to exist in public houses.

Upstairs, six days a week, you can get a good, solid lunch – for example, a cut off the joint, two vegetables and boiled jam roll – for about three shillings.

The special pleasure of this lunch is that you can have draught stout with it. I doubt whether as many as ten per cent of London pubs serve draught stout, but the Moon under Water is one of them. It is a soft, creamy sort of stout, and it goes better in a pewter pot.

They are particular about their drinking vessels at the Moon under Water and never, for example, make the mistake of serving a pint of beer in a handleless glass. Apart from glass and pewter mugs, they have some of those pleasant strawberry-pink china ones which are now seldom seen in London. China mugs went out about thirty years ago, because most people like their drink to be transparent, but in my opinion beer tastes better out of china.

The great surprise of the Moon under Water is its garden. You go through a narrow passage leading out of the saloon, and find yourself in a fairly large garden with plane trees under which there are little green tables with iron chairs round them. Up at one end of the garden there are swings and a chute for the children.

On summer evenings there are family parties, and you sit under the plane trees having beer or draught cider to the tune of delighted squeals from children going down the chute. The prams with the younger children are parked near the gate.

Many as are the virtues of the Moon under Water I think that the garden is its best feature, because it allows whole families to go there instead of Mum having to stay at home and mind the baby while Dad goes out alone.

And though, strictly speaking, they are only allowed in the garden, the children tend to seep into the pub and even to fetch drinks for their parents. This, I believe, is against the law, but it is a law that deserves to be broken, for it is the puritanical nonsense of excluding children – and therefore to some extent, women – from pubs that has turned these places into mere boozing-shops instead of the family gathering-places that they ought to be.

The Moon under Water is my ideal of what a pub should be – at any rate, in the London area. (The qualities one expects of a country pub are slightly different.)

But now is the time to reveal something which the discerning and disillusioned reader will probably have guessed already. There is no such place as the Moon under Water.

That is to say, there may well be a pub of that name, but I don't know of it, nor do I know any pub with just that combination of qualities.

I know pubs where the beer is good but you can't get meals, others where you can get meals but which are noisy and crowded, and others which are quiet but where the beer is generally sour. As for gardens, offhand I can only think of three London pubs that possess them.

But, to be fair, I do know of a few pubs that almost come up to the Moon under Water. I have mentioned above ten qualities that the perfect pub should have, and I know one pub that has eight of them. Even there, however, there is no draught stout and no china mugs.

And if anyone knows of a pub that has draught stout, open fires, cheap meals, a garden, motherly barmaids and no radio, I should be glad to hear of it, even though its name were something as prosaic as the Red Lion or the Railway Arms.

George Orwell *Evening Standard*, 9 February 1946

Arrers

Darts is the most popular of pub games. It may have originated in knife-throwing or some form of indoor archery using the end of a cask as the target. The archery theory receives some support from the fact that in London the darts are still called arrows – or, more correctly, 'arrers'. Darts only achieved real popularity in this century, developing into a national craze between the wars, and unfortunately sweeping out many older and localized games in the process. By the time of the Second World War the game had achieved such popularity that when Marmaduke A. Breckon beat Jim Pike at the Agricultural Hall, Islington, in 1939 he did so in front of a crowd of nearly 20,000. There are now reckoned to be some six or seven million regular players in the British Isles. There are a million registered league players, 750,000 of them being competition players. This means that darts surpasses even angling as the biggest participator sport in the country.

Until 1908 the legality of darts in pubs was in some doubt as it had not been established whether it was a game of skill or chance. Tom Barrett (himself twice winner of the *News of the World* Championship) describes in his book *Darts* (Pan, 1973) how the issue was settled by the Leeds Magistrates Court. A landlord called 'Foot' Anakin was prosecuted for allowing a game of chance, darts, to be played on his licensed premises. 'Foot' asked for permission to give a demonstration, and a dart board was brought into court. The highest number on the board is a twenty, and 'Foot' threw three of them. A junior clerk of the court was invited to try and missed the board altogether with two of his darts. The magistrates asked 'Foot' if he could repeat the performance. Now the highest possible score with one dart is not the bull (50) but the treble twenty (60). This is an area rather smaller than the edge of a matchbox. 'Foot's' first dart was a treble twenty, as was his second, and his third. The magistrate was satisfied. Darts is not a game of chance.

Richard Boston *Beer and Skittles*

Darts Night

'I bet I shall end As always on double one'

I will record that double top, treble
nineteen and outer bull in my diary
when I get home. It is my highest score
of the night, and it means I am winning,

however temporarily. You line up
your arm with your eye and throw.
A treble to take back the lead.
Is there something wrong with my beer?
I wonder, watching its sluggish flow
down the canal tunnel of my glass.

The squeak of chalk. My toe
feels for the slat screwed to the floor,
and I confront the board
spinning backwards into its stationary blur
like a casually swung propeller
to the engine-roar of laughter from the bar.

Dangerous throwing a dart into that, I think,
and, sure enough, it sparks on metal
and spits back out at me.
I shift my weight. I seem to be in trouble.
Conscious of the sweat mingling with chalk dust
in my palm, I fist my penultimate dart,

and, with all the inevitability of art,
leave myself MacNeice's ineluctable double.

Simon Rae

Inns

Third in our Borough's list appears the sign
Of a fair queen – the gracious Caroline;
But in decay – each feature in the face
Has stain of Time, and token of disgrace.
The storm of winter, and the summer-sun,
Have on that form their equal mischief done;
The features now are all disfigured seen,
And not one charm adorns th'insulted queen:
To this poor face was never paint applied,
Th'unseemly work of cruel Time to hide;
Here we may rightly such neglect upbraid,
Paint on such faces is by prudence laid.
Large the domain, but all within combine
To correspond with the dishonour'd sign;
And all around dilapidates; you call –
But none replies – they're inattentive all:
At length a ruin'd stable holds your steed,
While you through large and dirty rooms proceed,
Spacious and cold; a proof they once had been
In honour – now magnificently mean;
Till in some small half-furnish'd room you rest,
Whose dying fire denotes it had a guest.
In those you pass'd where former splendour reign'd,
You saw the carpets torn, the paper stain'd;
Squares of discordant glass in windows fix'd,
And paper oil'd in many a space betwixt;
A soil'd and broken sconce, a mirror crack'd,
With table underpropp'd, and chairs new-back'd;
A marble side-slab with ten thousand stains,

And all an ancient tavern's poor remains.
With much entreaty, they your food prepare,
And acid wine afford, with meagre fair;
Heartless you sup; and when a dozen times
You've read the fractured window's senseless rhymes;
Have been assured that Phœbe Green was fair,
And Peter Jackson took his supper there;
You reach a chilling chamber, where you dread
Damps, hot or cold, from a tremendous bed;
Late comes your sleep, and you are waken'd soon
By rustling tatters of the old festoon.
O'er this large building, thus by time defaced,
A servile couple has its owner placed,
Who not unmindful that its style is large,
To lost magnificence adapt their charge:
Thus an old beauty, who has long declined,
Keeps former dues and dignity in mind;
And wills that all attention should be paid
For graces vanish'd and for charms decay'd.
Few years have pass'd, since brightly 'cross the way,
Lights from each window shot the lengthen'd ray,
And busy looks in every face were seen,
Through the warm precincts of the reigning Queen:
There fires inviting blazed, and all around
Was heard the tinkling bells' seducing sound;
The nimble waiters to that sound from far
Sprang to the call, then hasten'd to the bar;
Where a glad priestess of the temple sway'd,
The most obedient, and the most obey'd;
Rosy and round, adorn'd in crimson vest,
And flaming ribands at her ample breast: –
She, skill'd like Circe, tried her guests to move,
With looks of welcome and with words of love;
And such her potent charms, that men unwise
Were soon transform'd and fitted for the sties.
Her port in bottles stood, a well-stain'd row,
Drawn for the evening from the pipe below;

Three powerful spirits fill'd a parted case,
Some cordial bottles stood in secret place;
Fair acid fruits in nets above were seen.
Her plate was splendid, and her glasses clean;
Basins and bowls were ready on the stand,
And measures clatter'd in her powerful hand.

George Crabbe *The Borough*

Villers

In the worst inn's worst room, with mat half-hung,
The floors of plaister, and the walls of dung,
On once a flock-bed, but repair'd with straw,
With tape-ty'd curtains, never meant to draw,
The George and Garter dangling from that bed
Where tawdry yellow strove with dirty red,
Great Villers lies – alas! how chang'd from him,
That life of pleasure, and that soul of whim!
Gallant and gay, in Cliveden's proud alcove,
The bow'r of wanton Shrewsbury and love;
Or just as gay, at Council, in a ring
Of mimick'd Statesmen, and their merry King.
No Wit to flatter, left to all his store!
No Fool to laugh at, which he valu'd more.
There, Victor of his health, of fortune, friends,
And fame; this lord of useless thousands ends.

Alexander Pope *Epistle to Bathurst*

The Village Inn

'The village inn, the dear old inn,
So ancient, clean and free from sin,
True centre of our rural life
Where Hodge sits down beside his wife
And talks of Marx and nuclear fission
With all a rustic's intuition.
Ah, more than church or school or hall,
The village inn's the heart of all.'
So spake the brewer's PRO,
A man who really ought to know,
For he is paid for saying so.
And then he kindly gave to me
A lovely coloured booklet free.
'Twas full of prose that sang the praise
Of coaching inns in Georgian days,
Showing how public-houses are
More modern than the motor-car,
More English than the weald or wold
And almost equally as old,
And run for love and not for gold
Until I felt a filthy swine
For loathing beer and liking wine,
And rotten to the very core
For thinking village inns a bore,
And village bores more sure to roam
To village inns than stay at home.
And then I thought I *must* be wrong,
So up I rose and went along
To that old village alehouse where
In neon lights is written 'Bear'.

Ah, where's the inn that once I knew
  With brick and chalky wall
Up which the knobbly pear-tree grew
  For fear the place would fall?

Oh, that old pot-house isn't there,
It wasn't worth our while;
You'll find we have rebuilt 'The Bear'
In Early Georgian style.

But winter jasmine used to cling
With golden stars a-shine
Where rain and wind would wash and swing
The crudely painted sign.

And where's the roof of golden thatch?
The chimney-stack of stone?
The crown-glass panes that used to match
Each sunset with their own?

Oh now the walls are red and smart,
The roof has emerald tiles.
The neon sign's a work of art
And visible for miles.

The bar inside was papered green,
The settles grained like oak,
The only light was paraffin,
The woodfire used to smoke.

And photographs from far and wide
Were hung around the room:
The hunt, the church, the football side,
And Kitchener of Khartoum.

Our air-conditioned bars are lined
With washable material,
The stools are steel, the taste refined,
Hygienic and ethereal.

Hurrah, hurrah, for hearts of oak!
Away with inhibitions!
For here's a place to sit and soak
In sanit'ry conditions.

John Betjeman

Good Mine Host

The Inn at Barnet. Enter HOST, FERRET.)
HOST: I am not pleased, indeed, you are i' the right;
Nor is my house pleased, if my sign could speak,
The sign o' the Light Heart. There, you may read it;
So may your master too, if he look on't.
A heart weighed with a feather, and outweighed too:
A brainchild o' mine own! And I am proud on't!
And if his worship think, here to be melancholy,
In spite of me or my wit, he is deceived;
I will maintain the rebus 'gainst all humours,
And all complexions i' the body of man,
That's my word, or i' the isle of Britain!
FERRET: You have reason good mine host.
HOST: Sir, I have rhyme too.
Whether it be by chance or art,
'A heavy purse makes a light Heart.'
There 'tis expressed! First, by a purse of gold,
'A heavy purse', and then two turtles, 'makes',
A heart with a light stuck in't, 'a light heart'!
Old Abbot Islip could not invent better,
Or Prior Bolton with his bolt and tun.
I am an innkeeper, and know my grounds,
And study 'em; brain o' man, I study 'em:
I must ha' jovial guests to drive my ploughs,
And whistling boys to bring my harvest home,
Or I shall hear no flails thwack. Here, your master
And you ha' been this fortnight, drawing fleas

Out of my mats and pounding 'em in cages
Cut out of cards, and those roped round with pack-thread,
Drawn thorough birdlime! A fine subtlety!
Or poring through a multiplying glass
Upon a captivated crab-louse, or a cheese-mite
To be dissected as the sports of nature,
With a neat Spanish needle! Speculations
That do become the age, I do confess!
As measuring an ant's eggs with the silkworm's
By a fantastic instrument of thread
Shall give you their just difference to a hair!
Or else recovering o' dead flies with crumbs!
(Another quaint conclusion i' the physics)
Which I ha' seen you busy at through the keyhole –
But never had the fate to see a fly –
(*Enter* LOVEL.)
Alive i' your cups, or once heard, 'Drink mine host',
Or such a cheerful chirping charm come from you.
LOVEL: What's that? What that?
FERRET: A buzzing of mine host
About a fly! A murmur that he has.
HOST: Sir, I am telling your stoat here, Monsieur Ferret,
(For that I hear's his name) and dare tell you, sir,
If you have a mind to be melancholy and musty,
There's Footman's Inn, at the town's end, the stocks,
Or Carrier's Place, at sign o' the Broken Wain,
Mansions of state! Take up your harbour there;
There are both flies and fleas, and all variety
Of vermin for inspection or dissection.
LOVEL: We ha' set our rest up here, sir, i' your Heart.
HOST: Sir set your heart at rest, you shall not do it:
Unless you can be jovial. Brain o' man,
Be jovial first, and drink, and dance, and drink.
Your lodging here and wi' your daily dumps
Is a mere libel 'gainst my house and me;
And, then, your scandalous commons.
LOVEL: How, mine host?

HOST: Sir, they do scandal me upo' the road, here.
A poor quotidian rack o' mutton, roasted,
Dry, to be grated! And that driven down
With beer and buttermilk mingled together,
Or clarified whey, instead of claret!
It is against my freehold, my inheritance,
My magna charta, *cor laetificat*,
To drink such balderdash, or bonny-clabber!
Gi' me good wine, or catholic or christian,
Wine is the word that glads the heart of man:
And mine's the house of wine, sack, says my bush,
'Be merry, and drink sherry'; that's my pot!
For I shall never joy i' my light heart
So long as I conceive a sullen guest,
Or anything that's earthy!
LOVEL: Humorous host.
HOST: I care not if I be.
LOVEL: But airy also,
Not to defraud you of your rights, or, trench
Upo' your privileges or great charter,
(For those are every ostler's language now)
Say you were born beneath those smiling stars
Have made you lord and owner of the Heart,
Of the Light Heart in Barnet, suffer us
Who are more saturnine, to enjoy the shade
Of your round roof yet.
HOST: Sir, I keep no shades
No shelters, I; for either owls or rearmice.

Ben Jonson *The New Inn*

McCabe

Though publicans come in all shapes, sizes and varieties there are certain requirements that they have in common, basic ones such as being prepared to sell alcoholic beverages during licensed hours for consumption on the premises. Or so I thought until I met James McCabe, landlord of the Red Lion.

Though his family had been in the village for several generations these dour Scots had never been properly assimilated into the easy-going Berkshire ways. Ownership of the pub would have had McCabe in trouble with the Wee Frees, but his mind-set was still by local standards positively Knoxite. James (call him Jim at your peril) McCabe was not only a teetotaller himself but made no secret of his disapproval of other people drinking. As for conviviality, his idea of conversation seemed to be that the other person listened while he delivered his bigoted opinions on the events of the day. These usually involved flogging and hanging: flog them first and then hang them. About once in five years a black person would pass through the village. This was enough to fuel McCabe's racism for the foreseeable future, providing as it did further proof that the country was being swamped by immigrants who should be sent back where they came from.

If it had been a tied house the brewery would have had him out on his ear in no time, but McCabe owned the pub, just as he did the village shop, the bakery, the milk and paper rounds, the post office, a few houses and joint-tenancy with a brother-in-law of the largest farm. On top of which, for as long as anyone could remember, he had been chairman of the parish council as well. Behind his back he was known as King Jim. No one, not even the squirearchy, could afford to offend him, unless they wanted to make tiresome alternative arrangements for their newspapers, bread, milk, eggs, paraffin and other essentials of rural life. King Jim could exert his power in ways that were not always obvious. A newcomer who made the mistake of falling out with him found it simply impossible to get domestic help. When his pipes burst the plumber never turned up, the local builder was always too busy to mend the roof and even the rat-catcher was unable to take on his vermin. The man was gone within a year.

Since the village is off the main road there is little passing trade, and that 'little' was not encouraged by King Jim. The weary traveller expecting a cheery welcome from a jovial ruddy-faced Mine Host wreathed in smiles at this charming unspoilt hostelry was in for a rude shock, and I mean rude.

A lorry-driver once breezed in and asked for, 'Pint of beer and a pork pie, mate.' King Jim replied, 'There are no pork pies and I'm not your mate' and went out of the back without serving him. Of course he was right. He was no man's mate, and there were no pork pies. There was a jar of pickled eggs though, but it had been there so long that no one had ever dared to try one.

King Jim just survived to see the early days of the Real Beer movement of the 1970s. Before buying a pint one itinerant beer-bore asked in a spirit of connoisseurship whose beer it was. 'It's my beer,' King Jim replied, 'And when you've paid for it, it'll be your beer.'

The pub was usually empty at lunchtime. My first visit was on a weekday at just after 1.45. Even after twenty years I can time it that precisely because the unmistakable sound of inane Archers conversation could be heard from a wireless (as McCabe would certainly have called it) at the back. Otherwise there was no sign of life. After about ten minutes I peered round an open door that gave on to the kitchen and saw King Jim asleep in a chair in front of the wireless. I tiptoed out.

I might have been less cautious if I hadn't heard what happened to someone else who had found himself in the identical situation. After a long wait he had rapped on the bar with a coin, first quietly and then more loudly. Finally McCabe appeared.

'Was that you rapping on the bar?'

'Yes,' the man said.

'Well, don't,' said King Jim and went back where he had come from.

In the evenings there actually were a few customers. These were mostly old villagers of McCabe's own age who drank mild. I think he quite approved of their drinking, his plan being to outlive them and thus prove that drink had been their downfall. There were old shepherds and gamekeepers and a village idiot and a man who kept a ferret in his pocket. This was only twenty years ago and it was like being in a time-warp. It was like something out of one of the gloomier bits of nineteenth-century Russian literature, but even McCabe couldn't entirely keep out the spirit of Chaucer, Shakespeare and Dickens. There would be times – a birthday, or a wedding or (best of all) some national festivity involving Royalty – when the place was packed and everyone was laughing and shouting and singing into the small hours: for all his faults one of the laws of the land that King Jim did not uphold was the one covering licensing hours.

The nearest house was occupied by a retired brigadier and his lady. Though the Brig, aged nearly ninety, had an impressive military bearing, bristling moustache and decorations for valour in the field in every war this century, he was the mildest of men, almost to the point of timidity. After one particularly raucous late-night session at the Red Lion even he was provoked to murmur in passing to McCabe that there had been rather a lot of noise last night.

'Was there?' said King Jim. 'None of my customers complained.'

Richard Boston

A Roach of the Taverns

i went into a
speakeasy the other night
with some of the
boys and we were all sitting
around under one of
the tables making
merry with crumbs and
cheese and what not but
after a while a strange
melancholy descended
upon the jolly crew and
one old brown veteran roach
said with a sigh well
boys eat drink and
be maudlin for
tomorrow we are dry the
shadow of the padlock

rushes toward us
like a sahara sandstorm
flinging itself at an oasis
for years myself and my
ancestors before me have
inhabited yonder ice box but
the day approaches
when our old homestead
will be taken away from
here and scalded out
yes says i soon there will
be nothing but that
eheu fugaces stuff
on every hand i
never drank it says he
what kind of a
drink is it
it is bitter as wormwood
says i and the
only chaser to it is
the lethean water
it is not the booze itself
that i regret so
much said the old brown
roach it is the
golden companionship of
the tavern myself
and my ancestors have been
chop house and tavern
roaches for hundreds of years
countless generations back
one of my elizabethan
forebears was plucked from
a can of ale in the
mermaid tavern by
will shakespeare and
put down kit marlowes back

what subtle wits they were in
those days said i yes
he said and later
another one of my
ancestors was
introduced into a larded
hare that addison
was eating by dicky steele
my ancestor came
scurrying forth dicky
said is that your own
hare joe or a wig a
thing which addison
never forgave yours is a
remarkable family
history i said yes he
said i am the last
of a memorable
line one of my
ancestors was found drowned
in the ink well
out of which poor
eddie poe wrote the
raven we have
always associated with wits
bohemians and bon
vivants my maternal
grandmother was slain by
john masefield with
a bung starter well well it
is sad i said the
glad days pass yes
he says soon we will all
be as dry as the
egyptian scarab that
lies in the sarcophagus
beside the mummy of rameses and

he hasnt had a
drink for four thousand
years it is sad for
you he continued but
think how much sadder it
is for me with
a family tradition such as
mine only one of my
ancestors cheese it i said
interrupting him i do
not wish to injure
your feelings but i weary
of your ancestors i
have often noticed that
ancestors never boast
of the descendants who boast
of ancestors i would
rather start a family than
finish one blood will tell but often
it tells too much

archy

Don Marquis

Lord Landlord

The author of *Rochester's Memoirs* reports that in one of these banishments from court Rochester and his friend Buckingham, (then too, a disgraced favourite), happened to learn that a certain inn was to be let on the road between London and Newmarket – the Green Mare Inn at Six Mile Bottom. They took it under feigned names, disguised themselves as inn-keepers and took turns in playing landlord. Trying to get as much sport out of this adventure as possible, they invited the whole countryside to frequent festivals and bouts, and, with the help of their neighbours, carried the escapade to a veritable comedy. At last Rochester fell in love with some pretty woman living in the neighbourhood. One day, when her husband, a jealous old miser, had come to drink in the bar of the inn, Rochester took his chance. He dressed himself up in women's clothes and, after giving his brother publican Buckingham a hint to make the man drunk and keep him in the inn as long as possible, went off to the house of the couple. Opposite its door he pretended to faint. The hospitable beauty, supposing him to be a woman, took him into the house, put him to bed, and nursed him carefully. By and by, Rochester lifted his mask, won her confidence, and 'was as happy as he could desire, and as long as he durst stay, for fear of the Husband's return.'

Eventually King Charles, on his way to Newmarket, stopped at the inn and discovered the hosts to be his own banished courtiers. Greatly delighted in the joke, he restored them to favour and took both of them with him to Newmarket.

Johannes Prinz *John Wilmot, Earl of Rochester, His Life and Writing*

The Maypole

'Halloa!' cried a voice he knew, as the man who spoke came cleaving through the throng. 'Where is he? Give him to me. Don't hurt him. How now, old Jack! Ha ha ha!'

Mr Willet looked at him, and saw it was Hugh; but he said nothing, and thought nothing.

'These lads are thirsty and must drink!' cried Hugh, thrusting him back towards the house. 'Bustle, Jack, bustle. Show us the best – the very best – the over-proof that you keep for your own drinking, Jack!'

John faintly articulated the words, 'Who's to pay?'

'He says, "Who's to pay?"' cried Hugh, with a roar of laughter which was loudly echoed by the crowd. Then turning to John, he added, 'Pay! Why, nobody.'

John stared round at the mass of faces – some grinning, some fierce, some lighted up by torches, some indistinct, some dusky and shadowy: some looking at him, some at his house, some at each other – and while he was, as he thought, in the very act of doing so, found himself, without any consciousness of having moved, in the bar; sitting down in an arm-chair, and watching the destruction of his property, as if it were some queer play or entertainment, of an astonishing and stupefying nature, but having no reference to himself – that he could make out – at all.

Yes. Here was the bar – the bar that the boldest never entered without special invitation – the sanctuary, the mystery, the hallowed ground: here it was, crammed with men, clubs, sticks, torches, pistols; filled with a deafening noise, oaths, shouts, screams, hootings; changed all at once into a bear-garden, a madhouse, an infernal temple: men darting in and out by door and window, smashing the glass, turning the taps, drinking liquor out of China punchbowls, sitting astride of casks, smoking private and personal pipes, cutting down the sacred grove of lemons, hacking and hewing at the celebrated cheese, breaking open inviolable drawers, putting things in their pockets which didn't belong to them, dividing his own money before his own eyes, wantonly wasting, breaking, pulling down and tearing up: nothing quiet, nothing private: men everywhere – above, below, overhead, in the bedrooms, in the kitchen, in the yard, in the stables – clambering in at windows when there were doors wide open; dropping out of windows when the stairs were handy; leaping over the banisters into chasms of passages: new faces and figures presenting themselves every instant – some yelling, some singing, some fighting, some breaking glass and crockery, some laying the dust with the liquor they couldn't drink, some ringing the bells till they pulled them down, others beating them with pokers till they beat them into fragments: more men still – more, more, more, – swarming on like insects: noise, smoke, light, darkness, frolic, anger, laughter, groans, plunder, fear, and ruin!

Nearly all the time while John looked on at this bewildering scene, Hugh kept near him; and though he was the loudest, wildest, most destructive villain there, he saved his old master's bones a score of times. Nay, even when Mr Tappertit, excited by liquor, came up, and in assertion of his prerogative politely kicked John Willet on the shins, Hugh bade him return the compliment; and if old John had had sufficient presence of mind to understand this whispered direction, and to profit by it, he might no doubt, under Hugh's protection, have done so with impunity.

At length the band began to re-assemble outside the house, and to call to those within to join them, for they were losing time. These murmurs increasing, and attaining a high pitch, Hugh, and some of those who yet lingered in the bar, and who plainly were the leaders of the troop, took counsel together, apart, as to what was to be done with John, to keep him quiet until their Chigwell work was over. Some proposed to set the house on fire and leave him in it; others, that he should be reduced to a state of temporary insensibility, by knocking on the head; others, that he should be sworn to sit where he was until to-morrow at the same hour; others again, that he should be gagged and taken off with them, under a sufficient guard. All these propositions being overruled, it was concluded, at last, to bind him in his chair, and the word was passed for Dennis.

'Look'ee here, Jack!' said Hugh, striding up to him: 'We are going to tie you, hand and foot, but otherwise you won't be hurt. D'ye hear?'

John Willet looked at another man, as if he didn't know which was the speaker, and muttered something about an ordinary every Sunday at two o'clock.

'You won't be hurt, I tell you, Jack – do you hear me?' roared Hugh, impressing the assurance upon him by means of a heavy blow on the back. 'He's so dead scared, he's woolgathering, I think. Give him a drop of something to drink here. Hand over, one of you.'

A glass of liquor being passed forward, Hugh poured the contents down old John's throat. Mr Willet feebly smacked his lips, thrust his hand into his pocket, and inquired what was to pay; adding, as he looked vacantly round, that he believed there was a trifle of broken glass –

'He's out of his senses for the time, it's my belief,' said Hugh, after shaking him, without any visible effect upon his system, until his keys rattled in his pocket.

'Where's that Dennis?'

The word was again passed, and presently Mr Dennis, with a

long cord bound about his middle, something after the manner of a friar, came hurrying in, attended by a body-guard of half-a-dozen of his men.

'Come! Be alive here!' cried Hugh, stamping his foot upon the ground. 'Make haste!'

Dennis, with a wink and a nod, unwound the cord from about his person, and raising his eyes to the ceiling, looked all over it, and round the walls and cornice, with a curious eye; then shook his head.

'Move, man, can't you!' cried Hugh, with another impatient stamp of his foot. 'Are we to wait here till the cry has gone for ten miles round, and our work's interrupted?'

'It's all very fine talking, brother,' answered Dennis, stepping towards him; 'but unless' – and here he whispered in his ear – 'unless we do it over the door, it can't be done at all in this here room.'

'What can't?' Hugh demanded.

'What can't!' retorted Dennis. 'Why, the old man can't.'

'Why, you weren't going to hang him!' cried Hugh.

'No, brother?' returned the hangman with a stare. 'What else?'

Hugh made no answer, but snatching the rope from his companion's hand, proceeded to bind old John himself; but his very first move was so bungling and unskilful, that Mr Dennis entreated, almost with tears in his eyes, that he might be permitted to perform the duty. Hugh consenting, he achieved it in a twinkling.

'There,' he said, looking mournfully at John Willet, who displayed no more emotion in his bonds than he had shown out of them. 'That's what I call pretty and workmanlike. He's quite a picter now. But, brother, just a word with you – now that he's ready trussed, as one may say, wouldn't it be better for all parties if we was to work him off? It would read uncommon well in the newspapers, it would indeed. The public would think a great deal more on us!'

Hugh, inferring what his companion meant, rather from his gestures than his technical mode of expressing himself (to which, as he was ignorant of his calling, he wanted the clue), rejected this proposition for the second time, and gave the word 'Forward!'

which was echoed by a hundred voices from without.

'To the Warren!' shouted Dennis as he ran out, followed by the rest. 'A witness's house, my lads!'

A loud yell followed, and the whole throng hurried off, mad for pillage and destruction. Hugh lingered behind for a few moments to stimulate himself with more drink, and to set all the taps running, a few of which had accidentally been spared; then, glancing round the despoiled and plundered room, through whose shattered window the rioters had thrust the Maypole itself, – for even that had been sawn down, – lighted a torch, clapped the mute and motionless John Willet on the back, and waving his light above his head, and uttering a fierce shout, hastened after his companions.

Charles Dickens *Barnaby Rudge*

BARS AND CAFÉS

Commodore Hotel Bar

The Lebanese were forever asking me whether I had visited Beirut before the civil war began.

'No,' I would say, 'I never had the pleasure.' Then they would get a faraway look, and a mist of reminiscence would fog their eyes, and they would wax eloquent about how 'life was so beautiful then – Lebanon really was the Switzerland of the Middle East.' It certainly looked that way on the postcards: snowcapped mountains towering over Beirut, a bank on every corner, and a parliament with all the trappings of a European-style democracy. But how could a city go from being a vision of heaven to a vision of hell practically overnight? Because it was too good to be true, because Beirut in its heyday was a city with a false bottom.

My first glimpse of Beirut's real bottom came at the Commodore Hotel bar on 7 February 1984 – the day after the Druse and Shiite Amal militias had seized control of West Beirut from the Lebanese army. Groups of Shiite militiamen belonging to the radical new pro-Iranian organization, Hizbullah, 'Party of God', had gone on a rampage that morning, ransacking heathen bars and whorehouses just off West Beirut's Hamra Street. Some they set ablaze, others they smashed apart with crowbars.

I was enjoying a 'quiet' lunch in the Commodore restaurant that day when I heard a ruckus coming from the lobby. I turned around and saw a tall, heavy-set Shiite militiaman with a black beard, a wild look in his eyes, and an M-16 in his hands, heading for the bar. It was clear he wasn't going for a drink. Anticipating such a visit, Yunis, the bartender, had hidden all the liquor bottles under the counter and had replaced them with cans of Pepsi-Cola and Perrier, which he had carefully stacked into a tall, rather absurd-looking pyramid. The militiaman wasn't fooled. He stalked behind the bar, shoved Yunis aside, and began smashing every liquor bottle and glass with his rifle butt. He didn't miss a single one. When he was done, he stalked out of the lobby, leaving behind a small lake of liquor on the floor and a stunned crowd of journalists frozen to their chairs.

The scene was terrifying on many levels. The relentless manner in which that gunman smashed bottle after bottle with the butt of his rifle left me with the uneasy feeling that he could easily have done the same to any human heads which might have stood in his way. He had Truth with a capital T, he was from the Party of God, and nothing could stop him. But what was no less unsettling to me, and I think many members of the Commodore staff who watched this scene with lips grimly pursed and arms folded across their chests, was that this man was our neighbor. He was not an invader from Syria or Israel. He was a Lebanese, probably a Beiruti. He had been living for years in the same city with us, maybe even in the same neighborhood, and we really never knew he was there – our fault not his. It was as though with his rifle butt he not only smashed the Commodore bar but also right through Beirut's false bottom. Suddenly what remained of the genteel Levantine spirit of Nabil Tabbara's drawings was torn aside, only to reveal a pool of tribal wrath that had been building in intensity for decades beneath the surface among all those Beirutis who were never really part of the Beirut game, or, if they were part of it, played it with a mask on.

This turbulent pool was made up largely of Lebanese Shiites. The Shiites of Lebanon were the country's perpetual underclass, a rural people who for centuries seemed to silently accept their role as Lebanon's beasts of burden. But the Palestinian–Israeli fighting in south Lebanon in the seventies and eighties drove thousands of these Shiites from their native villages in the south to shantytowns on the outskirts of Beirut, where their neighborhoods were aptly dubbed the 'Belt of Misery'. They lived at the gates of Beirut, but the city never really admitted them – not socially, not politically, and not economically. By the early 1980s, the Shiites of Lebanon were the largest single religious community in the country, making up close to half the total population, but they were represented in the government by corrupt feudal lords and were looked down on by the Sunni aristocracy as much as by the Maronites.

By 1984 the Shiites of Lebanon were tired of waiting for the city's gates to open. The Israeli invasion and the Shouf war had shown them how weak the Lebanese state was and the Iranian Islamic revolution had shown them the power which Shiites could exert in the world. Emboldened by the distant whistle of a pied piper named Khomeini, the Shiites of Lebanon decided that their days of violation and silence were over. It was time for a cleansing, time for a people who had always been denied to claim Beirut for themselves. And so they did. West Beirut has been dominated by the Shiites ever since.

The Shiite who broke up the Commodore bar, though, was not only taking revenge on the symbol of something he had been denied but also on the symbol of something he probably never really comprehended. What Nabil Tabbara and his friends did not understand was that the Levantine spirit which infused them – the most modern, secularized, urbanized classes in Lebanese society – had not penetrated many of their other countrymen – not just the Shiites from villages in south Lebanon, but all of those Lebanese Muslims and Christians living in the hinterlands, beyond the city limits, where the spirit of their ancestors continued to rule the day. They called themselves Beirutis or Lebanese, but these identities were just uniforms that many of them wore to work in the city centre. These people mimicked the genteel Levantine language when they walked the streets of Beirut, but at home they spoke a different vernacular. At moments of intercommunal tension, such as the Shouf war, they were always ready to answer the call of the tribe. For them Lebanon was never the Switzerland of the Middle East. It was always the Tower of Babel.

Thomas Friedman *From Beirut to Jerusalem*

Cocktail Hour

Night-life begins late in Beirut. Cocktail hour at the Commodore is 8 p.m., when US editors and network executives are safely at lunch (there's a seven-hour time difference). The Commodore is strictly neutral territory with only one rule. No guns at the bar. All sorts of raffish characters hang about, expatriates from Palestine, Libya and Iran, officers in mufti from both sides of the Lebanese army, and combatants of other stripes. I overheard one black Vietnam veteran loudly describe to two British girls how he teaches orthodox Muslim women to fight with knives. And there are diplomats, spooks and dealers in gold, arms and other things. At least that's what they seem to be. No one exactly announces his occupation – except the journalists, of course.

I met one young lady from Atlanta who worked on a CNN camera crew. She was twenty-six, cute, slightly plump and looked like she should have been head of the Georgia State pep squad. I sat next to her at the Commodore bar and watched her drink twenty-five gin and tonics in a row. She never got drunk, never slurred a word, but along about G&T number twenty-two out came the stories about dismembered babies and dead bodies flying all over the place and the Red Cross picking up hands and feet and heads from bomb blasts and putting them all in a trash dumpster. 'So I asked the Red Cross people,' she said, in the same sweet Dixie accent, 'like, what's this? Save 'em, collect 'em, trade 'em with your friends?'

Everyone in Beirut can hold his or her liquor. If you get queasy, Muhammad, the Commodore bartender, has a remedy rivalling Jeeves's in P. G. Wodehouse's novels. It will steady your stomach so you can drink more. You'll want to. No one in this part of the world is without a horror story, and, at the Commodore bar, you'll hear most of them.

P. J. O'Rorke *Holidays in Hell*

Two Young Men, 23 to 24 Years Old

He'd been sitting in the café since ten-thirty
expecting him to turn up any minute.
Midnight had gone, and he was still waiting for him.
It was now after one-thirty, and the café was almost deserted.
He'd grown tired of reading newspapers
mechanically. Of his three lonely shillings
only one was left: waiting that long,
he'd spent the others on coffees and brandy.

And he'd smoked all his cigarettes.
So much waiting had worn him out.
Because alone like that for so many hours,
he'd also begun to have disturbing thoughts
about the immoral life he was living.

But when he saw his friend come in –
weariness, boredom, thought all disappeared at once.

His friend brought unexpected news.
He'd won sixty pounds playing cards.

Their good looks, their exquisite youthfulness,
the sensitive love they shared
were refreshed, livened, invigorated
by the sixty pounds from the card table.

Now all joy and vitality, feeling and charm,
they went – not to the homes of their respectable families
(where they were no longer wanted anyway) –
they went to a familiar and very special
house of debauchery, and they asked for a bedroom
and expensive drinks, and they drank again.

And when the expensive drinks were finished
and it was close to four in the morning,
happy, they gave themselves to love.

C. P. Cavafy, trans. Edmund Keeley & Philip Sherrard

1 September 1939

I sit in one of the dives
On Fifty-Second Street
Uncertain and afraid
As the clever hopes expire

Of a low dishonest decade:
Waves of anger and fear
Circulate over the bright
And darkened lands of the earth,
Obsessing our private lives;
The unmentionable odour of death
Offends the September night.

Accurate scholarship can
Unearth the whole offence
From Luther until now
That has driven a culture mad,
Find what occurred at Linz,
What huge imago made
A psychopathic god:
I and the public know
What all schoolchildren learn,
Those to whom evil is done
Do evil in return.

Exiled Thucydides knew
All that a speech can say
About Democracy,
And what dictators do,
The elderly rubbish they talk
To an apathetic grave;
Analysed all in his book,
The enlightenment driven away,
The habit-forming pain,
Mismanagement and grief:
We must suffer them all again.

Into this neutral air
Where blind skyscrapers use
Their full height to proclaim
The strength of Collective Man,
Each language pours its vain

Competitive excuse:
But who can live for long
In an euphoric dream;
Out of the mirror they stare,
Imperialism's face
And the international wrong.

Faces along the bar
Cling to their average day:
The lights must never go out,
The music must always play,
All the conventions conspire
To make this fort assume
The furniture of home;
Lest we should see where we are,
Lost in a haunted wood,
Children afraid of the night
Who have never been happy or good.

The windiest militant trash
Important Persons shout
Is not so crude as our wish:
What mad Nijinsky wrote
About Diaghilev
Is true of the normal heart;
For the error bred in the bone
Of each woman and each man
Craves what it cannot have,
Not universal love
But to be loved alone.

From the conservative dark
Into the ethical life
The dense commuters come
Repeating their morning vow,
'I *will* be true to the wife,
I'll concentrate more on my work',

And helpless governors wake
To resume their compulsory game:
Who can release them now,
Who can reach the deaf,
Who can speak for the dumb?

All I have is a voice
To undo the folded lie,
The romantic lie in the brain
Of the sensual man-in-the-street
And the lie of Authority
Whose buildings grope the sky:
There is no such thing as the State
And no one exists alone;
Hunger allows no choice
To the citizen or the police;
We must love one another or die.

Defenceless under the night
Our world in stupor lies;
Yet, dotted everywhere,
Ironic points of light
Flash out wherever the Just
Exchange their messages:
May I, composed like them
Of Eros and of dust,
Beleaguered by the same
Negation and despair,
Show an affirming flame.

W. H. Auden

Cruising

Let's move on to a tour of the bars. Though it's only ten, don't worry, we won't be too early. The bars close at two and LA is an early-to-bed, early-to-rise sort of city.

Among the leather bars, the One Way is druggy, Griff's is for older numbers, the Stud is good on Sunday afternoons. At Larry's there is a ball and chain cast down on the bar, but it seems no more authentic than a spinning wheel in a Williamsburg eatery. In the back is a pool table where I chatted with a painter who's teaching at a nearby junior college. Up front, right beside the ball and chain, I met the young heir to a pasta fortune who tells me he's toured Europe often but never travelled in the States east of the Mississippi. Under a dim spot stands a tall, handsome blond in full leather; he's obviously aware of the exact nuances of his lighting. After a bit I overhear him say to a friend, 'I met this tall, handsome blond in full leather . . .'

My favourite tavern was the Detour, the easiest pickup place right now. It's a long, narrow room, the bar making it still narrower, and as you squeeze to the back you jostle past stoned smiles under ten-gallon hats that cast beguiling arcs of shadow over friendly eyes. Boots in pairs are suspended by their laces from the slats over the bar. In one corner hangs a glass ball in which the silhouette of a stagecoach slowly revolves. In the very back is a pool table. There is no room for playing a game since shirtless, sweating men, standing four deep, are boogying in place and sniffing poppers to the disco music.

Back on Santa Monica, across the street and two blocks down from Rascals, is the Blue Parrot. Here you can pick up the same beauties who snubbed you at Rascals earlier. But snubbing isn't all that fashionable in Los Angeles. People are friendly, and I doubt if the New York stare that says, 'I despise you but I might condescend to fuck you,' would ever go over very big out West. In LA there are no back rooms, the last resort in New York for those who spend all evening being overly fastidious but end up by being prodigally indiscriminate. And then, once you've driven forty miles to your suburban bungalow in LA, you're quite definitely *alone* for the night as you listen to the dog barking down the street and look at the blue gloom emanating from your neighbour's tube. Better to have someone, anyone, by your side.

Edmund White *States of Desire: Travels in Gay America*

At Six o'Clock

I lift – lift you five States away your glass,
Wide of this bar you never graced, where none
Ever I know came, where what work is done
Even by these men I know not, where a brass
Police-car sign peers in, wet strange cars pass,
Soiled hangs the rag of day out over this town,
A juke-box brains air where I drink alone,
The spruce barkeep sports a toupee alas –

My glass I lift at six o'clock, my darling,
As you plotted . . . Chinese couples shift in bed,
We shared today not even filthy weather,
Beasts in the hills their tigerish love are snarling,
Suddenly they clash, I blow my short ash red,
Grey eyes light! and we have our drink together.

John Berryman

The Terminal Bar

(for Philip Haas)

The television set hung
in its wire-net cage,
protected from the flung
bottle of casual rage,

is fetish and icon
providing all we want
of magic and redemption,
routine and sentiment.
The year-old tinsels hang
where an unclaimed no-hoper
trembles; fly-corpses cling
to the grimy fly-paper.
Manhattan snows swarm
on constellated waters,
steam trails from warm
subway ventilators . . .
Welcome to the planet,
its fluorescent beers
buzzing in the desolate
silence of the spheres.
Slam the door and knock
the snow from your shoe,
admit that the vast dark
at last defeated you –
nobody found the grail
or conquered outer space.
Join the clientele
watching itself increase.

Derek Mahon

CELEBRATIONS

Prayer for Patroclus

Before Achilles sailed to Troy
His women packed and put aboard his ship
A painted oak box filled with winter clothes;
Rugs for his feet, a fleece-lined windcheater –
You know the sort of thing. And in this box
He kept an eye bowl made from ivory and horn
Which he, and only he, used for Communion.
And having spoken to his troops he took it out,
Rubbed sulphur crystals on its inner face,
And washed and dried his hands before,
Spring water rinsed, brimming with altar-wine,
He held it at arm's length, and prayed:

'Our Father, Who rules the Heaven,
Because Your will is done where will may be,
Grant me this prayer
As You have granted other prayers of mine:
Give my Patroclus Your victory;
Let him show Hector he can win
Without me at his side;
And grant, above all else, O Lord,
That when the Trojans are defeated, he
Returns to me unharmed.'

God heard his prayer and granted half of it.
Patroclus would rout the Trojans; yes;
But not a word was said about his safe return.
No, my Achilles, God promised nothing of the kind,
As carefully you dried your cup,
As carefully replaced it in its box,
And stood outside your tent and watched
Your men and your Patroclus go by.

Christopher Logue *War Music*

Water into Wine

And the third day there was a marriage in Cana of Galilee; and the mother of Jesus was there: and both Jesus was called, and his disciples, to the marriage.

And when they wanted wine, the mother of Jesus saith unto him, They have no wine.

Jesus saith unto her, Woman, what have I to do with thee? mine hour is not yet come.

His mother saith unto the servants, Whatsoever he saith unto you, do *it*.

And there were set there six water-pots of stone, after the manner of the purifying of the Jews, containing two or three firkins apiece.

Jesus saith unto them, Fill the water-pots with water. And they filled them up to the brim.

And he saith unto them, Draw out now, and bear unto the governor of the feast. And they bare *it*.

When the ruler of the feast had tasted the water that was made wine, and knew not whence it was: (but the servants which drew the water knew;) the governor of the feast called the bridegroom.

And saith unto him, Every man at the beginning doth set forth good wine; and when men have well drunk, then that which is worse: *but* thou hast kept the good wine until now.

This beginning of miracles did Jesus in Cana of Galilee, and manifested forth his glory; and his disciples believed on him.

St John 2:1–11

Royal Wedding

The meeting between the prince and princess, as witnessed by Malmesbury later on that day, was certainly as unpropitious as their most cruelly disposed ill-wishers could have hoped. The princess knelt, as she had been instructed to do. The prince 'raised her (gracefully enough)'. He embraced her. But then, overcome by either the smell of her hair, the sight of her red face or by sudden self-pity at his unfortunate predicament, he soon turned away; and, without another word or a backward glance in her direction, he retreated to a far corner of the room where, beckoning Malmesbury towards him, he said, 'Harris, I am not well. Pray get me a glass of brandy.'

'Sir,' Malmesbury replied. 'Had you not better have a glass of water?'

Exasperated by this remark, the prince 'said with an oath, "*No.* I will go directly to the queen," and away he went. The princess, left during this short moment alone, was in a state of astonishment.'

'My God!' she exclaimed in French when the door had closed. 'Does the prince always act like this? I think he's very fat and he's nothing like as handsome as his portrait.'

The mutual antipathy intensified in the days before the marriage. In a sadly misguided and forlorn attempt to show that she did not care about the prince's attachment to Lady Jersey and his evident dislike of herself, Princess Caroline adopted a pert and bantering manner, making embarrassing 'attempts at cleverness and coarse sarcasm' which made the prince wince with irritation and distaste. When the dreaded morning of the wedding arrived he was 'like a man doing a thing in desperation', Lord Melbourne thought. 'It was like Macheath going to execution.' To brace himself for the ceremony he drank glass after glass of brandy, and by the time he entered the Chapel Royal, closely supported by two dukes who had difficulty in preventing him from falling over, he was obviously – as his future son-in-law, Prince Leopold, told Queen Victoria – '*extremely* DRUNK'. The bride appeared so, too. For her dress was so heavy that she also nearly fell over as she walked down the aisle, chatting away gustily to the Duke of Clarence.

The prince could not bring himself to look at her. During the service he suddenly stood up in the middle of a prayer and remained standing until his father stepped forward to whisper something in his ear. Later he burst into tears. According to the bride, he continued drinking after the service was over, and by nightfall was so intoxicated that he collapsed into their bedroom fireplace where she left him. Evidently he recovered sufficiently to climb into bed the next morning; and precisely nine months later the princess gave birth to what her husband described as 'an *immense* girl'.

Christopher Hibbert *Memoirs of Queen Caroline*

Divorce

We went down to our quarters. On the main deck we ran into Mr Hartford, the ex-tycoon from Delaware. He adjusted his hearing aid, embraced Artie, and boomed that we were just in time to celebrate. This was, he said, the seventeenth anniversary of his divorce, a happy day that called for champagne. Mr Hartford always found a pretext to celebrate. We went to the bar and had a bottle of champagne and another one. After that we forgot all about the captain and being restricted. Artie told Mr Hartford about our war against the *Azay-le-Rideau*. The ex-tycoon solemnly put his hand on Artie's shoulder. 'There's only one thing to do,' he said. 'Strike. Don't play any more.'

I pointed out that you don't strike aboard ship.

'All right, then,' Mr Hartford said. 'Why don't you throw your violin overboard? You can't play without a violin, can you?'

Artie said: 'It's no use. Two seamen have violins and the damned pharmacist carries a 'cello along, and – ' Artie stopped in the middle of his sentence and jumped up from his chair. 'There is only one piano aboard,' he said, in a soft, alien-sounding voice. 'Without a piano there won't be ten hours of music, as the madman said. In fact, there won't be any music at all.'

A solemn silence followed these words. The magnitude of the suggestion was crushing. It was a hot night. The bar-tender opened a third bottle of champagne.

'If the captain finds out about this, we'll be fired in Saigon,' I said. 'What are we going to do there?'

Artie shrugged magnanimously: 'We can open an opium den. Everybody smokes opium in Saigon. And if we fold up, we can always join the Foreign Legion in Tongking.'

Mr Hartford fussed with his hearing aid and said, would

somebody *please* speak up and tell him what it was all about? When we explained our plan, he nodded gravely. He got up and picked up one of the chairs. He lifted it, testing its weight, and suddenly threw it overboard. Everybody got very excited. Pedro threw a table and another chair after Mr Hartford's chair, 'for a mermaid who wants to furnish her room', and I joined in with all the glasses, match-holders, ash-trays, and bottles within reach.

Mr Hartford and Artie were already busy with the piano. Mr Hartford said the price of such a bad, old piano did not amount to anything in American money, and that he would gladly pay for it. We had another glass of cool champagne. We pushed the piano toward the railing. The bar-tender and the deck steward looked on, in utter consternation. Mr Hartford breathed hard and almost lost his hearing aid. Artie suggested that we should cover the instrument with a flag, a piano being worth almost as much as any human being and considerably more than some of them, but no one seconded the motion. We lifted the piano. It was only an upright Pleyel, but after all the drinks it seemed as heavy as a concert grand. A final effort and the instrument rolled over the railing. There was a short metallic protest and then the chords emitted what sounded like an almost human last cry. There was a big splash. Pedro, a devout Catholic, took off his Basque beret and moved his lips. Perhaps he said a prayer. There was nothing else to say. We went down to our rooms and lay down.

Joseph Wechsberg *Looking for a Bluebird*

Fleadh Cheoil*

Subtle capering on a simple thought,
the vindicated music soaring out
each other door in a mean twisting main street,
flute-player, fiddler and penny-whistler
concentrating on one sense only

*A music festival.

such a wild elegance of energy gay and sad
few clouds of lust or vanity could form;
the mind kept cool, the heart kept warm;
therein the miracle, three days and nights
so many dances played and so much drinking done,
so many voices raised in singing but none
in anger nor any fist in harm –
Saint Patrick's Day in Cambridge Circus might
have been some other nation's trough of shame.

Hotel-back-room, pub-snug, and large open lounges
and the mean street like a Latin fête,
music for once taking all harm out –
from even the bunting's pathetic blunderings
and the many mean publicans making money fast,
hand over fat fist, pouring the flat
western porter from black-chipped white enamel,
Dervorgilla's penitent chapel
crumbling arch archaic but east,
only music now releasing her people
like Sweeney's cousins on a branch unable
to find his words, but using music
for all articulateness.

But still the shabby county-town was full,
en fête; on fire with peace – for all
the black-and-white contortionists bred
from black and white enamel ever said.
From Easter Snow and Scartaglin
the men with nimble fingers came
in dowdy Sunday suits,
from Kirkintilloch and Ladbroke Grove came back
in flashy ties and frumpish hats,
to play an ancient music, make it new.
A stranger manner of telling than words can do,
a strange manner, both less and more than words or Bach,
but like, that Whitsuntide, stained-glass in summer,

high noon, rose window, Benedictbeuern pleasure,
and Seán Ó Neachtain's loving singing wood,
an Nollaig sa tSamhradh.*

Owls and eagles, clerks and navvies,
ex-British Tommies in drab civvies,
and glorious-patriots whose wild black brindled hair
stood up for the trench-coats they had no need to wear
that tranquil carnival weekend,
when all the boastful maladies got cured –
the faction-fighting magniloquence,
devoid of charity or amorous sense,
the sun-shunning pubs, the trips to Knock.

One said to me: 'There's heart in that',
pointing at: a thick-set man of middle age,
a thick red drinker's face,
and eyes as bright as good stained-glass,
who played on and on and on
a cheap tin-whistle, as if no race
for petty honours had ever come to pass
on earth, or his race to a stale pass;
tapping one black boot on a white flag,
and us crowding, craning, in at the door,
gaining, and storing up, the heart in that.
With him a boy about eighteen,
tall and thin, but, easy to be seen,
Clare still written all over him
despite his eighteen months among the trim
scaffoldings and grim digs of England;
resting his own tin-whistle for his mentor's riff,
pushing back, with a big red hand, the dank mousy quiff,
turning to me to say, 'You know what I think of it,
over there?
Over there, you're free.'

*Christmas in Summer.

Repeating the word 'free', as gay and sad as his music,
repeating the word, the large bright eyes convinced
of what the red mouth said, convinced beyond
shaming or furtiveness, a thousand preachers,
mothers and leader-writers wasting their breath
on the sweet, foggy, distant-city air.
Then he went on playing as if there never were
either a famed injustice or a parish glare.

Ennis

Pearse Hutchinson

Enlisted by Bacchus

If, my cultured Maecenas, old Cratínus was right,
poems written by water-drinkers will never enjoy
long life or acclaim. Since Bacchus enlisted frenzied
poets among his Satyrs and Fauns, the dulcet Muses
have usually smelt of drink first thing in the morning.
His praises of wine prove that Homer was fond of the grape;
father Ennius himself never sprang to his tale
of arms, unless he was drunk. 'The Stock Exchange and the City
shall be reserved for the sober; the stern are forbidden to sing' –
since I issued this edict, poets have never ceased
drinking in competition by night, and stinking by day.

Horace *Book 1 Epistle 19*, trans. Niall Rudd

A Reading

I was sitting with Isadora Duncan one evening in 'The Stable of Pegasus' café when the poets were having a party; that is to say one after another got up on a little stage at the end of the room and recited his own verses. That, it seems, is the poet's ideal of a party. Essenin had been sitting there rather drunker and more offensive than usual, which was saying a good deal, and when he left us just before his turn I couldn't help asking Isadora why on earth she married that one. She was not in the least offended. 'He's not at his best to-night, poor Sergei,' she admitted, 'but there's one thing I'd have you know, and it's this; that boy's a genius. All my lovers have been geniuses; it's the one thing upon which I insist.' Mentally I raised my eyebrows but I did not attempt to argue. A minute or two later Essenin reeled on to the stage to speak his piece. The café was full of a motley crowd, poets and their girl friends all talking at the top of their voices; just behind me a couple of prostitutes from the Tverskaya bargaining noisily with a reluctant client; in a corner near the door two drunks were having a wordy battle with a hack driver who demanded payment on account before he would agree to wait for them indefintely. Then Essenin began to recite one of his poems called 'The Black Man'. At first his voice was low and husky, but as the swing of the verses caught him it deepened and grew stronger.

The poem was raw and brutal but alive and true. It described the feelings of a drunkard on the verge of delirium tremens, who was haunted by the face of a negro grinning at him. The face was not unfriendly but it was everywhere – looking over his shoulder in the mirror when he shaved, beside him on the pillow in his bed, poised between his shoes in the morning when he got up to put them on.

I knew the story of this poem. The negro face was that of Claude McKay, the coloured poet who had visited Moscow a year or so before and had been a friend of Essenin. Essenin was then close to delirium tremens, and his verses were real; they expressed what he had felt and known.

As his voice rose there came utter silence in the café. Line after shattering line banged the consciousness of that motley crowd and froze them into horror. It was tremendous and terrible to hear the agony of the haunted wretch, and Essenin made us share it. A triumph of transmitted emotion from the Artist to the Public.

When he stopped there was not a sound. Everyone – cab-men, speculators, prostitutes, poets, drunkards – all sat frozen with pale faces, open mouths, and anguished eyes. Then Isadora, whom nothing could dismay, said to me quietly, 'Do you still think my little peasant boy has no genius?'

Walter Duranty *'I Write as I Please'*

Gargantua's Grief

When Pantagruel was born, there was none more astonished and perplexed than was his father Gargantua; for, of the one side, seeing his wife Badebec dead, and on the other side his son Pantagruel born, so fair and so great, he knew not what to say, nor what to do. And the doubt that troubled his brain was to know whether he should cry for the death of his wife, or laugh for the joy of his son. He was *hinc inde* choked with sophistical arguments, for he framed them very well *in modo et figura*, but he could not resolve them, remaining pestered and entangled by this means, like a mouse catch'd in a trap, or kite snared in a gin. Shall I weep? said he. Yes, for why? My so good wife is dead who was the most *this*, the most *that*, that was ever in the world. Never shall I see her, never shall I recover such another, it is unto me an inestimable loss! O my good God, what had I done that thou shouldest thus punish me? Why didst thou not take me away before her? Seeing for me to live without her is but to languish. Ah Badebec, Badebec, my minion, my dear heart, my sugar, my sweeting, my honey, my little C*** – yet it had in circumference full six acres, three rods, five poles, four yards, two foot, one inch and a half of good woodland measure – my tender peggy, my codpiece darling, my bob and hit, my slipshoe-lovey, never shall I see thee! Ah, poor Pantagruel, thou hast lost thy good mother, thy sweet nurse, thy well-beloved lady! O false death, how injurious and despiteful hast thou been to me! How malicious and outrageous have I found thee in taking her from me, my well-beloved wife, to whom immortality did of right belong!

With these words he did cry like a cow; but on a sudden fell a laughing like a calf, when Pantagruel came into his mind. Ha, my little son, said he, my childilolly, fedlifondy, dandlichucky, my ballocky, my pretty rogue! O how jolly thou art, and how much am I bound to my gracious God, that hath been pleased to bestow on me a son, so fair, so spriteful, so lively, so smiling, so pleasant, and so gentle! Ho, ho, ho, ho, how glad I am! Let us drink ho, and put away melancholy! Bring of the best, rinse the glasses, lay the cloth, drive out these dogs, blow this fire, light candles, shut that door there, cut this bread in sippets for brewis, send away these poor folks in giving them what they ask, hold my gown. I will strip myself into my doublet, (*én cuerpo*,) to make the gossips merry, and keep them company.

As he spake this, he heard the litanies and the mementos of the priests that carried his wife to be buried, upon which he left the good purpose he was in, and was suddenly ravished another way, saying, Lord God, must I again contrist myself? This grieves me. I am no longer young, I grow old, the weather is dangerous; I may perhaps take an ague, then shall I be foiled, if not quite undone. By the faith of a gentleman, it were better to cry less, and drink more. My wife is dead, well, by G— (*da jurandi*), I shall not raise her again by my crying: she is well, she is in Paradise at least, if she be no higher: she prayeth to God for us, she is happy, she is above the sense of our miseries, nor can our calamities reach her. What though she be dead, must not we also die? The same debt which she hath paid hangs over our heads; nature will require it of us, and we must all of us some day taste of the same sauce. Let her pass then, and the Lord preserve the survivors; for I must now cast about how to get another wife. But I will tell you what you shall do, said he to the midwives, in France called wise women (where be they? good folks, I cannot see them). Go you to my wife's interment, and I will the while rock my son; for I find myself somewhat altered and distempered, and should otherwise be in danger of falling sick; but drink one good draught first, you will be the better for it, and believe me upon mine honour. They at his request went to her burial and funeral obsequies.

François Rabelais *Gargantua and Pantagruel*,
trans. Sir Robert Urquhart

Wake

The inebriated chanting of professional mourners came wailing from 44 Cloncarragah Terrace. Inside the front room, propped by the fireplace, was the flower-bedecked coffin of Dan Doonan. Grouped around admiringly, reverently clutching their drinks, were friends and foes alike, and with drink they were all very much alike. Funeral clichés were flying in the teeth of the dear departed.

'A fine man, ma'am, it's a great day for him.'

'You must be proud of him, Mrs Doonan.'

'One of the finest dead men ter ever walk the earth.'

'I was sorry ter see him go!'

'So was I – he owed me a pound.'

'It's hard to believe he's dead.'

'Oh he's *dead* is he?' said Foggerty, who'd been speaking to him all evening.

The corpse looked fine, fine, fine. New suit, hair cut and greased, his boots highly polished and loaned by an anonymous donor were firmly nailed to the coffin for additional security. The tables in the next room were swollen high with the food. Two wooden tubs steamed with baked potatoes, their earthy jackets split and running with rivulets of melting butter. Hot pig slices, a quarter inch thick, were piled high on seventeen plates. In the middle, was one huge dish of brown pork sausages, and bacon, still bubbling from the pan. On the floor, floating in a bucket of vinegar, was a minefield of pickled onions. The temporary bar was serving drinks as fast as O'Toole could pour them.

'God, there hasn't been a night like this since the signing of the Treaty.'

Many people die of thirst but the Irish are born with one.

O'Connor the piper tucked his kilt between his legs, puffed the bladder of his pipes and droned them into life; soon the floor was lost in a sea of toiling, reeling legs. Uppity-hippity-juppity-ippity-dippity-dippity shook the house. The centre bulb danced like a freshly hanged man. There was a clapping a stamping-and-cries-of-encouragement. The faithful few in Dan's parlour soon deserted him for the dance. Alone in his room he stood, his body jerking to the rhythm now shaking the house. The party was swelled by the arrival of the victorious Puckoon Hurley team, many still unconscious from the game. These were dutifully laid on the floor beside Dan's coffin – the rest joined into the frenzied dance.

The Milligan pulled his trousers up and leaped into the middle, but he observed his legs and stopped. 'Hey, you said me legs would develop with the plot.'

'They will.'

'Den why are they still like a pair of dirty old pipe cleaners.'

'It's a transitional period.'

'Look, I don't want transitional legs.' He stood in the middle of the leaping bodies and spoke, 'What's dis book all about, here we are on page-page – ' he looked down, 'on page 80 – and all these bloody people comin' and goin', where's it all going to end?'

'I don't know. Believe me, I'm just as worried as you are.'

'Tell me why? – tell me – give me a sign!'

A bottle bounced off Milligan's head.

'The Queen,' he shouted and fell sideways like a poleaxed ox.

Three fights had broken out in the midst of the dancers but the difference was hard to tell. The whole house now trembled from roof to foundations. In the next room the great family bible shook from the shelf above the coffin and struck Dan Doonan, throwing him from the coffin and catapulting him from his boots. His wig, a life-long secret, shot from his head and slid under the table next to the cat. He fell among the unconscious members of the Hurley team, who were starting to recover. 'He's drunk as a lord,' they said, dragging him across the hall and tucking him in bed.

'Good God, look at the size of that rat,' one said, seeing the cat pass with a wig in its jaws. 'He mustha' put up a fight.'

Placing a bottle of whisky by the bed they drank it and stumbled from the room.

It was 4.32 in the morning as the crow flies. The last mourners had slobbered out their drunken farewells, their voices and great posterior blasts mingling into the night. Mrs Doonan drained an empty bottle, scratched her belly, and made for her bed.

Somewhere in the night, Milligan, drunk and with lumps on his head, was wandering through the braille-black countryside: in his path a carefully written well. Splash! it went on receipt of his body.

At 4.56 in the morning, the quietly patrolling constable Oaf was reduced to a kneeling-praying holy man by a leg-weakening shriek. The door of number 33 burst open and out screamed Mrs Doonan in unlaced corsets.

'There's a man in me bed, get him out!' she yelled, restraining her abounding bosoms.

'Madam, if you can't frighten him in that get-up, I certainly can't!'

'Do yer duty,' she said, ladling her bosoms back.

The constable unclipped his torch, took a firm grip on his truncheon and entered the house.

'In that room,' she whispered.

'Leave him to me,' said Oaf, pushing her in front. He shone his torch on the bed. Mrs Doonan gasped and let fall her bosoms. 'Holy Mary!' she gasped, 'It's me husband.'

She fainted, clutching the policeman's legs as she fell, bringing his trousers to the ground. Now then, who would have thought a constable would use green knotted string for garters and have red anchors tattooed on his knees? Ah, Ireland is still a land of mystery.

Spike Milligan *Puckoon*

PARTIES

Etiquette

ANTICLEON: Well now, come and lie down over here. (*He indicates the two couches.*) I'll show you how to behave at a fashionable drinking party.

PROCLEON: Lie down? How am I supposed to lie?

ANTICLEON: Just recline, gracefully.

(PROCLEON *clambers on to one of the couches and lies down on his back, with his knees up.*)

No, no, not like that, for heaven's sake!

PROCLEON: How, then? Show me.

ANTICLEON: You must straighten your knees – that's it – and sort of *pour* yourself back into the cushions with a supple athletic grace.

(ANTICLEON *demonstrates, taking up a reclining position on the other couch.* PROCLEON *practises 'pouring' himself into the cushions until* ANTICLEON *is satisfied.*)

Good. But now you should say something complimentary about the bronze ornaments – look up at the ceiling – admire the rugs on the wall.

(PROCLEON *mimes all this as instructed.* ANTICLEON *now claps his hands to summon the slaves, who have been briefed in advance. At each stage of the imaginary party* ANTICLEON *demonstrates the correct procedure and table manners.* PROCLEON *attempts to imitate his gestures.*)

Bring the finger-bowls!

(*The* SLAVES *do so.*)

Bring in the tables!

(*The* SLAVES *do so.*)

Now we eat . . . now wash hands again . . . now the libation.

(*The* SLAVES *whisk away the tables.*)

PROCLEON: Was I dreaming, or were we supposed to be having dinner?

ANTICLEON: Now, the flute-girl has played her piece, and you are drinking with – let's say – Theorus, Aeschines, Phanos, Cleon, and that foreign fellow, the son of Acestor. He's at Cleon's head. Can you take up a catch when it comes to your turn?

PROCLEON: Oh, yes, I'm good at that.

ANTICLEON: Well, we shall see. Now, I'm Cleon: suppose I start off with 'Harmodius': and you have to cap it (*Sings.*)

Such a man was never seen in Athens . . .

PROCLEON: (*Sings*):

Such a low-down, thieving little bastard . . .

ANTICLEON: If you sing that, you'll never survive the uproar: he'll swear to have your blood, he'll threaten to ruin you and drive you out of the city.

PROCLEON: If he threatens me, I've got another song for him: (*Sings*:)

Take care, if too high in the city you rise.
You'll make her top-heavy and then she'll capsize!

ANTICLEON: And now supposing Theorus, lying next to Cleon, takes his right hand and starts up this one: (*Sings.*)

It's wise, as Admetus found out in the end
To choose a good man for your very best friend.

How are you going to cap that?

PROCLEON: Oh, I've got something very poetical for that. (*Sings.*)

It isn't as easy, old boy, as it sounds
To run with the hare and to hunt with the hounds.

ANTICLEON: And now it's Aeschines's turn. He's a very learned, cultured sort of fellow – he'll start off with (*Sings rowdily*):

What a lot of money,
Power and propertee!
What a time we had of it,
Up in Thessalee!
Oh, we showed them what was what,
Clitagor and me –

PROCLEON: (*Sings*):

I can boast to you, dear,
And you can boast to me.

ANTICLEON: Well, you seem to have got the idea pretty well. All right, we'll go and have dinner at Philoctemon's (*He claps his hands.*) Boy! Pack up the food, we're going out on a binge for once in a while.

PROCLEON: No, I don't approve of drinking, I know what wine leads to: breaches of the peace, assault and battery – and a fine to pay before you've got rid of the hangover.

ANTICLEON: Not if you're drinking with real gentlemen. They'll pacify the victim for you – or you can smooth him down yourself: just come out with a neat quotation from Aesop, or one of the stories about the Sybarites – something you heard at the party. Make a joke of the whole thing, and he'll just go away quietly.

PROCLEON: I see I shall have to learn a lot of those stories, if I want to avoid getting fined in future. Well, my boy, what are we waiting for? Let's go.

Aristophanes *The Wasps*, trans. David Barrett

Dinner with Trimalchio

Trimalchio looked round at us with a gentle smile: 'If you don't like the wine, I'll have it changed. It is up to you to do it justice. I don't buy it, thank heaven. In fact, whatever wine really tickles your palate this evening, it comes from an estate of mine which as yet I haven't seen. It's said to join my estates at Tarracina and Tarentum. What I'd like to do now is add Sicily to my little bit of land, so that when I want to go to Africa, I could sail there without leaving my own property.

'But tell me, Agamemnon, what was your debate about today? Even though I don't go in for the law, still I've picked up enough education for home consumption. And don't you think I turn my nose up at studying, because I have two libraries, one Greek, one Latin. So tell us, just as a favour, what was the topic of your debate?'

Agamemnon was just beginning, 'A poor man and a rich man were enemies . . .' when Trimalchio said: 'What's a poor man?' 'Oh, witty!' said Agamemnon, and then told us about some fictitious case or other. Like lightning Trimalchio said: 'If this happened, it's not a fictitious case – if it didn't happen, then it's nothing at all.'

We greeted this witticism and several more like it with the greatest enthusiasm.

'Tell me, my dear Agamemnon,' continued Trimalchio, 'do you remember the twelve labours of Hercules and the story of Ulysses – how the Cyclops tore out his thumb with a pair of pincers. I used to read about them in Homer, when I was a boy. In fact, I actually saw the Sibyl at Cumae with my own eyes dangling in a bottle, and when the children asked her in Greek: "What do you want, Sybil?" she used to answer: "I want to die."'

He was still droning on when a server carrying the massive pig was put on the table. We started to express our amazement at this speed and swear that not even an ordinary rooster could be cooked so quickly, the more so as the pig appeared far larger than we remembered. Trimalchio looked closer and closer at it, and then shouted:

'What's this? Isn't this pig gutted? I'm damn certain it isn't. Call the chef in here, go on, call him!'

The downcast chef stood by the table and said he'd forgotten it.

'What, you forgot! shouted Trimalchio. 'You'd think he'd only left out the pepper and cumin. Strip him!'

In a second the chef was stripped and standing miserably between two men with whips. But everyone began pleading for him:

'It does tend to happen,' they said, 'do let him off, please. If he does it any more, none of us will stand up for him again.'

Personally, given my tough and ruthless temperament, I couldn't contain myself. I leaned over and whispered in Agamemnon's ear:

'How could anyone forget to clean a pig? I damn well wouldn't let him off if he forgot to clean a fish.'

But not Trimalchio. His face relaxed into a smile.

'Well,' he said, 'since you have such a bad memory, gut it in front of us.'

The chef recovered his shirt, took up a knife and with a nervous hand cut open the pig's belly left and right. Suddenly, as the slits widened with the pressure, out poured sausages and blood puddings.

The staff applauded this piece of ingenuity and gave a concerted cheer – 'Hurray for Gaius!' The chef of course was rewarded with a drink and a silver crown, and was also given a drinking cup on a tray of Corinthian bronze.

Petronius *The Satyricon*, trans. J. P. Sullivan

Who Goes There?

Yesterday, I dined out with a largeish party, where were Sheridan and Colman, Harry Harris of C[ovent] G[arden] and his brother, Sir Gilbert Heathcote, D[ougla]s Kinnaird, and others, of note and notoriety. Like other parties of the kind, it was first silent, then talky, then argumentative, then disputatious, then unintelligible, then altogethery, then inarticulate, and then drunk. When we had reached the last step of this glorious ladder, it was difficult to get down again without stumbling; – and, to crown all, Kinnaird and I had to conduct Sheridan down a d——d corkscrew staircase, which had certainly been constructed before the discovery of fermented liquors, and to which no legs, however crooked, could possibly accommodate themselves. We deposited him safe at home, where his man, evidently used to the business, waited to receive him in the hall.

Both he and Colman were, as usual, very good; but I carried away much wine, and the wine had previously carried away my memory; so that all was hiccup and happiness for the last hour or so, and I am not impregnated with any of the conversation. Perhaps you heard of a late answer of Sheridan to the watchman who found him bereft of that 'divine particle of air,' called reason, * * * * * *

* * * He, the watchman, found Sherry in the street, fuddled and bewildered, and almost insensible. 'Who are you, sir?' – no answer. 'What's your name?' – a hiccup. 'What's your name?' – Answer, in a slow, deliberate, and impassive tone – 'Wilberforce!!!'* Is not that Sherry all over? – and, to my mind, excellent. Poor fellow, *his* very dregs are better than the 'first sprightly runnings' of others.

My paper is full, and I have a grevious headache.

Lord Byron to Thomas Moore, 31 October 1815

Unmasked

The buoyant rhythm of a waltz and the rumour of talk and laughter drowned the tom-toms of Plessis as Berthe came downstairs to the lights of the ballroom. She found the Count standing in the hall, his hair ruffled and his eyebrows twisted up in obvious distress.

'Really, Berthe,' he said, leading her into an ante-chamber, 'of all the things to happen, just when everything was going so well!'

Berthe asked what was the matter but he appeared not to have heard her.

'The best ball we've ever had,' he went on, 'and now this comes along and ruins everything.' He lowered his tall body despondently onto a sofa and, leaning an elbow on his knee, rested his bearded chin on his fist in an attitude of bewildered pensiveness. Somebody must have told him about the duel, Berthe thought. But it soon turned out to be something else.

'I thought there was something queer about those black dominoes from the start,' he went on. Completely at sea, Berthe could stand it no longer. She sat down beside him on the sofa. 'What about the black dominoes, Cousin Agénor?'

'You haven't heard? Thank God for that! Well, you noticed those black dominoes who came in with the carnival masques – the drunkest of the lot? Well, when the time came to unmask at half

*William Wilberforce (1759–1833), chiefly noted as an anti-slavery advocate, became a strict Evangelical, one of the 'Clapham Sect', and was a teetotaller.

past two, I went down to their terrace with Gentilien to have a drink with the whole party. They did the usual *caleinda* and then off came the masks. Everything was very lively and gay. But the dominoes had all collected to one side and were about to slip away into the trees. The others saw them, and everyone shouted that the masks must all come off. A crowd of boys ran and pulled them back to the fireside. Everyone was laughing and Maman Zélie took charge and said they must each drink a full glass of rum as a forfeit. But they still refused to unmask and tried to run off again, so the others caught hold of them and the *Roi-Diable* ceremoniously threw back the first one's domino and lifted off his mask. And,' the Count lowered his voice, 'What do you think?' His voice fell still lower. 'It was a leper. And when the other five were unmasked, they all turned out to be lepers as well. There was a terrified silence at first. Then – you can imagine the uproar . . . I tried to calm everybody down and sent Gentilien back to the house for Dr Vamel. The lepers were in such a condition they could hardly articulate. They had been loose in the town for the past five days, drinking hard all the time and never daring to join in the meals in case they were discovered. As you can guess, they were all as drunk as Poles, and it was very hard to make out how they got here. It seems that they came from the Desirade.* One of them had been there seventeen years. Some time last week they stole a boat and headed for Marie Galante, meaning to hide there in the dominoes (which they had prepared beforehand) for the first few days of carnival. When the search for them in the Desirade and in Guadeloupe had died down, they planned to slip across and stow away on the Brest packet from Pointe-à-Pitre,† and make their way to France. A myth has apparently grown up in the Desirade that a new cure for the disease has been discovered in France which the local authorities know nothing about or are wilfully withholding. . . . At all events, off they set, steered much too far south, missed Marie Galante and finally landed here at

*La Desirade – the Deseada of the first Spanish Conquistadores – is the rocky coffin-shaped island some miles to the east of Guadeloupe and due north of Saint-Jacques. It is the principal leper colony of the French West Indies.

†The port of Guadeloupe.

Cap d'Ivry. They made their way to Plessis under cover of night, living on dasheen and yam and breadfruit they had uprooted from the plantations and lying up in the forest till it was dark, arriving here five days ago, when they were able to put on their dominoes and come out of hiding. . . .

'Dr Vamel was marvellous. He promised to see that they were properly looked after and I will do what I can for them as well. But, between ourselves, there is no hope. The cure is a complete legend,' the Count sighed. 'The masques behaved very well indeed. Dr Vamel told them, and I backed him up, that leprosy isn't usually contagious in the ordinary sense – not that you can ever be sure. You can touch people a hundred times without catching it. It is prolonged and intimate contacts that are the most dangerous, if you follow me; and that's half the trouble in this case. You know how drunk everybody gets and what goes on in carnival time. . . . The doctor said he would do what he could, with strong disinfectant, for anyone who felt himself or herself to be specially in danger. In the end, he left for his clinic with a very sad little procession of *Gwan-wobes*. . . . What a business! We all either danced with them or with people who *had*; so we are all potential lepers. Poor little Berthe! Toi et moi aussi, et la pauvre Mathilde et les enfants et le Capitaine et Gentilien et tous les invités et tous le noirs! But there's nothing to be done about it, absolutely nothing. The great thing is not to mention it to anybody, especially not to the *Metwopolitains*.'

'What has happened to them now?' Berthe asked.

'To the lepers? Gentilien and I locked them in the old coach house with a sucking pig and a demijohn of rum, poor fellows. We'll have to put our thinking caps on tomorrow. . . . Luckily,' he went on, waving to the ballroom, which seemed more densely and hilariously populated than ever, 'nobody seems to have heard yet and the best thing we can do is to forget all about it for the present.'

Patrick Leigh Fermor *The Violins of Saint-Jacques*

A Merrymaking in Question

'I will get a new string for my fiddle,
 And call to the neighbours to come,
And partners shall dance down the middle
 Until the old pewter-wares hum:
 And we'll sip the mead, cyder, and rum!'

From the night came the oddest of answers:
 A hollow wind, like a bassoon,
And headstones all ranged up as dancers,
 And cypresses droning a croon,
 And gurgoyles that mouthed to the tune.

Thomas Hardy

A Party on Lundy

Wednesday, 15 April 1925 Yesterday there was a most depraved scene. After a quiet evening in the canteen I went down to the villa and talked in Elizabeth's bedroom until about 11. I came back to find an amazing orgy in progress. Everyone drunk or pretending drunkenness, except —— who was sitting in the middle of it all unusually sedate. —— almost naked was being slapped on the buttocks and enjoying herself ecstatically. Every two minutes she ran to the lavatory and as soon as she was out of the room everyone said, 'My dear, the things we are finding out about ——.' It was all rather cruel. She looked so awful with enormous shining legs cut and bleeding in places and slapped rosy in others and her eyes shining with desire. She kept making the most terrible remarks, too, whether consciously or unconsciously I do not know, about blood and grease... These girls must talk a terrible lot of bawdy amongst themselves. David became quite incredibly obscene before the evening broke up and I went to bed, as always, with rather a heavy heart.

Evelyn Waugh *Diaries*

Wet, Beige Morning

Dear Oscar, Little dear Honourable Treasurer of mine, how are you? Did you discover Columbus well? and give my best to Long Don Drummond the Potent Man? I missed you a lot my last days, and was Lizzed away to the plane alone. I almost liked the plane-ride, though; it was stormy and dangerous, and only my iron will kept the big bird up; lightning looked wonderful through the little eyeholes in its underbelly; the bar was open all the way from Newfoundland; and the woman next to me was stone-deaf so I spoke to her all the way, more wildly and more wildly as the plane lurched on through dark and lion-thunder and the fire-water yelled through my blood like Sioux, and she unheard all my delirium with a smile; and then the Red Indians scalped me; and then it was London, and my iron will brought the bird down safely, with only one spine-cracking jar. And, queasy, purple, maggoty, scalped, I weak-wormed through festoons, bunting, flags, great roses, sad spangles, paste and tinsel, the million cardboard simpers and ogrish plaster statuettes of the nincompoop queen, I crawled as early as sin in the chilly weeping morning through the city's hushed hangover and all those miles of cock-deep orange-peel, nibbled sandwiches, broken bottles, discarded vests, vomit and condoms, lollipops, senile fish, blood lips, old towels, teeth, turds, soiled blowing newspapers by the unread mountain, all the spatter and bloody gravy and giant mousemess that go to show how a loyal and phlegmatic people – 'London can break it!' – enjoyed themselves like hell the day before. And, my God, wouldn't I have enjoyed it too! In the house where I stay in London, a party was still going on, at half-past seven in the wet, beige morning, that had started two nights before. Full of my news, of the latest American gossip from the intellectual underworld, of tall goings-on, of tiny victories and disasters, aching to gabble I found myself in a company of amiable, wrestling, maudlin, beetleskulled men, semi-men, and many kinds of women, who did not know or care I had been so far and wildly away but seemed to think I had been in the party all the whooping time. Sober, airsick, pancaked flat, I saw these intelligent old friends as a warrenfull of blockish stinkers, and sulked all morning over my warm beer as they clamoured and hiccupped, rolled rodgering down, fell gaily through windows, sang and splintered. And in the afternoon, I stood – I was the only one who could – alone and disillusioned among the snorers and the dead. They grunted all around me, or went soughing and green to their Maker. As the little murdered moles in the Scotch poem, like sma' Assyrians they lay. I was close to crying there, in the chaotic middle of anticlimax. It was all too sordid. Oh how I hated these recumbent Bohemians! Slowly, I went upstairs to bath. There was a man asleep in the bath. And tears ran down my cheeks. Two creatures stretched dead in my bed. And, now, rain was boo-hooing too all over London.

P.S. I am sorry to add to this that by the end of the day I was happy as a pig in shit myself, and conducted the singing of hymns with my broken arm, and chased people and was caught, and wound up snug as a bugger in Rugby. Oh, my immortal soul, and oh, my tissues!

Dylan Thomas to Oscar Williams, 22 June 1953

Vers de Société

My wife and I have asked a crowd of craps
To come and waste their time and ours: perhaps
You'd care to join us? In a pig's arse, friend.
Day comes to an end.
The gas fire breathes, the trees are darkly swayed.
And so *Dear Warlock-Williams: I'm afraid* –

Funny how hard it is to be alone.
I could spend half my evenings, if I wanted,
Holding a glass of washing sherry, canted
Over to catch the drivel of some bitch
Who's read nothing but *Which*;
Just think of all the spare time that has flown

Straight into nothingness by being filled
With forks and faces, rather than repaid
Under a lamp, hearing the noise of wind,
And looking out to see the moon thinned
To an air-sharpened blade.
A life, and yet how sternly it's instilled

All solitude is selfish. No one now
Believes the hermit with his gown and dish
Talking to God (who's gone too); the big wish
Is to have people nice to you, which means
Doing it back somehow.
Virtue is social. Are, then, these routines

Playing at goodness, like going to church?
Something that bores us, something we don't do well
(Asking that ass about his fool research)
But try to feel, because, however crudely,
It shows us what should be?
Too subtle, that. Too decent, too. Oh hell,

Only the young can be alone freely.
The time is shorter now for company,
And sitting by a lamp more often brings
Not peace, but other things.
Beyond the light stand failure and remorse
Whispering *Dear Warlock-Williams: Why, of course* –

Philip Larkin

Read Us Your Play

None of the Saltines played [tennis]. A delicate social line had early hardened and not been crossed. Instead, today they had taken Freddy Thorne who played terribly, out into the Bay for skin diving. It amused him to keep his wetsuit on. His appearance in the tight shiny skin of black rubber was disturbingly androgynous: he was revealed to have hips soft as a woman's and with the obscene delicacy of a hydra's predatory petals his long hands flitted bare from his sleeves' flexible carapace. This curvaceous rubber man had arisen from another element. Like a giant monocle his Cyclopean snorkeling mask jutted from his naked skull, and his spatulate foot flippers flopped grotesquely on the Constantines' threadbare Oriental rugs. When he sat in a doiliéd armchair and, twiddling a cigarette, jauntily crossed his legs, the effect was so outrageous and droll, monstrous and regal that even Piet Hanema laughed, feeling in Freddy's act life's bad dreams subdued.

'Read us your play,' Carol Constantine begged him. She wore a man's shirt over an orange bikini. Something had nerved her up tonight; a week ago, she had dyed her hair orange. 'Let's all take parts.'

All summer it had been rumoured that Freddy was writing a pornographic play. Now he pretended not to understand. 'What play?' he asked. Beneath the misted snorkel mask he missed his customary spectacles. His eyes were blind and furry; his lipless mouth bent in upon itself in a pleased yet baffled way.

'Freddy, I've *seen* it,' Janet Appleby said. 'I've seen the cast of characters.'

With the dignity of a senile monarch Freddy slowly stared toward her. 'Who are you? Oh, I know. You're Jan-Jan Applesauce. I didn't recognize you out of context. Where are your little friends?'

'They're in Maine, thank God.'

'Don't be your usual shitty self, Freddy,' Carol said, sitting on the arm of the chair and draping her gaunt arms around his rubber shoulders. The action tugged open her shirt. Piet, sitting cross-legged on the floor, saw her navel: a thick-lidded eye. Carol caressed Freddy's air hose, hung loose around his neck. 'We want to do your play,' she insisted.

'We can make a movie of it,' Eddie Constantine said. He flew in spells; he had been home three days. His growth of beard suggested a commando, cruel and sleepless. He held a beer can in each hand. Seeing his wife draped across Freddy, he had forgotten who he was fetching them for, his vacant eyes the tone of the same aluminium. Abruptly, as if tossing a grenade, he handed a can to Ben Saltz, who sat in the corner.

'I want to be the one who answers the door,' Carol said. 'Don't all dirty movies begin with a woman answering the door?'

Ben sat staring, his dark eyes moist with disquiet. He had recently shaved, and looked enfeebled, slack-chinned, mockingly costumed in sailing clothes – a boat-neck jersey, a wind-breaker, a white officer's cap, and suntans cut down to make shorts, fringed with loose threads. Ben's calves were heavily, mournfully hairy. Piet glimpsed himself in that old-fashioned male shagginess but his own body hair was reddish, lighter, gayer, springy. Ben's lank hairs ran together to make black seams, like sores down-running into the tops of his comically new topsiders, cup-soled, spandy-bright. Except for his sunburned nose, Ben's skin was pasty and nauseated. He had pockmarks. His wounded love of Carol weighed on the air of the room and gave the couples an agitated importance, like children in safe from a thunderstorm.

'What's a dirty movie?' Freddy asked, blinking, pretending to be confused.

'*Tom Jones*,' Terry Gallagher said.

Angela rose up unexpectedly and said, 'Come on Carol, let's undress him. I know he has the play in his pocket.'

'You think he takes it underwater with him?' Piet asked mildly, exchanging with Foxy a quizzical look over Angela's uncharacteristic display of flirtatious energy. They had become, these two, the parents of their spouses, whose faults they forgave and whose helplessness they cherished from the omniscient height of their adultery.

Foxy had come to the party without Ken, but with Terry Gallagher. Ken and Matt, having been easily beaten in North Mather, had played consolation singles together all afternoon on the Ongs' court. The two men, uncomfortable among the couples, were comfortable with each other. Foxy and Terry shared tallness and an elusive quality of reluctance, of faintly forbidding enchantment, reflected, perhaps, from their similar husbands. But Foxy was Snow White and Terry Rose Red – something Celtic strummed her full lips, her musical hands, the big muscles knitting her hips to her thighs. She stood tall and joined in the rape, asking Janet, 'Where are his pants? You told me he always carries it in his pants.'

'Upstairs,' Carol said brokenly, wrestling with Freddy's flailing arms, struggling to undo his jacket's rusty snaps. 'In Kevin's room. Don't wake him up.'

Janet, who had been in therapy two months now, watched the struggle and pronounced, 'This is childish.'

Angela tried to pin Freddy's ankles as he slid from the chair. One of his flippers kicked over a tabouret holding a crammed ashtray and a small vase of asters. Angela brushed up the ashes and butts with two copies of *Art News*, Eddie carefully poured beer over Freddy's head, and Ben Saltz sat dazed by the sight of Carol, her hair a colour no hair in nature ever was, writhing nearly nude in the man's black embrace. The rubber of his suit squeaked as her bare skin slid across his lap. Her shirt had ridden up to her armpits: her orange top twisted, and a slim breast flipped free. Crouching on the carpet, Carol quickly readjusted herself, but kneeled a while panting, daring to look nowhere. All these people had seen her nipple. It had been orangish.

In the front parlour, reached through a doorway hung with a beaded curtain, Irene Saltz's voice was saying, 'I can't believe you know what you're saying. Frank, I *know* you, and I *know* that you're a human being.' She was drunk.

His voice responded, heated and pained. 'It's *you* who want to keep them down, to give them on a platter everything everybody else in this country has had to work for.'

'Work! What honest work have you ever done?'

Janet Appleby shouted toward them, 'He's worked himself into an ulcer, Irene. Come on in here and take your husband home, he looks sick.'

The Constantines' house was large, but much of its space was consumed by magniloquent oak stairways and wide halls and cavernous closets, so that no single room was big enough to hold a party, which then overflowed into several, creating problems of traffic and acoustics. Janet was not heard, but Frank's voice came to them from the parlour clearly. 'The federal government was never meant to be a big mama every crybaby could run to. Minimal government was the founders' ideal. States' rights. Individual rights.'

Irene's voice in argument was slurred and even affectionate. 'Frank, suppose you were Mrs Medgar Evers. Would you want to cry or not?'

'Ask any intelligent Negro what the welfare cheque has done to his race. They hate it. It castrates. I agree with Malcolm X.'

'You're not answering me, Frank. What about Medgar Evers? What about the six Birmingham Sunday-school children?'

'They should have the protection of the law like everybody else, like everybody else,' Frank said, 'no more and no less. I don't approve of discriminatory legislation and that's what the Massachusetts Fair Housing Bill is. It deprives the homeowner of his right to choose. The constitution, my dear Irene, tries to guarantee equality of *opportunity*, not equality of status.'

Irene said, 'Status and opportunity are inseparable.'

'Can't we shut them up?' Eddie Constantine asked.

'It's sex for Irene,' Carol told him, standing and buttoning her shirt. 'Irene loves arguing with right-wing men. She thinks they have bigger pricks.'

Janet's lips opened but, eyes flicking from Carol to Freddy to Ben, she said nothing. Self-knowledge was turning her into a watcher, a hesitater.

Terry Gallagher came down the Constantines' grand staircase holding a single often-folded sheet of paper. 'It's nothing,' she said. 'It's not even begun. It's a cast of characters. Freddy, you're a fake.'

Freddy protested, 'But they're beautiful characters.'

Amid laughter and beer and white wine, through the odours of brine and tennis sweat, the play was passed around. It bore no title. The writing, beginning at the top as a careful ornamental print, degenerated into Freddy's formless hand, with no decided slant and a tendency for the terminal strokes to swing down depressively.

DRAMATIS PERSONÆ

Eric Shun, *hero*
Ora Fiss, *heroine*

Cunny Lingus, *a tricksome Irish lass*
Testy Cull, *a cranky old discard*

Anna L. Violation, Ona Nism, Labia Minoris — *nymphs*

Auntie Climax, *a rich and meaningful relation*

ACT I

ERIC (*entering*): !
ORA (*entered*): O!

'That's not fair,' Janet said. 'Nobody is really called Ora or Ona.'

'Maybe the problem,' Piet said, 'is that Eric enters too soon.'

'I was saving Auntie Climax for the third act,' Freddy said.

Terry said, 'I'm so glad Matt isn't here.'

Foxy said, 'Ken loves word games.'

'Good job, Freddy,' Eddie Constantine said. 'I'll buy it.' He clapped Ben Saltz on the back and held the paper in front of Ben's eyes. Ben's face had become white, whiter than his wife's sun-sensitive skin. Foxy went and, awkwardly pregnant, knelt beside him, tent-shaped, whispering.

Piet was busy improvising. The crude energy the others loved in him had been summoned. 'We need more plot,' he said. 'Maybe Ora Fiss should have a half-brother, P. Niss. Peter Niss. They did filthy things in the cradle together, and now he's returned from overseas.'

'From Titty City,' Eddie said. He was of all the men the least educated, the least removed in mentality from elementary school. Yet he had lifted and hurled thousands of lives safely across the continent. They accepted him.

Janet said, 'You're all fantastically disgusting. What infuriates me, I'm going to have to waste a whole twenty-dollar session on this grotesque evening.'

'Leave,' Carol told her.

Piet was continuing, gesturing expansively, red hair spinning from his broad arms. 'Ora is frightened by his return. Will the old magic still be there? Dear God, pray not! She takes one look. Alas! It is. "Ora!" he ejaculates. "Mrs Nism now," she responds coldly, yet trembling within.'

'You're mixing up my beautiful characters,' Freddy complained.

'Let's play some new game,' Carol said; she squatted down to gather the residue of the spilled ashes. Her slim breasts swung loose in Piet's eyes. Welcome to Titty, sombre city of unmockable suckableness: his heart surged forward and swamped Carol as she squatted. Love for her licked the serial bumps of her diapered crotch. Her bare feet, long-toed, stank like razor clams. Her painted hair downhung sticking drifting to her mouth. She stood, ashes and aster petals in her lily palm, and glared toward the corner where, beneath a Miró print, Foxy was ministering with words to the immobilized Ben Saltz.

'Let's not,' Freddy Thorne said to her. 'It's good. It's good for people to act out their fantasies.'

Angela leaped up, warm with wine, calling Freddy's bluff, and announced, 'I want to take off all my clothes!'

'Good, good,' Freddy said, nodding calmly. He stubbed out his cigarette on his own forehead, on the Cyclopean glass mask. It sizzled. His wise old woman's face with its inbent lips streamed with sweat.

Piet asked him, 'Shouldn't you take the outfit off? Don't you eventually die if the skin can't breathe?'

'It's me. Piet baby, this suit *is* my skin. I'm a monster from the deep.'

Angela's hand had halted halfway down the zipper at the back of her pleated white tennis dress. 'No one is watching,' she said. Piet touched her hand and redid the zipper, which made a quick kissing sound.

'Let her go, it's good,' Freddy said. 'She wants to share the glory. I've always wanted to see Angela undressed.'

'She's beautiful,' Piet told him.

'Jesu, I don't doubt it for a sec. Let her strip. She wants to, you don't understand your own wife. She's an exhibitionist. She's not this shy violet you think you're stuck with.'

'He's sick,' Foxy told Carol, of Ben, in self-defence.

'Maybe,' Carol said, 'he'd like to be left alone.'

'He says you all gave him lobster and rum for supper.'

Ben groaned. 'Don't mention.' Piet recognized a manoeuvring for attention, an economical use of misery. But Ben would play the game, Piet saw, too hard in his desire to succeed, and the game would end by playing him. The Jew's fierce face was waxen: dead Esau. Where his beard had been it was doubly pale.

'Shellfish,' Eddie explained to all of them. 'Not kosher.'

Carol said sharply, 'Foxy, let him sit it out. He can go upstairs to a bed if he has to.'

'Does he know where the beds are?' Freddy asked.

'Freddy, why don't you put that mask over your mouth?' Carol's skin was shivering as if each nerve were irritated. The holiday eve was turning chilly and the furnace had been shut off for the summer. Her lips were forced apart over clenched teeth like a child's after swimming and, touched and needing to touch her, Piet asked, 'Why are you being such a bitch tonight'?

'Because Braque just died.' Her walls were full of paintings, classic prints and her own humourless mediocre canvases, coarse in their colouring, modishly broad in their brushwork, showing her children on chairs, the Tarbox wharf and boatyard, Eddie in a turtleneck shirt, the graceless back view of the Congregational Church, houses, and trees seen from her studio windows and made garish, unreal, petulant. Cézanne and John Marin, Utrillo and Ben Shahn – her styles muddled theirs, and Piet thought how provincial, how mediocre and lost we all are.

Carol sensed that he thought this and turned on him. 'There's something I've been meaning to ask you for a long time, Piet, and now I've had just enough wine to do it. Why do you build such ugly houses? You're clever enough, you wouldn't have to.'

His eyes sought Foxy's seeking his. She would know that, hurt, he would seek her eyes. Their glances met, locked, burned, unlocked. He answered Carol, 'They're not ugly. They're just ordinary.'

'They're hideous. I think what you're doing to Indian Hill is a disgrace.'

She had, slim Carol, deliberately formed around her a ring of astonishment. For one of their unspoken rules was that professions were not criticized; one's job was a pact with the meaningless world beyond the ring of couples.

Terry Gallagher said, 'He builds what he and Matt think people want to buy.'

Freddy said, 'I *like* Piet's houses. They have a Dutch something, a fittingness. They remind me of teeth. Don't laugh, everybody, I mean it. Piet and I are spiritual brothers. I put silver in my cavities, he puts people in his. Jesus, you try to be serious in this crowd, everybody laughs.'

Angela said, 'Carol, you're absurd.'

Piet said, 'No, she's right. I hate my houses. God, I hate them.'

Janet Appleby said, 'Somebody else died last month. A poet, Marcia was very upset. She said he was America's greatest, and not that old.'

'Frost died last January,' Terry said.

'*Not* Frost. A German name. *Oh*, Marcia and Harold would know it. None of us *know* anything.'

'I thought you'd start to miss them,' Freddy said to her.

Janet, sitting on the floor, sleepily rested her head on a hassock. She had switched from twice-a-week therapy to analysis, and drove into Brookline at seven-thirty every weekday morning. It was rumoured that Frank had commenced therapy. 'We need a new game,' she said.

'Freddy, let's play Impressions,' Terry said.

'Let's think up more names for my play,' he said. 'They don't have to be dirty.' He squinted blindly into space, and came up with, 'Donovan U. Era.'

'You had that prepared,' Janet said. 'But Harold the other night did think of a good one. What was it, Frank?' With a rattle of wooden beads, the couple had returned from the political parlour. Frank looked sheepish, Irene's eyebrows and lips seemed heavily inked.

'León MacDouffe,' Frank pronounced, glancing toward Janet, wanting to go home.

John Updike *Couples*

The Select Party

Hands that wiped arses
are holding glasses,
lips that fellated
are intoxicated,
parts that were randy
have counterparts handy –

but the fact of a quorum
preserves decorum,
and the social unction
inhibits the function
of the natural passions
concealed by the fashions.

Tongues that licked scrota
don't move one iota
from the usual phrases
that the century praises,
the undisturbed labia
are deserted Arabia –

these cats are all mousers
but skirts and trousers
keep the lid on the kettle;
there are magnets, there's metal,
but they don't click together
thru nylon and leather.

Gavin Ewart

Party Politics

I never remember holding a full drink.
   My first look shows the level half-way down.
What next? Ration the rest, and try to think
   Of higher things, until mine host comes round?

Some people say, best show an empty glass:
   Someone will fill it. Well, I've tried that too.
You may get drunk, or dry half-hours may pass.
   It seems to turn on where you are. Or who.

Philip Larkin

TROUBLE

A Light Fantastic Round

Comus enters with a charming-rod in one hand, his glass in the other; with him a rout of monsters headed like sundry sorts of wild beasts, but otherwise like men and women, their apparel glistering. They come in making a riotous and unruly noise, with torches in their hands.

Comus. The star that bids the shepherd fold
Now the top of heav'n doth hold,
And the gilded car of day
His glowing axle doth allay
In the steep Atlantic stream;
And the slope sun his upward beam
Shoots against the dusky pole,
Pacing toward the other goal
Of his chamber in the east.
Meanwhile welcome joy and feast,
Midnight shout and revelry,
Tipsy dance and jollity.
Braid your locks with rosy twine
Dropping odors, dropping wine.
Rigor now is gone to bed,
And Advice with scrupulous head,
Strict Age, and sour Severity,
With their grave saws in slumber lie.
We that are of purer fire
Imitate the starry squire,
Who in their nightly watchful spheres
Lead in swift round the months and years.
The sounds and seas with all their finny drove
Now to the moon in wavering morris move,
And on the tawny sands and shelves

Rosy twine, intertwined roses; *finny drove*, in Spenser, *F.Q.* 3.8.29.9; *morris*, morris dance.

Trip the pert fairies and the dapper elves;
By dimpled brook and fountain brim
The wood-nymphs, decked with daisies trim,
Their merry wakes and pastimes keep:
What hath night to do with sleep?
Night hath better sweets to prove,
Venus now wakes, and wakens Love.
Come, let us our rites begin;
'Tis only daylight that makes sin,
Which these dun shades will ne'er report.
Hail, goddess of nocturnal sport,
Dark-veiled Cotytto, t' whom the secret flame
Of midnight torches burns; mysterious dame,
That ne'er art called but when the dragon womb
Of Stygian darkness spets her thickest gloom,
And makes one blot of all the air,
Stay thy cloudy ebon chair
Wherein thou rid'st with Hecat', and befriend
Us thy vowed priests, till utmost end
Of all thy dues be done, and none left out,
Ere the blabbing eastern scout,
The nice Morn on th' Indian steep,
From her cabined loop-hole peep,
And to the tell-tale Sun descry
Our concealed solemnity.
Come, knit hands, and beat the ground,
In a light fantastic round.

John Milton *Comus*

pert, lively; *dapper*, small and nimble; *Cotytto*, a Thracian divinity celebrated in licentious nocturnal rites; *spets*, spits; *Morn*, Aurora; *Indian steep*, cf. *A Midsummer Night's Dream* 2.1.69; *descry*, reveal.

A Bet

It was past one o'clock when Pierre left his friend. It was a cloudless, northern, summer night. Pierre took an open cab intending to drive straight home. But the nearer he drew to the house the more he felt the impossibility of going to sleep on such a night. It was light enough to see a long way in the deserted street and it seemed more like morning or evening than night. On the way Pierre remembered that Anatole Kurágin was expecting the usual set for cards that evening, after which there was generally a drinking bout, finishing with visits of a kind Pierre was very fond of.

'I should like to go to Kurágin's', thought he.

But he immediately recalled his promise to Prince Andrew not to go there. Then, as happens to people of weak character, he desired so passionately once more to enjoy that dissipation he was so accustomed to, that he decided to go. The thought immediately occurred to him that his promise to Prince Andrew was of no account, because before he gave it he had already promised Prince Anatole to come to his gathering; 'besides,' thought he, 'all such "words of honour" are conventional things with no definite meaning, especially if one considers that by tomorrow one may be dead, or something so extraordinary may happen to one that honour and dishonour will be all the same!' Pierre often indulged in reflections of this sort, nullifying all his decisions and intentions. He went to Kurágin's.

Reaching the large house near the Horse Guards' barracks, in which Anatole lived, Pierre entered the lighted porch, ascended the stairs, and went in at the open door. There was no one in the anteroom; empty bottles, cloaks, and over-shoes were lying about; there was a smell of alcohol, and sounds of voices and shouting in the distance.

Cards and supper were over, but the visitors had not yet dispersed. Pierre threw off his cloak and entered the first room, in which were the remains of supper. A footman, thinking no one saw him, was drinking on the sly what was left in the glasses. From the third room came sounds of laughter, the shouting of familiar voices, the growling of a bear, and general commotion. Some eight or nine young men were crowding anxiously round an open window. Three others were romping with a young bear, one pulling him by the chain and trying to set him at the others.

'I bet a hundred on Stevens!' shouted one.

'Mind, no holding on!' cried another.

'I bet on Dólokhov!' cried a third. 'Kurágin, you part our hands.'*

'There, leave Bruin alone; here's a bet on.'

'At one draught, or he loses!' shouted a fourth.

'Jacob, bring a bottle!' shouted the host, a tall handsome fellow who stood in the midst of the group, without a coat, and with his fine linen shirt unfastened in front. 'Wait a bit, you fellows. . . . Here is Pétya! Good man!' cried he, addressing Pierre.

Another voice, from a man of medium height with clear blue eyes, particularly striking among all these drunken voices by its sober ring, cried from the window: 'Come here; part the bets!' This was Dólokhov, an officer of the Semënov regiment, a notorious gambler and duellist, who was living with Anatole. Pierre smiled, looking about him merrily.

'I don't understand. What's it all about?'

'Wait a bit, he is not drunk yet! A bottle here,' said Anatole, and taking a glass from the table he went up to Pierre.

'First of all you must drink!'

Pierre drank one glass after another looking from under his brows at the tipsy guests who were again crowding round the window, and listening to their chatter. Anatole kept on refilling Pierre's glass while explaining that Dólokhov was betting with Stevens, an English naval officer, that he would drink a bottle of rum sitting on the outer ledge of the third-floor window with his legs hanging out.

'Go on, you must drink it all,' said Anatole, giving Pierre the last glass, 'or I won't let you go!'

'No, I won't,' said Pierre, pushing Anatole aside, and he went up to the window.

Dólokhov was holding the Englishman's hand and clearly and

*The Russian custom was to shake hands on a bet and for some third person, acting as a witness, to separate the hands.

distinctly repeating the terms of the bet, addressing himself particularly to Anatole and Pierre.

Dólokhov was of medium height, with curly hair and light blue eyes. He was about five-and-twenty. Like all infantry officers he wore no moustache, so that his mouth, the most striking feature of his face, was clearly seen. The lines of that mouth were remarkably finely curved. The middle of the upper lip formed a sharp wedge and closed firmly on the firm lower one, and something like two distinct smiles played continually round the two corners of the mouth; this, together with the resolute, insolent intelligence of his eyes, produced an effect which made it impossible not to notice his face. Dólokhov was a man of small means and no connexions. Yet though Anatole spent tens of thousands of rubles, Dólokhov lived with him and had placed himself on such a footing that all who knew them, including Anatole himself, respected him more than they did Anatole. Dólokhov could play all games and nearly always won. However much he drank he never lost his clear-headedness. Both Kurágin and Dólokhov were at that time notorious among the rakes and scapegraces of Petersburg.

The bottle of rum was brought. The window frame which prevented any one from sitting on the outer sill, was being forced out by two footmen, who were evidently flurried and intimidated by the directions and shouts of the gentlemen around.

Anatole with his swaggering air strode up to the window. He wanted to smash something. Pushing away the footmen he tugged at the frame, but could not move it. He smashed a pane.

'You have a try, Hercules,' said he, turning to Pierre.

Pierre seized the crossbeam, tugged, and wrenched the oak frame out with a crash.

'Take it right out, or they'll think I'm holding on,' said Dólokhov.

'Is the Englishman bragging. . . . Eh? Is it all right?' said Anatole.

'First rate,' said Pierre, looking at Dólokhov, who with a bottle of rum in his hand was approaching the window, from which the light of the sky, the dawn merging with the afterglow of sunset, was visible.

Dólokhov, the bottle of rum still in his hand, jumped on to the window-sill. 'Listen!' cried he, standing there and addressing those in the room. All were silent.

'I bet fifty imperials' – he spoke French that the Englishman might understand him but he did not speak it very well – 'I bet fifty imperials . . . or do you wish to make it a hundred?' added he, addressing the Englishman.

'No, fifty,' replied the latter.

'All right. Fifty imperials . . . that I will drink a whole bottle of rum without taking it from my mouth, sitting outside the window on this spot' (he stooped and pointed to the sloping ledge outside the window), 'and without holding on to anything. Is that right?'

'Quite right,' said the Englishman.

Anatole turned to the Englishman and taking him by one of the buttons of his coat and looking down at him – the Englishman was short – began repeating the terms of the wager to him in English.

'Wait!' cried Dólokhov, hammering with the bottle on the window-sill to attract attention. 'Wait a bit, Kurágin. Listen! If any one else does the same, I will pay him a hundred imperials. Do you understand?'

The Englishman nodded, but gave no indication whether he intended to accept this challenge or not. Anatole did not release him, and though he kept nodding to show that he understood, Anatole went on translating Dólokhov's words into English. A thin young lad, an hussar of the Life Guards, who had been losing that evening, climbed on the window-sill, leaned over, and looked down.

'Oh! Oh! Oh!' he muttered, looking down from the window at the stones of the pavement.

'Shut up!' cried Dólokhov, pushing him away from the window. The lad jumped awkwardly back into the room, tripping over his spurs.

Placing the bottle on the window-sill where he could reach it easily, Dólokhov climbed carefully and slowly through the window and lowered his legs. Pressing against both sides of the window, he adjusted himself on his seat, lowered his hands, moved a little to the right and then to the left and took up the bottle. Anatole brought two candles and placed them on the window-sill, though it was already quite light. Dólokhov's back in his white shirt, and his curly head, were lit up from both sides. Every one crowded to the window, the Englishman in front. Pierre stood smiling but silent. One man, older than the others present, suddenly pushed forward with a scared and angry look and wanted to seize hold of Dólokhov's shirt.

'I say, this is folly! He'll be killed,' said this more sensible man.

Anatole stopped him.

'Don't touch him! You'll startle him and then he'll be killed. Eh? . . . What then? . . . Eh?'

Dólokhov turned round, and again holding on with both hands, arranged himself on his seat.

'If any one comes meddling again,' said he, emitting the words separately through his thin compressed lips, 'I will throw him down there. Now then!'

Saying this he again turned round, dropped his hands, took the bottle and lifted it to his lips, threw back his head, and raised his free hand to balance himself. One of the footmen who had stooped to pick up some broken glass, remained in that position without taking his eyes from the window and from Dólokhov's back. Anatole stood erect with staring eyes. The Englishman looked on sideways pursing up his lips. The man who had wished to stop the affair ran to a corner of the room and threw himself on a sofa with his face to the wall. Pierre hid his face, from which a faint smile forgot to fade though his features now expressed horror and fear. All were still. Pierre took his hand from his eyes, Dólokhov still sat in the same position, only his head was thrown further back till his curly hair touched his shirt collar, and the hand holding the bottle was lifted higher and higher and trembled with the effort. The bottle was emptying perceptibly and rising still higher and his head tilting yet further back. 'Why is it so long?' thought Pierre. It seemed to him that more than half an hour had elapsed. Suddenly Dólokhov made a backward movement with his spine, and his arm trembled nervously; this was sufficient to cause his whole body to slip as he sat on the sloping ledge. As he began slipping down, his head and arm wavered still more with the strain. One hand moved as if to clutch the window-sill, but refrained from touching it. Pierre again covered his eyes and thought he would never open them again. Suddenly he was aware of a stir all around. He looked up: Dólokhov was standing on the window-sill with a pale but radiant face.

'It's empty!'

He threw the bottle to the Englishman, who caught it neatly. Dólokhov jumped down. He smelt strongly of rum.

'Well done! . . . Fine fellow! . . . There 's a bet for you! . . . Devil take you!' came from different sides.

The Englishman took out his purse and began counting out the money. Dólokhov stood frowning and did not speak. Pierre jumped upon the window-sill.

'Gentlemen, who wishes to bet with me? I'll do the same thing!' he suddenly cried. 'Even without a bet, there! Tell them to bring me a bottle. I'll do it. . . . Bring a bottle!'

'Let him do it, let him do it,' said Dólokhov, smiling.

'What next? Have you gone mad? . . . No one would let you! . . . Why, you go giddy even on a staircase,' exclaimed several voices.

'I'll drink it! Let's have a bottle of rum!' shouted Pierre, banging the table with a determined and drunken gesture and preparing to climb out of the window.

They seized him by his arms; but he was so strong that every one who touched him was sent flying.

'No, you'll never manage him that way,' said Anatole. 'Wait a bit and I'll get round him . . . Listen! I'll take your bet tomorrow, but now we are all going to —'s.'

'Come on then,' cried Pierre. 'Come on! . . . And we'll take Bruin with us.'

And he caught the bear, took it in his arms, lifted it from the ground, and began dancing round the room with it.

Leo Tolstoy *War and Peace*, trans. Louise & Aylmer Maude

A Bear

The bear-cub at the Kuriatins' was disappointingly small, and its head looked rather large for its body and seemed to weigh it down. The skin was very loose, as though the cub had not quite grown into it. The dense fur, dark, golden and ginger, grew at all angles, except along the spine which was neatly parted, and on the glovelike paws and hind feet. The protruding claws looked as if they were made of metal, and the bear itself was a dangerous toy. Both front and back legs were bent in an inward curve. The total effect was confused and amateurish, openly in need of protection for some time yet. Planting its feet on the ground in a straight line required thought from the bear, and was not always successful. When Mitya Kuriatin hit it with a billiard cue it turned its torpedo-shaped head from side to side and then fell over.

'Is that all it can do?' asked his sister Masha. 'You said it would dance.'

Mitya, humiliated in front of the English guests with whom he had intended to cut a dash, and by the presence of an animal when at the age of thirteen he would have so much preferred something mechanical, shouted 'Well then, music!' Masha went to the pianola, which Kuriatin had bought in Berlin with the idea that it would save the trouble of having his children taught to play the piano. Perhaps rightly, they took very little interest in it, and although they knew how to start and stop it they did not know how to change the music rolls. Now when Masha turned the switch the idiot contrivance began half way through. Masha flung herself across brocaded piano stool and pressed the key down to loudest. The bear withdrew to the farthest corner of the room. Turning round with a loud scratching of claws on the floorboards beyond the carpet, it faced all comers.

'It won't dance, it won't do anything, it's imbecile.'

They tried throwing cold water over it. The bear sneezed and shook itself, then tried to lick up the sparkling drops on the surface of its fur.

'It's thirsty,' said Dolly coldly. After glancing at it for a moment she and Ben stood together in isolation behind one of the curtains.

'What are you two talking about?' Mitya called out.

'We're saying that you should give it something to drink.'

'Yes, it's one of God's creatures,' said the treacherous Masha.

Mitya blundered out of the room, and came back with a bottle of vodka and a pale blue saucer of fine china with a gilt rim.

'Where did you get those?' asked Dolly.

'From the dining room. It's all laid out for some reception or other.'

'Are you allowed in there?' said Ben.

'My father's in Riga. I'm the master here!' Mitya's face was red with senseless excitement. He poured the vodka into the saucer and, slopping it over, carried it to the bear's far corner. For the first time its mouth opened and its long dark tongue came out. It tilted its head a little and licked the saucer dry. Mitya poured again, and this time screwing its head round the other way, the little animal drank again.

'Dance now,' shouted Mitya.

The bear got on to its hind legs and was as tall, suddenly, as Mitya, who retreated. Losing its perilous balance it held out its paws like small hands and reeled on to the carpet where its claws gave it a better hold, while a gush of urine sprayed across the pattern of red and blue. For some reason one of its ears had turned inside out, showing the lining of paler skin. It rolled over several times while the dark patch spread, then sidled at great speed out of the door. All the children laughed, Dasha and Ben as well, they were all laughing and disgusted together, the laughter had taken possession of them, broke them in half and squeezed the tears out of their eyes.

'It's gone into the dining room.'

Then they were silent and only Mitya went on grossly laughing as they followed clinging to each other to the front of the house and heard a tearing and rending, then a crash like the splintering of ice in the first spring thaw as the bear, and they could see it now reflected in the great mirrors on every wall, lumbered from end to end of the table making havoc among glass and silver, dragging at the bottle of vodka which stood in each place, upending them like ninepins and licking desperately at what was spilled. The service door flew open and the doorman, Sergei, came in, crossed himself, and without a moment's hesitation snatched up a shovel, opened the doors of the white porcelain stove and scooped out a heap of red-hot charcoal which he scattered over the bear. The tablecloth, soaked in spirits, sent up a sheet of flame. The bear screamed, its screams being like that of a human child. Already alight, it tried to protect its face with its front paws. Mitya was still doubled up with laughter when from the passage outside could be heard the roar of Kuriatin, pleased with himself because he had come home early as his wife had implored him. 'Devils, do I have to let myself into my own house?' He was at the door. 'Why is that bear on fire? I'll put it out of its misery. I'll spatter its brains out. I'll spatter the lot of you.'

Frank, quietly removing Dolly and Ben from the uproar, would have liked to know where Mrs Kuriatin had been all this time and why Sergei, half idiotic as he was, hadn't thrown water at the wretched animal instead of red-hot cinders. This was the only one of his questions that the children could answer. Sergei had known that bears were lovers of water. Water would never have stopped a bear.

'You told us you thought we could go there every day after school,' said Ben, 'as long as we were reasonably quiet.'

'I don't think that now.'

'What will you say?'

'I shall go round to Arkady Kuriatin's office tomorrow and offer to pay for some, not much, of the damage.'

'Will you ask him what happened to the bear?' asked Dolly.

'No.'

'Its face was burning.'

'I shan't ask him.'

Penelope Fitzgerald *The Beginning of Spring*

Night Club

After the legshows and the brandies
And all the pick-me-ups for tired
Men there is a feeling
Something more is required.

The lights go down and eyes
Look up across the room;
Salome comes on, bearing
The head of God knows whom.

Louis MacNeice

Dangerfield

The bar was filled with old men. Spitting secrets in each other's ears. Smoke coming over the top of all the snugs. Faces turning as Dangerfield comes in. The sound of corks ripped pop. Ends of bottles bang on the bar. Seaweedy foam rising in the wet glasses. Rudeness must be dealt with. Swiftly. Put them down, I say, not up, down and don't spare the clubs.

Sebastian stepped to the bar, stood dignified and quiet. Bartender removing bottles. Comes along up to him. His eyes meeting the red ones and he nods his head to this tall customer.

'Yes?'

'A double Gold Label.'

Bartender turns a few steps and back with the bottle, tense and pouring.

'Water?'

'Soda.'

Bartender goes, gets the soda bottle. Squirt, squirt. A blast coming out of it. Whoops. The whiskey shot up the sides of the glass, splashing on the bar.

'Sorry, sir.'

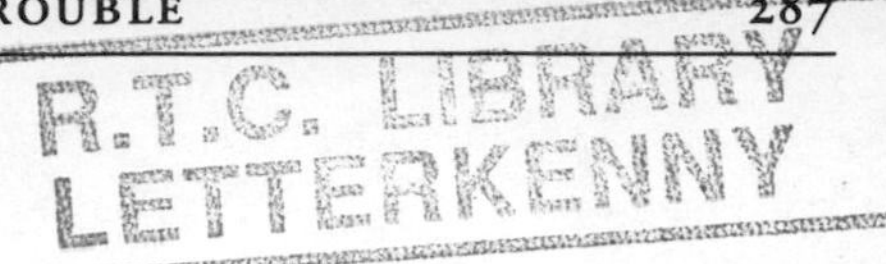

'Yes.'

'It's a new bottle.'

'Quite.'

Bartender puts away the bottle and comes back for the money. Stands embarrassed in front of Dangerfield. Licking his lips, ready to speak, but waits, says nothing. Dangerfield looking at him. The old men sensing disaster, turning on their stools to watch.

'Two shillings.'

'I was in this public house this afternoon about four o'clock. Do you remember?'

'I do.'

'And you refused to serve me.'

'Yes.'

'On the grounds that I was drunk. Is that correct?'

'That's correct.'

'Do you think I am drunk now?'

'That's not for me to decide.'

'You decided that this afternoon. I repeat. Do you think I am drunk now?'

'I want no trouble.'

'Half my whiskey is on the bar.'

'No trouble now.'

'Would you mind bringing me the bottle to replace the amount splashed in my face.'

Bartender in his white shirt and sleeves rolled up brings back the bottle. Sebastian taking out the cork and filling his glass to the brim.

'You can't do that. We don't have much of that.'

'I repeat. Do you think I'm drunk now.'

'Now peacefully, no trouble, no trouble, we don't want any trouble here. No, I don't think you're drunk. Not drunk. Little excited. No.'

'I'm a sensitive person. I hate abuse. Let them all hear.'

'Quietly now, peace.'

'Shut up while I'm talking.'

All the figures spinning about on their stools and flat feet.

'No trouble now, no trouble.'

'Shut up. Am I drunk? Am I drunk?'

'No.'

'Why you Celtic lout. I am. I'm drunk. Hear me, I'm drunk and I'm going to level this kip, level it to the ground, and anyone who doesn't want his neck broken get out.'

The whiskey bottle whistled past the bartender's head, splattering in a mass of glass and gin. Dangerfield drank off the whiskey in a gulp and a man up behind him with a stout bottle which he broke on Dangerfield's head, stout dripping over his ears and down his face, reflectively licking it from around his mouth. The man in horror ran from the building. The bartender went down the trap door in the floor. Sebastian over the bar standing on it. Selecting a bottle of brandy for further reference. Three brave figures at the door peering in upon the chaos and saying stop him, as this Danger made for the door and one man's hand reached out to grab him and it was quickly twisted till the fingers broke with his squeal of agony and the other two lay back to attack from behind and he jumped phoof on Dangerfield's shoulders and was flipped neatly on his arse five paces down the street. The rest had gone to doorways or posing that they were just out walking their dogs.

Dangerfield was running like a madman down the middle of the road with the cry get the guards pushing him faster. Into a laneway, bottle stuffed under his arm. More yells as they caught sight as he went round and down another street. Must for the love of God get hidden. Up these steps and got to get through this door somehow and out of sight quick.

Heart pounding, leaning on the wall for breath. A bicycle against the wall. Dark and racy for sure. Hope. Wait till they are by the house. Feet. I hear the heavy heels of a peeler. Pray for me. If they get me I'll be disgraced. Must avoid capture for the sake of the undesirable publicity it will produce. Or they may take clubs to me. Suffering shit.

The door opens slowly. Light shining in through the dark. Dangerfield moves cautiously behind the door as it widens against him. A small head peers in, hesitates. I must be upon him for the sake of safety. Sebastian drove his shoulder against the door pulling the figure in by the neck.

'If you so much as breathe I'll belt you to death.'

J. P. Donleavy *The Ginger Man*

Suck Hour

'Suck Hour!' screamed Ploy.

Which kind of broke the spell. The quick-thinking inmates of the Impulsive somehow coalesced in the sudden milling around of jolly jack tars, hoisted Ploy bodily and rushed with the little fellow toward the nearest nipple, in the van of the attack.

Mrs Buffo, poised on her rampart like the trumpeter of Cracow, took the full impact of the onslaught, toppling over backwards into an ice-tub as the first wave came hurtling over the bar. Ploy, hands outstretched, was propelled over the top. He caught on to one of the tap handles and simultaneously his shipmates let go; his momentum carried him and the handle in a downward arc: beer began to gush from the foam rubber breast in a white cascade, washing over Ploy, Mrs Buffo and two dozen sailors who had come around behind the bar in a flanking action and who were now battering one another into insensibility. The group who had carried Ploy over spread out and tried to corner more beer taps. Ploy's leading petty officer was on hands and knees holding Ploy's feet, ready to pull them out from under him and take his striker's place when Ploy had had enough. The Impulsive detachment in their charge had formed a flying wedge. In their wake and through the breach clambered at least sixty more slavering bluejackets, kicking, clawing, sidearming, bellowing uproariously; some swinging beer bottles to clear a path.

Profane sat at the end of the bar, watching hand-tooled sea boots, bell-bottoms, rolled up levi cuffs; every now and again a drooling face at the end of a fallen body; broken beer bottles, tiny sawdust storms.

Soon he looked over; Paola was there, arms around his leg, cheek pressed against the black denim.

'It's awful,' she said.

'Oh,' said Profane. He patted her head.

'Peace,' she sighed. 'Isn't that what we all want, Benny? Just a little peace. Nobody jumping out and biting you on the ass.'

'Hush,' said Profane, 'look: someone has just walloped Dewey Gland in the stomach with his own guitar.'

Paola murmured against his leg. They stay quiet, without raising their eyes to watch the carnage going on above them. Mrs Buffo had undertaken a crying jag. Inhuman blubberings beat against and rose from behind the old imitation mahogany of the bar.

Pig had moved aside two dozen beer glasses and seated himself on a ledge behind the bar. In times of crisis he preferred to sit in as voyeur. He gazed eagerly as his shipmates grappled shoatlike after the seven geysers below him. Beer had soaked down most of the sawdust behind the bar: skirmishes and amateur footwork were now scribbling it into alien hieroglyphics.

Outside came sirens, whistles, running feet. 'Oh, oh,' said Pig. He hopped down from the shelf, made his way around the end of the bar to Profane and Paola. 'Hey, ace,' he said, cool and slitting his eyes as if the wind blew into them. 'The sheriff is coming.'

'Back way,' said Profane.

'Bring the broad,' said Pig.

The three of them ran broken-field through a roomful of teeming bodies. On the way they picked up Dewey Gland. By the time the Shore Patrol had crashed into the Sailor's Grave, night sticks flailing, the four found themselves running down an alley parallel to East Main. 'Where we going,' Profane said. 'The way we're heading,' said Pig. 'Move your ass.'

Thomas Pynchon *V*

Frogs

In mid-morning the Model T truck rolled triumphantly home to Cannery Row and hopped the gutter and creaked up through the weeds to its place behind Lee Chong's. The boys blocked up the front wheels, drained what petrol was left into a five-gallon can, took their frogs, and went wearily home to the Palace Flophouse. Then Mack made a ceremonious visit to Lee Chong while the boys got a fire going in the big stove. Mack thanked Lee with dignity for lending the truck. He spoke of the great success of the trip, of the hundreds of frogs taken. Lee smiled shyly and waited for the inevitable.

'We're in the chips,' Mack said enthusiastically, 'Doc pays us a nickel a frog and we got about a thousand.'

Lee nodded. The price was standard. Everybody knew that.

'Doc's away,' said Mack. 'Jesus, is he gonna be happy when he sees all them frogs.'

Lee nodded again. He knew Doc was away and he also knew where the conversation was going.

'Say, by the way,' said Mack as though he had just thought of it. 'We're a little bit short right now . . .' He managed to make it sound like a very unusual situation.

'No whisky,' said Lee Chong, and he smiled.

Mack was outraged. 'What would we want whisky for? Why, we got a gallon of the finest whisky you ever laid a lip over – a whole full God-damned-running-over gallon. By the way,' he continued, 'I and the boys would like to have you just step up for a snort with us. They told me to ask you.'

In spite of himself Lee smiled with pleasure. They wouldn't offer it if they didn't have it.'

'No,' said Mack, 'I'll lay it on the line. I and the boys are pretty short and we're pretty hungry. You know the price of frogs is twenty for a buck. Now Doc is away and we're hungry. So what we thought is this. We don't want to see you lose nothing, so we'll make over to you twenty-five frogs for a buck. You got a five-frog profit there and nobody loses his shirt.'

'No,' said Lee. 'No money.'

'Well, hell, Lee, all we need is a little groceries. I'll tell you what – we want to give Doc a little party when he gets back. We got plenty of liquor, but we'd like to get maybe some steaks, and stuff like that. He's such a nice guy. Hell, when your wife had that bad tooth, who give her the laudanum?'

Mack had him. Lee was indebted to Doc – deeply indebted. What Lee was having trouble comprehending was how his indebtedness to Doc made it necessary that he give credit to Mack.

'We don't want you to have like a mortgage on frogs,' Mack went on. 'We will actually deliver right into your hands twenty-five frogs for every buck of groceries you let us have and you can come to the party too.'

Lee's mind nosed over the proposition like a mouse in a cheese cupboard. He could find nothing wrong with it. The whole thing was legitimate. Frogs *were* cash as far as Doc was concerned, the price was standard, and Lee had a double profit. He had his five-frog margin and also he had the grocery mark-up. The whole thing hinged on whether they actually had any frogs.

'We go see flog,' Lee said at last.

In front of the Palace he had a drink of the whisky, inspected the damp sacks of frogs, and agreed to the transaction. He stipulated, however, that he would take no dead frogs. Now Mack counted fifty frogs into a can and walked back to the grocery with Lee and got two dollars' worth of bacon and eggs and bread.

Lee, anticipating a brisk business, brought a big packing-case out and put it into the vegetable department. He emptied the fifty frogs into it and covered it with a wet gunny-sack to keep his charges happy.

And business was brisk. Eddie sauntered down and bought two frogs' worth of Bull Durham. Jones was outraged a little later when the price of Coca-Cola went up from one to two frogs. In fact bitterness arose as the day wore on and prices went up. Steak, for instance – the very best steak shouldn't have been more than ten frogs a pound, but Lee set it at twelve and a half. Canned peaches were sky high, eight frogs for a No. 2 can. Lee had a stranglehold on the consumers. He was pretty sure that the Thrift Market or Holman's would not approve of this new monetary system. If the boys wanted steak, they knew they had to pay Lee's prices. Feeling ran high when Hazel, who had coveted a pair of yellow silk arm-bands for a long time, was told that if he didn't want to pay thirty-five frogs for them he could go somewhere else. The poison of greed was already creeping into the innocent and laudable merchandising agreement. Bitterness was piling up. But in Lee's packing-case the frogs were piling up too.

Financial bitterness could not eat too deeply into Mack and the boys, for they were not mercantile men. They did not measure their joy in goods sold, their egos in bank balances, nor their loves in what they cost. While they were mildly irritated that Lee was taking them for an economic ride or perhaps hop, two dollars' worth of bacon and eggs was in their stomachs lying right on top of a fine slug of whisky and right on top of the breakfast was another slug of whisky. And they sat in their own chairs in their own house and watched Darling learning to drink canned milk out of a sardine can. Darling was and was destined to remain a very happy dog, for in the group of five men there were five distinct theories of dog training, theories which clashed so that Darling never got any training at all. From the first she was a precocious bitch. She slept on the bed of the man who had given her the last bribe. They really stole for her sometimes. They wooed her away from one another. Occasionally all five agreed that things had to change and that Darling must be disciplined, but in the discussion of method the intention invariably drifted away. They were in love with her. They found the little puddles she left on the floor charming. They bored all their acquaintances with her cuteness and they would have killed her with food if in the end she hadn't had better sense than they.

Jones made her a bed in the bottom of the grandfather clock, but Darling never used it. She slept with one or another of them as the fancy moved her. She chewed the blankets, tore the mattresses, sprayed the feathers out of the pillows. She coquetted and played her owners against one another. They thought she was wonderful. Mack intended to teach her tricks and go in vaudeville and he didn't even house-break her.

They sat in the afternoon, smoking, digesting, considering, and now and then having a delicate drink from the jug. And each time they warned that they must not take too much, for it was to be for Doc. They must not forget that for a minute.

'What time you figure he'll be back?' Eddie asked.

'Usually gets in about eight or nine o'clock,' said Mack. 'Now we got to figure when we're going to give it. I think we ought to give it tonight.'

'Sure,' the others agreed.

'Maybe he might be tired,' Hazel suggested. 'That's a long drive.'

'Hell,' said Jones, 'nothing rests you like a good party. I've been so dog-tired my pants was draggin' and then I've went to a party and felt fine.'

'We got to do some real thinkin',' said Mack. 'Where we going to give it – here?'

'Well, Doc, he likes his music. He's always got his phonograph going at a party. Maybe he'd be more happy if we give it over at his place.'

'You got something there,' said Mack. 'But I figure it ought to be like a surprise party. And how we going to make like it's a party and not just bringin' over a jug of whisky?'

'How about decorations?' Hughie suggested. 'Like Fourth of July or Hallowe'en.'

Mack's eyes looked off into space and his lips were parted. He could see it all. 'Hughie,' he said, 'I think you got something there. I never would of thought you could do it, but by God you really rang a duck that time.' His voice grew mellow and his eyes looked into the future. 'I can just see it,' he said. 'Doc comes home. He's tired. He drives up. The place is all lit up. He thinks somebody's broke in. He goes up the stairs, and by God the place has got the hell decorated out of it. There's crêpe paper and there's favours and a big cake. Jesus, he'd know it was a party then. And it wouldn't be no little mouse fart party neither. And we're kind of hiding so for a minute he don't know who done it. And then we come out yelling. Can't you see his face? By God, Hughie, I don't know how you thought of it.'

Hughie blushed. His conception had been much more conservative, based in fact on the New Year's party at 'La Ida', but if it was going to be like that, why Hughie was willing to take credit. 'I just thought it would be nice,' he said.

'Well, it's a pretty nice thing,' said Mack, 'and I don't mind saying when the surprise kind of wears off, I'm going to tell Doc who thought it up.' They leaned back and considered the thing.

And in their minds the decorated laboratory looked like the conservatory at the Hotel del Monte. They had a couple more drinks, just to savour the plan.

Lee Chong kept a very remarkable store. For instance, most stores buy yellow-and-black crêpe paper and black paper cats, masks and papier-mâché pumpkins in October. There is a brisk business for Hallowe'en and then these items disappear. Maybe they are sold or thrown out, but you can't buy them, say, in June. The same is true of Fourth of July equipment, flags and bunting and sky-rockets. Where are they in January? Gone – no one knows where. This was not Lee Chong's way. You could buy Valentines in November at Lee Chong's, shamrocks, hatchets, and paper cherry-trees in August. He had fire-crackers he had laid up in 1920. One of the mysteries was where he kept his stock since his was not a very large store. He had bathing-suits he had bought when long skirts and black stockings and head bandanas were in style. He had bicycle clips and tatting shuttles and Mah Jong sets. He had badges that said 'Remember the Maine' and felt pennants commemorating 'Fighting Bob'. He had mementos of the Panama Pacific International Exposition of 1915 – little towers of jewels. And there was one other unorthodoxy in Lee's way of doing business. He never had a sale, never reduced a price, and never remaindered. An article that cost thirty cents in 1912 still was thirty cents, although mice and moths might seem to some to have reduced its value. But there was no question about it. If you wanted to decorate a laboratory in a general way, not being specific about the season but giving the impression of a cross between Saturnalia and a pageant of the Flags of all Nations, Lee Chong's was the place to go for your stuff.

Mack and the boys knew that, but Mack said: 'Where we going to get a big cake? Lee hasn't got nothing but them little bakery cakes.'

Hughie had been so successful before he tried again. 'Why'n't Eddie bake a cake?' he suggested. 'Eddie used to be fry cook at the San Carlos for a while.'

The instant enthusiasm for the idea drove from Eddie's brain the admission that he had never baked a cake.

Mack put it on a sentimental basis besides. 'It would mean more to Doc,' he said. 'It wouldn't be like no God damned old soggy bought cake. It would have some heart in it.'

As the afternoon and the whisky went down the enthusiasm rose. There were endless trips to Lee Chong's. The frogs were gone from one sack and Lee's packing-case was getting crowded. By six o'clock they had finished the gallon of whisky and were buying half-pints of Old Tennis Shoes at fifteen frogs a crack, but the pile of decorating materials was heaped on the floor of the Palace Flophouse – miles of crêpe paper commemorating every holiday in vogue and some that had been abandoned.

Eddie watched his stove like a mother hen. He was baking a cake in a wash-basin. The recipe was guaranteed not to fail by the company which made the shortening. But from the first the cake had acted strangely. When the batter was completed it writhed and panted as though animals were squirming and crawling inside it. Once in the oven it put up a bubble like a baseball which grew tight and shiny and then collapsed with a hissing sound. This left such a crater that Eddie made a new batch of batter and filled in the hole. And now the cake was behaving very curiously, for while the bottom was burning and sending out a black smoke the top was rising and falling glueyly with a series of little explosions.

When Eddie finally put it out to cool, it looked like one of Bel Geddes's miniatures of a battlefield on a lava bed.

This cake was not fortunate, for while the boys were decorating the laboratory Darling ate what she could of it, was sick on it, and finally curled up in its still warm dough and went to sleep.

But Mack and the boys had taken the crêpe paper, the masks, the broomsticks and paper pumpkins, the red, white and blue bunting, and moved over the lot and across the street to the laboratory. They disposed of the last of the frogs for a quart of Old Tennis Shoes and two gallons of 49-cent wine.

'Doc is very fond of wine,' said Mack. 'I think he likes it even better than whisky.'

Doc never locked the laboratory. He went on the theory that anyone who really wanted to break in could easily do it, that people were essentially honest, and that finally there wasn't much the average person would want to steal there, anyway. The valuable things were books and records, surgical instruments and optical glass and such things that a practical working burglar wouldn't look at twice. His theory had been sound as far as burglars, snatch thieves, and kleptomaniacs were concerned, but it had been completely ineffective regarding his friends. Books were often 'borrowed'. No can of beans ever survived his absence, and on several occasions, returning late, he had found guests in his bed.

The boys piled the decorations in the ante-room and then Mack stopped them. 'What's going to make Doc happiest?' he asked.

'The party!' said Hazel.

'No,' said Mack.

'The decorations?' Hughie suggested. He felt responsible for the decorations.

'No,' said Mack, 'the frogs. That's going to make him feel best of all. And maybe by the time he gets here, Lee Chong might be closed and he can't even see his frogs until tomorrow. No, sir,' Mack cried. 'Them frogs ought to be right here, right in the middle of the room with a piece of bunting on it and a sign that says: "Welcome Home, Doc".'

The committee which visited Lee met with stern opposition. All sorts of possibilities suggested themselves to his suspicious brain. It was explained that he was going to be at the party so he could watch his property, that no one questioned that they were his. Mack wrote out a paper transferring the frogs to Lee in case there should be any question.

When his protests weakened a little they carried the packing-case over to the laboratory, tacked red, white, and blue bunting over it, lettered the big sign with iodine on a card, and they started the decorating from there. They had finished the whisky by now and they really felt in a party mood. They criss-crossed the crêpe paper, and put the pumpkins up. Passers-by in the street joined the party and rushed over to Lee's to get more to drink. Lee Chong joined the party for a while, but his stomach was notoriously weak and he got sick and had to go home. At eleven o'clock they fried the steaks and ate them. Someone digging through the records found an album of Count Basie and the great phonograph roared out. The noise could be heard from the boatworks to 'La Ida'. A group of customers from the Bear Flag mistook Western Biological for a rival house and charged up the stairs whooping with joy. They were evicted by the outraged hosts, but only after a long, happy, and bloody battle that took out the front door and broke two windows. The crashing of jars was unpleasant. Hazel going through the kitchen to the toilet tipped the frying-pan of hot grease on himself and the floor and was badly burned.

At one-thirty a drunk wandered in and passed a remark which was considered insulting to Doc. Mack hit him a clip which is still remembered and discussed. The man rose off his feet, described a small arc, and crashed through the packing-case in among the frogs. Someone trying to change a record dropped the tone arm down and broke the crystal.

No one has studied the psychology of a dying party. It may be raging, howling, boiling, and then a fever sets in and a little silence and then quickly quickly it is gone, the guests go home or go to sleep or wander away to some other affair and they leave a dead body.

The lights blazed in the laboratory. The front door hung sideways by one hinge. The floor was littered with broken glass. Phonograph records, some broken, some only nicked, were strewn about. The plates with pieces of steak ends and coagulating grease were on the floor, on top of the bookcases, under the bed. Whisky-glasses lay sadly on their sides. Someone trying to climb the bookcases had pulled out a whole section of books and spilled them in broken-backed confusion on the floor. And it was empty, it was over.

Through the broken end of the packing-case a frog hopped and sat feeling the air for danger, and then another joined him. They could smell the fine, damp, cool air coming in the door and in through the broken windows. One of them sat on the fallen card which said: 'Welcome Home, Doc.' And then the two hopping timidly toward the door.

For quite a while a little river of frogs hopped down the steps, a swirling, moving river. For quite a while Cannery Row crawled with frogs – was overrun with frogs. A taxi which brought a very late customer to the Bear Flag squashed five frogs in the street. But well before dawn they had all gone. Some found the sewer and some worked their way up the hill to the reservoir and some went into culverts and some only hid among the weeds in the vacant lot.

And the lights blazed in the quiet empty laboratory.

John Steinbeck *Cannery Row*

About Coronation Ale

In June 1911, during the preparations in Gildsey for celebrating the coronation of George V, amidst the hanging of flags, the building of bonfires, the arranging of floral mottoes and planning of banquets, my grandfather, the morose and unpopular brewer of the town, proposed to make his own contribution to the festivities by producing a commemorative bottled ale, to be called, appropriately enough, Coronation Ale; the first thousand bottles to be issued free, but no drop to pass any man's lips till the king was indeed crowned.

Though it had already passed, in a form known simply as 'Special', my grandfather's lips. And perhaps too the budding lips of Helen Atkinson, my mother.

Warmed by patriotic zeal and softened by a mood of reconciliation (so, when it comes to it, the peevish brewer can say his God Save the King like any man), the townspeople chose to forget for a moment their differences with Ernest Atkinson. The jubilant day drew near. They cast their minds back to other times when they had been licensed to swill beer in a noble cause; to the Diamond and Golden Jubilee Ales, even to the Grand '51, and so to those halcyon days when the fortunes of the town had bloomed. Had those days gone for ever? Could this National Occasion – so Ernest Atkinson ventured, addressing the Celebrations Committee, with no hint of politics but with a curious glint in his eye – not include a local one? For was it not, he pointed out, the glint becoming curiouser, almost exactly one hundred years ago that Thomas Atkinson received, to the great grudgingness (uneasy laughter amongst the committee members) of certain Gildsey factions, the Leem Navigation, thus inaugurating the process by which this once obscure Fenland town gained its place in the Nation – if not, indeed, the World?

What was in this Corontion Ale, offered in a dark brown bottle of a shape narrower and more elongated than the beer bottle of later days, with 'Atkinson – Gildsey' embossed upon it and a label bearing a large crown, centre, and a continuous border of alternating smaller crowns and union jacks? Nectar? Poison? Merriment? Madness? The bottled-up maniacs of His Majesty's subjects?

Rest assured, it was no ordinary ale that they drank by the Ouse while in Westminster crowds thronged, guns fired and the Abbey bells pealed. For when the men of Gildsey jostled into the Pike and Eel and the Jolly Bargeman to be amongst the privileged first one thousand to receive their bottle gratis and to raise their glasses in decent good cheer to toast the King, they discovered that this patriotic liquor hurled them with astonishing rapidity through the normally gradual and containable stages of intoxication: pleasure, satisfaction, well-being, elation, light-headedness, hot-headedness, befuddlement, distraction, delirium, irascibility, pugnaciousness, imbalance, incapacity – all in the gamut of a single bottle. And if a second bottle was broached –

Precise accounts of the events of that day are hard to track down. Partly because it was a day that Gildsey wished to forget; partly for the more pertinent reason that many of those who might have acted as reliable witnesses were, at the time, hopelessly drunk.

With alarming frequency the women of the town were called upon to restrain displays of intemperance in their menfolk, only to succumb themselves to the temptation of tasting this brew which had such remarkable effect. The landlords of the town's twenty-three public houses began to fear for the respectability and physical safety of their establishments. A parade of schoolchildren down Water Street demonstrating their innocent, flag-waving allegiance to the new Monarch, was marred by the raucous – and possibly obscene – choruses emanating from the Swan and the Pike and Eel. Sky-rockets and Roman candles intended for a dazzling evening display were let off in broad daylight and along alarming trajectories. A horrific incidence of shipwreck and drowning almost occurred when the *St Guthlac*, whose steersman had quaffed his bottle, as had a good many of his passengers, took a zig-zagging career across the river, pennants aflutter and steam-horn braying, and was almost run down by the *Fen Queen*, under a similar state of captaincy.

Drunkenness. While the bells of St Gunnhilda's ring in the new reign. Drunkenness in many sudden and wonderful forms.

A deputation of the two senior police officers of the town addressed themselves, in the canvas structure known as the 'Coronation Pavilion', to Ernest Atkinson, to express their urgent view that in the name of law and order the public houses of the town should be closed, and to ask, in the meantime, what on earth was in those bottles, and was there no antidote? To which Ernest is said to have replied, with a detectable mimicking of his election speech style, that it would be a most deplorable action, to suppress, on this of all days, a gesture intended only to do honour to King and Country; that though he was responsible for the beer, he could hardly be held responsible for those (these were his words) who did not drink it wisely. And to illustrate this latter point, he proceeded, before the eyes of the police chiefs, to drain in one draught a bottle of the ale in question (of which several crates had penetrated the Coronation Pavilion) without the slightest visible effect, thus giving the lie to the slanders made at that same election speech and proving the adage that it takes more than his own beer to get a brewer drunk. The officers were cordially invited to try for themselves. Being in their best ceremonial uniforms, they declined.

To these same senior officers it had soon regrettably to be reported that a number of their constables had yielded to the general intoxication and tasted the extraordinary potion. A young reveller had attempted to climb a flag-pole and broken a leg. The Processions and Events were falling into disarray. And numerous participating citizens who even on this day should have maintained a necessary degree of sobriety, had failed to do so, including the members of the Gildsey Free Trade Brass Band, whose much rehearsed programme suffered from wild improvisations and whose rendering of Elgar's Cockaigne Overture broke down irredeemably.

It was now a question of some difficulty, for those still able to judge the matter, whether prohibiting the supply of this by now clamoured-for beer might not lead to even greater uproar than that caused by its consumption.

During the course of this riotous afternoon several of those invited to attend the Coronation Banquet (at eight, in the Great Chamber of the Town Hall) began to wonder how (given that they too had drunk –) they might conceivably excuse themselves from such a dignified gathering. But no Coronation Banquet was to occur. For the worst of this outrageous day was yet to come.

No one knows how it started. Whether the alarm was first given by individuals (and was ignored as one of innumerable hoaxes and hallucinations) or whether the whole town as a body was suddenly aware of the palpable fact. But as twilight descended on this more than festive day it became evident that the brewery, the New Atkinson Brewery, built in 1849 by George and Alfred Atkinson, was on fire. Palls of thickening smoke were rapidly followed by leaping flames, then by the loud crackings and burstings that signal an advanced conflagration.

A crowd rushed and swarmed. The Coronation Banquet, in the face of such a dire emergency, was summarily cancelled. The Gildsey Fire Brigade (founder, Alfred Atkinson) was called out in full complement. But whether this stalwart body, with its three engines and two auxiliary tenders, was of any use on this disastrous night is to be doubted. For not only had the Fire Station been improvidently undermanned throughout the day (one of the engines having been decked out with ribbons and flags as part of the celebratory procession) but almost every fireman, struggling now just as much to sober himself as to get into his cumbersome fireman's garb, had drunk his share of the Ale; with the result that when the engines at last arrived, in ragged order, with much clanging of bells, and in one case still festooned with patriotic rosettes, the brewery was already past saving. And it was claimed by several eye-witnesses that the gallant crews devoted much more of their energy to a variety of insubordinate antics (such as playing their hoses upon the watching crowd) than they ever did to the fire.

So the fire burned. Subsuming all bonfires and all other pyrotechnic displays arranged for this joyous evening. The crowd, indeed, eyes glazed as much by their intake of ale as by the glare of the flames, watched as if this were not their town brewery being burnt to the ground but some elaborate spectacle expressly arranged for their delight and contemplation. And perhaps it was. The ineptitudes of the Fire Brigade were cheered and encouraged. Few accounts speak of dismay, of panic, even of apprehended danger. When the fire performed particularly impressive stunts (a row of upper windows bursting all at once like a ship's broadside) it did so amidst hearty applause; and when, at twelve midnight (for that was the last hour ever to be registered on its lofty clock face) the brewery chimney trembled, tottered and, with its Italianate friezes and paralysed iron clock-hands, sank swiftly, vertically, into the blazing shell of the brewery, it was to the accompaniment of a resounding ovation, notwithstanding the fact that if the chimney had chosen to adopt a different angle of collapse it might have crushed several score of the spectators.

An unearthly glare lit all that night the clustered rooftops of Gildsey. On the oily-black surface of the Ouse fiery necklaces scattered and rethreaded themselves. In the deserted, garlanded market-place the paving stones throbbed, and in the Town Hall where the places were laid for a banquet that was never to be, the shadows of the tall municipal window frames quivered on the walls. For miles around, across the flat unimpeded outlook of the Fens, the fire could be seen, like some meteoric visitation – a gift to Fenland superstition; and on the morning of the twenty-third of June, in place of the familiar chimney, a great cloud of smoke, lingering for many days.

Was it the case – for no sooner had the blaze gone out than the talk began to be fanned – that this Coronation Ale, which so fired internally those who drank it, had found a means to manifest its power externally and in a process of spontaneous combustion engulfed in flames its own source? Had this phenomenal ale, intended to regale the people on a day of national festivity, only exposed the inflammatory folly of their jingoistic ardour and revealed to them that they preferred destruction to rejoicing? And was that the meaning of Ernest's cryptic and bitter remark when in the autumn of 1914 he left Gildsey for ever: 'You have enjoyed one conflagration, you will see another'? Had the brewery fire been started – as was widely credited – by drunken revellers who, bursting into the buildings in search of further supplies of the ale and, accidentally or otherwise, starting a fire, had discovered a new and more consuming thirst? Or was the counter-theory true, that the fire was started by the town authorities as a desperate means both of preventing a night of wholesale lawlessness and of destroying at one go all stocks of the offending brew? For, indeed, after the razing of the brewery, no more Coronation Ale was ever seen (or drunk) again (with one exception). And the secret of its concoction – remained a secret.

Did the burning of the brewery give final and positive proof of the notion that a curse lay on the Atkinson family? Yet if it did, how did this accord with that other theory that sprang up quietly at first but with greater boldness in the ensuing years when Ernest, having made no plans to rebuild, sold his remaining business assets and retired – all too guiltily it seemed – to Kessling Hall? That Ernest himself, under cover of getting the whole town drunk, had set fire to the brewery. Because he wished to get his hands on the massive insurance sums.

And because, children (allow your history teacher his fanciful but not ill-researched surmise), far from being the victim of a curse he was glad to be its instrument. Because he saw no future for this firm of Atkinson and its one-time empire, let alone for these people who courted disaster. Because he wanted nothing better than to see this brewery utterly destroyed and finished with. To wipe the slate clean.

So, perhaps, he thought, that October day in 1914, in the ample back seat of a Daimler limousine, beside his only daughter (a beauty of eighteen), being driven from Gildsey to Kessling, where once there was no Hall, no Maltings and no barge-pool. So he pondered, passing through those flat fringes of the Leem so similar to the low country between the Lys and the Yser where so many lives were soon to be extinguished and where Henry Crick was to be wounded in the knee. What had the Atkinsons achieved, he perhaps asked himself, by bringing the wide world to a backwater?

And – I put it to you, children – were Ernest and all the beer-producing Atkinsons doing anything more, if on a grander scale, than what Freddie Parr's father did when he took to drink? Trying to assuage emptiness. Lifting sunken spirits. Kindling fire and ferment out of watery nothing . . .

The verdict of the official investigators and the insurance company inspectors: an accident.

Graham Swift *Waterland*

Bedlam Gates

The besiegers being now in complete possession of the house, spread themselves over it from garret to cellar, and plied their demon labours fiercely. While some small parties kindled bonfires underneath the windows, others broke up the furniture and cast the fragments down to feed the flames below; where the apertures in the wall (windows no longer) were large enough, they threw out tables, chests of drawers, beds, mirrors, pictures, and flung them whole into the fire; while every fresh addition to the blazing mass was received with shouts, and howls, and yells, which added new and dismal terrors to the conflagration. Those who had axes and had spent their fury on the movables, chopped and tore down the doors and window frames, broke up the flooring, hewed away the rafters, and buried men who lingered in the upper rooms, in heaps of ruins. Some searched the drawers, the chests, the boxes, writing-desks, and closets, for jewels, plate, and money; while others, less mindful of gain and more mad for destruction, cast their whole contents into the court-yard without examination, and called to those below to heap them on the blaze. Men who had been into the cellars, and had staved the casks, rushed to and fro stark mad, setting fire to all they saw – often to the dresses of their own friends – and kindling the building in so many parts that some had no time for escape, and were seen, with drooping hands and blackened faces, hanging senseless on the window-sills to which they had crawled, until they were sucked and drawn into the burning gulf. The more the fire crackled and raged, the wilder and more cruel the men grew; as though moving in that element they became fiends, and changed their earthly nature for the qualities that give delight in hell.

The burning pile, revealing rooms and passages red hot, through gaps made in the crumbling walls; the tributary fires that licked the outer bricks and stones with their long forked tongues, and ran up to meet the glowing mass within; the shining of the flames upon the villains who looked on and fed them; the roaring of the angry blaze, so bright and high that it seemed in its rapacity to have swallowed up the very smoke; the living flakes the wind bore rapidly away and hurried on with, like a storm of fiery snow; the noiseless breaking of great beams of wood, which fell like feathers on the heap of ashes, and crumbled in the very act to sparks and powder; the lurid tinge that overspread the sky, and the darkness, very deep by contrast, which prevailed around; the exposure to the coarse, common gaze, of every little nook which usages of home had made a sacred place, and the destruction by rude hands of every little household favourite which old associations make a dear and precious thing: all this taking place – not among pitying looks and friendly murmurs of compassion, but brutal shouts and exultations, which seemed to make the very rats who stood by the old house too long, creatures with some claim upon the pity and regard of those its roof had sheltered: – combined to form a scene never to be forgotten by those who saw it and were not actors in the work, so long as life endured.

And who were they? The alarm-bell rang – and it was pulled by no faint or hesitating hands – for a long time; but not a soul was seen. Some of the insurgents said that when it ceased, they heard the shrieks of women, and saw some garments fluttering in the air, as a party of men bore away no unresisting burdens. No one could say that this was true or false, in such an uproar; but where was Hugh? Who among them had seen him, since the forcing of the doors? The cry spread through the body. Where was Hugh!

'Here!' he hoarsely cried, appearing from the darkness; out of breath, and blackened with the smoke. 'We have done all we can; the fire is burning itself out; and even the corners where it hasn't spread, are nothing but heaps of ruins. Disperse, my lads, while the coast's clear; get back by different ways; and meet as usual!' With that, he disappeared again, – contrary to his wont, for he was always first to advance, and last to go away, – leaving them to follow homewards as they would.

It was not an easy task to draw off such a throng. If Bedlam gates had been flung open wide, there would not have issued forth such maniacs as the frenzy of that night had made. There were men there who danced and trampled on the beds of flowers as though they trod down human enemies, and wrenched them from the stalks, like savages who twisted human necks. There were men who cast their lighted torches in the air, and suffered them to fall upon their heads and faces, blistering the skin with deep unseemly burns. There were men who rushed up to the fire, and paddled in it with their hands as if in water; and others who were restrained by force from plunging in, to gratify their deadly longing. On the skull of one drunken lad – not twenty, by his looks – who lay upon the ground with a bottle to his mouth, the lead from the roof came streaming down in a shower of liquid fire, white hot; melting his head like wax. When the scattered parties were collected, men – living yet, but singed as with hot irons – were plucked out of the cellars, and carried off upon the shoulders of others, who strove to wake them as they went along with ribald jokes, and left them, dead, in the passages of hospitals. But of all the howling throng not one learnt mercy from, nor sickened at, these sights; nor was the fierce, besotted, senseless rage of one man glutted.

Slowly, and in small clusters, with hoarse hurrahs and repetitions of their usual cry, the assembly dropped away. The last few red-eyed stragglers reeled after those who had gone before; the distant noise of men calling to each other, and whistling for others whom they missed, grew fainter and fainter; at length even these sounds died away, and silence reigned alone.

Silence indeed! The glare of the flames had sunk into a fitful, flashing light; and the gentle stars, invisible till now, looked down upon the blackening heap. A dull smoke hung upon the ruin, as though to hide it from those eyes of Heaven; and the wind forbore to move it. Bare walls, roof open to the sky – chambers, where the beloved dead had, many and many a fair day, risen to new life and energy; where so many dear ones had been sad and merry; which were connected with so many thoughts and hopes, regrets and changes – all gone. Nothing left but a dull and dreary blank – a smouldering heap of dust and ashes – the silence and solitude of utter desolation.

The vintner's house, with half-a-dozen others near at hand, was one great, glowing blaze. All night, no one had essayed to quench the flames, or stop their progress; but now a body of soldiers were actively engaged in pulling down two old wooden houses, which were every moment in danger of taking fire, and which could scarcely fail, if they were left to burn, to extend the conflagration immensely. The tumbling down of nodding walls and heavy blocks of wood, the hooting and the execrations of the crowd, the distant firing of other military detachments, the distracted looks and cries of those whose habitations were in danger, the hurrying to and fro of frightened people with their goods; the reflections in every quarter of the sky of deep, red, soaring flames, as though the last day had come and the whole universe were burning; the dust, and smoke, and drift of fiery particles, scorching and kindling all it fell upon; the hot unwholesome vapour, the blight on everything; the stars, and moon, and very sky, obliterated; – made up such a sum of dreariness and ruin, that it seemed as if the face of Heaven were blotted out, and night, in its rest and quiet, and softened light, never could look upon the earth again.

But there was a worse spectacle than this – worse by far than fire and smoke, or even the rabble's unappeasable and maniac rage. The gutters of the street, and every crack and fissure in the stones, ran with scorching spirit, which being dammed up by busy hands, overflowed the road and pavement, and formed a great pool, into which the people dropped down dead by dozens. They lay in heaps all round this fearful pond, husbands and wives, fathers and sons, mothers and daughters, women with children in their arms and babies at their breasts, and drank until they died. While some stooped with their lips to the brink and never raised their heads again, others sprang up from their fiery draught, and danced, half in mad triumph, and half in the agony of suffocation, until they fell, and steeped their corpses in the liquor that had killed them. Nor was even this the worst or most appalling kind of death that happened on this fatal night. From the burning cellars, where they drank out of hats, pails, buckets, tubs, and shoes, some men were drawn alive, but all alight from head to foot; who, in their unendurable anguish and suffering, making for anything that had the look of water, rolled, hissing, in this hideous lake, and splashed up liquid fire which lapped in all it met with as it ran along the surface, and neither spared the living nor the dead. On this last night of the great riots – for the last night it was – the wretched victims of a senseless outcry became themselves the dust and ashes of the flames they had kindled, and strewed the public streets of London.

Charles Dickens *Barnaby Rudge*

EFFECTS

Blotto Motto

And wine can of their wits the wise beguile,
Make the sage frolic, and the serious smile,
The grave in memory measure frisk about,
And many a long-repented word bring out.

Homer *The Odyssey*, trans. Alexander Pope

Intoxication

I do not think that anyone completely understands its mechanism, but it is a fact that there are foreign substances which, when present in the blood or tissues, directly cause us pleasurable sensations; and they also so alter the conditions governing our sensibility that we become incapable of receiving unpleasurable impulses.

Sigmund Freud *Civilization and Its Discontents*, trans. Joan Riviere

Now and Then

(*Suggested by a passage from Laurence Sterne.*)

I love drinking now and then. It defecates the standing pool of thought. A man perpetually in the paroxysm and fears of inebriety is like a half-drowned stupid wretch condemned to labour unceasingly in water; but a now-and-then tribute to Bacchus is like the cold bath, bracing and invigorating.

Robert Burns *Life and Works* ed. Robert Chambers & William Wallace

Three Things

PORTER: (*Knocking within*) Anon, Anon! (*He opens the gate.*) I pray you remember the porter.

(*Enter MacDuff and Lennox.*)

MACDUFF: Was it so late, friend, ere you went to bed
That you do lie so late?

PORTER: Faith, sir, we were carousing till the second cock, and drink, sir, is a great provoker of three things.

MACDUFF: What three things does drink especially provoke?

PORTER: Marry, sir, nose-painting, sleep, and urine. Lechery, sir, it provokes and unprovokes: it provokes the desire but it takes away the performance. Therefore much drink may be said to be an equivocator with lechery: it makes him and mars him; it sets him on and it takes him off; it persuades him and disheartens him, makes him stand to and not stand to: in conclusion, equivocates him in a sleep, and, giving him the lie, leaves him.

MACDUFF: I believe drink gave thee the lie last night.

PORTER: That it did, sir, i'the very throat on me; but I requited him for his lie, and, I think, being too strong for him though he took up my legs sometime, yet I made a shift to cast him.

William Shakespeare *Macbeth*

Brewer's Droop

Why cannot the drunken have sexual intercourse? Is it because one part of the body must be hotter than the rest, which cannot be the case with the drunken owing to their excessive heat? So the heat caused by movement is quenched, being heated by the surrounding heat. Or is it because the lower parts require to be heated, but wine naturally travels upwards, so that it produces heat there and withdraws it from the other part? After food men are least inclined to intercourse, so that they recommend a large breakfast but a light dinner; for when food is undigested there is an upward travel of heat and moisture, but when digested downwards: and the production of semen is due to heat and moisture. The weary emit semen at night because weariness is warm and wet; if, then, there is any waste product in this place, emission occurs. It is for the same reason that it happens with those whose health is bad. Similarly also it occurs with those who are frightened or dying.

Aristotle *Problems*, trans. W. S. Hett

Wine as a Pick-lock

We talked of drinking wine. JOHNSON. 'I require wine, only when I am alone. I have then often wished for it, and often taken it.' SPOTTISWOODE. 'What, by way of a companion, Sir?' JOHNSON. 'To get rid of myself, to send myself away. Wine gives great pleasure; and every pleasure is of itself a good. It is a good, unless counterbalanced by evil. A man may have a strong reason not to drink wine; and that may be greater than the pleasure. Wine makes a man better pleased with himself. I do not say that it makes him more pleasing to others. Sometimes it does. But the danger is, that while a man grows better pleased with himself, he may be growing less pleasing to others. Wine gives a man nothing. It neither gives him knowledge nor wit; it only animates a man, and enables him to bring out what a dread of the company has repressed. It only puts in motion what has been locked up in frost. But this may be good, or it may be bad.' SPOTTISWOODE. 'So, Sir, wine is a key which opens a box; but this box may be either full or empty.' JOHNSON. 'Nay, Sir, conversation is the key: wine is a pick-lock, which forces open the box and injures it. A man should cultivate his mind so as to have that confidence and readiness without wine, which wine gives.'

James Boswell *Life of Johnson*

In Vino Veritas?

To say truth, nothing is more erroneous than the common observation, that men who are ill-natured and quarrelsome when they are drunk, are very worthy persons when they are sober: for drink, in reality, doth not reverse nature, or create passions in men which did not exist in them before. It takes away the guard of reason, and consequently forces us to produce those symptoms which many, when sober, have art enough to conceal. It heightens and inflames our passions, (generally indeed that passion which is uppermost in our mind) so that the angry temper, the amorous, the generous, the good-humoured, the avaricious, and all other dispositions of men, are in their cups heightened and exposed.

And yet as no nation produces so many drunken quarrels, especially among the lower people, as England; (for, indeed, with them, to drink and to fight together, are almost synonymous terms) I would not, methinks, have it thence concluded, that the English are the worst-natured people alive. Perhaps the love of glory only is at the bottom of this; so that the fair conclusion seems to be, that our countrymen have more of that love, and more of bravery, than any other plebeians. And this the rather, as there is seldom anything ungenerous, unfair or ill-natured, exercised on those occasions: nay, it is common for the combatants to express good-will for each other, even at the time of the conflict; and as their drunken mirth generally ends in a battle, so do most of their battles end in friendship.

Henry Fielding *Tom Jones*

In the Drink

(*Enter* STEPHANO, *singing:* [*a bottle in his hand*].)

STEPHANO: I shall no more to sea, to sea,
Here shall I die ashore, –

This is a very scurvy tune to sing at a man's funeral; well, here's my comfort. (*Drinks. Sings.*)

The master, the swabber, the boatswain, and I,
The gunner, and his mate,
Lov'd Mall, Meg, and Marian, and Margery,
But none of us car'd for Kate:
For she had a tongue with a tang,
Would cry to a sailor, Go hang!
She lov'd not the savour of tar nor of pitch;
Yet a tailor might scratch her where'er she did itch.
Then to sea, boys, and let her go hang!

This is a scurvy tune too: but here's my comfort. (*Drinks.*)

CALIBAN: Do not torment me: – O!

STEPHANO: What's the matter? Have we devils here? Do you put tricks upon's with salvages and men of Ind, ha? I have not scap'd drowning, to be afeard now of your four legs; for it hath been said, As proper a man as ever went on four legs cannot make him give ground; and it shall be said so again, while Stephano breathes at' nostrils.

CALIBAN: The spirit torments me: – O!

STEPHANO: This is some monster of the isle with four legs, who hath got, as I take it, an ague. Where the devil should he learn our language? I will give him some relief, if it be but for that. If I can recover him, and keep him tame, and get to Naples with him, he's a present for any emperor that ever trod on neat's-leather.

CALIBAN: Do not torment me, prithee; I'll bring my wood home faster.

STEPHANO: He's in his fit now, and does not talk after the wisest. He shall taste of my bottle: if he have never drunk wine afore, it will go near to remove his fit. If I can recover him, and keep him tame, I will not take too much for him; he shall pay for him that hath him and that soundly.

CALIBAN: Thou dost me yet but little hurt; thou wilt anon, I know it by thy trembling: now Prosper works upon thee.

STEPHANO: Come on your ways; open your mouth; here is that which will give language to you, cat: open your mouth; this will shake your shaking, I can tell you, and that soundly: you cannot tell who's your friend: open your chaps again.

TRINCULO: I should know that voice: it should be – but he is drowned; and these are devils: – O defend me!

STEPHANO: Four legs and two voices, – a most delicate monster! His forward voice, now, is to speak well of his friend; his backward voice is to utter foul speeches and to detract. If all the wine in my bottle will recover him, I will help his ague. Come: – Amen! I will pour some in thy other mouth.

TRINCULO: Stephano!

STEPHANO: Doth thy other mouth call me? Mercy, mercy! This is a devil, and no monster: I will leave him; I have no long spoon.

TRINCULO: Stephano! If thou beest Stephano, touch me, and speak to me; for I am Trinculo, – be not afeard, – thy good friend Trinculo.

STEPHANO: If thou beest Trinculo, come forth: I'll pull thee by the lesser legs: if any be Trinculo's legs, these are they. Thou art very Trinculo indeed! How cam'st thou to be the siege of this moon-calf? can he vent Trinculos?

TRINCULO: I took him to be kill'd with a thunder-stroke. But art thou not drown'd, Stephano? I hope, now, thou art not drown'd. Is the storm over-blown? I hid me under the dead moon-calf's gaberdine for fear of the storm. And art thou living, Stephano? O Stephano, two Neapolitans scap'd!

STEPHANO: Prithee, do not turn me about; my stomach is not constant.

CALIBAN: [*Aside*] These be fine things, an if they be not sprites.
That's a brave god, and bears celestial liquor:
I will kneel to him

STEPHANO: How didst thou scape? How cam'st thou hither? swear, by this bottle, how thou cam'st hither. I escap'd upon a butt of sack, which the sailors heaved o'erboard, by this bottle! which I made of the bark of a tree with mine own hands, since I was cast ashore.

CALIBAN: I'll swear, upon that bottle, to be thy true subject; for the liquor is not earthly.

STEPHANO: Here; swear, then, how thou escap'dst.

TRINCULO: Swum ashore, man, like a duck: I can swim like a duck, I'll be sworn.

STEPHANO: Here, kiss the book. Though thou canst swim like a duck, thou are made like a goose.

TRINCULO: O Stephano, hast any more of this?

STEPHANO: The whole butt, man: my cellar is in a rock by th' sea-side, where my wine is hid. How now, moon-calf! how does thine ague?

CALIBAN: Hast thou not dropp'd from heaven?

STEPHANO: Out o' the moon, I do assure thee: I was the man i' th' moon when time was.

CALIBAN: I have seen thee in her, and I do adore thee:
My mistress show'd me thee, and thy dog, and thy bush.

STEPHANO: Come, swear to that; kiss the book: I will furnish it anon with new contents: swear.

TRINCULO: By this good light, this is a very shallow monster;
I afeard of him? A very weak monster! The man i' th' moon! A most poor credulous monster! Well drawn, monster, in good sooth!

CALIBAN: I'll show thee every fertile inch o' th' island; and I will kiss thy foot: I prithee, be my god.

TRINCULO: By this light, a most perfidious and drunken monster! when's god's asleep, he'll rob his bottle.

CALIBAN: I'll kiss thy foot; I'll swear myself thy subject.

STEPHANO: Come on, then; down, and swear.

TRINCULO: I shall laugh myself to death at this puppy-headed monster. A most scurvy monster! I could find in my heart to beat him, –

STEPHANO: Come, kiss.

TRINCULO: But that the poor monster's in drink. An abominable monster!

CALIBAN: I'll show thee the best springs; I'll pluck thee berries;
I'll fish for thee, and get thee wood enough.
A plague upon the tyrant that I serve!

I'll bear him no more sticks, but follow thee,
Thou wondrous man.

TRINCULO: A most ridiculous monster, to make a wonder of a poor drunkard!

CALIBAN: I prithee, let me bring thee where crabs grow;
And I with my long nails will dig thee pig-nuts;
Show thee a jay's nest, and instruct thee how
To snare the nimble marmoset; I'll bring thee
To clustering filberts, and sometimes I'll get thee
Young scamels from the rock. Wilt thou go with me?

STEPHANO: I prithee now, lead the way, without any more talking. Trinculo, the King and all our company else being drown'd, we will inherit here: here; bear my bottle: fellow Trinculo, we'll fill him by and by again.

CALIBAN (*Sings drunkenly.*):

Farewell, master; farewell, farewell!

TRINCULO: A howling monster; a drunken monster!

CALIBAN: No more dams I'll make for fish;
Nor fetch in firing
At requiring;
Nor scrape trenchering, nor wash dish:
'Ban, 'Ban, Cacaliban
Has a new master: – get a new man.

Freedom, high-day! high-day, freedom! freedom, high-day, freedom!

STEPHANO: O brave monster! lead the way. (*Exeunt.*)

William Shakespeare *The Tempest*

Rotten Honey

The fire was still smouldering in a great ring of ash. The shelters were torn apart though the uprights still stood. As for the ground in the clearing it had been churned up as though a whole herd of cattle had stampeded there. Lok crept to the edge of the clearing while Fa hung back. He began to circle. In the centre of the clearing were the pictures and the gifts.

When Fa saw these she moved inward behind Lok, and they approached them spirally, ears cocked for the return of the new people. The pictures were confused by the fire where the stag's head still watched Lok inscrutably. There was a new stag now, spring-coloured and fat, but another figure lay across it. This figure was red, with enormous spreading arms and legs and the face glared up at him for the eyes were white pebbles. The hair stood out round the head as though the figure were in the act of some frantic cruelty, and through the figure, pinning it to the stag, was a stake driven deep, its end split and furred over. The two people retreated from it in awe, for they had never seen any thing like it. Then they returned timidly to the presents.

The whole haunch of a stag, raw but comparatively bloodless, hung from the top of the stake and an opened stone of honey-drink stood by the staring head. The scent of the honey rose out of it like the smoke and flame from a fire. Fa put out her hand and touched the meat which swung so that she snatched her hand back. Lok fetched another circle round the figure, his feet avoiding the out-stretched limbs while his hand moved out slowly. In a moment they were tearing at the present, ripping apart the muscle and cramming the raw meat into their mouths. They did not stop till they were skin tight with food and a shining white bone hung from the stake by a strip of hide.

At last Lok stood back and wiped his hands on his thighs. Still with nothing said they turned in towards each other and squatted by the pot. From far off on the slope leading to the terrace they could hear the old man.

'A-ho! A-ho! A-ho!'

The reek from the open mouth of the pot was thick. A fly meditated on the lip, then as Lok's breathing came closer, shuffled its wings, flew for a moment and landed again.

Fa put her hand on Lok's wrist.

'Do not touch it.'

But Lok's mouth was close to the pot, his nostrils wide, his breathing quick. He spoke in a loud cracked voice.

'Honey.'

All at once he ducked, thrust his mouth into the pot and sucked. The rotten honey burnt his mouth and tongue so that he somersaulted backwards and Fa fled from the pot round the ashes of the fire. She stood looking fearfully at him while he spat and began to crawl back stalking the pot that waited for him, reeking. He lowered himself cautiously and sipped. He smacked his lips and sucked again. He sat back and laughed in her face.

'Drink.'

Uncertainly she bent to the mouth of the pot and put her tongue in the stinging, sweet stuff. Lok suddenly knelt forward, talking, and pushed her away so that she was astonished and squatted, licking her lips and spitting. Lok burrowed into the pot and sucked three times; but at the third suck the surface of the honey slid out of reach so that he sucked air and choked explosively. He rolled on the ground, trying to get his breath. Fa tried for the honey but could not reach it with her tongue and spoke bitterly to him. She stood silent for a moment then picked up the pot and held it to her mouth as the new people did. Lok saw her with the great stone at her face and laughed and tried to tell her how funny she was. He remembered the honey in time, leapt up and tried to take the stone from her face. But it was stuck, glued, and as he dragged it down her face came with it. Then they were pulling and shouting at each other. Lok heard his voice coming out, high and loud and savage. He let go to examine this new voice and Fa staggered away with the pot. He found that the trees were moving very gently sideways and upwards. He had a magnificent picture that would put everything right and tried to describe it to Fa who would not listen. Then he had nothing but the picture of having had a picture and this made him furiously angry. He reached out after the picture with his voice and he heard it, disconnected from inside-Lok, laughing and quacking like a duck. But there was one word that was the beginning of the picture even though the picture itself had gone out of sight. He held on to the word. He stopped laughing and spoke very solemnly to Fa who was still standing with the stone at her face.

'Log!' he said. 'Log!'

Then he remembered the honey and indignantly pulled the stone from her. Immediately her red face came out of the pot she started to laugh and talk. Lok held the pot as the new people had held it and the honey flowed over his chest. He writhed his body until his face was under the pot and contrived to get the trickle into his mouth. Fa was shrieking with laughter. She fell over, rolled, and lay back kicking her legs in the air. Lok and the honey fire responded to this invitation clumsily. Then they both remembered the pot and were pulling and arguing once more. Fa managed to drink a little but the honey turned sulky and would not come out. Lok snatched the pot, wrestled with it, beat it with his fist, shouted; but there was no more honey. He hurled the pot at the ground in fury and it grinned open into two pieces. Lok and Fa flung themselves at the pieces, squatted, each licking and turning a piece over to find where the honey had gone. The fall was roaring in the clearing, inside Lok's head. The trees were moving faster. He sprang to his feet and found that the ground was as perilous as a log. He struck at a tree as it came past to keep it still and then he was lying on his back with the sky spinning over him. He turned over, and got up rump first, swaying like the new one. Fa was crawling round the ashes of the fire like a moth with a burnt wing. She was talking to herself about hyenas. All at once Lok discovered the power of the new people in him. He was one of them, there was nothing he could not do. There were many branches left in the clearing and unburnt logs. Lok ran sideways to a log and commanded it to move. He shouted.

'A-ho! A-ho! A-ho!'

The log was sliding like the trees but not fast enough. He went on shouting but the log would not move any faster. He seized a branch and struck again and again at the log as Tanakil had struck at Liku. He had a picture of people on either side of the log, straining, mouths open. He shouted at them like the old man.

Fa was crawling past. She was moving slowly, deliberately as the log and the trees. Lok swung the stick at her rump with a great yell and the splintered end of the branch flew off and bounded among the trees. Fa screeched and staggered to her feet so that Lok struck again and missed. She swung round and they were standing face to face, shouting and the trees were sliding. He saw her right breast move, her arm come up, her open palm in the air, a palm somehow of importance that any moment now would become a thing he must attend to. Then the side of his face was struck by lightning that dazzled the world and the earth stood up and hit his right side a thunderous blow. He leaned against this vertical ground while the side of his face opened and shut and flames burst out of it. Fa was lying down, receding and coming close. Then she was pulling him up or down, there was solid earth under his feet again and he was hanging on to her. They were weeping and laughing at each other and the fall was roaring in the clearing while the shock head of the dead tree was climbing away into the sky, only getting larger instead of smaller. He became frightened in a detached way, he knew it would be good to get close to her. He put aside the strangeness and sleepiness of his head; he peered for her, bored at her face which kept receding like the shock-headed tree. The trees were still sliding but steadily as though it had always been their nature to do so.

He spoke to her through the mists.

'I am one of the new people.'

This made him caper. Then he walked through the clearing with what he thought was the slow swaying carriage of the new people. The picture came to him that Fa must cut off his finger. He lumbered round the clearing, trying to find her and tell her so. He found her behind the tree near the edge of the river and she was being sick. He told her about the old woman in the water but she took no notice so he went back to the broken pot and licked the traces of decaying honey off it. The figure on the ground became the old man and Lok told him that there was now an addition to the new people. Then he felt very tired so that the ground became soft and the pictures in his head went round and round. He explained to the man that now Lok must go back to the overhang but that reminded him even with his spinning head that there was no overhang any more. He began to mourn, loudly and easily and the mourning was very pleasant. He found that when he looked at the trees they slid apart and could only be induced to come together with a great effort that he was not disposed to make. All at once there was nothing but sunlight and the voice of the woodpigeons over the drone of the fall. He lay back, his eyes open, watching the strange pattern that the doubled branches made against the sky. His eyes closed themselves and he fell down as over a cliff of sleep.

William Golding *The Inheritors*

Plunder

Strong beer, a liquor extracted with very little art from wheat or barley, and *corrupted* (as it is strongly expressed by Tacitus) into a certain semblance of wine, was sufficient for the gross purposes of German debauchery. But those who had tasted the rich wines of Italy, and afterwards of Gaul, sighed for that more delicious species of intoxication. They attempted not, however (as has since been executed with so much success), to naturalize the vine on the banks of the Rhine and Danube; nor did they endeavour to procure by industry the materials of an advantageous commerce. To solicit by labour what might be ravished by arms was esteemed unworthy of the German spirit. The intemperate thirst of strong liquors often urged the barbarians to invade the provinces on which art or nature had bestowed those much envied presents. The Tuscan who betrayed his country to the Celtic nations attracted them into Italy by the prospect of the rich fruits and delicious wines, the productions of a happier climate. And in the same manner the German auxiliaries, invited into France during the civil wars of the sixteenth century, were allured by the promise of plenteous quarters in the provinces of Champagne and Burgundy. Drunkenness, the most illiberal, but not the most dangerous, of *our* vices, was sometimes capable, in a less civilized state of mankind, of occasioning a battle, a war, or a revolution.

Edward Gibbon *The History of the Decline and Fall of the Roman Empire*

Prompting

Think of the wonders uncorked by wine! It opens secrets,
gives heart to our hopes, pushes the cowardly into battle,
lifts the load from anxious minds, and evokes talents.
Thanks to the bottle's prompting no one is lost for words,
no one who's cramped by poverty fails to find release.

Horace *Book I Epistle 5*, trans. Niall Rudd

Seeing Double

Why is it that to the drunk everything seems to travel in a circle, and that as drunkenness gets more hold men cannot count objects at a distance? For this reason some make this a test of drunkenness. Is it because the vision is considerably distorted by the heat of the wine?

Aristotle *Problems*, trans. W. S. Hett

And so to Bed

In a moment he'd taken a bottle of port from among the sherry, beer, and cider which filled half a shelf inside. It was from this very bottle that Welch had, the previous evening, poured Dixon the smallest drink he'd ever been seriously offered. Some of the writing on the label was in a Romance language, but not all. Just right: not too British, and not too foreign either. The cork came out with a festive, Yule-tide pop which made him wish he had some nuts and raisins; he drank deeply. Some of the liquor coursed refreshingly down his chin and under his shirt-collar. The bottle had been about three-quarters full when he started, and was about three-quarters empty when he stopped. He thumped and clinked it back into position, wiped his mouth on the sideboard-runner, and, feeling really splendid, gained his bedroom without opposition .

It wasn't as nice in the bathroom as it had been in the bedroom. Though it was a cool night for early summer, he found he felt hot and was sweating. He stood for some time in front of the wash-basin, trying to discover more about how he felt. His body seemed swollen below the chest and uneven in density. The stuff coming from the light seemed less like light than a very thin but cloudy phosphorescent gas; it gave a creamy hum. He turned on the cold tap and bent over the basin. When he did this, he had to correct an impulse to go on leaning forward until his head lay between the taps. He wetted his face, took a bakelite mug from the glass shelf above the basin, and drank a very great deal of water, which momentarily refreshed him, though it had some other effect as well which he couldn't at once identify. He cleaned his teeth with a lot of toothpaste, wetted his face again, refilled the mug, and ate some more toothpaste.

He stood brooding by his bed. His face was heavy, as if little bags of sand had been painlessly sewn into various parts of it, dragging the features away from the bones, if he still had bones in his face. Suddenly feeling worse, he heaved a shuddering sigh. Someone seemed to have leapt nimbly up behind him and encased him in a kind of diving-suit made of invisible cotton-wool. He gave a quiet groan; he didn't want to feel any worse than this.

He began getting into bed. His four surviving cigarettes – had he really smoked twelve that evening? – lay in their packet on a polished table at the bed-head, accompanied by matches, the bakelite mug of water, and an ashtray from the mantelpiece. A temporary inability to raise his second foot on to the bed let him know what had been the secondary effect of drinking all that water: it had made him drunk. This became a primary effect when he lay in bed. On the fluttering mantelpiece was a small china effigy, the representation, in a squatting position, of a well-known Oriental religious figure. Had Welch put it there as a silent sermon to him on the merits of the contemplative life? If so, the message had come too late. He reached up and turned off the light by the hanging switch above his head. The room began to rise upwards from the right-hand bottom corner of the bed, and yet seemed to keep in the same position. He threw back the covers and sat on the edge of the bed, his legs hanging. The room composed itself to rest. After a few moments he swung his legs back and lay down. The room lifted. He put his feet to the floor. The room stayed still. He put his legs on the bed but didn't lie down. The room moved. He sat on the edge of the bed. Nothing. He put one leg up on the bed. Something. In fact a great deal. He was evidently in a highly critical condition. Swearing hoarsely, he heaped up the pillows, half-lay, half-sat against them, and dangled his legs half-over the edge of the bed. In this position he was able to lower himself gingerly into sleep.

Kingsley Amis *Lucky Jim*

Drink Me

'When I have one martini I feel bigger, wiser, taller. When I have a second, I feel superlative. When I have more there's no holding me.'

Joseph Blotner *Faulkner, A Biography*

To William Godwin

Dear Godwin, The punch after the wine made me tipsy last night – this I mention, not that my head aches, or that I felt after I quitted you, any unpleasantness, or titubancy – ; but because tipsiness has, and has always, one unpleasant effect – that of making me talk *very* extravagantly / & as when sober, I talk extravagantly enough for any *common* Tipsiness, it becomes a matter of nicety in discrimination to know when I am or am not affected. – An idea starts up in my hand [head?] – away I follow it thro' thick & thin, Wood & Marsh, Brake and Briar – with all the apparent Interest of a man who was defending one of his old and long-established Principles – Exactly of this kind was the Conversation, with which I quitted you / I do not believe it possible for a human Being to have a greater horror of the Feelings that usually accompany such principles as I then supported, or a deeper Conviction of their irrationality than myself – but the whole Thinking of my Life will not bear me up against the accidental Press & Crowd of my mind, when it is elevated beyond its natural Pitch/. –

We shall talk wiselier with the Ladies on Tuesday – God bless you, & give your dear little ones a kiss a piece for me –

The Agnus Dei & the Virgin Mary desire their kind respects to *you*, you sad Atheist – ! Your's with affectionate / Esteem

Samuel Taylor Coleridge, 3 March 1800

To Robert Southey

Dear Southey, The affair with Godwin began thus: we were talking of Reviews, & bewailing their ill-effects – I detailed *my* plan for a Review viz. to occupy regularly the 4th side of an Evening paper &c &c – adding that it had [been] a favorite scheme with me for two years past. – Godwin very coolly observed – it was a plan which 'no man who had a spark of honest pride' could join with – 'no man, not the slave of the grossest Egotism, could write in – .['] Cool and civil! – I asked whether he & most others did not already do what I proposed in *Prefaces*. – 'Aye – in *prefaces* – that is quite a different Thing. – ['] I then adverted to the extreme rudeness of the Speech with regard to myself, & added that it was not only a very rough, but likewise a very mistaken opinion / for I was nearly if not quite sure, that it had received the approbation both of you & of Wordsworth – 'Yes – Sir! just so! – of Mr Southey – just what I said – ['] and so on mōrĕ Godwiniānō – in language so ridiculously and exclusively appropriate to himself, that it would have made you merry – it was even as if he was looking into a sort of moral Looking-Glass, without knowing what it was, & seeing his own very very Godwinship, had by a merry conceit christened it in your name, not without some annexment of me & Wordsworth. – I replyed by laughing in the first place at the capricious nature of his nicety – that what was gross in folio, should become double-refined in octavo fool's cap, or *pick-pocket* Quartos – blind slavish Egotism in small pica, manly discriminating Self-respect in double primer – / modest, as Maiden's blushes, between boards, or in Calf's skin / & only not obscene in naked Sheets – and then in a deep and somewhat sarcastic Tone tried to teach him to speak more reverentially of his Betters by stating what & who they were, by whom honored – & added that I would spare him the pain of detailing, by whom depreciated. – Well! this Gust died away – I was going home to look over his Duncity – he begged me to stay till his return – about ½ an hour——I meaning to take nothing more the whole evening took a crust of Bread, & Mary Lamb made me a glass of punch of most deceitful Strength – . Instead of ½ an hour Godwin stayed an hour & a half. – In came his wife, Mrs Fenwick, and four young Ladies – & just as Godwin returned, Supper came on and it was now useless to go – – At Supper I was rather a mirth-maker than merry – I was disgusted at Heart with the grossness & vulgar Insanocaecity of this dim-headed Prig of a Philosophicide – when after Supper his ill-stars impelled him to renew the contest – I begged him for his own sake not to goad me / for that I feared, my feelings would not long remain in his [my?] power – he (to my wonder & indignation: for I had not decyphered the cause) persisted – & then as he well said I did 'thunder & lighten at him' with a vengeance, for more than an hour & a half – every effort of self-defence only made him more ridiculous – If I had been Truth in person, I could not have spoken more accurately but it was Truth in a war-chariot drawn by the Three Furies, & the Reins had slipped out of the Goddess's Hands; [as the Maid was somewhat inebriated –] & yet he did not absolutely give way, till that stinging CONTRAST which I drew between him, as a Man, a writer, & a Benefactor of Society & those of whom he had spoken so irreverently. In short, I suspect, that I seldom at any time & for so great a length of time so continuously displayed so much power; & do hope & trust, that never never did I display one half the scorn & ferocity. The next morning the moment when I awoke O mercy! I did feel like a very Wretch. I got up, & immediately wrote & sent off by a Porter, a Letter – I dare affirm, an affecting & eloquent Letter to him / & since then have been working for him / for I was heart-smitten with the recollection, that I had said all, all in the presence of his *Wife*. – But if I had known all I now know, I will not say that I should not have apologized; but most certainly I should not have made such an apology – for he confessed to Lamb that he should [not] have persisted in irritating me but that Mrs Godwin had twitted him for his prostration before me – as if he was afraid to say his Life was his own in my presence – . He admitted too, that altho' he never to the very last suspected, that I was tipsy – yet he saw clearly, that something unusual ailed me, and that I had not been my natural Self the whole evening. What a poor Creature! to attack a man who had been so kind to him, at the instigation of such a Woman! and what a woman to instigate him to quarrel with *me*, who with as much power as any, & more than most of his acquaintances had been perhaps the only one, who had never made a Butt of him – who had uniformly spoken respectfully to him – But it is past! and I trust will teach me Wisdom in future.

Samuel Taylor Coleridge, 20 February 1804

My First Dissipation

Being a little embarrassed at first, and feeling much too young to preside, I made Steerforth take the head of the table when dinner was announced, and seated myself opposite to him. Everything was very good; we did not spare the wine; and he exerted himself so brilliantly to make the thing pass off well, that there was no pause in our festivity. I was not quite such good company during dinner as I could have wished to be, for my chair was opposite the door, and my attention was distracted by observing that the handy young man went out of the room very often, and that his shadow always presented itself, immediately afterwards, on the wall of the entry, with a bottle at its mouth. The 'young gal' likewise occasioned me some uneasiness: not so much by neglecting to wash the plates, as by breaking them. For being of an inquisitive disposition, and unable to confine herself (as her positive instructions were) to the pantry, she was constantly peering in at us, and constantly imagining herself detected; in which belief, she several times retired upon the plates (with which she had carefully paved the floor), and did a great deal of destruction.

These, however, were small drawbacks, and easily forgotten when the cloth was cleared, and the dessert put on the table; at which period of the entertainment the handy young man was discovered to be speechless. Giving him private directions to seek the society of Mrs Crupp, and to remove the 'young gal' to the basement also, I abandoned myself to enjoyment.

I began, by being singularly cheerful and light-hearted; all sorts of half-forgotten things to talk about, came rushing into my mind, and made me hold forth in a most unwonted manner. I laughed heartily at my own jokes, and everybody else's; called Steerforth to order for not passing the wine; made several engagements to go to Oxford; announced that I meant to have a dinner-party exactly like that, once a week, until further notice; and madly took so much snuff out of Grainger's box, that I was obliged to go into the pantry, and have a private fit of sneezing ten minutes long.

I went on, by passing the wine faster and faster yet, and continually starting up with a corkscrew to open more wine, long before any was needed. I proposed Steerforth's health. I said he was my dearest friend, the protector of my boyhood, and the companion of my prime. I said I was delighted to propose his health. I said I owed him more obligations than I could ever repay, and held him in a higher admiration than I could ever express. I finished by saying, 'I'll give you Steerforth! God bless him! Hurrah!' We gave him three times three, and another, and a good one to finish with. I broke my glass in going round the table to shake hands with him, and I said (in two words) 'Steerforth, you'retheguidingstarofmy-existence.'

I went on, by finding suddenly that somebody was in the middle of a song. Markham was the singer, and he sang 'When the heart of a man is depressed with care.' He said, when he had sung it, he would give us 'Woman!' I took objection to that, and I couldn't allow it. I said it was not a respectful way of proposing the toast, and I would never permit that toast to be drunk in my house otherwise than as 'The Ladies!' I was very high with him, mainly I think because I saw Steerforth and Grainger laughing at me – or at him – or at both of us. He said a man was not to be dictated to. I said a man *was*. He said a man was not to be insulted, then. I said he was right there – never under my roof, where the Lares were sacred, and the laws of hospitality paramount. He said it was no derogation from a man's dignity to confess that I was a devilish good fellow. I instantly proposed his health.

Somebody was smoking. We were all smoking. *I* was smoking, and trying to suppress a rising tendency to shudder. Steerforth had made a speech about me, in the course of which I had been affected almost to tears. I returned thanks, and hoped the present company would dine with me to-morrow, and the day after – each day at five o'clock, that we might enjoy the pleasures of conversation and society through a long evening. I felt called upon to propose an individual. I would give them my aunt. Miss Betsey Trotwood, the best of her sex!

Somebody was leaning out of my bedroom window, refreshing his forehead against the cool stone of the parapet, and feeling the air upon his face. It was myself. I was addressing myself as 'Copperfield,' and saying, 'Why did you try to smoke? You might have known you couldn't do it.' Now, somebody was unsteadily contemplating his features in the looking-glass. That was I too. I was very pale in the looking-glass; my eyes had a vacant appearance; and my hair – only my hair, nothing else – looked drunk.

Charles Dickens *David Copperfield*

Proof Reading

As I say, that afternoon life with Tania never had any bad effect upon me. Once in a while I'd get too much of a skinful and I'd have to stick my finger down my throat – because it's hard to read proof when you're not all there. It requires more concentration to detect a missing comma than to epitomize Nietzsche's philosophy. You can be brilliant sometimes, when you're drunk, but brilliance is out of place in the proof-reading department. Dates, fractions, semicolons

– these are the things that count. And these are the things that are most difficult to track down when your mind is all ablaze.

Henry Miller *Tropic of Cancer*

Behind Bars

Upon the first goblet he read this inscription: Monkey wine; upon the second: lion wine; upon the third: sheep wine; upon the fourth: swine wine. These four inscriptions expressed the four descending degrees of drunkenness: the first, that which enlivens; the second, that which irritates; the third, that which stupefies; finally the last, that which brutalizes.

Victor Hugo *Les Misérables*, trans. Charles E. Wilbour

Dutch Courage

'Yes, Jeeves?'

'Sir?'

'You have the air of one about to make a remark, Jeeves.'

'Oh, no sir. I note that you are in possession of Mr Fink-Nottle's orange juice. I was merely about to observe that in my opinion it would be injudicious to add spirit to it.'

'That is a remark, Jeeves, and it is precisely – '

'Because I have already attended to the matter, sir.'

'What?'

'Yes, sir. I decided, after all, to acquiesce in your wishes.'

I stared at the man, astounded. I was deeply moved. Well, I mean, wouldn't any chap who had been going about thinking that the old feudal spirit was dead and then suddenly found it wasn't have been deeply moved?

'Jeeves,' I said, 'I am touched.'

'Thank you, sir.'

'Touched and gratified.'

'Thank you very much, sir.'

'But what caused this change of heart?'

'I chanced to encounter Mr Fink-Nottle in the garden, sir, while you were still in bed, and we had a brief conversation.'

'And you came away feeling that he needed a bracer?'

'Very much so, sir. His attitude struck me as defeatist.'

I nodded.

'I felt the same. "Defeatist" sums it up to a nicety. Did you tell him his attitude struck you as defeatist?'

'Yes, sir.'

'But it didn't do any good?'

'No, sir.'

'Very well, then, Jeeves. We must act. How much gin did you put in the jug?'

'A liberal tumberful, sir.'

'Would that be a normal dose for an adult defeatist, do you think?'

'I fancy it should prove adequate, sir.'

'I wonder. We must not spoil the ship for a ha'porth of tar. I think I'll add just another fluid ounce or so.'

'I would not advocate it, sir. In the case of Lord Brancaster's parrot – '

'You are falling into your old error, Jeeves, of thinking that Gussie is a parrot. Fight against this. I shall add the oz.'

'Very good, sir.'

'And, by the way, Jeeves, Mr Fink-Nottle is in the market for bright, clean stories to use in his speech. Do you know any?'

'I know a story about two Irishmen, sir.'

'Pat and Mike?'

'Yes, sir.'

'Who were walking along Broadway?'

'Yes, sir.'

'Just what he wants. Any more?'

'No, sir.'

'Well, every little helps. You had better go and tell it to him.'

'Very good, sir.'

He passed from the room, and I unscrewed the flask and tilted into the jug a generous modicum of its contents. And scarcely had I done so, when there came to my ears the sound of footsteps without. I had only just time to shove the jug behind the photograph of Uncle Tom on the mantelpiece before the door opened and in came Gussie, curvetting like a circus horse.

'What-ho, Bertie,' he said. 'What-ho, what-ho, what-ho, and again what-ho. What a beautiful world this is, Bertie. One of the nicest I ever met.'

I stared at him, speechless. We Woosters are as quick as lightning, and I saw at once that something had happened.

I mean to say, I told you about him walking round in circles. I recorded what passed between us on the lawn. And if I portrayed the scene with anything like adequate skill, the picture you will have retained of this Fink-Nottle will have been that of a nervous wreck, sagging at the knees, green about the gills, and picking feverishly at the lapels of his coat in an ecstasy of craven fear. In a word, defeatist. Gussie, during that interview, had, in fine, exhibited all the earmarks of one licked to a custard.

Vastly different was the Gussie who stood before me now. Self-confidence seemed to ooze from the fellow's every pore. His face was flushed, there was a jovial light in his eyes, the lips were parted in a swashbuckling smile. And when with a genial hand he sloshed me on the back before I could sidestep, it was as if I had been kicked by a mule.

'Well, Bertie,' he proceeded, as blithely as a linnet without a thing on his mind, 'you will be glad to hear that you were right. Your theory has been tested and proved correct. I feel like a fighting cock.'

My brain ceased to reel. I saw all.

'Have you been having a drink?'

'I have. As you advised. Unpleasant stuff. Like medicine. Burns your throat, too, and makes one as thirsty as the dickens. How anyone can mop it up, as you do, for pleasure beats me. Still, I would be the last to deny that it tunes up the system. I could bite a tiger.'

'What did you have?'

'Whisky. At least, that was the label on the decanter, and I have no reason to suppose that a woman like your aunt – staunch, true-blue, British – would deliberately deceive the public. If she labels her decanters Whisky, then I consider that we know where we are.'

'A whisky and soda, eh? You couldn't have done better.'

'Soda?' said Gussie thoughtfully. 'I knew there was something I had forgotten.'

'Didn't you put any soda in it?'

'It never occurred to me. I just nipped into the dining-room and drank out of the decanter.'

'How much?'

'Oh, about ten swallows. Twelve, maybe. Or fourteen. Say sixteen medium-sized gulps. Gosh, I'm thirsty.'

He moved over to the wash-hand stand and drank deeply out of the water bottle. I cast a covert glance at Uncle Tom's photograph behind his back. For the first time since it had come into my life, I was glad that it was so large. It hid its secret well. If Gussie had caught sight of that jug of orange juice, he would unquestionably have been on to it like a knife.

'Well, I'm glad you're feeling braced,' I said.

He moved buoyantly from the wash-stand, and endeavoured to slosh me on the back again. Foiled by my nimble footwork, he staggered to the bed and sat down upon it.

'Braced? Did I say I could bite a tiger?'

'You did.'

'Make it two tigers. I could chew holes in a steel door. What an ass you must have thought me out there in the garden. I see now you were laughing in your sleeve.'

'No, no.'

'Yes,' insisted Gussie. 'That very sleeve,' he said, pointing. 'And I don't blame you. I can't imagine why I made all that fuss about a potty job like distributing prizes at a rotten little country grammar school. Can you imagine, Bertie?'

'No.'

'Exactly. Nor can I imagine. There's simply nothing to it. I just shin up on the platform, drop a few gracious words, hand the little blighters their prizes, and hop down again, admired by all. Not a suggestion of split trousers from start to finish. I mean, why should anybody split his trousers? I can't imagine. Can you imagine?'

'No.'

'Nor can I imagine. I shall be a riot. I know just the sort of stuff that's needed – simple, manly, optimistic stuff straight from the shoulder. This shoulder,' said Gussie, tapping. 'Why I was so nervous this morning I can't imagine. For anything simpler than distributing a few footling books to a bunch of grimy-faced kids I can't imagine. Still, for some reason I can't imagine, I was feeling a little nervous, but now I feel fine, Bertie – fine, fine, fine – and I say this to you as an old friend. Because that's what you are, old man, when all the smoke has cleared away – an old friend. I don't think I've ever met an older friend. How long have you been an old friend of mine, Bertie?'

'Oh, years and years.'

'Imagine! Though, of course, there must have been a time when you were a new friend. . . . Hullo, the luncheon gong. Come on, old friend.'

And, rising from the bed like a performing flea, he made for the door.

I followed rather pensively. What had occurred was, of course, so much velvet, as you might say. I mean, I had wanted a braced Fink-Nottle – indeed, all my plans had had a braced Fink-Nottle as their end and aim – but I found myself wondering a little whether the Fink-Nottle now sliding down the banister wasn't, perhaps, a shade too braced. His demeanour seemed to me that of a man who might easily throw bread about at lunch.

Fortunately, however, the settled gloom of those round him exercised a restraining effect upon him at the table. It would have needed a far more plastered man to have been rollicking at such a gathering. I had told the Bassett that there were aching hearts in Brinkley Court, and it now looked probable that there would shortly be aching tummies. Anatole, I learned, had retired to his bed with a fit of the vapours, and the meal now before us had been cooked by the kitchen maid – as C3 a performer as ever wielded a skillet.

This, coming on top of their other troubles, induced in the company a pretty unanimous silence – a solemn stillness, as you might say – which even Gussie did not seem prepared to break. Except, therefore, for one short snatch of song on his part, nothing untoward marked the occasion, and presently we rose, with instructions from Aunt Dahlia to put on festal raiment and be at Market Snodsbury not later than 3.30. This leaving me ample time to smoke a gasper or two in a shady bower beside the lake, I did so, repairing to my room round about the hour of three.

Jeeves was on the job, adding the final polish to the old topper, and I was about to apprise him of the latest developments in the matter of Gussie, when he forestalled me by observing that the latter had only just concluded an agreeable visit to the Wooster bed-chamber.

'I found Mr Fink-Nottle seated here when I arrived to lay out your clothes, sir.'

'Indeed, Jeeves? Gussie was in here, was he?'

'Yes, sir. He left only a few moments ago. He is driving to the school with Mr and Mrs Travers in the large car.'

'Did you give him your story of the two Irishmen?'

'Yes, sir. He laughed heartily.'

'Good. Had you any other contributions for him?'

'I ventured to suggest that he might mention to the young gentlemen that education is a drawing out, not a putting in. The late Lord Brancaster was much addicted to presenting prizes at schools, and he invariably employed this dictum.'

'And how did he react to that?'

'He laughed heartily, sir.'

'This surprised you, no doubt? This practically incessant merriment, I mean.'

'Yes, sir.'

'You thought it odd in one who, when you last saw him, was well up in Group A of the defeatists.'

'Yes, sir.'

'There is a ready explanation, Jeeves. Since you last saw him, Gussie has been on a bender. He's as tight as an owl.'

'Indeed, sir?'

'Absolutely. His nerve cracked under the strain, and he sneaked into the dining-room and started mopping the stuff up like a vacuum cleaner. Whisky would seem to be what he filled the radiator with. I gather that he used up most of the decanter. Golly, Jeeves, it's lucky he didn't get at that laced orange juice on top of that, what?'

'Extremely, sir.'

I eyed the jug. Uncle Tom's photograph had fallen into the fender, and it was standing there right out in the open, where Gussie couldn't have helped seeing it. Mercifully, it was empty now.

'It was a most prudent act on your part, if I may say so, sir, to dispose of the orange juice.'

I stared at the man.

'What? Didn't you?'

'No, sir.'

'Jeeves, let us get this clear. Was it not you who threw away that o.j.?'

'No, sir. I assumed, when I entered the room and found the pitcher empty, that you had done so.'

We looked at each other, awed. Two minds with but a single thought.

'I very much fear, sir – '

'So do I, Jeeves.'

'It would seem almost certain – '

'Quite certain. Weigh the facts. Sift the evidence. The jug was standing on the mantelpiece, for all eyes to behold. Gussie had been complaining of thirst. You found him in here, laughing heartily. I think that there can be little doubt, Jeeves, that the entire contents of that jug are at this moment reposing on top of the existing cargo in that already brilliantly lit man's interior. Disturbing, Jeeves.'

'Most disturbing, sir.'

'Let us face the position, forcing ourselves to be calm. You inserted in that jug – shall we say a tumblerful of the right stuff?'

'Fully a tumblerful, sir.'

'And I added of my plenty about the same amount.'

'Yes, sir.'

'And in two shakes of a duck's tail Gussie, with all that lapping about inside him, will be distributing the prizes at Market

Snodsbury Grammar School before an audience of all that is fairest and most refined in the county.'

'Yes, sir.'

'It seems to me, Jeeves, that the ceremony may be one fraught with considerable interest.'

'Yes, sir.'

'What, in your opinion, will the harvest be?'

'One finds it difficult to hazard a conjecture, sir.'

'You mean imagination boggles?'

'Yes, sir.'

I inspected my imagination. He was right. It boggled.

P. G. Wodehouse *Right Ho, Jeeves*

Chronic

More punch, more enthusiasm, more speeches. Everybody's health is drunk, saving the youngest gentleman's in company. He sits apart, with his elbow on the back of a vacant chair, and glares disdainfully at Jinkins. Gander, in a convulsing speech, gives them the health of Bailey junior; hiccups are heard; and a glass is broken. Mr Jinkins feels that it is time to join the ladies. He proposes, as a final sentiment, Mrs Todgers. She is worthy to be remembered separately. Hear, hear. So she is: no doubt of it. They all find fault with her at other times; but every man feels, now, that he could die in her defence.

They go upstairs, where they are not expected so soon; for Mrs Todgers is asleep, Miss Charity is adjusting her hair, and Mercy, who has made a sofa of one of the window-seats, is in a gracefully recumbent attitude. She is rising hastily, when Mr Jinkins implores her, for all their sakes, not to stir; she looks too graceful and too lovely, he remarks, to be disturbed. She laughs, and yields, and fans herself, and drops her fan, and there is a rush to pick it up. Being now installed, by one consent, as the beauty of the party, she is cruel and capricious, and sends gentlemen on messages to other gentlemen, and forgets all about them before they can return with the answer, and invents a thousand tortures, rending their hearts to pieces. Bailey brings up the tea and coffee. There is a small cluster of admirers round Charity; but they are only those who cannot get near her sister. The youngest gentleman in company is pale, but collected, and still sits apart; for his spirit loves to hold communion with itself, and his soul recoils from noisy revellers. She has a consciousness of his presence and adoration. He sees it flashing sometimes in the corner of her eye. Have a care, Jinkins, ere you provoke a desperate man to frenzy!

Mr Pecksniff had followed his younger friends upstairs, and taken a chair at the side of Mrs Todgers. He had also spilt a cup of coffee over his legs without appearing to be aware of the circumstance; nor did he seem to know that there was muffin on his knee.

'And how have they used you downstairs, sir?' asked the hostess.

'Their conduct has been such, my dear madam,' said Mr Pecksniff, 'as I can never think of without emotion, or remember without a tear. Oh, Mrs Todgers!'

'My goodness!' exclaimed that lady. 'How low you are in your spirits, sir!'

'I am a man, my dear madam,' said Mr Pecksniff, shedding tears, and speaking with an imperfect articulation, 'but I am also a father. I am also a widower. My feelings, Mrs Todgers, will not consent to be entirely smothered, like the young children in the Tower. They are grown up, and the more I press the bolster on them, the more they look round the corner of it.'

He suddenly became conscious of the bit of muffin, and stared at it intently: shaking his head the while, in a forlorn and imbecile manner, as if he regarded it as his evil genius, and mildly reproached it.

'She was beautiful, Mrs Todgers,' he said, turning his glazed eye again upon her, without the least preliminary notice. 'She had a small property.'

'So I have heard,' cried Mrs Todgers with great sympathy.

'Those are her daughters,' said Mr Pecksniff, pointing out the young ladies, with increased emotion.

Mrs Todgers had no doubt of it.

'Mercy and Charity,' said Mr Pecksniff, 'Charity and Mercy. Not unholy names, I hope?'

'Mr Pecksniff!' cried Mrs Todgers. 'What a ghastly smile! Are you ill, sir?'

He pressed his hand upon her arm, and answered in a solemn manner, and a faint voice, 'Chronic.'

'Cholic?' cried the frightened Mrs Todgers.

'Chron-ic,' he repeated with some difficulty. 'Chron-ic. A chronic disorder. I have been its victim from childhood. It is carrying me to my grave.'

'Heaven forbid!' cried Mrs Todgers.

'Yes, it is,' said Mr Pecksniff, reckless with despair. 'I am rather glad of it, upon the whole. You are like her, Mrs Todgers.'

'Don't squeeze me so tight, pray, Mr Pecksniff. If any of the gentlemen should notice us.'

'For her sake,' said Mr Pecksniff. 'Permit me. In honour of her memory. For the sake of a voice from the tomb. You are *very* like her, Mrs Todgers! What a world this is!'

'Ah! Indeed you may say that!' cried Mrs Todgers.

'I'm afraid it is a vain and thoughtless world,' said Mr Pecksniff, overflowing with despondency. 'These young people about us. Oh! what sense have they of their responsibilities? None. Give me your other hand, Mrs Todgers.'

That lady hesitated, and said 'she didn't like.'

'Has a voice from the grave no influence?' said Mr Pecksniff, with dismal tenderness. 'This is irreligious! My dear creature.'

'Hush!' urged Mrs Todgers. 'Really you mustn't.'

'It's not me,' said Mr Pecksniff. 'Don't suppose it's me: it's the voice; it's her voice.'

Mrs Pecksniff deceased, must have had an unusually thick and husky voice for a lady, and rather a stuttering voice, and to say the truth somewhat of a drunken voice, if it had ever borne much resemblance to that in which Mr Pecksniff spoke just then. But perhaps this was delusion on his part.

'It has been a day of enjoyment, Mrs Todgers, but still it has been a day of torture. It has reminded me of my loneliness. What am I in the world?'

'An excellent gentleman, Mr Pecksniff,' said Mrs Todgers.

'There is consolation in that too,' cried Mr Pecksniff. 'Am I?'

'There is no better man living,' said Mrs Todgers, 'I am sure.'

Mr Pecksniff smiled through his tears, and slightly shook his head. 'You are very good,' he said, 'thank you. It is a great happiness to me, Mrs Todgers, to make young people happy. The happiness of my pupils is my chief object. I dote upon 'em. They dote upon me too. Sometimes.'

'Always,' said Mrs Todgers.

'When they say they haven't improved, ma'am,' whispered Mr Pecksniff, looking at her with profound mystery, and motioning to her to advance her ear a little closer to his mouth. 'When they say they haven't improved, ma'am, and the premium was too high, they lie! I shouldn't wish it to be mentioned; you will understand me; but I say to you as to an old friend, they lie.'

'Base wretches they must be!' said Mrs Todgers.

'Madam,' said Mr Pecksniff, 'you are right. I respect you for that observation. A word in your ear. To Parents and Guardians. This is in confidence, Mrs Todgers?'

'The strictest, of course!' cried that lady.

'To Parents and Guardians,' repeated Mr Pecksniff. 'An eligible opportunity now offers, which unites the advantages of the best practical architectural education with the comforts of a home, and the constant association with some, who, however humble their sphere and limited their capacity – observe! – are not unmindful of their moral responsibilities.'

Mrs Todgers looked a little puzzled to know what this might mean, as well she might; for it was, as the reader may perchance remember, Mr Pecksniff's usual form of advertisement when he wanted a pupil; and seemed to have no particular reference, at present, to anything. But Mr Pecksniff held up his finger as a caution to her not to interrupt him.

'Do you know any parent or guardian, Mrs Todgers,' said Mr Pecksniff, 'who desires to avail himself of such an opportunity for a young gentleman? An orphan would be preferred. Do you know of any orphan with three or four hundred pound?'

Mrs Todgers reflected, and shook her head.

'When you hear of an orphan with three or four hundred pound,' said Mr Pecksniff,' let that dear orphan's friends apply, by letter post-paid, to S. P., Post Office, Salisbury. I don't know who he is, exactly. Don't be alarmed, Mrs Todgers,' said Mr Pecksniff, falling heavily against her: 'Chronic – chronic! Let's have a little drop of something to drink.'

'Bless my life, Miss Pecksniffs!' cried Mrs Todgers, aloud, 'your dear pa's took very poorly!'

Mr Pecksniff straightened himself by a surprising effort, as every one turned hastily toward him; and standing on his feet, regarded the assembly with a look of ineffable wisdom. Gradually it gave place to a smile; a feeble, helpless, melancholy smile; bland, almost to sickliness. 'Do not repine, my friends,' said Mr Pecksniff, tenderly. 'Do not weep for me. It is chronic.' And with these words, after making a futile attempt to pull off his shoes, he fell into the fireplace.

The youngest gentleman in company had him out in a second. Yes, before a hair upon his head was singed, he had him on the hearth-rug. – Her father!

She was almost beside herself. So was her sister. Jinkins consoled them both. They all consoled them. Everybody had something to say, except the youngest gentleman in company, who with a noble self-devotion did the heavy work, and held up Mr Pecksniff's head without being taken notice of by anybody. At last they gathered round, and agreed to carry him upstairs to bed. The youngest gentleman in company was rebuked by Jinkins for tearing Mr Pecksniff's coat! Ha, ha! But no matter.

They carried him upstairs, and crushed the youngest gentleman at every step. His bedroom was at the top of the house, and it was a long way; but they got him there in course of time. He asked them frequently on the road for a little drop of something to drink. It seemed an idiosyncrasy. The youngest gentleman in company proposed a draught of water. Mr Pecksniff called him opprobrious names for the suggestion.

Jinkins and Gander took the rest upon themselves, and made him as comfortable as they could, on the outside of his bed; and when he seemed disposed to sleep, they left him. But before they had all gained the bottom of the staircase, a vision of Mr Pecksniff, strangely attired, was seen to flutter on the top landing. He desired to collect their sentiments, it seemed, upon the nature of human life.

'My friends,' cried Mr Pecksniff, looking over the banisters, 'let us improve our minds by mutual inquiry and discussion. Let us be moral. Let us contemplate existence. Where is Jinkins?'

'Here,' cried that gentleman. 'Go to bed again!'

'To bed!' said Mr Pecksniff. 'Bed! 'Tis the voice of the sluggard, I hear him complain, you have woke me too soon, I must slumber again. If any young orphan will repeat the remainder of that simple piece from Doctor Watt's collection an eligible opportunity now offers.'

Nobody volunteered.

'This is very soothing,' said Mr Pecksniff, after a pause. 'Extremely so. Cool and refreshing; particularly to the legs! The legs of the human subject, my friends, are a beautiful production. Compare them with wooden legs, and observe the difference between the anatomy of nature and the anatomy of art. Do you know,' said Mr Pecksniff, leaning over the banisters, with an odd recollection of his familiar manner among new pupils at home, 'that I should very much like to see Mrs Todgers's notion of a wooden leg, if perfectly agreeable to herself!'

As it appeared impossible to entertain any reasonable hopes of him after this speech, Mr Jinkins and Mr Gander went upstairs again, and once more got him into bed. But they had not descended to the second floor before he was out again; nor, when they had repeated the process, had they descended the first flight, before he was out again. In a word, as often as he was shut up in his own room, he darted out afresh, charged with some new moral sentiment, which he continually repeated over the banisters, with extraordinary relish, and an irrepressible desire for the improvement of his fellow creatures that nothing could subdue.

Under these circumstances, when they had got him into bed for the thirtieth time or so, Mr Jinkins held him, while his companion went downstairs in search of Bailey junior, with whom he presently returned. That youth, having been apprised of the service required of him, was in great spirits, and brought up a stool, a candle, and his supper; to the end that he might keep watch outside the bedroom door with tolerable comfort.

Charles Dickens *Martin Chuzzlewit*

SIDE-EFFECTS

The Hellenistic Period

The wine, the toasts that could not be refused,
 her drowsy, trusting love for him,
lulled Aglaonice to sleep. She gives
 to Venus tokens of her first
surrender – dripping still with scent, and won
 with ease, her sandals and the band
that yielded her breasts – as witnesses
 of how she slept, and what he took from her.

Hedylos, trans. Adrian Wright

Sow's Ear

It was now a pleasant evening in the latter end of June, when our hero was walking in a most delicious grove, where the gentle breezes fanning the leaves, together with the sweet trilling of a murmuring stream, and the melodious notes of nightingales, formed all together the most enchanting harmony. In this scene, so sweetly accommodated to love, he meditated on his dear Sophia. While his wanton fancy roved unbounded over all her beauties, and his lively imagination painted the charming maid in various ravishing forms, his warm heart melted with tenderness, and at length throwing himself on the ground, by the side of a gently murmuring brook, he broke forth into the following ejaculation.

'Oh Sophia, would Heaven give thee to my arms, how blest would be my condition! Curst be that fortune which sets a distance between us. Was I but possessed of thee, one only suit of rags thy whole estate, is there a man on earth whom I would envy! How contemptible would the brightest Circassian beauty, drest in all the jewels of the Indies, appear to my eyes! But why do I mention another woman? Could I think my eyes capable of looking at any other with tenderness, these hands should tear them from my head.

No, my Sophia, if cruel fortune separates us for ever, my soul shall doat on thee alone. The chastest constancy will I ever preserve to thy image. Though I should never have possession of thy charming person, still shalt thou alone have possession of my thoughts, my love, my soul. Oh! my fond heart is so wrapt in that tender bosom, that the brightest beauties would for me have no charms, nor would a hermit be colder in their embraces. Sophia, Sophia alone shall be mine. What raptures are in that name! I will engrave it on every tree.'

At these words he started up, and beheld – not his Sophia – no, nor a Circassian maid richly and elegantly attired for the Grand Signior's seraglio. No; without a gown, in a shift that was somewhat of the coarsest, and none of the cleanest, bedewed likewise with some odoriferous effluvia, the produce of the day's labour, with a pitch-fork in her hand, Molly Seagrim approached. Our hero had his penknife in his hand, which he had drawn for the beforementioned purpose, of carving on the bark; when the girl coming near him, cry'd out with a smile, 'You don't intend to kill me, squire, I hope!' 'Why should you think I would kill you?' answered Jones. 'Nay,' replied she, 'after your cruel usage of me when I saw you last, killing me would, perhaps, be too great kindness for me to expect.'

Here ensued a parly, which, as I do not think myself obliged to relate, I shall omit. It is sufficient that it lasted a full quarter of an hour, at the conclusion of which they retired into the thickest part of the grove.

Some of my readers may be inclined to think this event unnatural. However, the fact is true; and, perhaps, may be sufficiently accounted for, by suggesting, that Jones probably thought one woman better than none, and Molly as probably imagined two men to be better than one. Besides the beforementioned motive assigned to the present behaviour of Jones, the reader will be likewise pleased to recollect in his favour, that he was not at this time perfect master of that wonderful power of reason, which so well enables grave and wise men to subdue their unruly passions, and to decline any of these prohibited amusements. Wine now had totally subdued this power in Jones. He was, indeed, in a condition, in which if reason had interposed, though only to advise, she might have received the answer which one Cleostratus gave many years ago to a silly fellow, who asked him if he was not ashamed to be drunk? 'Are not you,' said Cleostratus, 'ashamed to admonish a drunken man?' – To say the truth, in a court of justice, drunkenness must not be an excuse, yet in a court of conscience it is greatly so; and therefore Aristotle, who commends the laws of Pittacus, by which drunken men received double punishment for their crimes, allows there is more of policy than justice in that law. Now, if there are any transgressions pardonable from drunkenness, they are certainly such as Mr Jones was at present guilty of; on which head I could pour forth a vast profusion of learning, if I imagined it would either entertain my reader, or teach him anything more than he knows already. For his sake, therefore, I shall keep my learning to myself, and return to my history.

Henry Fielding *Tom Jones*

Drinking Song

He became more and more drunk
As the afternoon wore off.

Adrian Henri

Franglais

(Rap)

I should have had the savoir faire
To find out who you were
Before our affaire
Avait commencé.
Before I got turned on
by the Dom Perignon

I should have stopped to penser.

Ha Ha! Qui Moi? Tu m'aimes? Pourquoi?

Should have had more sang froid.
The night we enjoyed
What Freud
called the Auld Alliance.
Known your sexy joie de vivre
was toujours half seas ivre
a mere alcoholic compliance.

Ha Ha! Qui Moi? Tu m'aimes? Pourquoi?

Nouveau Beaujolais is thrilling
and Calvados is chilling.
The spirit makes you willing –
but it hampers . . .
The only objét trouvé
I could find under your duvet
was encore une bouteille de champers.

Ha Ha! Qui Moi? Tu m'aimes? Pourquoi?

If we hadn't mixed the grape and grain
we'd per'aps have come again
(amour is main-
ly for the frisky)
Oh, we'd've been tête a tête yet
If I hadn't let
you pour the nineteenth le scotch whisky.

Ha Ha! Qui Moi? Tu m'aimes? Pourquoi?

So I must say Au Revoir –
Tout fed up with Pas-Ce-Soir
I've-'ad-Far-Too-Much-to-Boire,

Josephine.
If we'd only stuck to Perrier . . .
You'd have loved me more and merrier
If that Vat Soixante-Neuf had not been
so beau . . . beauc . . . beaucoup your scene!

Liz Lochhead

Oozing Confidence

I restarted the car and began nipping home the back way. The Fiasco feels better on these side streets, where it can show off its acceleration. Then I noticed that a car was following me. I wasn't just being paranoid. It really was following me. It was flashing its lights and parping its horn and generally making with all the swear-words and V-signs in the motoring repertoire. I put my foot on the floor and jumped a junction or two at top speed. I must have been going flat out when the car stopped following me. It overtook me instead.

'Would you like to get out of the car, sir?'

The pigs, the fucking *pigs*. 'Sure,' I said, and climbed out. Annoyingly, I tripped and came a cropper on the kerb. But I got up again as quick as you like and dusted myself down, oozing confidence.

'Been drinking today, sir?'

I was ready for this, of course. Absolutely no problem at all. Over the years I've honed down the perfect answer to that question, and I let the pig have it pat. 'Ah now let me see,' I said, sonorously. 'I had a champagne perry and blackcurrant before lunch and, yeah, a glass of stout with my mutton vindaloo.' It's a good one, isn't it. None of this two-glasses-of-wine stuff. No, you see, the key to the whole gimmick is to confess quite cheerfully to a couple of unserious, feminine tipples, while at the same time deterring the law from smelling your breath. It's a *good* one, isn't it.

'Beg your pardon, sir? Here, Steve – it's not bad going, is it, for three o'clock in the afternoon?'

Annoyingly, I had fallen over again and was having a real spot of bother finding my feet.

'Would you like to come down to the station, sir, and have another go at saying that? Here, Steve, come on. Looks like we got a dead one.'

Martin Amis *Money*

Rough Seas

SEREZHA: (*After a longish pause*)
You think all men are brutes. We are.

SASHKA:
Not all of them. Just some of them.
I'm very fond of you,
(*Pause.*)
so *there.*
Let's get your trousers off and then
you'll see how much I fancy you.

(SEREZHA *kneels and* SASHKA *busies herself with his waistband and belt. The door bursts open and, after an interval,* SASHKA'S HUSBAND *enters, exits, and re-enters again. He is completely drunk and staggering like someone in a storm at sea.* SEREZHA *makes as if to go, but* SASHKA *puts a hand over his mouth and indicates they should watch the performance. Throughout his 'speech', the* HUSBAND *undresses clumsily, while* SEREZHA *gets into clothes behind him.*)

HUSBAND:
Mayday. Rough seas. Abandon ship.
This is your capstan calling all crew:
all hands on dick; all hands on dick.
(*Silent convulsed laughter at his own joke.*)
Women with chilblains first.
(*Delighted laughter ending in a coughing fit.*)
Oh dear . . .
Man the wifebelts.
(*Struggles into a corset of* SASHKA'*s and falls.*)

Man overboard.
He's in the drink.

(*More wheezing laughter.*)

He's in . . .

(*Convulsed again.*)

I'll steer.

(*Gets to his feet and mimics a helmsman.*)

Whoops! You'd need to be a whore
to handle all these prongs.

(*Loud belch.*)

Ale-force ten.
Oooh! fire amidships.

(*Ruefully pats stomach.*)

SASHKA: (*Clears her throat and coughs loudly.*)

HUSBAND: Pardon.

(*He freezes, then slowly unfreezes, picks up his shoes, and exits unsteadily, keeping his back to the bed, without another word.*)

SEREZHA:

I have to go. I can't stay now.

HUSBAND: (*Off.*)

Aye-aye, scupper.

SASHKA:

No, please stay.
Husbands! I could . . .

(*Makes strangling gesture.*)

HUSBAND: (*Off.*)

And there she blows!

SEREZHA:

Another night.

SASHKA:

I'll see you on the way.
Hang on. I'll just slip on a dress.

SEREZHA:

No, don't. You'll

(*Pause.*)

catch your death of cold.

(*Attempts to kiss her goodbye.*)

SASHKA: (*Seriously.*)

Then go.

(*Turns away from his kiss.*)

(*Exit* SEREZHA.)

SASHKA: (*Plaintively to the open door and the room in general*)
But don't you lose my address.

Craig Raine *The Electrification of the Soviet Union*

Was It the Cockles?

27 February 1821. Last night I suffered horribly – from an indigestion, I believe. I *never* sup – that is, never at home. But, last night, I was prevailed upon by the Countess Gamba's persuasion, and the strenuous example of her brother, to swallow, at supper, a quantity of boiled cockles, and to dilute them, *not* reluctantly, with some Imola wine. When I came home, apprehensive of the consequences, I swallowed three or four glasses of spirits, which men (the venders) call brandy, rum, or Hollands, but which Gods would entitle spirits of wine, coloured or sugared. All was pretty well till I got to bed, when I became somewhat swollen and considerably vertiginous. I got out, and mixing some soda-powders, drank them off. This brought on temporary relief. I returned to bed; but grew sick and sorry once and again. Took more soda-water. At last I fell into a dreary sleep. Woke, and was ill all day, till I had galloped a few miles. Query – was it the cockles, or what I took to correct them, that caused the commotion? I think both. I remarked in my illness the complete inertion, inaction, and destruction of my chief mental faculties. I tried to rouse them, and yet could not – and this is the *Soul*!!! I should believe that it was married to the body, if they did not sympathize so much with each other. If the one rose, when the other fell, it would be a sign that they longed for the natural state of divorce. But as it is, they seem to draw together like post-horses.

Lord Byron *Journal*

It Was the Excitement

Tuesday, 29 July 1947. 'It is not Christmas upsets the children but what they eat.' In this way, too, I explain the three or four days suffering which follow my rare visits to London. The symptoms are constant; insomnia, a disordered stomach, weakness at the knees, a trembling hand which becomes evident when I attempt to use the pen. They are at their worst on the day after my return home. I tell myself I have drunk too much, smoked too much and kept late hours. But I grow sceptical of this glib excuse. On this last occasion for instance, 23 July, I had an easy train journey as far as bodily comfort was concerned. I drank perhaps three cocktails before luncheon, lunched lightly, took things easy in the afternoon, drank perhaps three cocktails before dinner. From then onwards I drank fairly steadily – champagne, with a little brandy at the end of dinner – until four o'clock; but I doubt whether in those eight hours I consumed more than a bottle and a half. Next day I began drinking at eleven and drank two glasses of brandy and ginger ale, later two glasses of gin, and at luncheon practically nothing – half a glass of white Bordeaux and two tiny glasses of port. This is not enough to make a healthy middle-aged man ill for four days. No, it is the excitement –

Evelyn Waugh *Diaries*

It Was the Salmon

Eleven – twelve – one o'clock had struck, and the gentlemen had not arrived. Consternation sat on every face. Could they have been waylaid and robbed? Should they send men and lanterns in every direction by which they could be supposed likely to have travelled home? or should they – Hark! there they were. What could have made them so late? A strange voice, too! To whom could it belong? They rushed into the kitchen whither the truants had repaired, and at once obtained rather more than a glimmering of the real state of the case.

Mr Pickwick, with his hands in his pockets and his hat cocked completely over his left eye, was leaning against the dresser, shaking his head from side to side, and producing a constant succession of the blandest and most benevolent smiles without being moved thereunto by any discernible cause or pretence whatsoever; old Mr Wardle, with a highly-inflamed countenance, was grasping the hand of a strange gentleman muttering protestations of eternal friendship; Mr Winkle, supporting himself by the eight-day clock, was feebly invoking destruction upon the head of any member of the family who should suggest the propriety of his retiring for the night; and Mr Snodgrass had sunk into a chair, with an expression of the most abject and hopeless misery that the human mind can imagine, portrayed in every lineament of his expressive face.

'Is anything the matter?' inquired the three ladies.

'Nothing the matter,' replied Mr Pickwick. 'We – we're – all right. – I say, Wardle, we're all right, an't we?'

'I should think so,' replied the jolly host. – 'My dears, here's my friend, Mr Jingle – Mr Pickwick's friend, Mr Jingle, come 'pon – little visit.'

'Is anything the matter with Mr Snodgrass, sir?' inquired Emily, with great anxiety.

'Nothing the matter, ma'am,' replied the stranger. 'Cricket dinner – glorious party – capital songs – old port – claret – good – very good – wine, ma'am – wine.'

'It wasn't the wine,' murmured Mr Snodgrass, in a broken voice. 'It was the salmon.' (Somehow or other, it never *is* the wine, in these cases.)

'Hadn't they better go to bed, ma'am?' inquired Emma. 'Two of the boys will carry the gentlemen upstairs.'

'I won't go to bed,' said Mr Winkle, firmly.

'No living boy shall carry me,' said Mr Pickwick, stoutly; – and he went on smiling as before.

'Hurrah!' gasped Mr Winkle, faintly.

'Hurrah!' echoed Mr Pickwick, taking off his hat and dashing it on the floor, and insanely casting his spectacles into the middle of the kitchen. – At this humorous feat he laughed outright.

'Let's – have – 'nother – bottle,' cried Mr Winkle, commencing in a very loud key, and ending in a very faint one. His head dropped upon his breast; and, muttering his invincible determination not to go to his bed, and a sanguinary regret that he had not 'done for old Tupman' in the morning, he fell fast asleep; in which condition he was borne to his apartment by two young giants under the personal superintendence of the fat boy, to whose protecting care Mr Snodgrass shortly afterwards confided his own person. Mr Pickwick accepted the proffered arm of Mr Tupman and quietly disappeared, smiling more than ever; and Mr Wardle, after taking as affectionate a leave of the whole family as if he were ordered for immediate execution, consigned to Mr Trundle the honour of conveying him upstairs, and retired, with a very futile attempt to look impressively solemn and dignified.

'What a shocking scene!' said the spinster aunt.

'Dis – gusting!' ejaculated both the young ladies.

'Dreadful – dreadful!' said Jingle, looking very grave: he was about a bottle and a half ahead of any of his companions. 'Horrid spectacle – very!'

'What a nice man!' whispered the spinster aunt to Mr Tupman.

'Good-looking, too!' whispered Emily Wardle.

'Oh, decidedly,' observed the spinster aunt.

Charles Dickens *The Pickwick Papers*

It Was the Mixture

It was shortly before midnight in early March; I had been entertaining the college intellectuals to mulled claret; the fire was roaring, the air of my room heavy with smoke and spice, and my mind weary with metaphysics. I threw open my windows and from the quad outside came the not uncommon sounds of bibulous laughter and unsteady steps. A voice said: 'Hold up'; another, 'Come on'; another, 'Plenty of time . . . House . . . till Tom stops ringing'; and another, clearer than the rest, 'D'you know I feel most unaccountably unwell. I must leave you a minute,' and there appeared at my window the face I knew to be Sebastian's, but not, as I had formerly seen it, alive and alight with gaiety; he looked at me for a moment with unfocused eyes and then, leaning forward well into the room, he was sick.

It was not unusual for dinner parties to end in that way; there was in fact a recognized tariff for the scout on such occasions; we were all learning, by trial and error, to carry our wine. There was also a kind of insane and endearing orderliness about Sebastian's choice, in his extremity, of an open window. But, when all is said, it remained an unpropitious meeting.

His friends bore him to the gate and, in a few minutes, his host, an amiable Etonian of my year, returned to apologize. He, too, was tipsy and his explanations were repetitive and, towards the end, tearful. 'The wines were too various,' he said: 'it was neither the quality nor the quantity that was at fault. It was the mixture. Grasp that and you have the root of the matter. To understand all is to forgive all.'

Evelyn Waugh *Brideshead Revisited*

Small Tudor Windows

My readers . . . Sometimes I imagine them, sullen fleshy inarticulate men, stockbrokers, sellers of goods, living in thirty-year-old detached houses among the golf courses of Outer London, husbands of ageing and bitter wives they first seduced to Artie Shaw's 'Begin the Beguine' or The Squadronaires' 'The Nearness of You'; fathers of cold-eyed lascivious daughters on the pill, to whom Ramsay Macdonald is coeval with Rameses II, and cannabis-smoking jeans-and-bearded Stuart-haired sons whose oriental contempt for bread is equalled only by their insatiable demand for it; men in whom a pile of scratched coverless 78s in the attic can awaken memories of vomiting blindly from small Tudor windows to Muggsy Spanier's 'Sister Kate'.

Philip Larkin *All What Jazz*

The Orifice of the Throat

That same afternoon I was sitting on a stool in an intoxicated condition in Grogan's licensed premises. Adjacent stools bore the forms of Brinsley and Kelly, my two true friends. The three of us were occupied in putting glasses of stout into the interior of our bodies and expressing by fine disputation the resulting sense of physical and mental well-being. In my thigh pocket I had eleven and eightpence in a weighty pendulum of mixed coins. Each of the arranged bottles on the the shelves before me, narrow or squat-bellied, bore a dull picture of the gas bracket. Who can tell the stock of a public-house? Many no doubt are dummies, those especially within an arm-reach of the snug. The stout was of superior quality, soft against the tongue but sharp upon the orifice of the throat, softly efficient in its magical circulation through the conduits of the body. Half to myself, I said:

Do not let us forget that I have to buy *Die Harzreise*. Do not let us forget that.

Harzreise, said Brinsley. There is a house in Dalkey called Heartrise.

Brinsley then put his dark chin on the cup of a palm and leaned in thought on the counter, overlooking his drink, gazing beyond the frontier of the world.

What about another jar? said Kelly.

Ah, Lesbia, said Brinsley. The finest thing I ever wrote. How many kisses, Lesbia, you ask, would serve to sate this hungry love of mine? – As many as the Libyan sands that bask along Cyrene's shore where pine-trees wave, where burning Jupiter's untended shrine lies near to old King Battus' sacred grave:

Three stouts, called Kelly.

Let them be endless as the stars at night, that stare upon the lovers in a ditch – so often would lover-crazed Catullus bite your burning lips, that prying eyes should not have power to count, nor evil tongues bewitch, the frenzied kisses that you gave and got.

Before we die of thirst, called Kelly, will you bring us *three more stouts*. God, he said to me, it's in the desert you'd think we were.

That's good stuff, you know, I said to Brinsley.

A picture came before my mind of the lovers at their hedge-pleasure in the pale starlight, no sound from them, his fierce mouth burying into hers.

Bloody good stuff, I said.

Kelly, invisible to my left, made a slapping noise.

The best I ever drank, he said.

As I exchanged an eye-message with Brinsley, a wheezing beggar inserted his person at my side and said:

Buy a scapular or a stud, Sir.

This interruption I did not understand. Afterwards, near Lad Lane police station a small man in black fell in with us and tapping me often about the chest, talked to me earnestly on the subject of Rousseau, a member of the French nation. He was animated, his pale features striking in the starlight and voice going up and falling in the lilt of his argumentum. I did not understand his talk and was personally unacquainted with him. But Kelly was taking in all he said, for he stood near him, his taller head inclined in an attitude of close attention. Kelly then made a low noise and opened his mouth and covered the small man from shoulder to knee with a coating of unpleasant buff-coloured puke. Many other things happened on that night now imperfectly recorded in my memory but that incident is still very clear to me in my mind. Afterwards the small man was some distance from us in the lane, shaking his divested coat and rubbing it along the wall. He is a little man that the name of Rousseau will always recall to me. Conclusion of reminiscence.

Flann O'Brien *At Swim-Two-Birds*

Farewell to Paris

And it was down the Rue Bonaparte that only a year before Mona and I used to walk every night, after we had taken leave of Borowski. St Sulpice not meaning much to me then, nor anything in Paris. Washed out with talk. Sick of faces. Fed up with cathedrals and squares and menageries and what not. Picking up a book in the red bedroom and the cane chair uncomfortable; tired of sitting on my ass all day long, tired of red wallpaper, tired of seeing so many people jabbering away about nothing. The red bedroom and the trunk always open; her gowns lying about in a delirium of disorder. The red bedroom with my galoshes and canes, the notebooks I never touched, the manuscripts lying cold and dead. Paris! Meaning the Café Select, the Dôme, the Flea Market, the American Express. Paris! Meaning Borowski's canes, Borowski's hats, Borowski's *gouaches*, Borowski's prehistoric fish – and prehistoric jokes. In that Paris of '28 only one night stands out in my memory – the night before sailing for America. A rare night, with Borowski slightly pickled and a little disgusted with me because I'm dancing with every slut in the place. But we're leaving in the morning! That's what I tell every cunt I grab hold of – *leaving in the morning!* That's what I'm telling the blonde with agate-coloured eyes. And while I'm telling her she takes my hand and squeezes it between her legs. In the lavatory I stand before the bowl with a tremendous erection; it seems light and heavy at the same time, like a piece of lead with wings on it. And while I'm standing there like that two cunts sail in – Americans. I greet them cordially, prick in hand. They give me a wink and pass on. In the vestibule, as I'm buttoning my fly, I notice one of them waiting for her friend to come out of the can. The music is still playing and maybe Mona'll be coming to fetch me, or Borowski with his gold-knobbed cane, but I'm in her arms now and she has hold of me and I don't care who comes or what happens. We wriggle into the cabinet and there I stand her up, slap up against the wall, and I try to get it into her but it won't work and so we sit down on the seat and try it that way but it won't work either. No matter how we try it it won't work. And all the while she's got hold of my prick, she's clutching it like a lifesaver, but it's no use, we're too hot, too eager. The music is still playing and so we waltz out of the cabinet into the vestibule again and as we're dancing there in the shithouse I come all over her beautiful gown and she's sore as hell about it. I stumble back to the table and there's Borowski with his ruddy face and Mona with her disapproving eye. And Borowski says 'Let's all go to Brussels tomorrow,' and we agree, and when we get back to the hotel I vomit all over the place, in the bed, in the washbowl, over the suits and gowns and the galoshes and canes and the notebooks I never touched and the manuscripts cold and dead.

Henry Miller *Tropic of Cancer*

Unlucky for Some

For the third time he demanded a pint. His eyes were glazed with fatigue, and he would have let go the bar rail had not an ever-ready instinct of self-preservation leapt into his fist at the weakest moment and forced him to tighten his grip. He was beginning to feel sick, and in fighting this temptation his tiredness increased. He did not know whether he would go back upstairs to Brenda afterwards, or have his pint and get home to bed, the best place when you feel done-in, he muttered to himself.

The bartender placed a pint before him. He paid one-and-eightpence and drank it almost in a single gulp. His strength magically returned, and he shouted out for another, thinking: the thirteenth. Unlucky for some, but we'll see how it turns out. He received the pint and drank a little more slowly, but half way through it, the temptation to be sick became a necessity that beat insistently against the back of his throat. He fought it off and struggled to light a cigarette.

Smoke caught in his windpipe and he had just time enough to push his way back through the crush – nudging his elbow into standing people who unknowingly blocked his way, half choked by smoke now issuing from mouth and nostrils, feeling strangely taken up by a fierce power that he could not control – before he gave way to the temptation that had stood by him since falling down the stairs, and emitted a belching roar over a middle-aged man sitting with a woman on one of the green leather seats.

'My God!' the man cried. 'Look at this. Look at what the young bogger's gone and done. Would you believe it? My best suit. Only pressed and cleaned today. Who would credit such a thing? Oh dear. It cost me fifteen bob. As if money grows on trees. And suits as well. I wonder how I'll ever get the stains out? Oh dear.'

Alan Sillitoe *Saturday Night and Sunday Morning*

Observing the Decencies

'Crisis Diana' ended for good about a week later. There had been affection between Didi and me in the intervening days. I had written to Dr Cooper and had received a kind answer (although this was to come to nothing, because after half promising that he would visit the doctor, Didi slithered out of it), and Didi had again collapsed into tears and been comforted. He was drinking no less frantically, but he had suddenly become willing to bring his hang-overs home to me openly instead of hiding them in his room.

I was more worried over him than I had ever been, but at the same time I felt 'better in myself'. Instead of making him 'cringe', my physical presence had suddenly become benign to him, so that he sought it as a hurt child runs for comfort to its nurse or mother, and it was a relief to be rid of the disgusting image of myself which he had been reflecting, even though I hadn't believed in it. It was also a relief of a different kind – an unstoppering, as opposed to the removal of pressure from outside – to be able to indulge myself again in expressions of affection and gestures of comfort, even though I was unable to see how they could do any good.

This feeling of relief from pressure may have been the reason why I enjoyed far more than I expected a literary cocktail party to which I had to go. I went straight from my office, and expected to be back in the flat by about 8.30. I had not mentioned the party to Didi.

Instead of leaving early I stayed till the end, and went on after the party to have supper with friends. We sat talking until after mid-night, and we drank a great deal. I didn't realize how drunk I was until I was in the taxi on the way home and noticed that things were rocking slightly. 'Heavens!' I thought, 'it's at least twenty years since things last rocked – I must be hugely drunk,' and this was confirmed when I reached the flat by a mad burst of domestic energy. On the few occasions when I am so drunk that there is a chance I'll end by passing out, I usually go through a stage of euphoric energy during which I suddenly and perfectly efficiently do something like washing my hair or preparing a stew, knowing as I do it that I must be brisk and get it finished before the next stage sets in.

This time the energy went into doing the laundry – next day was clean-sheet day. Didi was out, so after I had stripped and made my bed I did his, wrote out the laundry list and packed up the box, pleased with myself at making such practical use of this stage of the drunkenness. Then I decided that there was enough of the energy left to see me through my bath, and I got myself undressed and bathed with undiminished competence. Coming out of the bathroom I bumped the wall and thought 'Oho, here we go! We're nearly into stage two,' and it occurred to me that although I was still feeling well and cheerful, I might be drunk enough to vomit later on.

I remember – although I hadn't thought of it for several years – that a previous lodger had once had a sick child to stay and had bought a chamber-pot for this emergency, which he had left behind and which had been at the back of my storage cupboard ever since. Infinitely clever, I felt, at remembering this pot, and cleverer still as I went down on hands and knees and burrowed my way into the cupboard to find it. I would put it beside my bed. Then, supposing I had to be sick and proved to be too far gone to get to the lavatory, it wouldn't matter. I knew that I was grinning and wagging my head in fatuous pride at having thought up this precaution, and the more I knew it the more I grinned. It was an amusing and agreeable drunkenness.

Indeed it was so agreeable that I was spared not only nausea, but even what had seemed the inevitable vertigo on lying down. I was ready to sit up again and to stare hard at my chest of drawers in order to keep the bed still, but instead I was out as soon as my head touched the pillow.

The next thing I knew was that my bedroom door had opened and that the light had been switched on. 'People are coming into my room,' I thought distinctly, without moving or opening my eyes because I couldn't. Then the light went off and the door clicked shut, and with relief I thought 'People gone away again – good.' I didn't even speculate as to who 'people' were or what they were doing. I was sunk so deep in a deliciously warm and dark well of sleep that anything beyond the registering of a sound or movement was impossible.

Perhaps – very likely – it was only a few seconds later that the side of my mattress was depressed, but I had been down to the bottom of the lovely well again, so it might have been hours for all I knew. 'People' hadn't gone away again, it seemed: they were in my room and had just sat down on my bed at a level with my waist. After what may have been quite a long time it occurred to me that I ought to open my eyes and try to see who 'they' were. I sleep with my curtains open and it was not a dark night, so I recognized the silhouette of the silent figure at once, and with a renewal of relief. It was Didi – I needn't do anything about *him*. He appeared to be naked, which was odd, but I couldn't be bothered with details and I shut my eyes again.

Then, tiresomely, he spoke.

'What's that horrible thing doing there?' he said.

I had no idea what he was talking about. What horrible thing? He was drunk, of course, and I needn't answer.

'What's that horrible thing doing there?' he said again. 'What's it doing?' And no sooner had I sunk back into oblivion than his voice dragged me up, again – 'that horrible thing'? What a bore he was being.

At last I heaved my eyelids up again, and this time he made a movement with his foot as he asked his parrotlike question, kicking the chamber-pot. Understanding enlivened me a little, and for the first time I spoke.

'I'm drunk,' I said. 'Thought I might be sick.'

There was the sound of a match: Didi had lit a cigarette. He was going to stay there. It didn't seem that he wanted to cry, but perhaps he was going to talk. He'd been talking a lot lately.

'What do you want to talk about?' I asked. I still hadn't moved a muscle and I had opened my eyes only twice. If he wanted to talk, let him; I could sink back into the well while he was doing so. He said: 'Sh, don't talk.'

He must have smoked all his cigarette because there was only a tiny butt in the chamber-pot next morning. Then I felt my mattress rise as he stood up, and I heard him say: 'I'm glad you're drunk. Let me get in.'

I found that I could move after all. It was possible to edge myself over a few inches to make room for him, and the effort enlivened me again so that when he was lying beside me I repeated 'What do you want to talk about?' Again he said 'Sh, don't talk.' And a few moments later he turned towards me, put an arm over me, and began to stroke my naked back very slowly, from the nape of my neck down to my buttocks. God bless my soul, I thought dreamily, he's going to make love to me!

The sensation of his stroking was delicious, perfectly in tune with the relaxation of my body. I was too nearly out to experience any specifically sexual reaction, but warmth and softness, softness and warmth – let them go on, part of the softness and warmth I was in already. The utter physical relaxation which is supposed to enable a drunk person to fall down a flight of stairs without hurting himself: that was what I was in, and it was blissful. When Didi moved to lie on top of me and pushed my legs apart with his, it came to me dimly that I was so far from being sexually excited that he might not be able to get further, but I didn't see what I could do about that, and anyway he managed it after a while, and there we were, Didi and I, making love.

It was entirely agreeable, gentle and tender. As it went on more of my consciousness surfaced, but not much of it, only enough for me to move my hands so that I was holding his shoulders and caressing his head and neck, and to know that I was glad that he didn't want to kiss me on the mouth – we must both be smelling disgustingly of stale drink and smoke. He gave me light kisses round the face and on the neck and breasts, murmuring 'You're so beautiful, so beautiful' – ritual words, nothing to do with me, I understood and accepted them as such. And I understood, too, that I mustn't murmur in return the words which would have come out if I had opened my mouth, which would have been: 'My little one, my baby.' It was, however, pleasant to say them to myself, to let tenderness move my hands, and to feel with sleepy amusement that what I had once wanted was now happening, and that although I no longer wanted it, it was in some mysterious way not without meaning: that this once, at least, Didi and I were expressing in a loving way – were perhaps dreaming? – the secret which lay between us.

My drunkenness had been restricting the range of my consciousness, but it hadn't been distorting it. Now, as activity gradually widened the range of what I could perceive, it was my ordinary self perceiving it and I knew that it would be a pity to spoil what was happening by letting it go on too long. Tenderness would soon be counteracted by the weariness of my unaroused body, so I had better end this love-making by faking a climax and bringing Didi to his. When that was done there was a moment of quite sober anxiety in which I feared that he might pass out and remain in my bed all night, but when I whispered 'Bed too small' he sat up and started to scrabble at something near his feet. 'What you doing?' I mumbled. 'Trying to put on these bloody underpants,' he said. 'Why?' – 'Must observe the decencies.' Yes – he certainly was very drunk indeed, perhaps even drunker than I was. I was asleep again within a few seconds of his leaving my room.

Diana Athill *After a Funeral*

Bedroom Farce

Two Cambridge students, Aleyn and John, have been sent with the college corn to Simkin, the dishonest miller, who distracts them from their watch by letting loose their horse, Bayard. After recapturing him they return to the mill exhausted and plead for a night's lodging . . .

Wery and weet, as beste is in the reyn,
Comth sely John, and with him comth Aleyn.
'Allas,' quod John, 'the day that I was born!
Now are we drive til hething and til scorn.
Our corn is stole, men wil us foles calle,

Bathe the wardeyn and our felawes alle,
And namely the miller; weylaway!'
  Thus pleyneth John as he goth by the way
Toward the mille, and Bayard in his hond.
The miller sitting by the fyr he fond,
For it was night, and forther mighte they noght;
But, for the love of god, they him bisoght.
Of herberwe and of ese, as for hir peny.
  The miller seyde agayn, 'if ther be eny,
Swich as it is, yet shal ye have your part.
Myn hous is streit, but ye han lerned art;
Ye conne by argumentes make a place
A myle brood of twenty foot of space.
Lat see now if this place may suffyse,
Or make it roum with speche, as is youre gyse.'
  'Now, Symond,' seyde John, 'by seint Cutberd,
Ay is thou mery, and this is faire answerd.
I have herd seyd, man sal taa of twa thinges
Slyk as he fyndes, or taa slyk as he bringes.
But specially, I pray thee, hoste dere,
Get us som mete and drinke, and make us chere,
And we wil payen trewely atte fulle.
With empty hand men may na haukes tulle;
Lo here our silver, redy for to spende.'
  This miller in-to toun his doghter sende
For ale and breed, and rosted hem a goos,
And bond hir hors, it sholde nat gon loos;
And in his owne chambre hem made a bed
With shetes and with chalons faire y-spred,
Noght from his own bed ten foot or twelve.
His doghter hadde a bed, al by hir-selve,
Right in the same chambre, by and by;
It mighte be no bet, and cause why,

herbewe, lodging; *ese*, refreshment; *man sal taa of twa thinges/Slyk as he fyndes, or taa slyk as he bringes*, A man must take one of two things – what he finds, or what he brings with him; *tulle*, entice; *chalons*, blankets.

Ther was no roumer herberwe in the place.
They soupen and they speke, hem to solace,
And drinken ever strong ale atte beste.
Aboute midnight wente they to reste.
  Wel hath this miller vernisshed his heed;
Ful pale he was for-dronken, and nat reed.
He yexeth, and he speketh thurgh the nose
As he were on the quakke, or on the pose.
To bedde he gooth, and with him goth his wyf.
As any jay she light was and jolyf,
So was hir joly whistle wel y-wet.
The cradel at hir beddes feet is set,
To rokken, and to yeve the child to souke.
And whan that dronken al was in the crouke,
To bedde went the doghter right anon;
To bedde gooth Aleyn and also John;
Ther nas na more, hem nedede no dwale.
This miller hath so wisly bibbed ale,
That as an hors he snorteth in his sleep,
Ne of his tayl bihinde he took no keep.
His wyf bar him a burdon, a ful strong,
Men mighte hir routing here two furlong;
The wenche routeth eek *par companye.*
  Aleyn the clerk, that herd this melodye,
He poked John, and seyde, 'slepestow?
Herdestow ever slyk a sang er now?
Lo, whilk a compline is y-mel hem alle!
A wilde fyr up-on thair bodyes falle!
Wha herkned ever slyk a ferly thing?
Ye, they sal have the flour of il ending.
This lange night ther tydes me na reste;
But yet, na fors; al sal be for the beste.
For John,' seyde he, 'als ever moot I thryve
If that I may, yon wenche wil I swyve.

vernisshed his heed, varnished his head – got drunk; *quakke*, hoarseness; *pose*, cold; *souke*, such; *crouke*, jug; *dwale*, sleeping draught; *y-mel*, among; *ferly*, extraordinary; *the flour of il ending*, the best of a bad end; *na fors*, nevertheless.

Som esement has lawe y-shapen us;
For John, ther is a lawe that says thus,
That gif a man in a point be y-greved,
That in another he sal be releved.
Our corn is stoln, shortly, it is na nay,
And we han had an il fit al this day.
And sin I sal have neen amendement,
Agayn my los I wil have esement.
By goddes saule, it sal neen other be!'
This John answerde, 'Alayn, avyse thee,
The miller is a perilous man,' he seyde,
'And gif that he out of his sleep abreyde
He mighte doon us bathe a vileinye.'
Aleyn answerde, 'I count him nat a flye;'
And up he rist, and by the wenche he crepte.
This wenche lay upright, and faste slepte,
Til he so ny was, er she mighte espye,
That it had been to late for to crye,
And shortly for to seyn, they were at on;
Now pley, Aleyn! for I wol speke of John.
This John lyth stille a furlong-wey or two,
And to him-self he maketh routhe and wo:
'Allas!' quod he, 'this is a wikked jape;
Now may I seyn that I is but an ape.
Yet has my felawe som-what for his harm;
He has the milleris doghter in his arm.
He auntred him, and has his nedes sped,
And I lye as a draf-sek in my bed;
And when this jape is tald another day,
I sal been halde a daf, a cokenay!
I wil aryse, and auntre it, by my fayth!
"Unhardy is unsely," thus men sayth.'
And up he roos and softely he wente
Un-to the cradel, and in his hand it hente,
And baar it softe un-to his beddes feet.

upright, supine; *at on*, united; *routhe*, lamentation; *auntred him*, took the risk; *draf-sak*, sack of husks; *daf*, fool; *Unhardy is unsely*, the coward is unfortunate.

Sone after this the wyf hir routing leet,
And gan awake, and wente hir out to pisse,
And cam agayn, and gan hir cradel misse,
And groped heer and ther, but she fond noon.
'Allas!' quod she, 'I hadde almost misgoon;
I hadde almost gon to the clerkes bed.
Ey, *ben'cite!* thanne hadde I foule y-sped:'
And forth she gooth til she the cradel fond.
She gropeth alwey forther with hir hond,
And fond the bed, and thoghte noght but good,
By-cause that the cradel by it stood,
And niste wher she was, for it was derk;
But faire and wel she creep in to the clerk,
And lyth ful stille, and wolde han caught a sleep.
With-inne a whyl this John the clerk up leep,
And on this gode wyf he leyth on sore.
So mery a fit ne hadde she nat ful yore;
He priketh harde and depe as he were mad.
This joly lyf han thise two clerkes lad
Til that the thridde cok bigan to singe.
Aleyn wex wery in the daweninge,
For he had swonken all the longe night;
And seyde, 'far wel, Malin, swete wight!
The day is come, I may no lenger byde;
But evermo, wher so I go or ryde,
I is thyn awen clerk, swa have I seel!'
'Now dere lemman,' quod she, 'go, far weel!
But er thou go, o thing I wol thee telle,
Whan that thou wendest homward by the melle,
Right at the entree of the dore bihinde,
Thou shalt a cake of half a busshel finde
That was y-maked of thyn owne mele,
Which that I heelp my fader for to stele.
And, gode lemman, god thee save and kepe!'
And with that word almost she gan to wepe.
Aleyn up-rist, and thoughte, 'er that it dawe,

routing, snoring; *leet*, cease; *sore*, fiercely; *swonken*, laboured.

I wol go crepen in by my felawe;'
And fond the cradel with his hand anon.
'By god,' thoghte he, 'al wrang I have misgon;
Myn heed is toty of my swink to-night,
That maketh me that I go nat aright.
I woot wel by the cradel, I have misgo,
Heer lyth the miller and his wyf also.'
And forth he goth, a twenty devel way,
Un-to the bed ther-as the miller lay.
He wende have cropen by his felawe John;
And by the miller in he creep anon.
And caught hym by the nekke, and softe he spak:
He seyde, 'thou, John, thou swynes-heed, awak
For Christes saule, and heer a noble game.
For by that lord that called is seint Jame,
As I have thryes, in this shorte night,
Swyved the milleres doghter bolt-upright,
Whyl thow hast as a coward been agast.'
'Ye, false harlot,' quod the miller, 'hast?
A! false traitour! false clerk!' quod he,
'Thou shalt be deed, by goddes dignitee!
Who dorste be so bold to disparage
My doghter, that is come of swich linage?'
And by the throte-bolle he caughte Alayn.
And he hente hym despitously agayn,
And on the nose he smoot him with his fest.
Doun ran the blody streem up-on his brest;
And in the floor, with nose and mouth to-broke,
They walwe as doon two pigges in a poke.
And up they goon, and doun agayn anon,
Til that the miller sporned at a stoon,
And doun he fil bakward up-on his wyf,
That wiste no-thing of this nyce stryf;
For she was falle aslepe a lyte wight
With John the clerk, that waked hadde al night.
And with the fal, out of his sleep she breyde –

toty, dizzy; *sporned*, stumbled.

'Help, holy croys of Bromeholm,' she seyde,
'*In manus tuas!* lord, to thee I calle!
Awak, Symond! the feend is on us falle,
Myne herte is broken, help, I nam but deed;
There lyth oon up my wombe and up myn heed;
Help, Simkin, for the false clerkes fighte.'
This John sterte up as faste as ever he mighte,
And graspeth by the walles to and fro,
To finde a staf; and she sterte up also,
And knew the estres bet than dide this John,
And by the wal a staff she fond anon.
And saugh a litel shimering of a light,
For at an hole in shoon the mone bright;
And by that light she saugh hem bothe two,
But sikerly she niste who was who,
But as she saugh a whyt thing in hir yë.
And whan she gan the whyte thing espye,
She wende the clerk hadde wered a volupeer.
And with the staf she drough ay neer and neer,
And wende han hit this Aleyn at the fulle,
And smoot the miller on the pyled skulle,
That doun he gooth and cryde, 'harrow! I dye!'
Thise clerkes bete him weel and lete him lye;
And greythen hem, and toke hir hors anon,
And eek hir mele, and on hir wey they gon.
And at the mille yet they toke hir cake
Of half a busshel flour, ful wel y-bake.
Thus is the proude miller wel y-bete,
And hath y-lost the grinding of the whete,
And payed for the soper every-deel
Of Aleyn and of John, that bette him weel.
His wyf is swyved, and his doghter als;
Lo, swich it is a miller to be fals!

Geoffrey Chaucer 'The Reeve's Tale'

estres, interior; *wende*, assumed; *volupeer*, night-cap; *pyled*, bald; *harrow!*, help!; *greythen*, prepare; *every-deel*, completely.

7 Eccles Street

What parallel courses did Bloom and Stephen follow returning? Starting united both at normal walking pace from Beresford place then followed in the order named Lower and Middle Gardiner streets and Mountjoy square, west: then, at reduced pace, each bearing left, Gardiner's place by an inadvertence as far as the farther corner of Temple street, north: then at reduced pace with interruptions of halt, bearing right, Temple street, north, as far as Hardwicke place. Approaching, disparate, at relaxed walking pace they crossed both the circus before George's church diametrically, the chord in any circle being less than the arc which it subtends.

Of what did the duumvirate deliberate during their itinerary?

Music, literature, Ireland, Dublin, Paris, friendship, woman, prostitution, diet, the influence of gaslight or the light of arc and glowlamps on the growth of adjoining paraheliotropic trees, exposed corporation emergency dustbuckets, the Roman catholic church, ecclesiastical celibacy, the Irish nation, jesuit education, careers, the study of medicine, the past day, the maleficent influence of the presabbath, Stephen's collapse.

Did Bloom discover common factors of similarity between their respective like and unlike reactions to experience?

Both were sensitive to artistic impressions musical in preference to plastic or pictorial. Both preferred a continental to an insular manner of life, a cisatlantic to a transatlantic place of residence. Both indurated by early domestic training and an inherited tenacity of heterodox resistance professed their disbelief in many orthodox religious, national, social and ethical doctrines. Both admitted the alternately stimulating and obtunding influence of heterosexual magnetism.

Were their views on some points divergent?

Stephen dissented openly from Bloom's views on the importance of dietary and civic selfhelp while Bloom dissented tacitly from Stephen's views on the eternal affirmation of the spirit of man in literature. Bloom assented covertly to Stephen's rectification of the anachronism involved in assigning the date of the conversion of the Irish nation to christianity from druidism by Patrick son of Calpornus, son of Potitus, son of Odyssus, sent by pope Celestine I in the year 432 in the reign of Leary to the year 260 or thereabouts in the reign of Cormac MacArt († 266 A.D.) suffocated by imperfect deglutition of aliment at Sletty and interred at Rossnaree. The collapse which Bloom ascribed to gastric inanition and certain chemical compounds of varying degrees of adulteration and alcoholic strength, accelerated by mental exertion and the velocity of rapid circular motion in a relaxing atmosphere, Stephen attributed to the reapparition of a matutinal cloud (perceived by both from two different points of observation, Sandycove and Dublin) at first no bigger than a woman's hand.

Was there one point on which their views were equal and negative?

The influence of gaslight or electric light on the growth of adjoining paraheliotropic trees.

Had Bloom discussed similar subjects during nocturnal perambulations in the past?

In 1884 with Owen Goldberg and Cecil Turnbull at night on public thoroughfares between Longwood avenue and Leonard's corner and Leonard's corner and Synge street and Synge street and Bloomfield avenue. In 1885 with Percy Apjohn in the evenings, reclined against the wall between Gibraltar villa and Bloomfield house in Crumlin, barony of Uppercross. In 1886 occasionally with casual acquaintances and prospective purchasers on doorsteps, in front parlours, in third class railway carriage of suburban lines. In 1888 frequently with major Brian Tweedy and his daughter Miss Marion Tweedy together and separately on the lounge in Matthew Dillon's house in Roundtown. Once in 1892 and once in 1893 with Julius Mastiansky, on both occasions in the parlour of his (Bloom's) house in Lombard street, west.

What reflection concerning the irregular sequence of dates 1884, 1885, 1886, 1888, 1892, 1893, 1904 did Bloom make before their arrival at their destination?

He reflected that the progressive extension of the field of individual development and experience was regressively accompanied by a restriction of the converse domain of interindividual relations.

As in what ways?

From inexistence to existence he came to many and was as one received: existence with existence he was with any as any with any: from existence to nonexistence gone he would be by all as none perceived.

What action did Bloom make on their arrival at their destination?

At the housesteps of the 4th of the equidifferent uneven numbers, number 7 Eccles street, he inserted his hand mechanically into the back pocket of his trousers to obtain his latchkey.

Was it there?

It was in the corresponding pocket of the trousers which he had worn on the day but one preceding.

Why was he doubly irritated?

Because he had forgotten and because he remembered that he had reminded himself twice not to forget.

What were then the alternatives before the, premeditatedly (respectively) and inadvertently, keyless couple?

To enter or not to enter. To knock or not to knock.

Bloom's decision?

A stratagem. Resting his feet on the dwarf wall, he climbed over the area railings, compressed his hat on his head, grasped two points at the lower union of rails and stiles, lowered his body gradually by its length of five feet nine inches and a half to within two feet ten inches of the area pavement, and allowed his body to move freely in space by separating himself from the railings and crouching in preparation for the impact of the fall.

Did he fall?

By his body's known weight of eleven stone and four pounds in avoirdupois measure, as certified by the graduated machine for periodical selfweighing in the premises of Francis Frœdman, pharmaceutical chemist of 19 Frederick street, north, on the last feast of the Ascension, to wit, the twelfth day of May of the bissextile year one thousand nine hundred and four of the christian era (jewish era five thousand six hundred and sixtyfour, mohammedan era one thousand three hundred and twentytwo), golden number 5, epact 13, solar cycle 9, dominical letters C B, Roman indication 2, Julian period 6617 MXMIV.

Did he rise uninjured by concussion?

Regaining new stable equilibrium he rose uninjured though concussed by the impact, raised the latch of the area door by the exertion of force at its freely moving flange and by leverage of the first kind applied at its fulcrum gained retarded access to the kitchen through the subadjacent scullery, ignited a lucifer match by friction, set free inflammable coal gas by turning on the ventcock, lit a high flame which, by regulating, he reduced to quiescent candescence and lit finally a portable candle.

What discrete succession of images did Stephen meanwhile perceive?

Reclined against the area railings he perceived through the transparent kitchen panes a man regulating a gasflame of 14 CP, a man lighting a candle, a man removing in turn each of his two boots, a man leaving the kitchen holding a candle of 1 CP.

Did the man reappear elsewhere?

After a lapse of four minutes the glimmer of his candle was discernible through the semitransparent semicircular glass fanlight over the halldoor. The hall door turned gradually on its hinges. In the open space of the doorway the man reappeared without his hat, with his candle.

Did Stephen obey his sign?

Yes, entering softly, he helped to close and chain the door and followed softly along the hallway the man's back and listed feet and lighted candle past a lighted crevice of doorway on the left and carefully down a turning staircase of more than five steps into the kitchen of Bloom's house.

James Joyce *Ulysses*

Brook Green, Hammersmith

'Where d'you live?' I demanded.

'Brugglesmith,' was the answer.

'What's that?' I said to Dempsey, more skilled than I in portmanteau words.

'Brook Green, 'Ammersmith,' Dempsey translated promptly.

'Of course,' I said. 'That's just the sort of place he would choose to live in. I only wonder that it was not Kew.'

'Are you going to wheel him 'ome, sir,' said Dempsey.

'I'd wheel him home if he lived in —— Paradise. He's not going to get out this ambulance while I'm here. He'd drag me into a murder for tuppence.'

'Then strap 'im up an' make sure,' said Dempsey and he deftly buckled two straps that hung by the side of the ambulance over the man's body. Brugglesmith – I know not his other name – was sleeping deeply. He even smiled in his sleep.

'That's all right,' said Dempsey, and I moved off wheeling my devil's perambulator before me. Trafalgar Square was empty except for the few that slept in the open. One of these wretches ranged alongside and begged for money, asserting that he had been a gentleman once.

'So have I,' I said. 'That was long ago. I'll give you a shilling if you'll help me to push this thing.'

'Is it a murder?' said the vagabond, shrinking back. 'I've not got to *that* yet.'

'No, it's going to be one,' I answered. 'I have.'

The man slunk back into the darkness and I pressed on, through Cockspur Street, and up to Piccadilly Circus, wondering what I should do with my treasure. All London was asleep, and I had only this drunken carcass to bear me company. It was silent – silent as chaste Piccadilly. A young man of my acquaintance came out of a pink brick club as I passed. A faded carnation drooped from his buttonhole; he had been playing cards, and was walking home before the dawn, when he overtook me.

'What are you doing?' he said.

I was far beyond any feeling of shame. 'It's for a bet,' said I. 'Come and help.'

'Laddie, who's yon?' said the voice beneath the hood.

'Good Lord!' said the young man, leaping across the pavement. Perhaps card-losses had told on his nerves. Mine were steel that night.

'The Lord, The Lord?' the passionless incurious voice went on. 'Dinna be profane, laddie. He'll come in His ain good time.'

The young man looked at me with horror.

'It's all part of the bet,' I answered. 'Do come and push!'

'W – where are you going to?' said he.

'Brugglesmith,' said the voice within. 'Laddie, d'ye ken my wife?'

'No,' said I.

'Well, she's just a tremenjus wumman. Laddie, I want a drink. Knock at one o' those braw houses laddie, an' – an' – ye may kiss the girl for your pains.'

'Lie still, or I'll gag you,' I said, savagely.

The young man with the carnation crossed to the other side of Piccadilly, and hailed the only hansom visible for miles. What he thought I cannot tell.

I pressed on – wheeling, eternally wheeling – to Brook Green, Hammersmith. There I would abandon Brugglesmith to the gods of that desolate land. We had been through so much together that I could not leave him bound in the street. Besides, he would call after me, and oh! it is a shameful thing to hear one's name ringing down the emptiness of London in the dawn.

So I went on, past Apsley House, even to the coffee-stall, but there was no coffee for Brugglesmith. And into Knightsbridge – respectable Knightsbridge – I wheeled my burden, the body of Brugglesmith.

'Laddie, what are ye going to do wi' me?' he said when opposite the barracks.

'Kill you,' I said briefly, 'or hand you over to your wife. Be quiet.'

He would not obey. He talked incessantly – sliding in one sentence from clear cut dialect to wild and drunken jumble. At the Albert Hall he said that I was the 'Hattle Gardle buggle,' which I apprehend is the Hatton Garden burglar. At Kensington High Street he loved me as a son, but when my weary legs came to the Addison Road Bridge he implored me with tears to unloose the straps and to fight against the sin of vanity. No man molested us. It was as though a bar had been set between myself and all humanity till I had cleared my account with Brugglesmith. The glimmering of light grew in the sky; the cloudy brown of the wood pavement turned to heather-purple; I made no doubt that I should be allowed vengeance on Brugglesmith ere the evening.

At Hammersmith the heavens were steel-gray, and the day came weeping. All the tides of the sadness of an unprofitable dawning poured into the soul of Brugglesmith. He wept bitterly, because the puddles looked cold and houseless. I entered a half-waked public-house – in evening dress and an ulster, I marched to the bar – and got him whisky on condition that he should cease kicking at the canvas of the ambulance. Then he wept more bitterly, for that he had ever been associated with me, and so seduced into stealing the *Breslau's* dinghy.

The day was white and wan when I reached my long journey's end, and, putting back the hood, bade Brugglesmith declare where he lived. His eyes wandered disconsolately round the red and gray houses till they fell on a villa in whose garden stood a staggering board with the legend 'To Let'. It needed only this to break him down utterly, and with the breakage fled his fine fluency in his guttural northern tongue; for liquor levels all.

'Olely lil while,' he sobbed. 'Olely lil while. Home – falmy – besht of falmies – wife too – *you* dole know my wife! Left them all a lill while ago. Now everything's sold – all sold. Wife – falmy – all sold. Lemmegellup!'

I unbuckled the straps cautiously. Brugglesmith rolled off his resting-place and staggered to the house.

'Wattle I do?' he said.

Then I understood the baser depths in the mind of Mephistopheles.

'Ring,' I said; 'perhaps they are in the attic or the cellar.'

'You do' know my wife. She shleeps on soful in the dorlin' room, waiting meculhome. *You* do' know my wife.'

He took off his boots, covered them with his tall hat, and craftily as a Red Indian picked his way up the garden path and smote the bell marked 'Visitors' a severe blow with the clenched fist.

'Bell sole too. Sole electick bell! Wassor bell this? I can't riggle bell,' he moaned despairingly.

'You pull it – pull it hard,' I repeated, keeping a wary eye down the road. Vengeance was coming and I desired no witnesses.

'Yes, I'll pull it hard.' He slapped his forehead with inspiration. 'I'll pull it out.'

Leaning back he grasped the knob with both hands and pulled. A wild ringing in the kitchen was his answer. Spitting on his hands he pulled with renewed strength, and shouted for his wife. Then he bent his ear to the knob, shook his head, drew out an enormous yellow and red handkerchief, tied it round the knob, turned his back to the door, and pulled over his shoulder.

Either the handkerchief or the wire, it seemed to me, was bound to give way. But I had forgotten the bell. Something cracked in the kitchen, and Brugglesmith moved slowly down the doorsteps, pulling valiantly. Three feet of wire followed him.

'Pull, oh pull!' I cried. 'It's coming now.'

'Qui' ri',' he said. '*I'll* riggle bell.'

He bowed forward, the wire creaking and straining behind him, the bell-knob clasped to his bosom, and from the noises within I fancied the bell was taking away with it half the wood-work of the kitchen and all the basement banisters.

'Get a purchase on her,' I shouted, and he spun round, lapping that good copper wire about him. I opened the garden gate politely, and he passed out, spinning his own cocoon. Still the bell came up, hand over hand, and still the wire held fast. He was in the middle of the road now, whirling like an impaled cockchafer, and shouting madly for his wife and family. There he met with the ambulance, the bell within the house gave one last peal, and bounded from the far end of the hall to the inner side of the hall-door, where it stayed fast. So did not my friend Brugglesmith. He fell upon his face, embracing the ambulance as he did so, and the two turned over together in the toils of the never-sufficiently-to-be-advertised copper wire.

'Laddie,' he gasped, his speech returning, 'have I a legal remedy?'

'I will go and look for one,' I said, and, departing, found two policemen. These I told that daylight had surprised a burglar in Brook Green while he was engaged in stealing lead from an empty house. Perhaps they had better take care of that bootless thief. He seemed to be in difficulties.

I led the way to the spot, and behold! in the splendour of the dawning, the ambulance, wheels upper-most, was walking down the muddy road on two stockinged feet – was shuffling to and fro in a quarter of a circle whose radius was copper wire, and whose centre was the bell-plate of the empty house.

Next to the amazing ingenuity with which Brugglesmith had contrived to lash himself under the ambulance, the thing that appeared to impress the constables most was the fact of the St Clement Danes ambulance being at Brook Green, Hammersmith.

They even asked me, of all people in the world, whether I knew anything about it!

They extricated him; not without pain and dirt. He explained that he was repelling boarding-attacks by a 'Hattle Gardle buggle' who had sold his house, wife, and family. As to the bell-wire, he offered no explanation, and was borne off shoulder-high between the two policemen. Though his feet were not within six inches of the ground, they paddled swiftly, and I saw that in his magnificent mind he was running – furiously running.

Sometimes I have wondered whether he wished to find me.

Rudyard Kipling 'Brugglesmith'

AFTER-EFFECTS

All At Sea

Said John Quinn:
There once was a pore honest sailor, a heavy drinker,
A hell of a cuss, a rowster, a boozer, and
The drink finally sent him to hospital,
And they operated, and there was a poor whore in
The woman's ward had a kid, while
They were fixing the sailor, and they brought him the kid
When he came to, and said:
'Here! this is what we took out of you.'

An' he looked at it, an' he got better,
And when he left the hospital, quit the drink,
And when he was well enough
signed on with another ship
And saved up his pay money,
and kept on savin' his pay money,
And bought a share in the ship,
and finally had half shares,
Then a ship
and in time a whole line of steamers;
And educated the kid,
and when the kid was in college,
The ole sailor was again taken bad
and the doctors said he was dying,
And the boy came to the bedside,
and the old sailor said:
'Boy, I'm sorry I can't hang on a bit longer,
'You're young yet.
I leave you re-sponsa-bilities.
'Wish I could ha' waited till you were older,
'more fit to take over the bisness . . .'
'But, father,
'Don't, don't talk about me, I'm all right.

It's you, father.'
'That's it, boy, you said it.
'You call me your father, and I ain't.
'I ain't your dad, no,
'I am not your fader but your moder,' quod he,
'Your fader was a rich merchant in Stambouli.'

Ezra Pound *Canto XII*

The Drunken Swine

The drunkard now supinely snores,
His load of ale sweats through his pores,
Yet when he wakes the swine shall find,
A crapula remains behind.

Charles Cotton

Alive Again

Dixon was alive again. Consciousness was upon him before he could get out of the way; not for him the slow, gracious wandering from the halls of sleep, but a summary, forcible ejection. He lay sprawled, too wicked to move, spewed up like a broken spider-crab on the tarry shingle of the morning. The light did him harm, but not as much as looking at things did; he resolved, having done it once, never to move his eyeballs again. A dusty thudding in his head made the scene before him beat like a pulse. His mouth had been used as a latrine by some small creature of the night, and then as its mausoleum. During the night, too, he'd somehow been on a cross-country run and then been expertly beaten up by secret police. He felt bad.

Kingsley Amis *Lucky Jim*

I Am Ill

Fa was shaking him.

'They are going away.'

Hands not Fa's hands were gripped round his head, producing a hot pain. He groaned and rolled away from the hands but they held on, squeezing until the pain was inside his head.

'The new people are going away. They are taking their hollow logs up the slope to the terrace.'

Lok opened his eyes and yelped with pain for he seemed to be looking straight into the sun. Water ran out of his eyes and blazed fiercely between the lids. Fa shook him again. He felt for the ground with his hands and feet and lifted himself a little way from it. His stomach contracted and all at once he was sick. His stomach had a life of its own; it rose in a hard knot, would have nothing to do with this evil, honey-smelling stuff and rejected it. Fa was taking by his shoulder.

'My stomach has been sick too.'

He turned over again, and squatted laboriously without opening his eyes. He could feel the sunlight burning down one side of his face.

'They are going away. We must take back the new one.'

Lok prised open his eyes, looked out cautiously between gummed-up lids to see what had happened to the world. It was brighter. The earth and the trees were made of nothing but colour and swayed so that he shut his eyes again.

'I am ill.'

For a while she said nothing. Lok discovered that the hands holding his head were inside it and they squeezed so tightly that he could feel blood pulsing through his brain. He opened his eyes, blinked, and the world settled a little. There were still the blazing colours but they were not swaying. In front of him the earth was rich brown and red, the trees were silver and green and the branches were covered with spurts of green fire. He squatted, blinking, feeling the tenderness of his face while Fa went on speaking.

'I was sick and you would not wake up. I went to see the new people. Their hollow logs have moved up the slope. The new people are frightened. They stand and move like people who are frightened. They heave and sweat and watch the forest over their backs. But there is no danger in the forest. They are frightened of the air where there is nothing. Now we must get the new one from them.'

Lok put his hands to the earth on either side of him. The sky was bright and the world blazed with colour, but it was still the world he knew.

'We must take Liku from them.'

Fa stood up and ran round the clearing. She came back and looked down at him. He got up carefully.

'Fa says "Do this!"'

He waited obediently. Mal had gone out of his head.

'Here is a picture. Lok goes up the path by the cliff where the people cannot see him. Fa goes round and climbs to the mountain above the people. They will follow. The men will follow. Then Lok takes the new one from the fat woman and runs.'

She took hold of him by the arms and looked imploringly into his face.

'There will be a fire again. And I shall have children.'

A picture came into Lok's head.

'I will do so,' he said sturdily, 'and when I see Liku I will take her also.'

There were things in Fa's face, not for the first time, that he could not understand.

William Golding *The Inheritors*

Darkness At Noon

Dr Johnson went to bed soon. When one bowl of punch was finished, I rose, and was near the door, in my way upstairs to bed; but Corrichatachin said, it was the first time Col had been in his house, and he should have his bowl; – and would not I join in drinking it? The heartiness of my honest landlord, and the desire of doing social honour to our very obliging conductor, induced me to sit down again. Col's bowl was finished; and by that time we were well warmed. A third bowl was soon made, and that too was finished. We were cordial, and merry to a high degree; but of what passed I have no recollection, with any accuracy. I remember calling Corrichatachin by the familiar appellation of Corri, which his friends do. A fourth bowl was made, by which time Col, and young M'Kinnon, Corrichatachin's son, slipped away to bed. I continued a little with *Corri* and *Knockow*; but at last I left them. It was near five in the morning when I got to bed.

Sunday, 26 September I awaked at noon, with a severe head-ach. I was much vexed that I should have been guilty of such a riot, and afraid of a reproof from Dr Johnson. I thought it very inconsistent with that conduct which I ought to maintain, while the companion of the Rambler. About one he came into my room, and accosted me, 'What, drunk yet?' – His tone of voice was not that of severe upbraiding; so I was relieved a little, – 'Sir, (said I,) they kept me up.' – He answered, 'No, you kept them up, you drunken dog:' – This he said with good-humoured *English* pleasantry. Soon afterwards, Corrichatachin, Col, and other friends assembled round my bed. *Corri* had a brandy-bottle and glass with him, and insisted I should take a dram. – 'Ay, (said Dr Johnson,) fill him drunk again. Do it in the morning, that we may laugh at him all day. It is a poor thing for a fellow to get drunk at night, and sculk to bed, and let his friends have no sport.' – Finding him thus jocular, I became quite easy; and when I offered to get up, he very good-naturedly said, 'You need be in no such hurry now.' – I took my host's advice, and drank some brandy, which I found an effectual cure for my headach. When I rose, I went into Dr Johnson's room, and taking up Mrs M'Kinnon's Prayer-book, I opened it at the twentieth Sunday after Trinity, in the epistle for which I read, 'And be not drunk with wine, wherein there is excess.' Some would have taken this as a divine interposition.

James Boswell *A Tour of the Western Isles and Hebrides*

The Morning After

Morning came, and I got up ... That doesn't sound particularly interesting or difficult, now does it? I bet you do it all the time. Listen though – I had a problem here. For instance, I was lying face-down under a hedge or bush or some blighted shrub in a soaked allotment full of nettles, crushed cigarette packs, used condoms and empty beercans. It was quite an appropriate place for me to be born again, which is what it felt like. Obviously it hurts, being born: that's why you scream and weep. Next, I had to frisk myself, to make sure I still had my wallet, limbs, face, dick, being. Next, I had to run crying through the concrete concourses in dawn rain until my panic slowed and I recognized the city and myself in the matt and muffled streets. Then I had to find a cab and get back here. The guy wouldn't take me until I showed him money. I didn't blame him. I had dreamed – and who needs dreams with this kind of nightlife? – of torture, laughter, pincer-grips on the frail-tubed spine.

In the bathroom I stripped slowly before the mirror. Face first: there was a grey swelling over my left eye, and my rug was quite badly singed on the same side. A fight? I didn't think so. If there'd been a fight, then I must have won it. My body was all there, trembling, whimpering in the graphic light, but all there. I turned – and gasped. *Dah* ... Oh, Christ. My back, my great white back was scored with thirty or forty sharp red welts, regularly patterned, as if I'd slept on a bed of nails. Taking a two-fisted grip on my spare tyre, I was able to wrench round some flesh and get a good look at one of these bloodless wounds. An indentation, a red hole: I could insert my quivering pinkie to half-nail depth. I stepped back. No other damage. No new damage. My bumf-crammed wallet was intact: credit cards, eighty-odd dollars, thirty-odd pounds. My hangover was fine. My hangover had come through okay.

So I had spent the night, or part of it, on a patch of earth in alphabet-land! – Avenue B, deep down on the East Side. After an evening of pleasure and profit with my friends in Bank Street, I had clearly gone out for a drink or two. Bad idea! Oh very bad!

Someone, at some stage, had worked me over with a tool, a spike or a blunt shiv. My shirt was punctured in places, but not my jacket – my good, my best jacket. It was now eight-thirty. I bathed my face with water and felt hot fingers beginning to tickle my back. For ten minutes I vomited elaborately, with steamhammer convulsions that I had no strength to resist or contain. Then for twice that long I sat twitching on the shower's deck, the silver snout tuned to full heat and heft but doing nothing much to wash off my rot. I must be *very unhappy*. That's the only way I can explain my behaviour. Oh man, I must be so depressed. I must be fucking suicidal. And I wish I knew *why*.

Look at my life. I know what you're thinking. You're thinking: But it's terrific! It's great! You're thinking: Some guys have all the luck! Well, I suppose it must look quite cool, what with the airplane tickets and the restaurants, the cabs, the filmstars, Selina, the Fiasco, the money. But my life is also my private culture – that's what I'm showing you, after all, that's what I'm letting you into, my private culture. And I mean *look* at my private culture. Look at the state of it. It really isn't very nice in here. And that is why I long to burst out of the world of money and into – into what? Into the world of thought and fascination. How do I get there? Tell me, please. I'll never make it by myself. I just don't know the way.

Martin Amis *Money*

Blah Blah Blah

'Norman,' said de Sousa as the coffee and brandy were being poured, 'I wonder if we ought perhaps to have just a tiny natter about the programme.'

'I think that would be an awfully good idea, Jack,' said Westerman. He took some cyclostyled papers out of his pocket and looked at them. 'Well, as I understand it, Jack – tell me if I'm wrong – we open with the credits on telecine. Right?'

'Right,' said de Sousa, lighting a small cigar.

'Then we come up on me in the studio. I say, "Good evening.

The film you're about to see is the record of a remarkable experiment in blah blah blah . . ."'

'All on Autocue.'

'All on Autocue. Then we have the film. Then we come back to me in the studio and I say, "The film you have just seen was an attempt to blah blah blah. Now we have here in the studio tonight four people who are vitally and personally concerned with the problems of living in a multiracial community. On my right is Lord Boddy, who was a member of the Royal Commission on blah blah blah . . ."'

'And you go right round the table.'

'And I go right round the table. Then I'll turn to you, Frank, and say, "Lord Boddy, what do you think of the experiment we have just seen? Do you think it holds out a ray of hope among the problems which perplex us all so sorely today?"'

'I say blah blah blah,' said Lord Boddy.

'You say blah blah blah. Then we all join in blah blah blah. Then when I get the sign from the studio manager I wind up and say, "Well, then, the conclusions we seem to have reached tonight are blah blah blah."'

'All on Autocue,' said de Sousa.

'All on Autocue. I think that's all fairly well tied up, isn't it, Jack?'

'I think so. Is everybody happy?'

'Indeed, indeed, indeed,' said Dyson. 'I don't think I've ever enjoyed myself so much in my life.'

They trooped down to the studio for the line-up, taking their glasses of brandy with them. A little of the festive warmth seemed to die out of the air as they took their places around the low coffee table in the corner of the great hangar. Williamson kept clearing his throat. Miss Drax smiled unhappily about her. Even Boddy, who had been telling Westerman as they came down the stairs how he had been at Bad Godesberg in 1938 just two days after Hitler and Chamberlain had left, trailed away into silence. Only Dyson lost none of his elation. When the studio manager asked him to say something to check the microphone levels, he recited the first few lines of 'The Wreck of the Deutschland' with appropriate gestures.

It seemed to amuse the studio crew. Really, he thought, this was his evening.

By the time they had been to make-up, and tramped back up the stairs to have another drink, a definite uneasiness was beginning to settle over the whole company. The men with the Brigade ties and their friends were running out of potential mutual acquaintances to describe. Miss Drax seemed to have caught the frog Williamson had had in his throat. Williamson, coming back from his second trip to the lavatory, passed Boddy on the way out for his third. Westerman, shuffling the cyclostyled papers about in his hands, dropped his glass, and filled his shoes with brandy. Dyson watched them all with amazement. He himself was greatly excited, but not nervous in the least.

'The public just don't realize,' said Williamson to him gloomily, 'the terrific amount of work that goes into making one short half-hour of television.'

'Work?' said Dyson. 'It's pure pleasure. I've never enjoyed anything so much in all my life. I'm absolutely bubbling over. I simply can't wait to get on.'

'Good God,' said Williamson.

One of the financial figures, still smiling deferentially, poured them both more brandy.

'I wonder if you could try and keep the bottle away from Lord Boddy,' he said quietly. 'I think perhaps he's had almost enough.'

How interesting it was, thought Dyson, how extraordinarily intriguing, to find that out of the whole team the only one who was actually turning up trumps was himself.

'I think perhaps we might go down now,' said de Sousa.

'I shan't be able to watch,' said Jannie, as the film sequence in the first half of John's programme unreeled meaninglessly in front of her. 'Honestly, Bob, I shan't be able to watch. I know something awful will happen. Oh, Bob, supposing he's had too much to drink?'

'He'll be fine, Jannie,' said Bob. 'Stop fussing.'

Jannie gripped the arms of her chair, trying to stop herself jumping out of it.

'What on earth's this stuff they're showing us now?' she demanded irritably.

'It's the film they're going to discuss.'

'Oh God, I know he's going to make a fool of himself. I know it, I know it, I know it!'

When the film ended, and the face of the chairman appeared again, she put her hand over her eyes, unable to watch the screen. The chairman was introducing Lord Boddy. She had a vision of John sitting hunched up in his chair, as he did at home sometimes when things were going wrong, all dark and gaunt and unhappy. Oh, poor John! Poor John! But where was he? The chairman had been introducing people for an eternity, and still no sign of him. Perhaps he was ill. She imagined him standing in some white-tiled institutional lavatory, suffering from nervous nausea. Had he taken the bismuth with him? But better for him to be in a lavatory somewhere than for him to be sick on the programme! Of course, they would turn the cameras . . .

'And on her left,' said the chairman, 'is Mr John Dyson, a journalist and broadcaster who lives . . .'

And there he was! Involuntarily she reached out and gripped Bob's hand. And what in the name of God was John up to? He was smiling and waving!

'What's he doing?' she cried, agonized, as the picture cut back to the chairman. 'It's not that sort of programme!'

'I don't know whether you noticed,' said Bob, 'but he was smoking.'

'Smoking?'

'Didn't you see? He had a cigarette between his fingers.'

'Don't be crazy, Bob. John hasn't smoked since he was an undergraduate.'

'Well, he's smoking now, Jannie.'

'Oh god!' said Jannie, holding Bob's hand very tight. 'I shan't be able to watch, Bob!'

'You're all right now, Jan. Lord Boddy's set for the night.'

But someone was saying something at the same time as Lord Boddy, making him falter and finally stop in midstride. The cameras hunted round the team, trying to locate the intruder. They were all smoking, observed Jannie, but John, as she saw when the camera finally settled on him, was smoking more than most. He was smoking and talking simultaneously, taking little melodramatic puffs between phrases.

'If I might butt in here,' he was saying (puff). 'If I might possibly butt in a moment . . . (puff, puff) I should just like to say that I find what Lord Boddy is saying extraordinarily interesting. *Extraordinarily* interesting.'

He took another energetic puff, and blew out a dense cloud of smoke at the camera as Lord Boddy resumed his discourse.

'Oh God,' said Jannie.

'Sh!' said Bob. Dyson was back in the conversation again.

'That is fascinating,' he was saying. 'Most fascinating. I find that absolutely fascinating.'

Jannie squeezed Bob's hand so hard that he flinched.

'Poor John!' she said.

When Miss Drax's turn to speak came, Dyson was fascinated by her thesis, too.

'Indeed!' he kept murmuring. 'Indeed, indeed!'

'Why is he behaving like this!' cried Jannie. 'Why is he smoking, and waving his arms about in that awful way?'

'He waves his arms about at the office sometimes,' said Bob. 'I don't object to that.'

'But why does he keep saying things like "extraordinarily interesting" and "indeed, indeed"? I've never heard him say anything like that before.'

'I've never heard him say "indeed, indeed", I must admit.'

Williamson was talking. Dyson turned out to be extraordinarily interested in his views, as well.

'Indeed,' he murmured. 'Indeed . . . indeed . . . Oh God, indeed!'

Jannie sank down into her chair, trying to work out who would be watching the programme. All John's family, of course. All *her* family. Her parents had invited the neighbours in to see it, too. Her friend Belinda Charles – she'd rung up to say she'd seen John's name in an article about the programme in the paper. Out of nowhere the idea came to her that Lionel Marcus might be watching. Please God, not Lionel Marcus!

'John Dyson,' the chairman was saying, 'do you, as a journalist, agree with the suggestion that what we need is for the Press to take a firm moral lead and play down all news to do with race relations?'

Dyson did not answer at once. He frowned, then leaned forward and stubbed out his cigarette thoughtfully in the ashtray.

'He's got a sense of timing, anyway,' said Bob.

'I can't bear it,' said Jannie.

Dyson sat back and put his fingertips together, as if about to deliver his verdict. But at the last moment he changed his mind, and instead leaned forward again and took another cigarette out of the box on the table.

'Oh God, Bob!' said Jannie.

Dyson picked up the table-lighter, and with an absolutely steady hand lit the cigarette. Then he snapped the top of the lighter down, drew in a mouthful of smoke, and let it out again slowly and meditatively.

'I think it's an extraordinarily interesting idea,' he said.

Jannie put her spare hand over her eyes as if shielding them from the sun, and closed out the sight of her husband.

'You're exaggerating, Jannie,' said Bob.

Later he said: 'People who don't know him wouldn't get the same impression at all.'

Later still he said: 'Honestly, Jannie, nobody watches this sort of programme apart from the relatives of the performers.'

It seemed to Jannie that the noise of John blowing cigarette smoke out almost drowned the conversation. She kept her hand over her eyes until at last Westerman halted the discussion and summed up. He paused before saying good night, and a voice from off-screen cut in at once.

'That is absolutely fascinating, Norman,' it said.

Jannie put her head on Bob's shoulder and wept.

Dyson walked up and down the bedroom in his overcoat, making large gestures, and trailing in his wake the cosy smell of digested alcohol. Jannie lay in bed, looking at him over the edge of the covers. It was after midnight.

'Honestly, Jannie,' said Dyson excitedly, 'I astonished myself! I simply didn't know I had it in me! How did it look?'

'Very good, John.'

'Really? You're not just saying that?'

'No, John.'

'I actually *enjoyed* it, Jannie, that was the thing. I was amazed! The others were all shaking with nerves! Even hardened television performers like Norman and Frank. But honestly, I could have gone on all night. I didn't use my notes at all.'

'I thought you didn't.'

'Didn't touch them – didn't even think about them. I was absolutely in my element! How did I come over, Jannie?'

'I told you – very well.'

'I didn't cut in and argue too much?'

'I don't think so.'

'I thought perhaps I was overdoing the controversy a bit?'

'No, no.'

Dyson stopped and gazed at Jannie seriously.

'I feel I've at last found what I really want to do in life, Jannie,' he said. 'It's so much more alive and vital than journalism. Honestly, Jannie, I'm so exhilarated . . .!'

He began to stride up and down the room again, smiling at himself. He glanced in the mirror as he passed it and straightened his glasses.

'What did Bob think?' he asked. 'Did he think I was all right?'

'He thought you were fine.'

Dyson stopped again, smiling reflectively.

'Frank Boddy is an absolute poppet,' he said warmly. 'He really is. Oh, Jannie, I adore television! I can't tell you . . .! You really think I looked all right?'

Later, as he was crawling about the floor in his underclothes, looking under the bed for his slippers, Jannie asked:

'Why were you smoking, John?'

He straightened up and gazed anxiously over the end of the bed at her.

'You thought it looked odd?' he said.

'No, no.'

'You don't think it seemed rather mannered?'

'Of course not, John. I just wondered how you came to think of it.'

Dyson smiled with pleasure as he remembered.

'It was sheer inspiration on the spur of the moment,' he said. 'I just saw the box of cigarettes lying there on the table, and everybody else smoking, and I just knew inside me with absolute certainty that I should smoke, too. I think it absolutely *made* my performance.'

He fell asleep almost as soon as the light was out, and woke up again about an hour later, his mouth parching, his whole being troubled with a great sense of unease. What was occupying his mind, as vividly as if it was even now taking place, was the moment when he had said, 'That is absolutely fascinating, Norman,' and then realized it was supposed to be the end of the programme. Had he *really* done that? How terrible. How absolutely terrible.

He sat up and drank some water. Still, one little slip in an otherwise faultless performance ... Then with great clarity and anguish he remembered the moment when Westerman had put his question about a moral lead from the Press, and instead of answering at once the idea had come to him of leaning forward and judiciously stubbing out his cigarette. It had been scarcely a quarter smoked! He lay down in bed again slowly and unhappily.

All the same, when he had finished stubbing the cigarette out he had given a very shrewd and pertinent answer ... No, he hadn't! He'd taken another cigarette! In absolute silence, in full view of the whole population of Britain, he had stubbed out a quarter-smoked cigarette and lit a fresh one!

He turned on to his right side, then he turned on to his left, wracked with the shamefulness of the memory. It was strange; everything he had done on the programme had seemed at the time to be imbued with an exact sense of logic and purposiveness, but now that he looked back on it, all the logical connections had disappeared, like secret writing when the special lamp is taken away.

And what about the time he had interrupted Lord Boddy, and then realized that all he had wanted to say was that it was interesting? *Extraordinarily* interesting ... Had he *really* said that? He himself? The occupant of the tense body now lying obscurely and privately in the dark bedroom of a crumbling Victorian house in Spadina Road, SW23? Was that slightly pooped gentleman with the waving arms who had (oh God!) told Lord Boddy that his views were absolutely fascinating, and (oh God oh God!) lit another of the television company's cigarettes with their silver butane table-lighter every time he had seen the red light come up on the camera pointing at him – was that exuberantly shameful figure really identical with the anguished mortal man who now lay here stretched as taut as a piano-string in the dark?

'Jannie,' he groaned. 'Are you awake, Jannie?'

There was no reply. He turned on to his right side. He turned back on to his left. He hurled himself on to his face.

Michael Frayn *Towards the End of the Morning*

Spellbound

The goddess rising, asks her guests to stay,
Who blindly follow where she leads the way.
Eurylochus alone of all the band,
Suspecting fraud, more prudently remain'd.
On thrones around with downy coverings grac'd,
With semblance fair, the unhappy men she plac'd.
Milk newly press'd, the sacred flour of wheat,
And honey fresh, and Pramnian wines the treat:
But venom'd was the bread, and mix'd the bowl,
With drugs of force to darken all the soul:
Soon in the luscious feast themselves they lost,
And drank oblivion of their native coast.
Instant her circling wand the goddess waves,
To hogs transforms them, and the sty receives.
No more was seen the human form divine;
Head, face, and members, bristle into swine:
Still curst with sense, their minds remain alone,
And their own voice affrights them when they groan.

Meanwhile the goddess in disdain bestows
The mast and acorn, brutal food! and strows
The fruits of cornel, as their feast, around;
Now prone and groveling on unsavoury ground.

Homer *The Odyssey*, trans. Alexander Pope

You Were Perfectly Fine

The pale young man eased himself carefully into the low chair, and rolled his head to the side, so that the cool chintz comforted his cheek and temple.

'Oh, dear,' he said. 'Oh, dear, oh, dear, oh, dear. Oh.'

The clear-eyed girl, sitting light and erect on the couch, smiled brightly at him.

'Not feeling so well today?' she said.

'Oh, I'm great,' he said. 'Corking, I am. Know what time I got up? Four o'clock this afternoon, sharp. I kept trying to make it, and every time I took my head off the pillow, it would roll under the bed. This isn't my head I've got on now. I think this is something that used to belong to Walt Whitman. Oh, dear, oh, dear, oh, dear.'

'Do you think maybe a drink would make you feel better?' she said.

'The hair of the mastiff that bit me?' he said. 'Oh, no, thank you. Please never speak of anything like that again. I'm through. I'm all, all through. Look at that hand; steady as a humming-bird. Tell me, was I very terrible last night?'

'Oh, goodness,' she said, 'everybody was feeling pretty high. You were all right.'

'Yeah,' he said. 'I must have been dandy. Is everybody sore at me?'

'Good heavens, no,' she said. 'Everyone thought you were terribly funny. Of course, Jim Pierson was a little stuffy, there, for a minute at dinner. But people sort of held him back in his chair, and got him calmed down. I don't think anybody at the other tables noticed it at all. Hardly anybody.'

'He was going to sock me?' he said. 'Oh, Lord. What did I do to him?'

'Why, you didn't do a thing,' she said. 'You were perfectly fine. But you know how silly Jim gets, when he thinks anybody is making too much fuss over Elinor.'

'Was I making a pass at Elinor?' he said. 'Did I do that?'

'Of course you didn't,' she said. 'You were only fooling, that's all. She thought you were awfully amusing. She was having a marvellous time. She only got a little tiny bit annoyed just once, when you poured the clam-juice down her back.'

'My God,' he said, 'Clam-juice down that back. And every vertebra a little Cabot. Dear God. What'll I ever do?'

'Oh, she'll be all right,' she said. 'Just send her some flowers, or something. Don't worry about it. It isn't anything.'

'No, I won't worry,' he said. 'I haven't got a care in the world. I'm sitting pretty. Oh, dear, oh, dear. Did I do any other fascinating tricks at dinner?'

'You were fine,' she said. 'Don't be so foolish about it. Everybody was crazy about you. The *maître d'hôtel* was a little worried because you wouldn't stop singing, but he really didn't mind. All he said was, he was afraid they'd close the place again, if there was so much noise. But he didn't care a bit, himself. I think he loved seeing you have such a good time. Oh, you were just singing away, there, for about an hour. It wasn't so terribly loud, at all.'

'So I sang,' he said. 'That must have been a treat. I sang.'

'Don't you remember?' she said. 'You just sang one song after another. Everybody in the place was listening. They loved it. Only you kept insisting that you wanted to sing some song about some kind of fusiliers or other, and everybody kept shushing you, and you'd keep trying to start it again. You were wonderful. We were all trying to make you stop singing for a minute, and eat something, but you wouldn't hear of it. My, you were funny.'

'Didn't I eat any dinner?' he said.

'Oh, not a thing,' she said. 'Every time the waiter would offer you something, you'd give it right back to him, because you said that he was your long-lost brother, changed in the cradle by a gypsy band, and that anything you had was his. You had him simply roaring at you.'

'I bet I did,' he said. 'I bet I was comical. Society's Pet, I must have been. And what happened then, after my overwhelming success with the waiter?'

'Why, nothing much,' she said. 'You took a sort of dislike to some old man with white hair, sitting across the room, because you didn't like his necktie and you wanted to tell him about it. But we got you out before he got really mad.'

'Oh, we got out,' he said. 'Did I walk?'

'Walk! Of course you did,' she said. 'You were absolutely all right. There was that nasty stretch of ice on the sidewalk, and you did sit down awfully hard, you poor dear. But good heavens, that might have happened to anybody.'

'Oh, sure,' he said 'Louisa Alcott or anybody. So I fell down on the sidewalk. That would explain what's the matter with my – Yes. I see. And then what, if you don't mind?'

'Ah, now, Peter!' she said. 'You can't sit there and say you don't remember what happened after that! I did think that maybe you were just a little tight at dinner – oh, you were perfectly all right, and all that, but I did know you were feeling pretty gay. But you were so serious, from the time you fell down – I never knew you to be that way. Don't you know, how you told me I had never seen your real self before? Oh, Peter, I just couldn't bear it, if you didn't remember that lovely long ride we took together in the taxi! Please, you do remember that, don't you? I think it would simply kill me, if you didn't.'

'Oh, yes,' he said. 'Riding in the taxi. Oh, yes, sure. Pretty long ride, hmm?'

'Round and round and round the park,' she said. 'Oh, and the trees were shining so in the moonlight. And you said you never knew before that you really had a soul.'

'Yes,' he said. 'I said that. That was me.'

'You said such lovely, lovely things,' she said. 'And I'd never known, all this time, how you had been feeling about me, and I'd never dared to let you see how I felt about you. And then last night – oh, Peter dear, I think that taxi ride was the most important thing that ever happened to us in our lives.'

'Yes,' he said. 'I guess it must have been.'

'And we're going to be so happy,' she said. 'Oh, I just want to tell everybody! But I don't know – I think maybe it would be sweeter to keep it all to ourselves.'

'I think it would be,' he said.

'Isn't it lovely?' she said.

'Yes,' he said. 'Great.'

'Lovely!' she said.

'Look here,' he said, 'do you mind if I have a drink? I mean, just medicinally, you know I'm off the stuff for life, so help me. But I think I feel a collapse coming on.'

'Oh, I think it would do you good,' she said. 'You poor boy, it's a shame you feel so awful. I'll go make you a whisky and soda.'

'Honestly,' he said, 'I don't see how you could ever want to speak to me again, after I made such a fool of myself, last night. I think I'd better go join a monastery in Tibet.'

'You crazy idiot!' she said. 'As if I could ever let you go away now! Stop talking like that. You were perfectly fine.'

She jumped up from the couch, kissed him quickly on the forehead, and ran out of the room.

The pale young man looked after her and shook his head long and slowly, then dropped it in his damp and trembling hands.

'Oh, dear,' he said. 'Oh, dear, oh, dear, oh, dear.'

Dorothy Parker *The Penguin Dorothy Parker*

The Skip

I took my life and threw it on the skip,
Reckoning the next-door neighbours wouldn't mind
If my life hitched a lift to the council tip
With their dry rot and rubble. What you find

With skips is – the whole community joins in.
Old mattresses appear, doors kind of drift
Along with all that won't fit in the bin
And what the bin-men can't be fished to shift.

I threw away my life, and there it lay
And grew quite sodden. 'What a dreadful shame,'
Clucked some old bag and sucked her teeth: 'The way
The young these days . . . no values . . . me, I blame . . .'

But I blamed no one. Quality control
Had loused it up, and that was that. 'Nough said.
I couldn't stick at home. I took a stroll
And passed the skip, and left my life for dead.

Without my life, the beer was just as foul,
The landlord still as filthy as his wife,
The chicken in the basket was an owl,
And no one said: 'Ee, Jim-lad, whur's thee life?'

Well, I got back that night the worse for wear,
But still just capable of single vision;
Looked in the skip; my life – it wasn't there!
Some bugger'd nicked it – *without* my permission.

Okay, so I got angry and began
To shout, and woke the street. Okay, *Okay!*
And I was sick all down the neighbour's van,
And I disgraced myself on the par-*kay*.

And then . . . you know how if you've had a few
You'll wake at dawn, all healthy, like sea breezes,
Raring to go, and thinking: 'Clever you!
You've got away with it.' And then, oh Jesus,

It hits you. Well, that morning, just at six
I woke, got up and looked down at the skip.
There lay my life, still sodden, on the bricks;
There lay my poor old life, arse over tip.

Or was it mine? Still dressed, I went downstairs
And took a long cool look. The truth was dawning.
Someone had just exchanged my life for theirs.
Poor fool, I thought – I should have left a warning.

Some bastard saw my life and thought it nicer
Than what he had. Yet what he'd had seemed fine.
He'd never caught his fingers in the slicer
The way I'd managed in that life of mine.

His life lay glistening in the rain, neglected,
Yet still a decent, an authentic life.
Some people I can think of, I reflected
Would take that thing as soon as you'd say Knife.

It seemed a shame to miss a chance like that.
I brought the life in, dried it by the stove.
It looked so fetching, stretched out on the mat,
I tried it on. It fitted, like a glove.

And now, when some local bat drops off the twig
And new folk take the house, and pull up floors
And knock down walls and hire some kind of big
Container (say, a skip) for their old doors,

I'll watch it like a hawk, and every day
I'll make at least – oh – half a dozen trips.
I've furnished an existence in that way.
You'd not believe the things you find on skips.

James Fenton

If Grant Had Been Drinking at Appomattox

Scribner's Magazine *published a series of three articles: 'If Booth Had Missed Lincoln,' 'If Lee Had Not Won The Battle of Gettysburg,' and 'If Napoleon Had Escaped to America.' This is the fourth.*

The morning of the ninth of April, 1865, dawned beautifully. General Meade was up with the first streaks of crimson in the eastern sky. General Hooker and General Burnside were up, and had breakfasted, by a quarter after eight. The day continued beautiful. It drew on toward eleven o'clock. General Ulysses S. Grant was still not up. He was asleep in his famous old navy hammock, swung high above the floor of his headquarters' bedroom. Headquarters was distressingly disarranged: papers were strewn on the floor; confidential notes from spies scurried here and there in the breeze from an open window; the dregs of an overturned bottle of wine flowed pinkly across an important military map.

Corporal Shultz, of the Sixty-fifth Ohio Volunteer Infantry, aide to General Grant, came into the outer room, looked around him, and sighed. He entered the bedroom and shook the General's hammock roughly. General Ulysses S. Grant opened one eye.

'Pardon, sir,' said Corporal Shultz, 'but this is the day of surrender. You ought to be up, sir.'

'Don't swing me,' said Grant, sharply, for his aide was making the hammock sway gently. 'I feel terrible,' he added, and he turned over and closed his eye again.

'General Lee will be here any minute now,' said the Corporal firmly, swinging the hammock again.

'Will you cut that out!' roared Grant. 'D'ya want to make me sick, or what?' Schultz clicked his heels and saluted. 'What's he coming here for?' asked the General.

'This is the day of surrender, sir,' said Shultz. Grant grunted bitterly.

'Three hundred and fifty generals in the Northern armies,' said Grant, 'and he has to come to *me* about this. What time is it?'

'You're the Commander-in-Chief, that's why,' said Corporal Shultz. 'It's eleven twenty-five, sir.'

'Don't be crazy,' said Grant. 'Lincoln is the Commander-in-Chief. Nobody in the history of the world ever surrendered before lunch. Doesn't he know that an army surrenders on its stomach?' He pulled a blanket up over his head and settled himself again.

'The generals of the Confederacy will be here any minute now,' said the Corporal. 'You really ought to be up, sir.'

Grant stretched his arms above his head and yawned.

'All right, all right,' he said. He rose to a sitting position and stared about the room. 'This place looks awful,' he growled.

'You must have had quite a time of it last night, sir,' ventured Shultz.

'Yeh,' said General Grant, looking around for his clothes. 'I was wrassling some general. Some general with a beard.'

Shultz helped the commander of the Northern armies in the field to find his clothes.

'Where's my other sock?' demanded Grant. Shultz began to look around for it. The General walked uncertainly to a table and poured a drink from a bottle.

'I don't think it wise to drink, sir,' said Shultz.

'Nev' mind about me,' said Grant, helping himself to a second, 'I can take it or let it alone. Didn' ya ever hear the story about the fella went to Lincoln to complain about me drinking too much?' "So-and-So says Grant drinks too much," this fella said. "So-and-So is a fool," said Lincoln. So this fella went to What's-His-Name and told him what Lincoln said and he came roarin' to Lincoln about it. "Did you tell So-and-So I was a fool?" he said. "No," said Lincoln, "I thought he knew it."' The General smiled, reminiscently, and had another drink. '*That's* how I stand with Lincoln,' he said, proudly.

The soft thudding sound of horses' hooves came through the open window. Shultz hurriedly walked over and looked out.

'Hoof steps,' said Grant, with a curious chortle.

'It is General Lee and his staff,' said Shultz.

'Show him in,' said the General, taking another drink. 'And see what the boys in the back room will have.'

Shultz walked smartly over to the door opened it, saluted, and stood aside. General Lee, dignified against the blue of the April sky, magnificent in his dress uniform, stood for a moment framed in the doorway. He walked in, followed by his staff. They bowed, and stood silent. General Grant stared at them. He only had one boot on and his jacket was unbuttoned.

'I know who you are,' said Grant. 'You're Robert Browning, the poet.'

'This is General Robert E. Lee,' said one of his staff, coldly.

'Oh,' said Grant. 'I thought he was Robert Browning. He certainly looks like Robert Browning. There was a poet for you, Lee: Browning. Did ja ever read "How They Brought the Good News from Ghent to Aix"? "Up Derek, to saddle, up Derek, away; up Dunder, up Blitzen, up Prancer, up Dancer, up Bouncer, up Vixen, up –"'

'Shall we proceed at once to the matter in hand?' asked General Lee, his eyes disdainfully taking in the disordered room.

'Some of the boys was wrassling here last night,' explained Grant. 'I threw Sherman, or some general a whole lot like Sherman. It was pretty dark.' He handed a bottle of Scotch to the commanding officer of the southern armies, who stood holding it, in amazement and discomfiture. 'Get a glass, somebody,' said Grant, looking straight at General Longstreet. 'Didn't I meet you at Cold Harbour?' he asked. General Longstreet did not answer.

'I should like to have this over with as soon as possible,' said Lee. Grant looked vaguely at Shultz, who walked up close to him, frowning.

'The surrender, sir, the surrender,' said Corporal Shultz in a whisper.

'Oh sure, sure,' said Grant. He took another drink. 'All right,' he said. 'Here we go.' Slowly, sadly, he unbuckled his sword. Then he handed it to the astonished Lee. 'There you are, General,' said Grant. 'We dam' near licked you. If I'd been feeling better we *would* of licked you.'

James Thurber *Vintage Thurber*

TLS

Animal Henry sat reading the *Times Literary Supplement*
with a large Jameson & a worse hangover.
Who will his demon lover
today become, he queried. Having made a dent
in the world, he insisted on special treatment,
massage at all hours.

Love in the shadows where the animals *come*
tickled his nerves' ends. He put down *The Times*
& began a salvage operation,
killing that is the partly incoherent,
saving the mostly fine, polishing the surfaces.
Brain- & instinct-work.

On all fours he danced about his cage, poor Henry
for whom, my love, too much was never enough.
Massage me in Kyoto's air.
The Japanese women are better than the Swedes,
more rhythmical, more piercing.
Somewhere, everywhere
a girl is taking her clothes off.

John Berryman

The Hangover

What a subject! And, in very truth, for once, a 'strangely neglected' one. Oh, I know you can hardly open a newspaper or magazine without coming across a set of instructions – most of them unoriginal, some of them quite unhelpful and one or two of them actually harmful – on how to cure this virtually pandemic ailment. But such discussions concentrate exclusively on physical manifestations, as if one were treating a mere illness. They omit altogether the psychological, moral, emotional, spiritual aspects: all that vast, vague, awful, shimmering metaphysical superstructure that makes the hangover a (fortunately) unique route to self-knowledge and self-realization.

Imaginative literature is not much better. There are poems and songs about drinking, of course, but none to speak of about getting drunk, let alone having been drunk. Novelists go into the subject more deeply and extensively, but tend to straddle the target, either polishing off the hero's hangover in a few sentences or, so to speak, making it the whole of the novel. In the latter case, the hero will almost certainly be a dipsomaniac, who is not as most men are and never less so than on the morning after. This vital difference, together with much else, is firmly brought out in Charles Jackson's marvellous and horrifying *The Lost Weekend*, still the best fictional account of alcoholism I have read.

A few writers can be taken as metaphorically illuminating the world of the hangover while ostensibly dealing with something else. Parts of Dostoevsky can be read in this way. Some of Poe's Tales convey perfectly the prevailing gloomy uneasiness and sudden fits of outlandish dread so many of us could recognize, and Poe himself had a drink problem; contrary to popular belief, he was not a dipsomaniac, but his system was abnormally intolerant of alcohol, so that just a couple of slugs would lay him on his back, no doubt with a real premature-burial of a hangover to follow. Perhaps Kafka's story *The Metamorphosis*, which starts with the hero waking up one morning and finding he has turned into a man-sized cockroach, is the best literary treatment of all. The central image could hardly be better chosen, and there is a telling touch in the nasty way everybody goes on at the chap. (I can find no information about Kafka's drinking history.)

It is not my job, or anyway I absolutely decline, to attempt a full, direct description of the metaphysical hangover: no fun to write or read. But I hope something of this will emerge by implication from my list of counter-measures. Before I get on to that, however, I must deal with the physical hangover, which is in any case the logical one to tackle first, and the dispersal of which will notably alleviate the other – mind and body, as we have already seen, being nowhere more intimately connected than in the sphere of drink. Here, then, is how to cope with

THE PHYSICAL HANGOVER

1 Immediately on waking, start telling yourself how lucky you are to be feeling so bloody awful. This, known as George Gale's Paradox, recognizes the truth that if you do *not* feel bloody awful after a hefty night then you are still drunk, and must sober up in a waking state before hangover dawns.

2 If your wife or other partner is beside you, and (of course) is willing, perform the sexual act as vigorously as you can. The exercise will do you good, and – on the assumption that you enjoy sex – you will feel toned up emotionally, thus delivering a hit-and-run raid on your metaphysical hangover (MH) before you formally declare war on it.

Warnings (i) If you are in bed with somebody you should not be in bed with, and have *in the least degree* a bad conscience about this, abstain. Guilt and shame are prominent constituents of the MH, and will certainly be sharpened by indulgence on such an occasion.

(ii) For the same generic reason, do not take the matter into your own hands if you awake by yourself.

3 Having of course omitted to drink all that water before retiring, drink a lot of it now, more than you need to satisfy your immediate thirst. Alcohol is a notorious dehydrant, and a considerable part of your physical hangover (PH) comes from the lack of water in your cells.

At this point I must assume that you can devote at least a good part of the day to yourself and your condition. Those who inescapably have to get up and do something can only stay in bed as long as they dare, get up, shave, take a hot bath or shower (more of this later), breakfast off an unsweetened grapefruit (m.o.t.l.) and coffee, and clear off, with the intention of getting as drunk at lunchtime as they dare. Others can read on – but let me just observe in passing that the reason why so many professional artists drink a lot is not necessarily very much to do with the artistic temperament, etc. It is simply that they can afford to, because they can normally take a large part of a day off to deal with the ravages. So, then,

4 Stay in bed until you can stand it no longer. Simple fatigue is another great constituent of the PH.

5 Refrain at all costs from taking a cold shower. It may bring temporary relief, but in my own and others' experience it will give your MH a tremendous boost after about half an hour, in extreme cases making you feel like a creature from another planet. Perhaps this is the result of having dealt another shock to your already shocked system. The ideal arrangement, very much worth the trouble and expense if you are anything of a serious drinker, is a shower fixed over the bath. Run a bath as hot as you can bear and lie in it as long as you can bear. When it becomes too much, stand up and have a hot shower, then lie down again and repeat the sequence. This is time well spent.

Warning Do not do this unless you are quite sure your heart and the rest of you will stand it. I would find it most disagreeable to be accused of precipitating your death, especially in court.

6 Shave. A drag, true, and you may well cut yourself, but it is a calming exercise and will lift your morale (another sideswipe at your MH).

7 Whatever the state of your stomach, do not take an alkalizing agent such as bicarbonate of soda. There is some of this in most hangover remedies but not enough to do you any harm, and the bubbling is cheerful. Better to take unsweetened fruit juice or a grapefruit without sugar. The reasoning behind this, known as Philip Hope-Wallace's Syndrome, is that your stomach, on receiving a further dose of acid, will say to itself, 'Oh, I see: we need more alkaline,' and proceed to neutralize itself. Bicarbonate will make it say, 'Oh, I see: we need more acid,' and do you further damage.

If you find this unconvincing, take heed of what happened one morning when, with a kingly hangover, I took bicarbonate with a vodka chaser. My companion said 'Let's see what's happening in your stomach,' and poured the remnant of the vodka into the remnant of the bicarbonate solution. The mixture turned black and gave off smoke.

8 Eat nothing, or nothing else. Give your digestion the morning off. You may drink coffee, though do not expect this to do anything for you beyond making you feel more wide-awake.

9 Try not to smoke. That nicotine has contributed to your PH is a view held by many people, including myself.

10 By now you will have shot a good deal of the morning. Get through the rest of it somehow, avoiding the society of your fellows. Talk is tiring. Go for a walk, or sit or lie about in the fresh air. At eleven or so, see if you fancy the idea of a Polish Bison (hot Bovril and vodka). It is still worth while without the vodka. You can start working on your MH any time you like.

11 About twelve-thirty, firmly take a hair (or better, in Cyril Connolly's phrase, a tuft) of the dog that bit you. The dog, by the way, is of no particular breed: there is no obligation to go for the same drink as the one you were mainly punishing the night before. Many will favour the Bloody Mary, though see my remarks on this in the Drinks section. Others swear by the Underburg. For the ignorant, this is a highly alcoholic bitters rather resembling Fernet Branca, but in my experience more usually effective. It comes in miniature bottles holding about a pub double, and should be put down in one. The effect on one's insides, after a few seconds, is rather like that of throwing a cricket-ball into an empty bath, and the resulting mild convulsions and cries of shock are well worth witnessing. But thereafter a comforting glow supervenes, and very often a marked turn for the better. By now, one way or another, you will be readier to face the rest of mankind and a convivial lunchtime can well result. Eat what you like within reason, avoiding anything greasy or rich. If your PH is still with you afterwards, go to bed.

Before going on to the MH, I will, for completeness' sake, mention three supposed hangover cures, all described as infallible by those who told me about them, though I have not tried any of the three. The first two are hard to come by.

12 Go down the mine on the early-morning shift at the coal-face.

13 Go up for half an hour in an open aeroplane, needless to say with a non-hungover person at the controls.

14 Known as Donald Watt's Jolt, this consists of a tumbler of

some sweet liqueur, Bénédictine or Grand Marnier, taken in lieu of breakfast. Its inventor told me that with one of them inside him he once spent three-quarters of an hour at a freezing bus-stop 'without turning a hair'. It is true that the sugar in the drink will give you energy and the alcohol alcohol.

At this point, younger readers may relax the unremitting attention with which they have followed the above. They are mostly strangers to the MH. But they will grin or jeer at their peril. Let them rest assured that, as they grow older, the MH will more and more come to fill the gap left by their progressively less severe PH. And, of the two, incomparably the more dreadful is

THE METAPHYSICAL HANGOVER

1 Deal thoroughly with your PH.

2 When that ineffable compound of depression, sadness (these two are not the same), anxiety, self-hatred, sense of failure and fear for the future begins to steal over you, start telling yourself that what you have is a hangover. You are not sickening for anything, you have not suffered a minor brain lesion, you are not all that bad at your job, your family and friends are not leagued in a conspiracy of barely maintained silence about what a shit you are, you have not come at last to see life as it really is, and there is no use crying over spilt milk. If this works, if you can convince yourself, you need do no more, as provided in the markedly philosophical

General Principle 9: *He who truly believes he has a hangover has no hangover.*

Kingsley Amis *On Drink*

Tissue-Restorer

I reached out a hand from under the blankets, and rang the bell for Jeeves.

'Good evening, Jeeves.'

'Good morning, sir.'

This surprised me.

'Is it morning?'

'Yes, sir.'

'Are you sure? It seems very dark outside.'

'There is a fog, sir. If you will recollect, we are now in autumn – season of mists and mellow fruitfulness.'

'Season of what?'

'Mists, sir, and mellow fruitfulness.'

'Oh? Yes. Yes, I see. Well, be that as it may, get me one of those bracers of yours, will you?'

'I have one in readiness, sir, in the ice box.'

He shimmered out, and I sat up in bed with that rather unpleasant feeling you get sometimes that you're going to die in about five minutes. On the previous night, I had given a little dinner at the Drones to Gussie Fink-Nottle as a friendly send-off before his approaching nuptials with Madeline, only daughter of Sir Watkyn Bassett, CBE, and these things take their toll. Indeed, just before Jeeves came in, I had been dreaming that some bounder was driving spikes through my head – not just ordinary spikes, as used by Jael the wife of Heber, but red-hot ones.

He returned with the tissue-restorer. I loosed it down the hatch, and after undergoing the passing discomfort, unavoidable when you drink Jeeves's patent morning revivers, of having the top of the skull fly up to the ceiling and the eyes shoot out of their sockets and rebound from the opposite wall like racquet balls, felt better. It would have been overstating it to say that even now Bertram was back again in mid-season form, but I had at least slid into the convalescent class and was equal to a spot of conversation.

'Ha!' I said, retrieving the eyeballs and replacing them in position. 'Well, Jeeves, what goes on in the great world? Is that the paper you have there?'

P. G. Wodehouse *The Code of the Woosters*

ILL-EFFECTS

All His Own Work?

He reached out for and put on his glasses. At once he saw that something was wrong with the bedclothes immediately before his face. Endangering his chance of survival, he sat up a little, and what met his bursting eyes roused to a frenzy the timpanist in his head. A large, irregular area of the turned-back part of the sheet was missing; a smaller but still considerable area of the turned-back part of the blanket was missing; an area about the size of the palm of his hand in the main part of the top blanket was missing. Through the three holes, which, appropriately enough, had black borders, he could see a dark brown mark on the second blanket. He ran a finger round a bit of the hole in the sheet, and when he looked at his finger it bore a dark-grey stain. That meant ash; ash meant burning; burning must mean cigarettes. Had this cigarette burnt itself out on the blanket? If not, where was it now? Nowhere on the bed; nor in it. He leaned over the side, gritting his teeth; a sunken brown channel, ending in a fragment of discoloured paper, lay across a light patch in the pattern of a valuable-looking rug. This made him feel very unhappy, a feeling sensibly increased when he looked at the bedside table. This was marked by two black, charred grooves, greyish and shiny in parts, lying at right angles and stopping well short of the ashtray, which held a single used match. On the table were two unused matches; the remainder lay with the empty cigarette packet on the floor. The bakelite mug was nowhere to be seen.

Had he done all this himself? Or had a wayfarer, a burglar, camped out in his room? Or was he the victim of some Horla fond of tobacco? He thought that on the whole he must have done it himself, and wished he hadn't. Surely this would mean the loss of his job, especially if he failed to go to Mrs Welch and confess what he'd done, and he knew already that he wouldn't be able to do that. There was no excuse which didn't consist of the inexcusable: an incendiary was no more pardonable when revealed as a drunkard as well – so much of a drunkard, moreover, that obligations to hosts and fellow-guests and the counter-attraction of a chamber-concert were as nothing compared with the lure of the drink. The only hope was that Welch wouldn't notice what his wife would presumably tell him about the burning of the bedclothes. But Welch had been known to notice things, the attack on his pupil's book in that essay, for example. But that had really been an attack on Welch himself; he couldn't much care what happened to sheets and blankets which he wasn't actually using at the time. Dixon remembered thinking on an earlier occasion that to yaw drunkenly round the Common Room in Welch's presence screeching obscenities, punching out the window-panes, fouling the periodicals, would escape Welch's notice altogether, provided his own person remained inviolate. The memory in turn reminded him of a sentence in a book of Alfred Beesley's he'd once glanced at: 'A stimulus cannot be received by the mind unless it serves some need of the organism.' He began laughing, an action he soon modified to a wince.

He got out of bed and went into the bathroom. After a minute or two he returned, eating toothpaste and carrying a safety-razor blade. He started carefully cutting round the edges of the burnt areas of the bedclothes with the blade. He didn't know why he did this, but the operation did seem to improve the look of things: the cause of the disaster wasn't so immediately apparent. When all the edges were smooth and regular, he knelt down slowly, as if he'd all at once become a very old man, and shaved the appropriate part of the rug. The debris from these modifications he stuffed into his jacket pocket, thinking that he'd have a bath and then go downstairs and phone Bill Atkinson and ask him to come through with his message about the senior Dixons a good deal earlier than had been arranged. He sat on the bed for a moment to recover from his vertiginous exertions with the rug, then, before he could rise, somebody, soon identifiable as male, came into the bathroom next door. He heard the clinking of a plug-chain, then the swishing of tap-water. Welch, or his son, or Johns was about to take a bath. Which one it was was soon settled by the upsurge of a deep, untrained voice into song. The piece was recognizable to Dixon as some skein of untiring facetiousness by filthy Mozart. Bertrand was surely unlikely to sing anything at all, and Johns made no secret of his indifference to anything earlier than Richard Strauss. Very slowly, like a forest giant under the axe, Dixon heeled over sideways and came to rest with his hot face on the pillow.

Kingsley Amis *Lucky Jim*

An Eye for an Eye

He comes with evening: all his fleecy flock
Before him march, and pour into the rock:
Not one, or male or female, staid behind
(So fortune chanc'd, or so some god design'd);
Then heaving high the stone's unwieldy weight,
He roll'd it on the cave, and clos'd the gate.
First down he sits, to milk the woolly dams,
And then permits their udder to the lambs.
Next seiz'd two wretches more, and headlong cast,
Brain'd on the rock; his second dire repast.
I then approach'd him reeking with their gore,
And held the brimming goblet foaming o'er;
Cyclop! since human flesh has been thy feast,
Now drain this goblet, potent to digest;
Know hence what treasures in our ship we lost,
And what rich liquors other climates boast.
We to thy shore the precious freight shall bear,
If home thou send us, and vouchsafe to spare.
But oh! thus furious, thirsting thus for gore,
The sons of men shall ne'er approach thy shore,
And never shalt thou taste this nectar more.
  He heard, he took, and pouring down his throat,
Delighted, swill'd the large luxurious draught.
More! give me more, he cry'd: the boon be thine,
Whoe'er thou art that bear'st celestial wine!
Declare thy name; not mortal is this juice,
Such as th'unblest Cyclopean climes produce

(Though sure our vine the largest cluster yields,
And Jove's scorn'd thunder serves to drench our fields);
But this descended from the blest abodes,
A rill of nectar, streaming from the gods.
He said, and greedy grasp'd the heady bowl,
Thrice drain'd, and pour'd the deluge on his soul.
His sense lay cover'd with the dozy fume;
While thus my fraudful speech I re-assume.
Thy promis'd boon, O Cyclop! now I claim,
And plead my title; Noman is my name.
By that distinguish'd from my tender years,
'Tis what my parents call me, and my peers.
The giant then: our promis'd grace receive,
The hospitable boon we mean to give:
When all thy wretched crew have felt my power,
Noman shall be the last I will devour.
He said; then nodding with the fumes of wine
Dropt his huge head, and snorting lay supine.
His neck obliquely o'er his shoulders hung,
Prest with the weight of sleep that tames the strong!
There belcht the mingled streams of wine and blood,
And human flesh, his indigested food.
Sudden I stir the embers, and inspire
With animating breath the seeds of fire;
Each drooping spirit with bold words repair,
And urge my train the dreadful deed to dare.
The stake now glow'd beneath the burning bed
(Green as it was) and sparkled fiery red.
Then forth the vengeful instrument I bring;
With beating hearts my fellows form a ring.
Urg'd by some present god, they swift let fall
The pointed torment on his visual ball.
Myself above them from a rising ground
Guide the sharp stake, and twirl it round and round.
As when a shipwright stands his workmen o'er,
Who ply the wimble, some huge beam to bore;
Urg'd on all hands, it nimbly spins about,

The grain deep-piercing till it scoops it out:
In the broad eye so whirls the fiery wood;
From the pierc'd pupil spouts the boiling blood;
Sing'd are his brows; the scorching lids grow black;
The jelly bubbles, and the fibres crack.
And as when armourers temper in the ford
The keen-edg'd pole-ax, or the shining sword,
The red-hot metal hisses in the lake,
Thus in his eye-ball hiss'd the plunging stake.
He sends a dreadful groan: the rocks around
Through all the inmost winding caves resound.

Homer *The Odyssey*, trans. Alexander Pope

Trappist Silence Broken in Shoot-Out as Monks Defend Monastery Wine

Our Paris Correspondent

Trappist monks forgot their vows of silence and fought a gun battle with masked burglars in the Gothic surroundings of Nôtre Dame des Neiges in the southern French department of the Ardèche.

Although lips were sealed again yesterday after the father superior prayed for forgiveness at Matins, the local gendarmerie released details of the showdown in the cloisters in which at least eighteen shots were exchanged.

The monks, members of the strict reformed Cistercian order, were woken by the alarm in one of the abbey's dormitories at 3 a.m. Three monks put on their habits to investigate, and one of them grabbed a shotgun.

'There were three or four burglars, all of them masked and carrying guns, including three rifles and a pistol,' a gendarme said. 'They were hiding out in one of the abbey buildings and there was a prolonged exchange of fire before the burglars took to their heels.'

One of the monks was hit in the foot and flown to hospital at

Puy-en-Velay in the Haute Loire. The burglars were suspected of trying to steal the monks' most famous product – an old wine.

Guardian, 7 November 1990

The Wine of Astonishment

Thou hast shewed thy people hard things: thou hast made us to drink the wine of astonishment.

Psalms 60:3

Desire of Wine

Desire of wine and all delicious drinks,
Which many a famous
Warrior overturns.

John Milton *Samson Agonistes*

As Lords

Lords are lordliest in their wine.

John Milton *Samson Agonistes*

Wine

Reading a life of Alexander the Great, Alexander
whose rough father, Philip, hired Aristotle to tutor
the young scion and warrior, to put some polish
on his smooth shoulders. Alexander who, later
on the campaign trail into Persia, carried a copy of

The Iliad in a velvet-lined box, he loved that book so
much. He loved to fight and drink, too.
I came to that place in the life where Alexander, after
a long night of carousing, a wine-drunk (the worst kind of drunk –
hangovers you don't forget), threw the first brand
to start a fire that burned Persepolis, capital of the Persian Empire
(ancient even in Alexander's day).
Razed it right to the ground. Later, of course,
next morning – maybe even while the fire roared – he was
remorseful. But nothing like the remorse felt
the next evening when, during a disgreement that turned ugly
and, on Alexander's part, overbearing, his face flushed
from too many bowls of uncut wine, Alexander rose drunkenly to
his feet,
grabbed a spear and drove it through the breast
of his friend, Cletus, who'd saved his life at Granicus.

For three days Alexander mourned. Wept. Refused food. 'Refused
to see to his bodily needs.' He even promised
to give up wine forever.
(I've heard such promises and the lamentations that go with them.)
Needless to say, life for the army came to a full stop
as Alexander gave himself over to his grief.
But at the end of those three days, the fearsome heat
beginning to take its toll on the body of his dead friend,
Alexander was persuaded to take action. Pulling himself together
and leaving his tent, he took out his copy of Homer, untied it,
began to turn the pages. Finally he gave orders that the funeral
rites described for Patroklos be followed to the letter:
he wanted Cletus to have the biggest possible send-off.
And when the pyre was burning and the bowls of wine were
passed his way during the ceremony? Of course, what do you
think? Alexander drank his fill and passed
out. He had to be carried to his tent. He had to be lifted, to be put
into his bed.

Raymond Carver

Erred Through Wine

But they also have erred through wine, and through strong drink are out of the way: the priest and the prophet have erred through strong drink, they are swallowed up of wine, they are out of the way through strong drink; they err in vision, they stumble in judgement.

For all the tables are full of vomit and filthiness, so that there is no place clean.

Isaiah 28:7–8

Opiates of the People

Besides these, there are other influences which enfeeble the health of a great number of workers, intemperance most of all. All possible temptations, all allurements combine to bring the workers to drunkenness. Liquor is almost their only source of pleasure, and all things conspire to make it accessible to them. The working-man comes from his work tired, exhausted, finds his home comfortless, damp, dirty, repulsive; he has urgent need of recreation, he *must* have something to make work worth his trouble, to make the prospect of the next day endurable. His unnerved, uncomfortable, hypochondriac state of mind and body arising from his unhealthy condition, and especially from indigestion, is aggravated beyond endurance by the general conditions of his life, the uncertainty of his existence, his dependence upon all possible accidents and chances, and his inability to do anything towards gaining an assured position. His enfeebled frame, weakened by bad air and bad food, violently demands some external stimulus; his social need can be gratified only in the public-house, he has absolutely no other place where he can meet his friends. How can he be expected to resist the temptation? It is morally and physically inevitable that, under such circumstances, a very large number of working-men should fall into intemperance. And apart from the chiefly physical influences which drive the working-man into drunkenness, there is the example of the great mass, the neglected education, the impossibility of protecting the young from temptation, in many cases the direct influence of intemperate parents, who give their own children liquor, the certainty of forgetting for an hour or two the wretchedness and burden of life, and a hundred other circumstances so mighty that the workers can, in truth, hardly be blamed for yielding to such overwhelming pressure. Drunkenness has here ceased to be a vice, for which the vicious can be held responsible; it becomes a phenomenon, the necessary, inevitable effect of certain conditions upon an object possessed of no volition in relation to those conditions. They who have degraded the working-man to a mere object have the responsibility to bear. But as inevitably as a great number of working-men fall a prey to drink, just so inevitably does it manifest its ruinous influence upon the body and mind of its victims. All the tendencies to disease arising from the conditions of life of the workers are promoted by it, it stimulates in the highest degree the development of lung and digestive troubles, the rise and spread of typhus epidemics.

Friedrich Engels *The Condition of the Working Classes in England*

Miracle

They're on a one-way flight, bound from LAX
to SFO, both of them drunk and strung-out
having just squirmed through the hearing,
their second bankruptcy in seven years.
And who knows what, if anything, was said
on the plane, or who said it?
It could have been accumulation
of the day's events, or years on years
of failure and corruption that triggered violence.

Earlier, turned inside out, crucified and left
for dead, they'd been dropped like so much

garbage in front of the terminal. But
once inside they found their bearings,
took refuge in an airport lounge where they tossed
back doubles under a banner that read *Go Dodgers!*
They were plastered, as usual, as they buckled
into their seats and, as always, ready to assume
it was the universal human condition, this battle
waged continually with forces past all reckoning,
forces beyond mere human understanding.

But she's cracking. She can't take any more
and soon, without a word, she turns
in her seat and drills him. Punches him and
punches him, and he takes it.
Knowing deep down he deserves it ten times over –
whatever she wants to dish out – he is being
deservedly beaten for something, there are
good reasons. All the while his head is pummelled,
buffeted back and forth, her fists falling
against his ear, his lips, his jaw, he protects
his whiskey. Grips that plastic glass as if, yes,
it's the long-sought treasure right there
on the tray in front of him.

She keeps on until his nose begins to bleed
and it's then he asks her to stop. *Please, baby,*
for Christ's sake, stop. It may be his plea
reaches her as a faint signal from another
galaxy, a dying star, for this is what it is,
a coded sign from some other time and place
needling her brain, reminding her of something
so lost it's gone forever. In any event, she stops
hitting him, goes back to her drink. Why
does she stop? Because she remembers
the fat years preceding the lean? All that history
they'd shared, sticking it out together, the two
of them against the world? No way. If she'd truly

remembered everything and those years had dropped
smack into her lap all at once,
she would've killed him on the spot.

Maybe her arms are tired, that's why she stops.
Say she's tired then. So she stops. He picks up
his drink almost as if nothing's happened
though it has, of course, and his head aches
and reels with it. She goes back to her whiskey
without a word, not even so much as the usual
'bastard' or 'son of a bitch'. Dead quiet.
He's silent as lice. Holds the drink
napkin under his nose to catch the blood,
turns his head slowly to look out.

Far below, the small steady lights in houses
up and down some coastal valley. It's
the dinner hour down there. People pushing
up to a full table, grace being said,
hands joined together under roofs so solid
they will never blow off those houses – houses where,
he imagines, decent people live and eat, pray
and pull together. People who, if they left
their tables and looked up from the dining
room windows, could see a harvest moon and,
just below, like a lighted insect, the dim glow
of a jetliner. He strains to see over
the wing and beyond, to the myriad lights
of the city they are rapidly approaching,
the place where they live with others of their kind,
the place they call home.

He looks around the cabin. Other people,
that's all. People like themselves
in a way, male or female, one sex
or the other, people not entirely unlike
themselves – hair, ears, eyes, nose, shoulders,

genitals – my God, even the clothes they wear
are similar, and there's that identifying strap
around the middle. But he knows he and she
are not like those others though he'd like it,
and she too, if they were.

Blood soaks his napkin. His head rings and rings
but he can't answer it. And what would he say
if he could? *I'm sorry they're not in. They left*
here, and there too, years ago. They tear
through the thin night air, belted in, bloody husband
and wife, both so still and pale they could be
dead. But they're not, and that's part of
the miracle. All this is one more giant step
into the mysterious experience of their lives.
Who could have foretold any of it years back when,
their hands guiding the knife, they made
that first cut deep into the wedding cake?
Then the next. Who would have listened?
Anyone bringing such tidings of the future
would have been scourged from the gate.

The plane lifts, then banks sharply. He touches
her arm. She lets him. She even takes his hand.
They were made for each other, right? It's fate.
They'll survive. They'll land and pull themselves
together, walk away from this awful fix –
they simply have to, they must.
There's lots in store for them yet, so many fierce
surprises, such exquisite turnings. It's now
they have to account for, the blood
on his collar, the dark smudge of it
staining her cuff.

Raymond Carver

Amid the Horrors

Amid the horrors of penitence, regret, remorse, headache, nausea, and all the rest of the hounds of hell that beset a poor wretch who has been guilty of the sin of drunkenness – Can you speak peace to a troubled soul?

My wife scolds me! my business torments me, and my sins come staring me in the face, every one telling the more bitter tale than his fellow. When I confess to you that even C— has lost its power to please, you will guess something of my hell within, and all around me. I began 'ELLIBANKS AND ELLIBRAES' but the stanzas fell unenjoyed and unfinished from my listless tongue.

Robert Burns to Robert Ainslie, November 1791

Past All Surgery

(*Exeunt all but* IAGO *and* CASSIO.)

IAGO: What, are you hurt, Lieutenant?

CASSIO: Ay, past all surgery.

IAGO: Marry, God forbid!

CASSIO: Reputation, reputation, reputation! O, I have lost my reputation! I have lost the immortal part of myself, and what remains is bestial. My reputation, Iago, my reputation!

IAGO: As I am an honest man I thought you had received some bodily wound: there is more of sense in that than in reputation. Reputation is an idle and most false imposition; oft got without merit and lost without deserving. You have lost no reputation at all, unless you repute yourself such a loser. What, man! There are ways to recover the General again. You are but now cast in his mood – a punishment more in policy than in malice – even so as one would beat his offenceless dog to affright an imperious lion. Sue to him again, and he's yours.

CASSIO: I will rather sue to be despised than to deceive so good a commander with so slight, so drunken, and so indiscreet an officer. Drunk! And speak parrot! And squabble! Swagger! Swear! And discourse fustian with one's own shadow! O, thou invisible spirit of wine, if thou hast no name to be known by, let us call thee devil.

IAGO: What was he that you followed with your sword? What had he done to you?

CASSIO: I know not.

IAGO: Is't possible?

CASSIO: I remember a mass of things, but nothing distinctly: a quarrel, but nothing wherefore. O God, that men should put an enemy in their mouths to steal away their brains! That we should with joy, pleasance, revel and applause transform ourselves into beasts!

IAGO: Why, but you are now well enough! How came you thus recovered?

CASSIO: It hath pleased the devil drunknness to give place to the devil wrath: one unperfectness shows me another, to make me frankly despise myself.

IAGO: Come, you are too severe a moraller. As the time, the place and the condition of this country stands, I could heartily wish this had not so befallen: but since it is as it is, mend it for your own good.

CASSIO: I will ask him for my place again; he shall tell me I am a drunkard. Had I as many mouths as Hydra, such an answer would stop them all. To be now a sensible man, by and by a fool, and presently a beast! O, strange! Every inordinate cup is unblessed and the ingredience is a devil.

IAGO: Come , come; good wine is a good familiar creature if it be well used: exclaim no more against it. And, good Lieutenant, I think you think I love you.

CASSIO: I have well approved it, sir. I drunk!

IAGO: You or any man living may be drunk at a time, man.

William Shakespeare *Othello*

Pure Genius

A drunken bank robber who gave a teller his name and then spilled £6,000 of his haul on the pavement was jailed for five years yesterday.

James McGuinness, 42, of no settled address, was arrested after the manager of the National Westminster Bank in Praed Street, Paddington, West London, arranged for a clerk to bring him a bag for the money, Knightsbridge Crown Court was told.

Daily Telegraph, 18 May 1991

ADMONITIONS

Wine Hath Destroyed Many

Shew not thy valiantness in wine; for wine hath destroyed many.

The furnace proveth the edge by dipping: so doth wine the hearts of the proud by drunkenness.

Wine is as good as life to a man, if it be drunk moderately: what life is then to a man that is without wine? for it was made to make men glad.

Wine measurably drunk and in season bringeth gladness of the heart, and cheerfulness of the mind: but wine drunken with excess maketh bitterness of the mind, with brawling and quarrelling.

Drunkenness increaseth the rage of a fool till he offend: it diminisheth strength, and maketh wounds.

Rebuke not thy neighbour at the wine, and despise him not in his mirth: give him no despiteful words, and press not upon him with urging him [to drink].

Ecclesiasticus 34:25–31

It Is Not for Kings

It is not for kings, O Lemuel, it is not for kings to drink wine, nor for princes strong drink;

lest they drink, and forget the law, and pervert the judgement of any of the afflicted.

Give strong drink unto him that is ready to perish, and wine unto those that be of heavy hearts.

Let him drink, and forget his poverty, and remember his misery no more.

Proverbs 31:4–7

Stanzas from *The Church-Porch*

Drink not the third glass, which thou canst not tame,
When once it is within thee; but before
Mayst rule it, as thou list; and poure the shame,
Which it would poure on thee, upon the floore.
  It is most just to throw that on the ground,
  Which would throw me there, if I keep the round.

He that is drunken, may his mother kill
Bigge with his sister: he hath lost the reins,
Is outlaw'd by himself: all kinde of ill
Did with his liquor slide into his veins.
  The drunkard forfets Man, and doth devest
  All worldly right, save what he hath by beast.

Shall I, to please anothers wine-sprung minde,
Lose all mine own? God hath giv'n me a measure
Short of his canne, and bodie; must I finde
A pain in that, wherein he findes a pleasure?
  Stay at the third glass: if thou lose thy hold,
  Then thou are modest, and the wine grows bold.

If reason move not Gallants, quit the room,
(All in a shipwrack shift their severall way)
Let not a common ruine thee intombe:
Be not a beast in courtesie; but stay,
  Stay at the third cup, or forgo the place.
  Wine above all things doth Gods stamp deface.

Yet, if thou sinne in wine or wantonnesse,
Boast not thereof; nor make thy shame thy glorie.
Frailtie gets pardon by submissivenesse;
But he that boasts, shuts that out of his storie.
  He makes flat warre with God, and doth defie
  With his poore clod of earth the spacious sky.

George Herbert

The Art of Getting Drunk

Saturday, 24 April 1779. Talking of the effects of drinking, he said, 'Drinking may be practised with great prudence; a man who exposes himself when he is intoxicated, has not the art of getting drunk; a sober man who happens occasionally to get drunk, readily enough goes into a new company, which a man who has been drinking should never do. Such a man will undertake any thing; he is without skill in inebriation. I used to slink home, when I had drunk too much. A man accustomed to self-examination will be conscious when he is drunk, though an habitual drunkard will not be conscious of it. I knew a physician who for twenty years was not sober; yet in a pamphlet, which he wrote upon fevers, he appealed to Garrick and me for his vindication from a charge of drunkenness. A bookseller (naming him,) who got a large fortune by trade, was so habitually and equably drunk, that his most intimate friends never perceived that he was more sober at one time than another.'

James Boswell *Life of Johnson*

Take My Advice

'Son, you look to me like a man of two great weaknesses, either one of which may ruin you. Women and whiskey, in that order. Take my advice, if you don't want to wind up being one more Barney Google like me. First thing you ought to do is throw away that shirt. Never wear light colors. They catch the sun. Blue is best – mailman blue. The whole secret of not ending up an O-Daddy on a line is to look as much like a mailman as possible – who knows what the mailman *looks* like? Who'd recognize him if he changed suits? Get a cap with a peak that shadows the eyes. Wear glasses that throw back the light. Grow a mustache but don't go into bars. If you must drink, lock the door and drink by yourself. Conviviality leads to fist-fighting, fist-fighting leads to rage. Look out for rage, son. People never forget a man they've seen in a rage.'

Nelson Algren *A Walk on the Wild Side*

RESOLUTIONS

Beer Only

All right, Geoffrey: suppose we forget it until you're feeling better: we can cope with it in a day or two, when you're sober.'

'But good lord!'

The Consul sat perfectly still staring at the floor while the enormity of the insult passed into his soul. As if, as if, he were not sober now! Yet there was some elusive subtlety in the impeachment that still escaped him. For he was not sober. No, he was not, not at this very moment he wasn't! But what had that to do with a minute before, or half an hour ago? And what right had Yvonne to assume it, assume either that he was not sober now, or that, far worse, in a day or two he *would* be sober? And even if he were not sober now, by what fabulous stages, comparable indeed only to the paths and spheres of the Holy Cabbala itself, had he reached *this* stage again, touched briefly once before this morning, this stage at which alone he could, as she put it, 'cope', this precarious precious stage, so arduous to maintain, of being drunk in which alone he was sober! What right had she, when he had sat suffering the tortures of the damned and the madhouse on her behalf for fully twenty-five minutes on end without having a decent drink, even to hint that he was anything but, to her eyes, sober? Ah, a woman could not know the perils, the complications, yes, the *importance* of a drunkard's life! From what conceivable standpoint of rectitude did she imagine she could judge what was anterior to her arrival? And she knew nothing whatever of what all too recently he had gone through, his fall in the Calle Nicaragua, his aplomb, coolness, even bravery there – the Burke's Irish whiskey! What a world! And the trouble was she had now spoiled the moment. Because the Consul now felt that he might have been capable, remembering Yvonne's 'perhaps I'll have one after breakfast', and all that implied, of saying, in a minute (but for her remark and yes, in spite of any salvation), 'Yes by all means you are right: let us go!' But who could agree with someone who was so certain you were going to be sober the day after tomorrow? It wasn't as though either, upon the most superficial plane, it were not well known that no one could tell when he was drunk. Just like the Taskersons: God bless them. He was not the person to be seen reeling about in the street. True he might lie down in the street, if need be, like a gentleman, but he would not reel. Ah, what a world it was, that trampled down the truth and drunkards alike! A world full of bloodthirsty people, no less! Bloodthirsty, did I hear you say bloodthirsty, Commander Firmin?

'But my lord, Yvonne, surely you know by this time I can't get drunk however much I drink,' he said almost tragically, taking an abrupt swallow of strychnine. 'Why, do you think I *like* swilling down this awful *nux vomica* or belladonna or whatever it is of Hugh's?' The Consul got up with his empty glass and began to walk around the room. He was not so much aware of having done by default anything fatal (it wasn't as if, for instance, he'd thrown his whole life away) as something merely foolish, and at the same time, as it were, sad. Yet there seemed a call for some amends. He either thought or said:

'Well, tomorrow perhaps I'll drink beer only. There's nothing like beer to straighten you out, and a little more strychnine, and then the next day just beer – I'm sure no one will object if I drink beer. This Mexican stuff is particularly full of vitamins, I gather . . . For I can see it really is going to be somewhat of an occasion, this reunion of us all, and then perhaps when my nerves are back to normal again, I'll go off it completely. And then, who knows,' he brought up by the door, 'I might get down to work again and finish my book!'

Malcolm Lowry *Under the Volcano*

Giving Up

I felt my heart curl and my scalp hum. Why? I gave up spirits three days ago. Giving up spirits is okay so long as you drink an incredible amount of beer, sherry, wine and port and can cope with especially bad hangovers. I think I had an especially bad hangover.

Martin Amis *Money*

Bad Practice

Boswell, a notable drinker by any standards, exemplifies even more than Pepys the diarist's naive faith in his own willpower, despite the innumerable times he is proved wrong. His journals are a compendium of good intentions whose shelf-life can be as little as twenty-four hours. Here is a series of entries from 1777, when Boswell was at home in Scotland, pursuing his career as a lawyer.

Tuesday, 4 February. Dined at Lord Monboddo's with a good deal of company; drank rather too much. Called in on my way home at Mr John Syme's to consult the cause, Cuttar against Rae. He followed the old method, and read over my paper from beginning to end. I was intoxicated to a certain degree. Met in the street with a coarse strumpet, went to the Castle Hill, was lascivious with her, but had prudence enough to prevent me from embarking. Was vexed that I had begun bad practices in 1777. Home and finished a paper.

Wednesday, 5 February. Dined with my wife and Miss Cuninghame at Mr Claud Boswell's. Drank a good deal too much. Tea there. At night was in a certain degree of intoxication; made Cameron, the chairman, send Peggie Dundas to me to the Castle Hill, where I lay with her without fear because I had been once safe; and such was my state of mind that at the time I felt no check of conscience but enjoyed her with appetite. No sooner was I at home than I was sadly vexed at what I had done, and my dearest wife saw from my countenance what had happened. I at once confessed. She was more seriously affected than I ever saw her. Dr and Mrs and Miss Grant, Burnett, Andrew Stewart, Junior, Bob Craig from Irvine, Hallglenmuir, and Knocktoon supped.

Thursday, 6 February. Was vexed at the recollection of last night, and despaired almost of acting properly. We dined at Sir George Preston's. Captain Brisbane, who was wounded at Bunker's Hill, was there, and gave such an account of wounds and death as shocked me.

Monday, 10 February. Mr Claud Boswell, his sister Miss Merrie, Lady Wallace, and Miss Susie Dunlop dined with us. I drank a bottle and a half of claret, which was too much. But I considered that I had a branch of our ancient family with me, and I would be cordial with him. I however found that he had nothing of family spirit in him, so that even wine could not unite him and me.

Tuesday, 11 February. For several days my dear wife had been distant to me, and no wonder. This day she abated of her displeasure. I was in remarkable vigour of health and spirits, as I have sometimes been after drinking freely. I was early out of Court, and walked with my wife in the New Town, and looked at a house which was to sell.

Wednesday, 12 February. M. Dupont and Grange drank tea with us. Surgeon Wood and his wife and daughter and brother in partnership with him, whom I had not seen before, and Grange supped. I was in a flow of spirits, and though I was to open Sir Allan Maclean's cause against the Duke of Argyll next day, and had not made out notes for it, I most improperly pushed about the port wine, and drank till between two and three in the morning. I deluded myself by imagining that I was thinking of the Cause and brightening my ideas. I was much intoxicated.

Thursday, 13 February. Could not get up till it was nearly nine, and was very sick and confused and had a violent headache. I was truly miserable, and shocked at my inexcusable ill-timed excess. I was for two hours in a wretched state; could get no rest for sickness and pain. The hearing did not come on till between twelve and one. I said to Mr Lawrie, 'This is terrible. It is like going into battle.' I had, however, a wonderful indifference as to the appearance which I was to make. I thought McQueen's Information had stated the cause ably. I could not therefore go wrong if I kept to it; and indeed it might save me the exertion of finding out arguments of my own ... I would have asked to have the cause put off by pleading indisposition; but I thought the real fact would come out, and my character as a practitioner would be hurt. I spoke about an hour and a half, and though I had not a single note, I really went tolerably through the cause . . . To get through at all decently was a great deal. This must be a warning to me for the future . . .

Friday, 14 February. This day was passed in the usual indistinguished way. I laboured well.

Saturday 15 February. Lady Colville, Lady Anne, and Captain Erskin dined with us. Mr Andrew was engaged. It was a calm, agreeable party. Lady Colville insisted on my attending her to the play. It was *The Clandestine Marriage.* I had company to sup with me, so came out at eight. I was a little elevated with wine, and picked up a girl in the street, with whom I went to the Meadow and had some lascivious sport, but did not embark. I was ashamed of my low appetite immediately. Mrs Dunlop of Dunlop, who was in town for a little, and her daughters Susie and Fannie, young Vans Agnew, who was to be married to the latter, Lady Wallace, Miss Mattie Graham of Dougalston, and Bute Lindsay supped with us. It was a cheerful meeting.

James Boswell

ROCK BOTTOM

Brief Reality

In the middle of the night you wake up. You start to cry. What's happening to me? Oh, my life, oh, my youth. . . . .

There's some wine left in the bottle. You drink it. The clock ticks. Sleep. . . .

Jean Rhys *Good Morning, Midnight*

The Black Man

Ah friend, my friend,
how sick I am. Nor do I know
whence came this sickness.
Either the wind whistles
over the desolate unpeopled field,
or like a September copse
alcohol assaults my brain.

My head waves my ears
like a bird its wings.
Unendurably it looms on my neck
when I walk.
The black
black
black man
sits by me on the bed all night
won't let me sleep.

This black man
runs his fingers down a vile book,
and, twanging over me
like a sleepy monk
indicts the life

of some drunken wretch,
filling my heart with longing and despair.
A black man
oh a black black man.

'Listen, listen, –'
he mutters to me –
'the book is full of beautiful
plans and resolutions.
This fellow lived
his life in a land
of the most repulsive
thieves and charlatans.

And in that land the December snow
is pure as the very devil,
and the snowstorms drive
merry spinning-wheels.
This man was a chancer,
though of the highest
and best quality.
Oh he was elegant,
– and a poet at that –
albeit of a slight
but penetrating gift,
he called some woman
– forty or so – his
"filthy whore", his
"beloved".

Happiness – he said
is quickness of hand and mind.
Slow fools are always
known for unhappy.
Heartaches, we know,
derive
from broken lying gestures

and into thunder and tempest,
and the world's coldheartedness
at times of heavy loss,
and when you are sad
it seems laughably simple –
the best of life is Art.'

'Black man!
This is no laughing matter.
You do not live as
deep-sea diver.
What's the life
of a scandalous poet to me?
Please read the tale
of someone else.'

The black man
Looks me straight in the eye
and his eyes screen
vomit-blue – as though
he wanted to tell me
I'm a thief and rogue
who'd robbed a man
openly without shame.

Ah friend, my friend,
how sick I am. Nor do I know
whence came this sickness.
Either the wind whistles
over the desolate unpeopled field
Or like a September copse
alcohol assaults my brain.
The night is freezing.
Still peace at the crossroads
I am alone at the window
expecting neither visitor nor friend.
The whole plain is covered

with soft quick-lime,
and the trees like riders
in our garden conspire.

Somewhere a night-bird
ill-omened is sobbing.
The wooden riders
scatter hoofbeats.
And again the black man
in sitting in my chair,
lifts his top-hat
and, casual, takes off his cape.
'Listen, listen,'
he cries, eyes on my face,
all the time leaning closer.
'I never knew one
of these rogues
stupidly, pointlessly,
suffer insomnia.

Well, I could be wrong.
There is a moon tonight.
What more is needful
in your drunken world than sleep?
Perhaps She will come,
with her fat thighs,
in secret, and you read
your languid carrion
verse to her.

Ah, how I love these poets!
A holy race!
I always find in them
a story known to my heart.
Such as a long-haired monster
sweating sexual lassitude
breathes to a pimply student.

I don't know, don't remember,
in some village,
Kaluga perhaps, or
maybe Ryazan,
there lived a boy
of simple peasant stock,
blonde-haired
and angel-eyed.

And he grew up,
grew up into a poet
of slight but
penetrating talent,
and some woman
of forty or so
called his filthy girl,
his loved one.'

'Black man!
An odious guest!
This ill-fame
is old talk of you.'
Enraged, possessed,
I let him have it –
my cane flies
straight across
the bridge of his nose.

. . .

The moon has died.
Dawn glimmers in the window.
Ah, you, night,
what have you covered up all night?
I stand top-hatted;
no one is with me,
I am alone,
and the mirror is broken.

Sergei Esenin *The Black Man*, trans. Geoffrey Thurley

Committed

'They say we have weak wills. Do you know about the two drunks who went to the film of *The Lost Weekend*. Came staggering out. "My God I'll never take another drink," said the first. "My God I'll never go to another movie." How's that for commitment? one-track all-powerful, same energy do the *Critique of Practical Reason*. Protecting his habit. Plink.'

John Berryman *Recovery*

Bottle

A telephone was ringing somewhere. He opened his eyes. Where was he. Home? His mother's? Oh. Here.

He listened to the phone. It rang six or seven times and then stopped. He closed his eyes, relieved.

It began to ring again. It rang out from the bedroom, stinging him like some nasty metallic kind of gnat, impossible to fight off. Whoever it was had thought, maybe, they'd got the wrong number, maybe, and tried again. He had no intention of answering it so that didn't matter, but he was fully awake now and that did.

The telephone finally stopped ringing and then didn't ring any more. He looked at the clock. It was half-past nine. The room was filled with light, a kind of glare reflected from the bright sun on the back of the apartment building across the garden. He turned his head on the pillow and looked around to see where the bottle was and found it. Oh, there it was; all right. On the table. A great big quart. Large as life and twice as empty.

Was he ever going to learn? Ever be wise and smart and sober enough one night, or one day, to see that he had something put by for tomorrow? Did he always have to drink it all up? Was he going to keep on for ever and ever being trapped for a fool, by no one but himself?

He got up to see if it was really empty, but really empty he meant of the last little sip. It was. Trust him. Trust the drunken hog of the night before. And the stupid fool. *Never put off till tomorrow what you can drink today,* that's me. As he stood at the table, he realized how weak he was. This was hangover. But the real thing. Thank God, he was dressed, he wouldn't have the dressing to go through, the fumbling with buttons, the insoluble puzzle that would be the shoelaces. He trembled like a high-strung terrier – shook all over with little fine tremors, a minute palsy. Not so damned minute either. *Now* what was he going to do?

Charles Jackson *The Lost Weekend*

Small Hours

In the real dark night of the soul it is always three o'clock in the morning.

F. Scott Fitzgerald *The Crack-Up*

The Fell of Dark

'No sedatives in the daytime. We try to maintain or restore the normal sleep-cycle, you see – make them stay awake during the day. Put them to sleep now and they'll be raising hell all night. That fellow over there took a running jump at the wall around three-thirty this morning and got a terrible shaking-up. Thought it was the ocean and wanted to jump in. That wouldn't have happened in the daytime. Delirium is a disease of the night.'

Charles Jackson *The Lost Weekend*

Why?

'Never ask me why. I don't know the answer. If I did, I wouldn't do it.'

Joseph Blotner: *Faulkner, A Biography*

Terminal

I should like to sit down with half a dozen close companions and drink myself to death but I am sick alike of life, liquor and literature.

F. Scott Fitzgerald to Maxwell Perkins, August 1921

Step One

Here is the text of Berryman's Step One:

> Social drinking until 1947 during a long & terrible love affair, my first infidelity to my wife after 5 years of marriage. My mistress drank heavily & I drank w. her. Guilt, murderous & suicidal. Hallucinations one day walking home. Heard voices. 7 years of psychoanalysis & group therapy in NY. Walked up & down drunk on a foot-wide parapet 8 stories high. Passes at women drunk, often successful. Wife left me after 11 yrs of marriage bec. of drinking. Despair, heavy drinking alone, jobless, penniless, in NY. Lost when blacked-out the most important professional letter I have ever received. Seduced students drunk. Made homosexual advances drunk, 4 or 5 times. Antabuse once for a few days, agony on floor after a beer. Quarrel w. landlord drunk at midnight over the key to my apartment, he called police, spent the night in jail, news somehow reached press & radio, forced to resign. Two months of intense self-analysis-dream-

interpretations etc. Remarried. My chairman told me I had called up a student drunk at midnight & threatened to kill her. Wife left me bec. of drinking. Gave a public lecture drunk. Drunk in Calcutta, wandered streets lost all night, unable to remember my address. Married present wife 8 yrs ago. Many barbiturates & tranquilizers off & on over last 10 yrs. Many hospitalizations. Many alibis for drinking, lying abt it. Severe memory-loss, memory distortions. DT's once in Abbott, lasted hours. Quart of whisky a day for months in Dublin working hard on a long poem. Dry 4 months 2 years ago. Wife hiding bottles, myself hiding bottles. Wet bed drunk in London hotel, manager furious, had to pay for new mattress, $100. Lectured too weak to stand, had to sit. Lectured badly prepared. Too ill to give an examination, colleague gave it. Too ill to lecture one day. Literary work stalled for months. Quart of whiskey a day for months. Wife desperate, threatened to leave unless I stopped. Two doctors drove me to Hazelden last November, 1 week intensive care unit, 5 wks treatment. AA 3 times, bored, made no friends. First drink at Newlbars' party. Two months' light drinking, hard biographical work. Suddenly began new poems 9 weeks ago, heavier & heavier drinking more & more, up to a quart a day. Defecated uncontrollably in a University corridor, got home unnoticed. Book finished in outburst of five weeks, most intense work in my whole life exc. maybe first two months of 1953. My wife said St Mary's or else. Came here.

Worst temptations to drinking:
parties, poetry-readings – refuse both for a year – & verse-writing: problem won't come up for 18 months or 2 years.

Replacements for drinking:
work on my Shakespeare biography morning & afternoons – I drink v. little when doing scholarly work or writing prose: 2 or 3 drinks a day. Evenings: reading or music or conversation. Need more social life, tho' not parties.
Absolutely certain my wife will leave me if I start drinking again; afraid I might then kill myself.
Absolutely certain any more drinking will mean insanity or suicide, perh. quite soon, 2 or 3 years.

Hopes for sobriety: a reformed marriage, trust in Jim, reliance on God: outpatient treatment, AA.

John Haffenden *The Life of John Berryman*

Pulley

O'Neill would prop himself against the bar and order his shot. The bartender knew him, and would place the glass in front of him, toss a towel across the bar, as though absent-mindedly forgetting it, and move away. Arranging the towel around his neck, O'Neill would grasp the glass of whiskey and an end of the towel in one hand and clutch the other end of the towel with his other hand. Using the towel as a pulley, he would laboriously hoist the glass to his lips. His hands trembled so violently that even with this aid he could scarcely pour the whiskey down his throat, and often spilled part of it.

Arthur and Barbara Gelb *O'Neill*

Bellevue and Back

'I really was in bad shape at the time,' he went on. 'Underweight, a bad cough, and of course blotto whenever I could be, which meant whenever one of the remittance derelicts got a cheque – we would immediately drink it up! It sure was lousy stuff that Jimmy served. So I again asked the folks for money, putting it so strong that I was sure this time they'd send a cheque – at least enough to get me to New London where they were going to spend the summer.'

Gene shivered, got up and looked out of the window at the windswept rainy bay, and then came back and suggested that we have some more coffee in a little while. 'I didn't know it, but they'd gone away for a couple of weeks, taking Jamie with them. However, I did get a letter – it seemed that Kathleen wanted a divorce. I didn't answer; then I thought it over. I decided to take matters in my own hands. . . .'

A day or so later Gene found himself in a room with a sordid blonde who sat on the edge of the bed and smoked one cigarette after another, while he nervously paced the floor. She finally got up and casually removed most of her clothes – meantime telling him the story of her life – so that by the time a detective came in Gene was as sorry for her as for himself. After that there was nothing for him to do but return to Jimmy the Priest's, feeling utterly sick, degraded and – without a drink. He had a desperate hope that the expected cheque would be there from his father, but it wasn't. Everyone was broke and sitting around with the jitters, just about as he described it later in a scene in *The Iceman Cometh*. Gene spent a nickel of the small amount he had left and made a collect call to New London – no answer! Jimmy refused any more drinks to anyone. He was in a bad mood that night and even hinted to Gene that he pay up his room rent or leave the next morning. Gene went up to his dusty dismal room, sat on the cot and brooded. Somehow this whole episode with the prostitute, the connection of all of it with the nice and really innocent Kathleen, whom he now for some reason recalled regretfully and who seemed like himself just another pawn of fate; the rejection of him by his parents (for of this he was sure now) and no Jamie there to talk things over with – all this threw him into a depth of despair from which he could not or did not want to emerge. He had enough change for another drink or so, but he knew from experience that a couple of drinks would not help him. Besides, could he drink in front of the others downstairs while they were suffering – they who had always shared with him?

So, determined to end it all, and no doubt somewhat comforted by the thought of the horrible effect on his parents when they found that their refusal to send more money had caused his death, and also, he said, because he couldn't stand his thoughts any longer, he went out, unseen by the others, and bought a lot of veronal tablets. At that time, according to newspaper stories, this was an often used way of ending one's life. Determined to make a good job of it and never again wake up, he took all the tablets, washed down by a glass of dirty water, put the hook on the inside of the door and passed out without even having time, first, to experience that glimpse of eternity or nothingness which he had expected and was waiting for. . . .

'I must have been there twenty-four hours, maybe longer,' Gene told me. 'I vaguely remembered coming to, hearing a knocking on the door, then silence. . . . This happened a number of times, but I paid no attention to it. It didn't occur to me that I was alive – after all those pills! At first I probably thought I was still on my way, not dead yet, but getting there. Perhaps I didn't think at all, just felt resentful that the veronal hadn't yet completely put me out and that I could hear the knocks. . . .

'Then a horrible thought came to me – I *was* dead, of course, *and death was nothing but a continuation of life as it had been when one left it!* A wheel that turned endlessly round and round back to the same old situation! This was what purgatory was – or was it hell itself? My body was dead, but *I* was there too. Frozen in a sort of motionless unbearable horror, I went into a stupor, hardly conscious – at least that was an escape from purgatory, or hell, whichever it was. . . . At last – how long I don't know – the knocking came again. This time there were loud bangs and oaths. Someone pushed hard against the door and then the flimsy hook loosened. I sat up. I knew then that I wasn't dead, for my old pals from below were all there, in the room, in the hall outside. They looked worried and excited and all badly in need of a drink and old ——, who came in first, held a letter which he waved at me – from my father. *He* opened it. There was a cheque for twenty five dollars.'

Gene paused a moment. . . .

'Jimmy deducted the room rent when he cashed it for me – and then drinks were on the house.' He shook his head. '*Wow!* What a celebration.'

'But *you* – you mean you got right up and went down and drank?'

'No – I'm coming to that. I tried to stand up, couldn't make it. They propped me up on the bed and brought me a drink, but that didn't do any good. They told how they'd been trying to get to me for hours – every once in a while somebody'd come up and bang on the door. Then they decided maybe I was dead and they'd break in. Then the major saw the empty pill bottles and I had to tell them what had happened. That's how the celebration began – they celebrated my return to life! The Boer War colonel endorsed the cheque for me, and they went down to the bar and began to drink. But there was a brotherly love behind it – they had to get rid of their shakes in order to be able to take me to the hospital. Jimmy himself insisted on this. I think he still was afraid that I was going to die at his place. Every half hour or so he'd come up to see how I was feeling. Finally they got me downstairs. Jimmy called Bellevue and found out I'd live because I'd taken an overdose, but I should go over at once and let them look at me. ... By this time I was feeling a little better, and so the gang had another round to celebrate *that!* I was able to keep down a drink myself.

'Anyway, to make a long story short, we didn't get going for a couple of hours or more. Jimmy would start to call a taxi, then put it off. At last we made it. The taxi got there, but Jimmy couldn't leave, and I was still rather weak and they thought I shouldn't go without them being along to take care of me. So five of them climbed into the taxi along with me. Jimmy Tomorrow brought a bottle along. We stopped on the way up twice, and the taxi driver had a couple of drinks – he didn't know what it was all about but he thought it was a good joke anyway. ... Jimmy Tomorrow passed out on the way over, then the general, and when we got there I was the only one sober. Ole Olson and Pete were hardly able to get out of the cab and had to be dragged out forcibly by the taxi driver. It seems' – Gene laughed wickedly – 'that he had taken us to the entrance of the alcoholic ward!

'First thing they did was to take away the bottle, which had a couple of drinks left in it. I was still in a sort of daze when I heard the intern telling me he'd take care of them – they'd get the works and be all right in a few days. I found myself alone at the desk. They'd all been taken away protesting incoherently, of course, and I was trying to explain without saying a word. 'Tough job you had!' the intern said politely. The taxi man was grinning; he evidently thought I'd had a tough job too. I got into the taxi and drove back to Jimmy the Priest's and managed to get potted to the gills. We all thought it was the biggest joke in the whole damn world.'

'Oh God – those old days. Nobody'd believe it. Nobody'd understand it. . . .'

Agnes Boulton *Part of a Long Story*

Ecce Homo

'So be it! "Behold the man!" Excuse me, young man, can you . . . No, to put it more strongly and more distinctly: not *can* you but *dare* you, looking upon me, assert that I am not a pig?'

The young man did not answer a word.

'Well,' the orator began again stolidly and with even increased dignity, after waiting for the laughter in the room to subside. 'Well, so be it, I am a pig, but she is a lady! I have the semblance of a beast, but Katerina Ivanovna, my spouse, is a person of education and an officer's daughter. Granted, granted, I am a scoundrel, but she is a woman of a noble heart, full of sentiments, refined by education. And yet . . . oh, if only she felt for me! Honoured sir, honoured sir, you know every man ought to have at least one place where people feel for him! But Katerina Ivanovna, though she is magnanimous, she is unjust. . . . And yet, although I realize that when she pulls my hair she only does it out of pity – for I repeat without being ashamed, she pulls my hair, young man,' he declared, with redoubled dignity, hearing the sniggering again – 'but, my God, if she would but once . . . But no, no! It's all in vain and it's no use talking! No use talking! For more than once, my wish did come true and more than once she has felt for me but . . . such is my fate and I am a beast by nature!'

'Rather!' assented the innkeeper, yawning. Marmeladov struck his fist resolutely on the table.

'Such is my fate! Do you know, sir, do you know, I have sold her very stockings for drink? Not her shoes – that would be more or less in the order of things, but her stockings, her stockings I have sold for drink! Her mohair shawl I sold for drink, a present to her long ago, her own property, not mine; and we live in a cold room and she caught cold this winter and has begun coughing and spitting blood too. We have three little children and Katerina Ivanovna is at work from morning till night; she is scrubbing and cleaning and washing the children, for she's been used to cleanliness from a child. But her chest is weak and she has a tendency to consumption and I feel it! Do you suppose I don't feel it? And the more I drink the more I feel it. That's why I drink too. I try to find sympathy and feeling in drink . . . I drink so that I may suffer twice as much!' And as though in despair he laid his head down on the table.

Fyodor Dostoevsky *Crime and Punishment*, trans. Constance Garnett

A Green Song

to sing at the bottle-bank

One green bottle,
Drop it in the bank.
Ten green bottles,
What a lot we drank.
Heaps of bottles
And yesterday's a blank
But we'll save the planet,
Tinkle, tinkle, clank!

We've got bottles –
Nice, percussive trash.
Bags of bottles
Cleaned us out of cash.
Empty bottles,
We love to hear them smash
And we'll save the planet,
Tinkle, tinkle, crash!

Wendy Cope

Rough Stuff

I began getting memory blackouts far quicker and for much longer stretches. It started to worry me – waking up not knowing what I'd done the day before, who I was with, where I'd been, whether I'd committed a crime. I usually had. But had it been a big or a little one? I also began wetting the bed.

One afternoon, after the pubs closed at 3 p.m., I bought a bottle of Scotch and went into the park to drink it. In about ten minutes I was surrounded by a load of winos and alcoholics. They were the roughest-looking people I had ever seen, and I was no stranger to mangled features. I sent for more drink and one of them brought back a few bottles of wine. I woke up in the park with them the next morning and found about £12 down my sock. They knew where to get a drink even at that early hour and it wasn't long before the party was in full swing again. We all drank fast . . . their conversation coming suddenly in violent bursts, raw and cutting.

One thing that impressed me about these winos was that they did not care what anyone had done in drink or otherwise the day before. They were immune to shock. I remember one instance. A guy called Mills, who they told me was a bit of a psychopath, fell over at the height of the afternoon's drinking and damaged his wrist and ankle. He was lying moaning on the ground when his troubles came to the attention of one of the Scotch blokes. The little Jock was smaller than Mills and, I was told, had been beaten up by him several times in the past. Here was the chance to even the score a little. He did – by kicking most of Mills' front teeth out as he lay writhing in agony. He had further plans for Mills too, but fell down drunk before he could carry them out.

John Healy *The Grass Arena*

Haven

Under the concreted cantilevered
haven of arty
spans of the *Bibliothek*,
shivering dossers each evening repose in
newspaper bivvies.
Mornings, they head for the park.

Slats of the frost-crusted park benches steam in
8 a.m. sunlight.
Scavenging corvine-clawed men
rifle each *Abfalleimer*, greedily
glean after rye crusts
flung for gross ducks near the lake,

swig the sour dregs of the bottle-bank empties,
Tafelwein, Schaumwein,
Spätlese, Steinhäger, Schnapps.
Today I have planted a two-kilo *Schinken*
where they will find it
[hooray for the secular saint].

Peter Reading *Perduta Gente*

Sneaking a Shit

Someone had go at the toilet attendant once: after that he left the shithouse locked so no strange dossers could sneak a shit. Mad Gerry didn't worry. He just shit on the washroom floor. We look at people with only one thought in mind: how can we get the price of a drink out of them? Even when sick, shuffling along, heads bent, we are always alert, ever aware like half-tamed animals. We cannot switch off.

Woke up feeling terrible – had a fuzziness in my head, everything seemed blurred, out of shape, odd, like looking through wet glass. I could not remember anything about the last few days. That's the trouble with drink, it ruins your brain cells and when that happens regularly you can get a wet brain. Then you're in a horrible fucking position. Mad Rafferty is curled up like a dog in the corner: bearded, straggle-haired, alive with lice, tattered clothes ripped and stained. He's never been the same since the gypos took him into the country working, never paid him, and tied him under a caravan with a chain each night for a week. He wakes up with a sort of alky shrug, enquiring with a roar if there's any drink . . . nothing.

'Fuck it to hell,' he says. 'I wish I knew where there was a good ironmonger's that'd give us a bottle of blue.'* We make up the price of a bottle of surgical spirits and head for the chemist. I went in alone. Mad Dog was too dirty, but here it wouldn't have mattered.

The chemist was a German or something. He said, 'Yes, how many bottles you vant?' He's all eyes: you can't nick anything.

We could get no water to mix with it, so we went in the church and filled a milk bottle out of the holy water font and started slowly to swallow it. But it's hard to get down first thing in the day – any time for that matter. Bastard stuff. It either makes you dead sleepy and fit for nothing, or drives you mad and ready to kill some cunt. We finished the bottle and were trying to open the collection box when this bloke comes in with a camera round his neck and asks Mad Dog if he can take his photo. Well, the only thing that stands between us reaching tomorrow is a drink, so I said we should go out to the porch, we did not want to be disrespectful in God's house. We went into it, and as he was lining the Dog up, I jumped on his back, arms round his neck. We went down in a heap. Mad Dog dropped, and was down his pockets straight away, but he was skint. All the time the bloke was trying to scream and wouldn't keep still. The Dog gave him a few kicks in the head and he went quiet as we were taking the camera off his neck. An old lady came to the door, she blessed herself, said something in a foreign language and fucked off quickly.

John Healy *The Grass Arena*

*Methylated spirits.

Fuel

Melted-down boot polish, eau de Cologne, meths,
    surgical spirit,
  kerosene, car diesel, derv . . .

When the St Mungo lot roll up with hot soup
    what you should do is
  keep back the slice of dry bread;

after they've fucked off, plaster the one side
    thick with the Brasso –
  goes down a regular treat.

  After a gobble of meths,
  crunch up a Trebor Mint fast –
  takes off the heat and the taste.

Peter Reading

PRO AND CON

Legacy

Coming of a temperance family, drunkenness had always been for me a symbol of freedom.

Louis MacNeice *The Strings Are False*

Because Thou Art Virtuous

(*Enter* MARIA.)

MARIA: What a caterwauling do you keep here! If my lady have not called up her steward Malvolio and bid him turn you out of doors, never trust me.

SIR TOBY: My lady's a Cathayan, we are politicians, Malvolio's a Peg-o'-Ramsey, and 'Three merry men be we'. Am not I consanguineous? Am I not of her blood? Tilly-vally – 'lady'! 'There dwelt a man in Babylon, lady, lady.'

FESTE: Beshrew me, the knight's in admirable fooling.

SIR ANDREW: Ay, he does well enough if he be disposed, and so do I, too. He does it with a better grace, but I do it more natural.

SIR TOBY:
'O' the twelfth day of December' –

MARIA: For the love o' God, peace.

(*Enter* MALVOLIO.)

MALVOLIO: My masters, are you mad? Or what are you? Have you no wit, manners, nor honesty, but to gabble like tinkers at this time of night? Do ye make an alehouse of my lady's house, that ye squeak out your cozier's catches without any mitigation or remorse of voice? Is there no respect of place, persons, nor time in you?

SIR TOBY: We did keep time, sir, in our catches. Sneck up!

MALVOLIO: Sir Toby, I must be round with you. My lady bade me tell you that though she harbours you as her kinsman she's nothing allied to your disorders. If you can separate yourself and your misdemeanours you are welcome to the house. If not, an it would please you to take leave of her she is very willing to bid you farewell.

SIR TOBY:

'Farewell, dear heart, since I must needs be gone.'

MARIA: Nay, good Sir Toby.

FESTE:

'His eyes do show his days are almost done.'

MALVOLIO: Is't even so?

SIR TOBY:

'But I will never die.'

FESTE:

'Sir Toby, there you lie.'

MALVOLIO: This is much credit to you.

SIR TOBY:

'Shall I bid him go?'

FESTE:

'What an if you do?'

SIR TOBY:

'Shall I bid him go, and spare not?'

FESTE:

'O no, no, no, no, you dare not.'

SIR TOBY: Out o' tune, sir, ye lie. (*To* MALVOLIO) Art any more than a steward? Dost thou think because thou art virtuous there shall be no more cakes and ale?

FESTE: Yes, by Saint Anne, and ginger shall be hot i'th' mouth, too.

SIR TOBY: Thou'rt i'th' right. (*To* MALVOLIO) Go, sir, rub your chain with crumbs. (*To* MARIA) A stoup of wine, Maria.

MALVOLIO: Mistress Mary, if you prized my lady's favour at anything more than contempt you would not give means for this uncivil rule. She shall know of it, by this hand. (*Exit.*)

MARIA: Go shake your ears.

William Shakespeare *Twelfth Night*

Benevolence

Tuesday, 28 April 1778. BOSWELL. 'The great difficulty of resisting wine is from benevolence. For instance, a good worthy man asks you to taste his wine, which he has had twenty years in his cellar.' JOHNSON. 'Sir, all this notion about benevolence arises from a man's imagining himself to be of more importance to others, than he really is. They don't care a farthing whether he drinks wine or not.' SIR JOSHUA REYNOLDS. 'Yes, they do for the time. JOHNSON. 'For the time! – If they care this minute, they forget it the next. And as for the good worthy man; how do you know he is good and worthy? No good and worthy man will insist upon another man's drinking wine. As to the wine twenty years in the cellar, – of ten men, three say this, merely because they must say something; – three are telling a lie, when they say they have had the wine twenty years; – three would rather save the wine; – one, perhaps, cares. I allow it is something to please one's company: and people are always pleased with those who partake pleasure with them. But after a man has brought himself to relinquish the great personal pleasure which arises from drinking wine, any other consideration is a trifle. To please others by drinking wine, is something, only if there be nothing against it. I should, however, be sorry to offend worthy men: –

> "Curst be the verse, how well so e'er it flow,
> That tends to make one worthy man my foe."'

BOSWELL. 'Curst be the *spring*, the *water*.' JOHNSON. 'But let us consider what a sad thing it would be, if we were obliged to drink or do any thing else that may happen to be agreeable to the company where we are.' LANGTON. 'By the same rule you must join with a gang of cut-purses.' JOHNSON. 'Yes, Sir: but yet we must do justice to wine; we must allow it the power it possesses. To make a man pleased with himself, let me tell you, is doing a very great thing;

"*Si patriæ volumus, si* Nobis *vivere cari.*"'*

I was at this time myself a water-drinker, upon trial, by Johnson's recommendation. JOHNSON. 'Boswell is a bolder combatant than Sir Joshua: he argues for wine without the help of wine; but Sir Joshua with it.' SIR JOSHUA REYNOLDS. 'But to please one's company is a strong motive.' JOHNSON. (who, from drinking only water, supposed every body who drank wine to be elevated,) 'I won't argue any more with you, Sir. You are too far gone.' SIR JOSHUA. 'I should have thought so indeed, Sir, had I made such a speech as you have now done.' JOHNSON. (drawing himself in, and, I really thought blushing,) 'Nay, don't be angry. I did not mean to offend you.' SIR JOSHUA. 'At first the taste of wine was disagreeable to me; but I brought myself to drink it, that I might be like other people. The pleasure of drinking wine is so connected with pleasing your company, that altogether there is something of social goodness in it.' JOHNSON. 'Sir, this is only saying the same thing over again.' SIR JOSHUA. 'No, this is new.' JOHNSON. 'You put it in new words, but it is an old thought. This is one of the disadvantages of wine. It makes a man mistake words for thoughts.' BOSWELL. 'I think it is a new thought; at least, it is in a new *attitude*,' JOHNSON. 'Nay, Sir, it is only in a new coat; or an old coat with a new facing. (Then laughing heartily,) It is the old dog in a new doublet. – An extraordinary instance however may occur where a man's patron will do nothing for him, unless he will drink: *there* may be a good reason for drinking.'

I mentioned a nobleman, who I believed was really uneasy if his company would not drink hard. JOHNSON. 'That is from having had people about him whom he has been accustomed to command.' BOSWELL. 'Supposing I should be *tête-a-tête* with him at table.' JOHNSON. 'Sir, there is no more reason for your drinking with *him*, than his being sober with *you*.' BOSWELL. 'Why, that is true; for it would do him less hurt to be sober, than it would do me to get drunk.' JOHNSON. 'Yes, Sir; and from what I have heard of him,

*'If we could make our life of value to our country *and to ourselves*.' Horace, *Epistles* i.3.29.

one would not wish to sacrifice himself to such a man. If he must always have somebody to drink with, he should buy a slave, and then he would be sure to have it. They who submit to drink as another pleases, make themselves his slaves.' BOSWELL. 'But, Sir, you will surely make allowance for the duty of hospitality. A gentleman who loves drinking, comes to visit me.' JOHNSON. 'Sir, a man knows whom he visits; he comes to the table of a sober man.' BOSWELL. 'But, Sir, you and I should not have been so well received in the Highlands and Hebrides, if I had not drunk with our worthy friends. Had I drunk water only as you did, they would not have been so cordial.' JOHNSON. 'Sir William Temple mentions that in his travels through the Netherlands he had two or three gentlemen with him; and when a bumper was necessary, he put it on *them*. Were I to travel again through the islands, I would have Sir Joshua with me to take the bumpers.' BOSWELL. 'But, Sir, let me put a case. Suppose Sir Joshua should take a jaunt into Scotland; he does me the honour to pay me a visit at my house in the country; I am overjoyed at seeing him; we are quite by ourselves, shall I unsociably and churlishly let him sit drinking by himself? No, no, my dear Sir Joshua, you shall not be treated so, I *will* take a bottle with you.'

James Boswell *Life of Johnson*

Bob Polter

BOB POLTER was a navvy, and
His hands were coarse, and dirty too,
His homely face was rough and tanned,
His time of life was thirty-two.

He lived among a working clan
(A wife he hadn't got at all),
A decent, steady, sober man –
No saint, however – not at all.

He smoked, but in a modest way,
Because he thought he needed it;
He drank a pot of beer a day,
And sometimes he exceeded it.

At times he'd pass with other men
A loud convivial night or two,
With, very likely, now and then,
On Saturdays, a fight or two.

But still he was a sober soul,
A labour-never-shrinking man,
Who paid his way – upon the whole,
A decent English working-man.

One day, when at the Nelson's Head
(For which he may be blamed of you),
A holy man appeared and said,
'Oh, ROBERT, I'm ashamed of you.'

He laid his hand on Robert's beer
Before he could drink up any,
And on the floor, with sigh and tear,
He poured the pot of 'thruppenny.'

'Oh, ROBERT, at this very bar,
A truth you'll be discovering,
A good and evil genius are
Around your noddle hovering.

'They both are here to bid you shun
The other one's society,
For Total Abstinence is one,
The other, Inebriety.'

He waved his hand – a vapour came –
  A wizard, Polter reckoned him:
A bogy rose and called his name,
  And with his finger beckoned him.

The monster's salient points to sum,
  His breath was hot as cautery;
His glowing nose suggested rum;
  His eyes were gin-and-watery.

His dress was torn – for dregs of ale
  And slops of gin had rusted it;
His pimpled face was wan and pale,
  Where filth had not encrusted it.

'Come, POLTER,' said the fiend, 'begin,
  And keep the bowl a-flowing on –
A working-man needs pints of gin
  To keep his clockwork going on.'

BOB shuddered: 'Ah, you've made a miss,
  If you take me for one of you –
You filthy brute, get out of this –
  BOB POLTER don't want none of you.'

The demon gave a drunken shriek,
  And crept away in stealthiness,
And lo, instead, a person sleek
  Who seemed to burst with healthiness.

'In me, as your adviser hints,
  Of Abstinence you've got a type –
Of MR TWEEDIE's pretty prints
  I am the happy prototype.

'If you abjure the social toast,
   And pipes, and such frivolities,
You possibly some day may boast
   My prepossessing qualities!'

Bob rubbed his eyes, and made 'em blink,
   'You almost make me tremble, you!
If I abjure fermented drink,
   Shall I, indeed, resemble you?

'And will my whiskers curl so tight?
   My cheeks grow smug and muttony?
My face become so pink and white?
   My coat so blue and buttony?

'Will trousers, such as yours, array
   Extremities inferior?
Will chubbiness assert its sway
   All over my exterior?

'In this, my unenlightened state,
   To work in heavy boots I comes –
Will pumps henceforward decorate
   My tiddle toddle tootsicums?

'And shall I get so plump and fresh,
   And look no longer seedily?
My skin will henceforth fit my flesh
   So tightly and so Tweedie-ly?'

The phantom said, 'You'll have all this,
   You'll have no kind of huffiness,
Your life will be one chubby bliss,
   One long unruffled puffiness!'

'Be off,' said irritated BOB,
  'Why come you here to bother one?
You pharisaical old snob,
  You're wuss, almost, than t'other one!

'I takes my pipe – I takes my pot,
  And drunk I'm never seen to be
I'm no teetotaller or sot,
  And as I am I mean to be!'

W. S. Gilbert

The Road that Leads from Competence and Peace

Pass where we may, through city or through town,
Village, or hamlet, of this merry land,
Though lean and beggared, every twentieth pace
Conducts the unguarded nose to such a whiff
Of stale debauch, forth-issuing from the styes,
That law has licensed, as makes temperance reel.
There sit, involved and lost in curling clouds
Of Indian fume, and guzzling deep, the boor,
The lackey, and the groom: the craftsman there
Takes Lethean leave of all his toil!
Smith, cobbler, joiner, he that plies the shears,
And he that kneads the dough; all loud alike,
All learned, and all drunk! The fiddle screams,
Plaintive and piteous, as it wept and wailed
Its wasted tones and harmony unheard:
Fierce the dispute whate'er the theme; while she,
Fell discord, arbitress of such debate,
Perched on the sign-post, holds with even hand
Her undecisive scales. In this she lays
A weight of ignorance; in that, of pride;

And smiles delighted with the eternal poise.
Dire is the frequent curse, and its twin sound
The cheek-distending oath, not to be praised
As ornamental, musical, polite,
Like those, which modern senators employ,
Whose oath is rhetoric, and who swears for fame!
Behold the schools, in which plebeian minds
Once simple are initiated in arts,
Which some may practise with politer grace,
But none with readier skill! – 'tis here they learn
The road, that leads from competence and peace
To indigence and rapine; till at last
Society, grown weary of the load,
Shakes her incumbered lap, and casts them out.
But censure profits little: vain the attempt
To advertise in verse a public pest,
That like the filth, with which the peasant feeds
His hungry acres, stinks, and is of use.
The excise is fattened with the rich result
Of all this riot; and ten thousand casks,
For ever dribbling out their base contents,
Touched by the Midas finger of the state,
Bleed gold for minister to sport away.
Drink, and be mad then; 'tis your country bids!
Gloriously drunk obey the important call!
Her cause demands the assistance of your throats; –
Ye all can swallow, and she asks no more.

William Cowper *The Task*

Resources

If all the world
Should in a pet of temperance feed on pulse,
Drink the clear stream, and nothing wear but frieze,
Th' All-giver would be unthanked, would be unpraised,

Not half his riches known, and yet despised,
And we should serve him as a grudging master,
As a penurious niggard of his wealth,
And live like Nature's bastards, not her sons,
Who would be quite surcharged with her own weight,
And strangled with her waste fertility;

John Milton *Comus*

Little Song

1

One time there was a man
Whose drinking bouts began
When he was eighteen . . . So
That was what laid him low.
He died in his eightieth year:
What of, is crystal clear.

2

One time there was a child
Which died when one year old
Quite prematurely . . . So
That was what laid it low.
It never drank, that's clear.
And died aged just one year.

3

Which helps you to assess
Alcohol's harmlessness.

Bertolt Brecht, trans. Edith Anderson,
Lee Bremner, John Cullen *et al*

Your Good Elf

If you drink a bottle of wine a day (or five pints of beer or ten pub whiskies) you're more or less an alcoholic, according to *Tonight*'s documentary on drinking (BBC1 Thursday). Over the past five years the consumption of beer has risen by 12 per cent, spirits by 60 per cent, wine by 'a staggering' 73 per cent. A bottle of Scotch now costs half what it did in the thirties. Housewives are boozing more these days; children are boozing more; we all are. I am an alcoholic, for instance. You probably are too.

Bestial drunks brawled in a hospital casualty ward ('I'll fuckin' whack you right where you are, you cunt'); an apologetic Irishman had a Guinness bottle removed from his crown ('I sort of fell over backwards on top of it, Doctor'); battered wives told of nightly atrocities; dazed tramps staggered backwards from camera; wrecked liver fizzed in a medic's discard tray. The point of the programme, apparently, was to show that social drinking and alcoholism are not so sharply differentiated as closet alcoholics like ourselves wish to believe. But the images of impending Yahooism were too garish to convince. As one hard-drinking tot pointed out, 'I see blokes drinking tons of pints – and drinking really *fast* – and they're in the best of elf.' Or, as a liver expert more vindictively explained, 'Some of them get away with heavy drinking – that's the problem.' The problem? Admonitory documentation of this kind ought to try to be less scary if they really want to scare anyone.

Martin Amis *New Statesman*, 12 September 1975

ABSTINENCE
and
TEMPERANCE

The Hissing Urn

Now stir the fire, and close the shutters fast,
Let fall the curtains, wheel the sofa round,
And while the bubbling and loud hissing urn
Throws up a steamy column, and the cups,
That cheer but not inebriate, wait on each,
So let us welcome peaceful evening in.

William Cowper *The Task*

Pleasure versus Happiness

Talking of drinking wine, he said, 'I did not leave off wine because I could not bear it; I have drunk three bottles of port without being the worse for it. University College has witnessed this.' BOSWELL. 'Why then, Sir, did you leave it off?' JOHNSON. 'Why, Sir, because it is so much better for a man to be sure that he is never to be intoxicated, never to lose the power over himself. I shall not begin to drink wine again, till I grow old, and want it.' BOSWELL. 'I think, Sir, you once said to me, that not to drink wine was a great deduction from life.' JOHNSON. 'It is a diminution of pleasure, to be sure; but I do not say a diminution of happiness. There is more happiness in being rational.'

James Boswell *Life of Johnson*

Cumberland Water Authority

Where once the Dove and Olive-Bough
Offered a greeting of good ale
To all who entered Grasmere Vale;
And called on him who must depart

To leave it with a jovial heart;
There, where the Dove and Olive-Bough
Once hung, a Poet harbours now,
A simple water-drinking Bard . . .

William Wordsworth *The Waggoner*

His Fare-well to Sack

Farewell thou Thing, time-past so knowne, so deare
To me, as blood of life and spirit: Neare,
Nay, thou more neare then kindred, friend, man, wife,
Male to the female, soule to body: Life
To quick action, or the warme soft side
Of the resigning, yet resisting Bride.
The kisse of Virgins; First-fruits of the bed;
Soft speech, smooth touch, the lips, the Maiden-head:
These, and a thousand sweets, co'd never be
So neare, or deare, as thou wast once to me.
O thou the drink of Gods, and Angels! Wine
That scatter'st Spirit and Lust; whose purest shine,
More radiant then the Summers Sun-beams shows;
Each way illustrious, brave; and like to those
Comets we see by night; whose shagg'd portents
Fore-tell the comming of some dire events:
Or some full flame, which with a pride aspires,
Throwing about his wild, and active fires.
'Tis thou, above Nectar, O Divinest soule!
(Eternall in thy self) that canst controule
That, which subverts whole nature, grief and care;
Vexation of the mind, and damn'd Despaire.
'Tis thou, alone, who with thy Mistick Fan,
Work'st more then Wisdome, Art or Nature can,
To rouze the sacred madnesse; and awake
The frost-bound-blood, and spirits; and to make
Them frantick with thy raptures, flashing through

The soule, like lightning, and as active too.
'Tis not *Apollo* can, or those thrice three
Castalian Sisters, sing, if wanting thee.
Horace, *Anacreon* both had lost their fame,
Had'st thou not fill'd them with thy fire and flame.
Phœbean splendour! and thou *Thespian* spring!
Of which, sweet Swans must drink, before they sing
Their true-pac'd-Numbers, and their Holy-Layes,
Which makes them worthy *Cedar*, and the *Bayes*.
But why? why longer doe I gaze upon
Thee with the eye of admiration?
Since I must leave thee; and enforc'd, must say
To all thy witching beauties, Goe, Away.
But if thy whimpring looks doe ask me why?
Then know, that Nature bids thee goe, not I.
'Tis her erroneous self has made a braine
Uncapable of such a Soveraigne,
As is thy powerfull selfe. Prethee not smile;
Or smile more inly; lest thy looks beguile
My vowes denounc'd in zeale, which thus much show thee,
That I have sworn, but by thy looks to know thee.
Let others drink thee freely; and desire
Thee and their lips espous'd; while I admire,
And love thee; but not taste thee. Let my Muse
Faile of thy former helps; and onely use
Her inadult'rate strength: what's done by me
Hereafter, shall smell of the Lamp, not thee.

Robert Herrick

Pulse Rate

DRINK SHORTENS LIFE. – An ingenious author, from this circumstance makes the following calculations: – 'If we allow seventy years for the usual age of man, and sixty pulsations in a minute for the common measure of pulses of a temperate person, the number of pulsations in his whole life would amount to 2,207,520,000. If, by intemperance, he force his blood into a more rapid motion, so as to give seventy-five pulses in a minute, the same number of pulses would be completed in fifty-six years. His life, by this means, would be reduced fourteen years. The celebrated physician, Dr Hufeland, appears to lay much stress on the circulation with respect to longevity. He remarks that 'a slow uniform pulse is a strong sign of long life, and a great means to promote it;' and again, 'A principal cause of our internal consumption, or spontaneous wasting, lies in the continual circulation of the blood. He who has a hundred pulsations in a minute may be wasted far more quickly than he who has only fifty. Those, therefore, whose pulse is always quick, and in whom every trifling agitation of the mind, or every additional drop of wine, increases the motion of the heart, are unfortunate candidates for longevity, since their whole life is a continual fever.' – *Hufeland, on Long Life.*

The Temperance Handbook

Death by Alcohol is Murder

'If penal legislation be justified in any case, why not in this in which we seek to direct it? What is there to exempt this case? If it be penal to kill your neighbour with a bullet, why should it not be penal to kill him with the bowl? If it be penal to take away his life by poison which does its work in six hours, why not penal to do so by one that takes six years for its deadly operation? Would you not measure the guilt of an act by the amount of suffering it causes? If, then, that which we work against, causes tenfold suffering, should not its punishment be tenfold in severity? Alcohol produces ten times the amount of suffering that arsenic does. The latter destroys life; a few brief hours of agony, and its work is done; but the agony caused by alcohol, extending over months to years, torments its victim with more than tenfold cruelty. Arsenic takes away animal life merely; it touches not the soul; while alcohol gives, not only ten times the amount of animal agony, but also destroys the soul, sapping all moral feeling, quenching all intellectual light. Therefore, I ask a more severe punishment for that crime which works the moral and immortal ruin, than for that whose touch overturns a mere tenement of clay.' – *Rev John Pierpoint.*

The Temperance Handbook

The Brick Lane Branch

The monthly meetings of the Brick Lane Branch of the United Grand Junction Ebenezer Temperance Association, were held in a large room, pleasantly and airily situated at the top of a safe and commodious ladder. The president was the straight-walking Mr Anthony Humm, a converted fireman, now a schoolmaster, and occasionally an itinerant preacher; and the secretary was Mr Jonas Mudge, chandler's shop-keeper, an enthusiastic and disinterested vessel, who sold tea to the members. Previous to the commencement of business, the ladies sat upon forms, and drank tea, till such time as they considered it expedient to leave off; and a large wooden money-box was conspicuously placed upon the green baize cloth of the business table, behind which the secretary stood, and acknowledged, with a gracious smile, every addition to the rich vein of copper which lay concealed within.

On this particular occasion the women drank tea to a most alarming extent; greatly to the horror of Mr Weller senior, who, utterly regardless of all Sam's admonitory nudgings, stared about him in every direction with the most undisguised astonishment.

'Sammy,' whispered Mr Weller, 'if some o' these here people don't want tappin' to-morrow mornin', I ain't your father, and that's wot it is. Why, this here old lady next me is a drowndin' herself in tea.'

'Be quiet, can't you,' murmured Sam.

'Sam,' whispered Mr Weller, a moment afterwards, in a tone of deep agitation, 'mark my words, my boy. If that 'ere secretary fellow keeps on for only five minutes more, he'll blow hisself up with toast and water.'

'Well, let him, if he likes,' replied Sam; 'it ain't no bis'ness o' yourn.'

'If this here lasts much longer, Sammy,' said Mr Weller, in the same low voice, 'I shall feel it my duty, as a human bein', to rise and address the cheer. There's a young 'ooman on the next form but two, as has drunk nine breakfast cups and a half; and she's a-swellin' wisibly before my wery eyes.'

There is little doubt that Mr Weller would have carried his benevolent intention into immediate execution, if a great noise, occasioned by putting up the cups and saucers, had not very fortunately announced that the tea-drinking was over. The crockery having been removed, the table with the green baize cover was carried out into the centre of the room, and the business of the evening was commenced by a little emphatic man, with a bald head, and drab shorts, who suddenly rushed up the ladder, at the imminent peril of snapping the two little legs encased in the drab shorts, and said:

'Ladies and gentlemen, I move our excellent brother, Mr Anthony Humm, into the chair.'

The ladies waved a choice collection of pocket-handkerchiefs at this proposition: and the impetuous little man literally moved Mr Humm into the chair, by taking him by the shoulders and thrusting him into a mahogany-frame which had once represented that article of furniture. The waving of handkerchiefs was renewed; and Mr Humm, who was a sleek, white-faced man, in a perpetual perspiration, bowed meekly, to the great admiration of the females, and formally took his seat. Silence was then proclaimed by the little man in the drab shorts, and Mr Humm rose and said – That, with the permission of his Brick Lane Branch brothers and sisters, then and there present, the secretary would read the report of the Brick Lane Branch committee; a proposition which was again received with a demonstration of pocket-handkerchiefs.

The secretary having sneezed in a very impressive manner, and the cough which always seizes an assembly, when anything particular is going to be done, having been duly performed, the following document was read: 'Report of the Committee of the Brick Lane Branch of the United Grand Junction Ebenezer Temperance Association.'

'Your committee have pursued their grateful labours during the past month, and have the unspeakable pleasure of reporting the following additional cases of converts to Temperance.

'H. Walker, tailor, wife, and two children. When in better circumstances, owns to having been in the constant habit of drinking ale and beer; says he is not certain whether he did not twice a week, for twenty years, taste 'dog's nose,' which your committee find upon inquiry, to be compounded of warm porter, moist sugar, gin, and nutmeg (a groan, and "So it is!" from an elderly female.) Is now out of work and penniless; thinks it must be the porter (cheers) or the loss of the use of his right hand; is not certain which, but thinks it very likely that, if he had drank nothing but water all his life, his fellow workman would never have stuck a rusty needle in him, and thereby occasioned his accident (tremendous cheering). Has nothing but cold water to drink, and never feels thirsty (great applause).

'Betsy Martin, widow, one child, and one eye. Goes out charing and washing, by the day; never had more than one eye, but knows her mother drank bottled stout, and shouldn't wonder if that caused it (immense cheering). Thinks it not impossible that if she had always abstained from spirits, she might have had two eyes by this time (tremendous applause). Used at every place she went to, to have eighteen pence a day, a pint of porter, and a glass of spirits; but since she became a member of the Brick Lane Branch, has always demanded three and sixpence instead (the announcement of this most interesting fact was received with deafening enthusiasm).

'Henry Beller was for many years toast-master at various corporation dinners, during which time he drank a great deal of foreign wine; may sometimes have carried a bottle or two home with him; is not quite certain of that, but is sure if he did, that he drank the contents. Feels very low and melancholy, is very feverish, and has a constant thirst upon him; thinks it must be the wine he used to drink (cheers). Is out of employ now: and never touches a drop of foreign wine by any chance (tremendous plaudits).

'Thomas Burton is purveyor of cat's meat to the Lord Mayor and Sheriffs, and several members of the Common Council (the announcement of this gentleman's name was received with breathless interest). Has a wooden leg; finds a wooden leg expensive, going over the stones; used to wear second-hand wooden legs, and drink a glass of hot gin and water regularly every night – sometimes two (deep sighs). Found the second-hand wooden legs split and rot very quickly; is firmly persuaded that their constitution was undermined by the gin and water (prolonged cheering). Buys new wooden legs now, and drinks nothing but water and weak tea. The new legs last twice as long as the others used to do, and he attributes this solely to his temperate habits (triumphant cheers).'

Anthony Humm now moved that the assembly do regale itself with a song. With a view to their rational and moral enjoyment, brother Mordlin had adapted the beautiful words of 'Who hasn't heard of a Jolly Young Waterman?' to the tune of the Old Hundredth, which he would request them to join him in singing (great applause). He might take that opportunity of expressing his firm persuasion that the late Mr Dibdin, seeing the errors of his former life, had written that song to show the advantages of abstinence. It was a temperance song (whirlwinds of cheers). The neatness of the young man's attire, the dexterity of his feathering, the enviable state of mind which enabled him in the beautiful words of the poet, to

'Row along, thinking of nothing at all,'

all combined to prove that he must have been a water-drinker (cheers). Oh, what a state of virtuous jollity! (rapturous cheering.) And what was the young man's reward? Let all young men present mark this:

'The maidens all flock'd to his boat so readily.'

(Loud cheers, in which the ladies joined.) What a bright example! The sisterhood, the maidens, flocking round the young waterman, and urging him along the stream of duty and of temperance. But, was it the maidens of humble life only, who soothed, consoled, and supported him? No!

'He was always first oars with the fine city ladies.'

(immense cheering.) The soft sex to a man – he begged pardon, to a female – rallied round the young waterman, and turned with disgust from the drinker of spirits (cheers). The Brick Lane Branch brothers were watermen (cheers and laughter). That room was their boat; that audience were the maidens; and he (Mr Anthony Humm), however unworthily, was 'first oars' (unbounded applause).

'Wot does he mean by the soft sex, Sammy?' inquired Mr Weller, in a whisper.

'The womin,' said Sam, in the same tone.

'He ain't far out there, Sammy,' replied Mr Weller; 'they *must* be a soft sex, – a wery soft sex, indeed – if they let themselves be gammoned by such fellers as him.'

Any further observations from the indignant old gentleman were cut short by the announcement of the song, which Mr Anthony Humm gave out, two lines at a time, for the information of such of his hearers as were unacquainted with the legend. While it was being sung, the little man with the drab shorts disappeared; he returned immediately on its conclusion, and whispered Mr Anthony Humm, with a face of the deepest importance.

'My friends,' said Mr Humm, holding up his hand in a deprecatory manner, to bespeak the silence of such of the stout old ladies as were yet a line or two behind; 'my friends, a delegate from the Dorking branch of our Society, Brother Stiggins, attends below.'

Out came the pocket-handkerchiefs again, in greater force than ever; for Mr Stiggins was excessively popular among the female constituency of Brick Lane.

'He may approach, I think,' said Humm, looking round him, with a fat smile. 'Brother Tadger, let him come forth and greet us.'

The little man in the drab shorts who answered to the name of Brother Tadger, bustled down the ladder with great speed, and was immediately afterwards heard tumbling up with the reverend Mr Stiggins.

'He's a-comin', Sammy,' whispered Mr Weller, purple in the countenance with suppressed laughter.'

'Don't say nothin' to me,' replied Sam, 'for I can't bear it. He's close to the door. I heard him a-knockin' his head again the lath and plaster now.'

As Sam Weller spoke, the little door flew open, and brother Tadger appeared, closely followed by the reverend Mr Stiggins, who no sooner entered, than there was a great clapping of hands, and stamping of feet, and flourishing of handkerchiefs; to all of which manifestations of delight, Brother Stiggins returned no other acknowledgement than staring with a wild eye, and a fixed smile, at the extreme top of the wick of the candle on the table: swaying his body to and fro, meanwhile, in a very unsteady and uncertain manner.

'Are you unwell, brother Stiggins?' whispered Mr Anthony Humm.

'I am all right, sir,' replied Mr Stiggins, in a tone in which ferocity was blended with an extreme thickness of utterance; 'I am all right, sir.'

'Oh, very well,' rejoined Mr Anthony Humm, retreating a few paces.

'I believe no man here, has ventured to say that I am *not* all right, sir?' said Mr Stiggins.

'Oh, certainly not,' said Mr Humm.

'I should advise him not to, sir; I should advise him not,' said Mr Stiggins.

By this time the audience were perfectly silent, and waited with some anxiety for the resumption of business.

'Will you address the meeting, brother?' said Mr Humm, with a smile of invitation.

'No, sir,' rejoined Mr Stiggins; 'No, sir. I will not, sir.'

The meeting looked at each other with raised eye-lids; and a murmur of astonishment ran through the room.

'It's my opinion, sir,' said Mr Stiggins, unbuttoning his coat, and speaking very loudly; 'it's my opinion, sir, that this meeting is drunk, sir. Brother Tadger, sir!' said Mr Stiggins, suddenly increasing in ferocity, and turning sharp round on the little man in the drab shorts, '*you* are drunk, sir!' With this, Mr Stiggins, entertaining a praiseworthy desire to promote the sobriety of the meeting, and to exclude therefrom all improper characters, hit brother

Tadger on the summit of the nose with such unerring aim, that the drab shorts disappeared like a flash of lightning. Brother Tadger had been knocked, head first, down the ladder.

Upon this, the women set up a loud and dismal screaming; and rushing in small parties before their favourite brothers, flung their arms around them to preserve them from danger. An instance of affection, which had nearly proved fatal to Humm, who, being extremely popular, was all but suffocated, by the crowd of female devotees that hung about his neck, and heaped caresses upon him. The greater part of the lights were quickly put out, and nothing but noise and confusion resounded on all sides.

'Now, Sammy,' said Mr Weller, taking off his great coat with much deliberation, 'just you step out, and fetch in a watchman.'

'And wot are you a-goin' to do, the while?' inquired Sam.

'Never you mind me, Sammy,' replied the old gentleman; 'I shall ockipy myself in havin' a small settlement with that 'ere Stiggins.' Before Sam could interfere to prevent it, his heroic parent had penetrated into a remote corner of the room, and attacked the reverend Mr Stiggins with manual dexterity.

'Come off!' said Sam.

'Come on!' cried Mr Weller; and without further invitation he gave the reverend Mr Stiggins a preliminary tap on the head, and began dancing round him in a buoyant and cork-like manner, which in a gentleman at his time of life was a perfect marvel to behold.

Finding all remonstrance unavailing, Sam pulled his hat firmly on, threw his father's coat over his arm, and taking the old man round the waist, forcibly dragged him down the ladder, and into the street; never releasing his hold, or permitting him to stop, until they reached the corner. As they gained it, they could hear the shouts of the populace, who were witnessing the removal of the reverend Mr Stiggins to strong lodgings for the night: and could hear the noise occasioned by the dispersion in various directions of the members of the Brick Lane Branch of the United Grand Junction Ebenezer Temperance Association.

Charles Dickens *The Pickwick Papers*

LIQUOR AND THE LAW

III.—The [illegible]

[illegible] paper, and [illegible]

[illegible] on the table [illegible]

[illegible] child [illegible]

How His Cold Was Cured

He had finished supper, and was not in the least anticipating Mrs Newberry again that night, when she tapped and entered as before. Stockdale's gratified look told that she had lost nothing by not appearing when expected. It happened that the cold in the head from which the young man suffered had increased with the approach of night, and before she had spoken he was seized with a violent fit of sneezing which he could not anyhow repress.

Mrs Newberry looked full of pity. 'Your cold is very bad to-night, Mr Stockdale.'

Stockdale replied that it was rather troublesome.

'And I've a good mind –' she added archly, looking at the cheerless glass of water on the table, which the abstemious minister was going to drink.

'Yes, Mrs Newberry?'

'I've a good mind that you should have something more likely to cure it than that cold stuff.'

'Well,' said Stockdale, looking down at the glass, 'as there is no inn here, and nothing better to be got in the village, of course it will do.'

To this she replied, 'There is something better, nor far off, though not in the house. I really think you must try it, or you may be ill. Yes, Mr Stockdale, you shall.' She held up her finger, seeing that he was about to speak. 'Don't ask what it is; wait, and you shall see.'

Lizzy went away, and Stockdale waited in a pleasant mood. Presently she returned with her bonnet and cloak on, saying, 'I am so sorry, but you must help me to get it. Mother has gone to bed. Will you wrap yourself up, and come this way, and please bring that cup with you?'

Stockdale, a lonely young fellow, who had for weeks felt a great craving for somebody on whom to throw away superfluous interest, and even tenderness, was not sorry to join her; and followed his guide through the back door, across the garden, to the bottom, where the boundary was a wall. This wall was low, and beyond it Stockdale discerned in the night shades several grey headstones, and the outlines of the church roof and tower.

'It is easy to get up this way,' she said, stepping upon a bank which abutted on the wall; then putting her foot on the top of the stonework, and descending by a spring inside, where the ground was much higher, as is the manner of graveyards to be. Stockdale did the same, and followed her in the dusk across the irregular ground till they came to the tower door, which, when they had entered, she softly closed behind them.

'You can keep a secret?' she said, in a musical voice.

'Like an iron chest!' said he fervently.

Then from under her cloak she produced a small lighted lantern, which the minister had not noticed that she carried at all. The light showed them to be close to the singing-gallery stairs, under which lay a heap of lumber of all sorts, but consisting mostly of decayed framework, pews, panels, and pieces of flooring, that from time to time had been removed from their original fixings in the body of the edifice and replaced by new.

'Perhaps you will drag some of those boards aside?' she said, holding the lantern over her head to light him better. 'Or will you take the lantern while I move them?'

'I can manage it,' said the young man, and acting as she ordered, he uncovered, to his surprise, a row of little barrels bound with wood hoops, each barrel being about as large as the nave of a heavy waggon-wheel. When they were laid open Lizzy fixed her eyes on him, as if she wondered what he would say.

'You know what they are?' she asked, finding that he did not speak.

'Yes, barrels,' said Stockdale simply. He was an inland man, the son of highly respectable parents, and brought up with a single eye to the ministry; and the sight suggested nothing beyond the fact that such articles were there.

'You are quite right, they are barrels,' she said, in an emphatic tone of candour that was not without a touch of irony.

Stockdale looked at her with an eye of sudden misgiving. 'Not smugglers' liquor?' he said.

'Yes,' said she. 'They are tubs of spirit that have accidentally floated over in the dark from France.'

In Nether-Moynton and its vicinity at this date people always smiled at the sort of sin called in the outside world illicit trading; and these little kegs of gin and brandy were as well known to the inhabitants as turnips. So that Stockdale's innocent ignorance, and his look of alarm when he guessed the sinister mystery, seemed to strike Lizzy first as ludicrous, and then as very awkward for the good impression that she wished to produce upon him.

'Smuggling is carried on here by some of the people,' she said in a gentle, apologetic voice. 'It has been their practice for generations, and they think it no harm. Now, will you roll out one of the tubs?'

'What to do with it?' said the minister.

'To draw a little from it to cure your cold,' she answered. 'It is so 'nation strong that it drives away that sort of thing in a jiffy. O, it is all right about our taking it. I may have what I like; the owner of the tubs says so. I ought to have had some in the house, and then I shouldn't ha' been put to this trouble; but I drink none myself, and so I often forget to keep it indoors.'

'You are allowed to help yourself, I suppose, that you may not inform where their hiding-place is?'

'Well, no; not that particularly; but I may take any if I want it. So help yourself.'

'I will, to oblige you, since you have a right to it,' murmured the minister; and though he was not quite satisfied with his part in the performance, he rolled one of the 'tubs' out from the corner into the middle of the tower floor. 'How do you wish me to get it out – with a gimlet, I suppose?'

'No, I'll show you,' said his interesting companion; and she held up with her other hand a shoemaker's awl and a hammer. 'You must never do these things with a gimlet, because the wood-dust gets in; and when the buyers pour out the brandy that would tell them that the tub had been broached. An awl makes no dust, and the hole nearly closes up again. Now tap one of the hoops forward.'

Stockdale took the hammer and did so.

'Now make the hole in the part that was covered by the hoop.'

He made the hole as directed. 'It won't run out,' he said.

'O yes it will,' said she. 'Take the tub between your knees, and squeeze the heads; and I'll hold the cup.'

Stockdale obeyed; and the pressure taking effect upon the tub, which seemed to be thin, the spirit spirted out in a stream. When the cup was full he ceased pressing, and the flow immediately stopped. 'Now we must fill up the keg with water,' said Lizzy, 'or it will cluck like forty hens when it is handled, and show that 'tis not full.'

'But they tell you you may take it?'

'Yes, the *smugglers*; but the *buyers* must not know that the smugglers have been kind to me at their expense.'

'I see,' said Stockdale doubtfully. 'I much question the honesty of this proceeding.'

By her direction he held the tub with the hole upwards, and while he went through the process of alternately pressing and ceasing to press, she produced a bottle of water, from which she took mouthfuls, conveying each to the keg by putting her pretty lips to the hole, where it was sucked in at each recovery of the cask from pressure. When it was again full he plugged the hole, knocked the hoop down to its place, and buried the tub in the lumber as before.

'Aren't the smugglers afraid that you will tell?' he asked, as they recrossed the churchyard.

'O no; they are not afraid of that, I couldn't do such a thing.'

'They have put you into a very awkward corner,' said Stockdale emphatically. 'You must, of course, as an honest person, sometimes feel that it is your duty to inform – really you must.'

'Well, I have never particularly felt it as a duty; and, besides, my first husband –' She stopped, and there was some confusion in her voice. Stockdale was so honest and unsophisticated that he did not at once discern why she paused: but at last he did perceive that the words were a slip, and that no woman would have uttered 'first husband' by accident unless she had thought pretty frequently of a second. He felt for her confusion, and allowed her time to recover and proceed. 'My husband,' she said, in a self-corrected tone, 'used to know of their doings, and so did my father, and kept the secret. I cannot inform, in fact, against anybody.'

'I see the hardness of it,' he continued, like a man who looked far into the moral of things. 'And it is very cruel that you should be tossed and tantalized between your memories and your conscience. I do hope, Mrs Newberry, that you will soon see your way out of this unpleasant position.'

'Well, I don't just now,' she murmured.

By this time they had passed over the wall and entered the house, where she brought him a glass and hot water, and left him to his own reflections. He looked after her vanishing form, asking himself whether he, as a respectable man, and a minister, and a shining light, even though as yet only the half-penny-candle sort, were quite justified in doing this thing. A sneeze settled the question; and he found that when the fiery liquor was lowered by the addition of twice or thrice the quantity of water, it was one of the prettiest cures for a cold in the head that he had ever known, particularly at this chilly time of the year.

Thomas Hardy *The Distracted Preacher*

A Smuggler's Song

If you wake at midnight, and hear a horse's feet,
Don't go drawing back the blind, or looking in the street,
Them that asks no questions isn't told a lie.
Watch the wall, my darling, while the Gentlemen go by!
    Five and twenty ponies
    Trotting through the dark –
    Brandy for the Parson,
    'Baccy for the Clerk;
    Laces for a lady, letters for a spy,
And watch the wall, my darling, while the Gentlemen go by!

Running round the woodlump if you chance to find
Little barrels, roped and tarred, all full of brandy-wine,
Don't you shout to come and look, nor use 'em for your play.
Put the brishwood back again – and they'll be gone next day!

If you see the stable-door setting open wide;
If you see a tired horse lying down inside;
If your mother mends a coat cut about and tore;
If the lining's wet and warm – don't you ask no more!

If you meet King George's men, dressed in blue and red,
You be careful what you say, and mindful what is said.
If they call you 'pretty maid', and chuck you 'neath the chin,
Don't you tell where no one is, nor yet where no one's been!

Knocks and footsteps round the house – whistles after dark –
You've no call for running out till the house-dogs bark.
Trusty's here, and *Pincher*'s here, and see how dumb they lie –
They don't fret to follow when the Gentlemen go by!

If you do as you've been told, 'likely there's a chance,
You'll be give a dainty doll, all the way from France,
With a cap of Valenciennes, and a velvet hood –
A present from the Gentlemen, along o' being good!
Five and twenty ponies
Trotting through the dark –
Brandy for the Parson,
'Baccy for the Clerk.
Them that asks no questions isn't told a lie –
Watch the wall, my darling, while the Gentlemen go by!

Rudyard Kipling

Bootlegging in Slobodka

Formerly there was widespread bootlegging of alcohol in Slobodka. The import and sale of alcohol are strictly forbidden on Sakhalin, and these prohibitions gave rise to peculiar methods of acquiring contraband. The alcohol was smuggled into the island in tin cans meant to hold sugar loaves and in samovars, and the smugglers were very nearly carrying it in their belts, but most frequently it was delivered in barrels and in the usual bottles since the lower officials were bribed and the higher officials looked the other way.

In Slobodka, a bottle of cheap vodka was sold for six and even ten roubles. It was from here that all the prisons of Northern Sakhalin obtained their vodka. Even the drunkards among the officials were not squeamish about it. I know one official who was on a drinking spree and gave all the money he had to some prisoners for a bottle of spirits.

Anton Chekhov *The Island of Sakhalin*, trans. Luba & Michael Terpak

Gulag

One such amazing story explained how zeks manage to get strictly forbidden alcohol into the camps. The more 'trustworthy' criminals are taken daily to work on sites outside the camp: doing their bit to get the agriculture of the Motherland going, chop wood for the bosses, wash dishes and so on. At night, they are marched back to their zone, and manage to bring in up to three litres of alcohol without its being found. How do they manage that? There is a special complex system to carry out this operation. A condom is hermetically attached to a long piece of thin plastic tubing. The zek then swallows it, leaving only one end of the tube in his mouth. To avoid swallowing it by accident, he wedges it in between two teeth: there are not likely to be any zeks in existence with a full set of thirty-two teeth. Then, with the help of a syringe, up to three litres of spirit are pumped into the condom via the plastic tubing – and the zek goes back to his zone. If the bonding has been badly done, or if the condom happens to burst in the zek's stomach, that means certain and painful death. Despite it, they run the risk: three litres of spirit makes seven litres of vodka! When the 'hero' returns to the zone, his impatiently waiting cronies start the 'emptying' process. He is hung head-down from a beam under the barracks roof and the end of the plastic tubing is held over a dish until every drop has been retrieved. Then the empty condom is hauled out: it's done its job, and the whole barracks binges.

Irina Ratushinskaya *Grey is the Colour of Hope*,
trans. Alyona Kojevnika

Prohibition

At exactly 12.01 a.m. on 17 January 1920, constitutional prohibition went into effect everywhere in the United States, and the American people, 105,000,000 strong, began the joyous march into the never-never land of the Eighteenth Amendment and the Volstead Act. Everything was ready for the great transformation. More than fifteen hundred enforcement agents, badges shined, guns oiled, and fingers trembling upon the triggers, were on their toes, ready to pounce upon the rum demon wherever he showed his ugly mug. The Coast Guard, the Customs Service, and the various agencies of the Bureau of Internal Revenue were standing by. The police of a thousand cities and the sheriffs of a thousand counties were on the alert. Judges were pondering the probability of history-making decisions, and prosecuting attorneys were thumbing their law-books and briefing their publicity staffs. Political bosses were happily grabbing jobs for the faithful in the many departments of the new Prohibition Bureau. Statements, predictions, and pronunciamentos were flying thick and fast. And behind this imposing array, their nostrils quivering eagerly to catch the first faint whiffs of illegal hooch, crouched the Allied Citizens of America and the embattled members of the Women's Christian Temperance Union, the latter more dangerous to the politicians than ever, now that Congress had passed the woman-suffrage amendment to the constitution and submitted it to the states for ratification. The Allied Citizens, formed by the Anti-Saloon League to help the government enforce the law, had long since served notice upon prospective evil-doers that it was a militant organization that would tolerate no nonsense.

In thousands of Protestant churches throughout the country, and in every town which had a chapter of the WCTU, the drys greeted the coming of the great day with thanksgiving and watch-night services, at which the Lord was publicly praised for His share in the victory. In Tennessee there were parades and mass meetings as well. In Denver and San Francisco the ceremonies were elaborate and the meetings remained in session for several days; in the latter city a national official of the WCTU described prohibition as 'God's present to the nation', and the head of the California State Anti-Saloon League declared that San Francisco was 'complacently joyful that John Barleycorn had been laid to rest'. In Chicago the WCTU announced that, having brought prohibition to America, it would now proceed to dry up the rest of the world.

As the fateful hour approached, many of the activities of the liquor people took on a quality of desperation. A brewery in Providence, Rhode Island, announced that in lieu of a final dividend, two barrels of beer would be shipped to every stockholder. 'Many members of the General Assembly,' said the New York *Tribune*, 'also shared in the distribution, being among the first to be cared for.' In New Jersey a brewer threatened to dump his entire stock into the Passaic River, whereupon hundreds of men hurried to the stream with buckets and pans, hoping to salvage at least a little foam. However, the brewer changed his mind and said that instead he would 'de-authorize' his beer. In Denver bootleggers said that they 'were through with the game forever', and would sell their liquors at reduced prices; they changed their minds also. In California the owner of a vineyard, convinced that prohibition would bankrupt him and every other grape grower in the country, committed suicide; he had failed to foresee the golden years that lay ahead. In New York two prohibition agents were threatened by a crowd when they seized a truck loaded with twenty thousand dollars' worth of whiskey; but it was never clear whether the crowd wanted to manhandle the officers or grab the liquor. Another hopeful crowd gathered on a Hudson River pier when a big cake of ice sank a barge loaded with whiskey worth one hundred and fifty thousand dollars. The owners of the liquor, the Green River Distilling Company, tried desperately to raise the barge and get it out of the harbour before prohibition became effective. They failed, and the liquor was confiscated by the government.

When the prohibition authorities notified the vintners of western New York State that they could legally sell their stocks of wine, thousands of motorists set out for the wine districts with the enthusiasm of prospectors rushing to a new Klondike. Many headed for the village of Hammondsport, in Steuben County, where seventy thousand cases of champagne had been placed on sale, but found the highways blocked by the heaviest snowfall of the year. Their yelps of despair were heard by the State Highway Department, and crews and emergency equipment were hurriedly sent to clear the roads. In the forlorn hope that something might happen, members of retail liquor dealers' associations in New Jersey decided to keep their saloons open and sell near beer, an insipid but legal beverage containing a maximum of one half of one per cent of alcohol. More general, however, was the feeling expressed by John S. Bennett, counsel for saloonkeepers' organizations in Brooklyn, which before prohibition had supported some two thousand saloons. Bennett declared that at least 75 per cent of the Brooklyn saloon-keepers would close their doors. 'As sensible men,' he said, 'most of our members know that the public will not buy this one half of one per cent stuff. As law-abiding citizens they cannot sell anything else. So there is nothing to do but close up.'

Everybody expected that on the night of 16 January 1920 saloons, cafés, cabarets, restaurants, and hotels all over the country would be crowded with liquor slaves having a last fling before prohibition settled 'like a blight upon the entire joyous side of human existence', as Senator W. Cabell Bruce of Maryland put it in testifying before a congressional committee in 1926. But the nation-wide binge failed to occur. Newspaper reports described the last fling as 'very tame', even in such notoriously wet cities as New York, Chicago, Detroit, Louisville, Baltimore, New Orleans, Philadelphia, and San Francisco. In Boston it was excessively tame; policemen were stationed in all of the well-known drinking places to prevent guzzling after midnight, and to seize all liquor on tables or otherwise in sight after that hour. In Atlantic City, home of the famous boardwalk and as wet a town as could be found anywhere, virtually every place that sold liquor closed at midnight after a quiet evening; some of the resorts gave their customers milk bottles as souvenirs. Things were a little better in San Francisco; the *Chronicle* reported that many 'saw it through with glorious festivals wherein corks popped and siphons fizzled and glasses clinked long after the legal hour'. Nothing out of the ordinary occurred in New Orleans; that city simply ignored prohibition, both on the night of January 16 and thereafter. In Washington DC, the saloons were crowded all day and all evening, especially those of the Wet Mile, a stretch of Pennsylvania Avenue between the Capitol and the White House, which boasted forty-seven bar-rooms. When midnight struck on 16 January, a final toast was drunk, and glasses and partially emptied bottles were given to favourite customers with the compliments of the saloonkeepers. The bars of the Willard, the Raleigh, and other big Washington hotels had closed several days before the Eighteenth Amendment became effective.

A dispatch to the New York *Times* said that in Chicago drinkers 'cheered the final moments of a moist United States in a more or less tame celebration in the cafés and restaurants'. But a gang of six masked men gave Chicago a foretaste of what was to come within another few years; they invaded a railroad yard, bound and gagged a yardmaster and a watchman, locked six trainmen in a shanty, and stole whiskey valued at one hundred thousand dollars from two box-cars. In a smaller enterprise of the same sort, several men held up a watchman and rolled four barrels of alcohol from a warehouse into a truck. More than a hundred thefts of large quantities of liquor had been reported during the two or three months prior to the advent of constitutional prohibition; the authorities at Washington admitted that they were investigating seventy-five cases in which whiskey worth several hundred thousand dollars had been stolen, or at least removed, from warehouses heavily guarded by watchmen and enforcement agents. In one of these thefts sixty-one barrels of fine bourbon, valued at one hundred and fifty thousand dollars, disappeared from a government warehouse at Bardstown, Kentucky. The news that so much good liquor had fallen into the hands of men who, presumably, would sell it was greeted by drinkers with quiet chuckles of contentment, but screams of anguish came from the distillers who owned the whiskey. Under the bond placing the liquor in the warehouses, they were required to pay a tax of $6.40 a gallon if it was withdrawn for sale. The Prohibition Bureau ruled that thefts would count as withdrawals.

Almost everywhere the drinking on the last night of the old order was dull, dogged, and expensive, and the celebrants, or mourners, seemed tired and discouraged. They had already participated in three farewells to liquor – when wartime prohibition went into effect on 1 July 1919, when the Volstead Act was passed by Congress late in October, and on New Year's Eve, just sixteen days before the Eighteenth Amendment superseded the wartime act. Physically and financially, they were beginning to feel the strain. Moreoever, there seems to have been a shortage of booze, which fortunately proved to be only temporary. The operators of cabarets and restaurants in many cities declared that the previous celebrations, particularly that of New Year's Eve, had exhausted their stock of potables, and that they had been unable to obtain fresh supplies, largely because of the frantic private buying that had been going on for several months. At three of New York's best-known hotels – the McAlpin, the Claridge, and the Waldorf-Astoria – a pint of champagne was given free on New Year's Eve to each pair of diners. The managers of these places were quoted in the New York *Tribune* of 16 January as saying that their cellars were empty, and that on prohibition night they would having nothing but soft drinks for sale. Many resort owners were afraid to sell, although the government had let it be known that there would be no raids until after dawn on 17 January, and in several large cities the police had refused to assist in the enforcement of the Volstead Act.

No one who wished to observe the passing of the old era away from home could be certain of getting a drink unless he carried his own liquor, and Americans had not yet acquired the habits of lugging bottles and pocket flasks. Nor had they become accustomed to paying dollars for drinks which only a few years before could be had for nickels. When the United States entered the first World War the standard price of a cocktail or a highbll at first-class bars was fifteen cents or two for a quarter. On the night of 16 January 1920, an ounce or so of dubious whiskey cost from forty to sixty cents in the cheapest saloons, and from one to three dollars in the swank cabarets and restaurants. The price of a fifth of whiskey ranged from twelve to eighteen dollars in New York, and from ten to fifteen dollars in San Francisco. In some of the southern cities rotgut moonshine, considered very choice stuff within another year, was available at from four to six dollars a bottle.

John Asbury *The Great Illusion*

Organized Crime

Throughout the fourteen years of prohibition, which the Anti-Saloon League had hailed joyfully as 'an era of clear thinking and clean living', and for several years afterward, virtually all of New York's best-known drinking and dancing resorts were dominated by big-shot criminals. These men controlled the flow of liquor into the metropolis and managed its distribution and sale; they operated or financed night clubs partly to provide good outlets for their booze and partly for reasons of vanity. They were the real top-drawer crooks of the period; they ran the whole criminal set-up in New York, and their alliances, especially in liquor, extended northward to Chicago and Detroit, southward to New Orleans and Miami, and westward to Los Angeles and San Francisco. Among other things, they planned and directed the New York liquor wars in which a thousand gangsters and bootleggers were killed. The gunmen who handled these murders, which to them were just so many jobs, never received as much publicity as their colleagues in Chicago, nor did they reach the heights of cruelty achieved by the killers who followed the banners of Johnny Torrio, Al Capone and Dion O'Banion. Nevertheless they frequently displayed considerable imagination, and are said to have invented many of the methods used with such spectacular success in Chicago, Detroit, and elsewhere.

Jack Diamond, Dutch Schultz, Charley Luciano, Lepke Buchalter, Bugsy Siegel, Jake Gurrah Shapiro, and Meyer Lansky, together with many others whose names were less familar, all helped finance night clubs at various times, and provided gunmen to protect the resorts in which they were interested and to discourage rivals with whom they were at war. (A classic example of discouragement occurred on 13 July 1929, when Jack Diamond put the Hotsy Totsy Club out of business by shooting down two of its owners on a crowded dance floor.) Their main interests, however, were in rum-running and bootlegging, and in the related fields of murder, hijacking, narcotics, prostitution, crooked gambling, racketeering, robbery and extortion. The only one of this group who invested heavily in the nightclub business was Arthur Flegenheimer, better known as Dutch Schultz, who was the beer baron of the Bronx and boss of the numbers or policy racket. His principal partner and protector in the latter enterprise was James J. Hines, a well-known Tammany politician who was sent to prison in 1939.

During the final years of prohibition Schultz owned the Embassy Club, a very plush night spot which catered to the high-class, or Park Avenue, trade. In return for paying exorbitant prices for poor food and bad liquor, which did them little harm, the Park Avenuers rubbed elbows with top-flight gangsters, which thrilled them, and listened to the singing of Helen Morgan, Morton Downey and the Yacht Club Boys, which amused them. Dutch Schultz was also distinguished in the underworld as the first employer of Vincent Coll, the so-called 'mad dog of gangland', who was probably the most brutal killer of his time, at least in New York. Coll loved to kill, and did so on the slightest provocation. He put several notches on his gun during a war with the Jack Diamond gang, but later broke with Schultz, organized his own mob, and begn hijacking his former boss's liquor trucks. Schultz immediately offered to pay fifty thousand dollars to any man who would kill Coll, and every free-lance gunman in New York went on the prowl, eager to earn the money. On the night of 7 February 1932, one of Schultz's own killers trapped Coll in a telephone booth in a drugstore on West Twenty-third Street, near Ninth Avenue, and poured fifty bullets from a submachine gun through the glass doors. Most of the slugs lodged in Coll's body between the head and the knees. The mad dog had just passed his twenty-third birthday.

John Asbury *The Great Illusion*

Disorganized Crime

In 1913 he bought a piece of land near Valleyfield, Quebec, and failed as a farmer. Then he came into town and failed as a baker; failed in the dry-goods business; failed as a jobber; failed as a sack manufacturer in the War, when no one else failed. He failed as a junk dealer. Then he became a marriage broker and failed – too short-tempered and blunt. And now he was failing as a bootlegger, on the run from the provincial Liquor Commission. Making a bit of a living.

In haste and defiantly, with a clear tense face, walking with mingled desperation and high style, a little awkwardly dropping his weight on one heel as he went, his coat, once lined with fox, turned dry and bald, the red hide cracking. This coat sweeping open as he walked, or marched his one-hand Jewish march, he was saturated with the odour of the Caporals he smoked as he covered Montreal in his swing – Papineau, Mile-End, Verdun, Lachine, Point St Charles. He looked for business opportunities – bankruptcies, job lots, mergers, fire sales, produce – to rescue him from illegality. He could calculate percentages mentally at high speed, but he lacked the cheating imagination of a successful businessman. And so he kept a little still in Mile-End, where goats fed in the empty lots. He travelled on the tramcar. He sold a bottle here and there and waited for his main chance. American rum-runners would buy the stuff from you at the border, any amount, spot cash, if you could get it there. Meanwhile he smoked cigarettes on the cold platforms of streetcars. The Revenue was trying to catch him. Spotters were after him. On the roads to the border were hijackers. On Napoleon Street he had five mouths to feed. Willie and Moses were sickly. Helen studied the piano. Shura was fat, greedy, disobedient, a plotting boy. The rent, back rent, notes due, doctors' bills to pay, and he had no English, no friends, no influence, no trade, no assets but his still – no help in all the world. His sister Zipporah in St Anne was rich, very rich, which only made matters worse.

Papa had forged labels. He would say cheerfully, 'Well, children, what shall it be – White Horse? Johnnie Walker?' Then we'd all call out our favourites. The paste pot was on the table.

Of course Zipporah, that realist, was right to refuse Father Herzog. He wanted to run bootleg whiskey to the border, and get into the big time. He and Voplonsky borrowed from money-lenders, and loaded a truck with cases. But they never reached Rouses Point. They were hijacked, beaten up, and left in a ditch. Father Herzog took the worse beating because he resisted. The hijackers tore his clothes, knocked out one of his teeth and trampled him.

He and Voplonsky the blacksmith returned to Montreal on foot. He stopped at Voplonsky's shop to clean up, but there was not much he could do about his swollen bloody eye. He had a gap in his teeth. His coat was torn and his shirt and undergarment were blood-stained.

That was how he entered the dark kitchen on Napoleon Street. We were all there. It was gloomy March, and anyway the light seldom reached that room. It was like a cavern. We were like cave dwellers. 'Sarah!' he said. 'Children!' He showed his cut face. He spread his arms so we could see his tatters, and the white of his body under them. Then he turned his pockets inside out – empty. As he did this, he began to cry, and the children standing about him all cried. It was more than I could bear that anyone should lay violent hands on him – a father, a sacred being, a king. Yes, he was a king to us. My heart was suffocated by this horror. I thought I would die of it. Whom did I ever love as I loved them?

Then Father Herzog told his story.

'They were waiting for us. The road was blocked. They dragged us from the truck. They took everything.'

'Why did you fight?' said Mother Herzog.

'Everything we had . . . all I borrowed!'

'They might have killed you.'

'They had handkerchiefs over their faces. I thought I recognized . . .'

Mama was incredulous. '*Landtsleit?* Impossible. No Jews could do this to a Jew.

'No?' cried Papa. 'Why not! Who says not! Why shouldn't they!'

'Not Jews! Never!' Mama said. 'Never. Never! They couldn't have the heart. Never!'

'Children – don't cry. And poor Voplonsky – he could barely creep into bed.'

'Yonah,' said Mama, 'you must give up this whole thing.'

'How will we live? We have to live.'

How did Papa feel when he found that Voplonsky was in cahoots with the hi-jackers? He never said.

Saul Bellow *Herzog*

A Raid

'Hit it again! Straight on through that wall!'

Frank didn't question me. He threw the truck into low gear, and again there was a grinding crash, only not as loud this time as the black wall collapsed.

It went down in a shower of dust and splinters, as if some giant hand had drawn a curtain aside to disclose a tableau. Five men stood there, frozen. As I leaped from the truck before it even stopped rolling, one of them, a huge, grizzled man, started to reach for the gun in his shoulder holster.

My Colt was in my hand, and as he made his move I triggered a shot over his head. His hand dropped away as I shouted over the hollow echo of the shot:

'Hold it! This is a federal raid!'

A man standing at the back inside one of the three trucks ducked, then made a dash towards the rear. Chapman started after him when there was a smacking sound and a groan. Seconds later, Sam Seager appeared out of the shadows, dragging the man by the collar of his coat.

'Guess he didn't hear us coming in the back, you were making so much noise with that truck,' Sam grinned. 'So I fetched him one to let him know the rest of the Marines had landed.'

The man Sam had collared, nursing an eye that was going to have purplish overtones next day, was shoved into line with the other four. They were searched for weapons but only one was armed.

I was jubilant as I looked them over. We had made quite a haul.

The armed man was Frank Conta, Scarface's old assistant. The burly, round-shouldered man standing sullenly next to him was Steve Svoboda, Capone's ace brewer. The other three were truck drivers. For some reason, they were shorthanded this particular night, but we had netted two big ones, at least. Nobody had escaped.

I climbed a rickety stairway, obviously an escape route to the roof, and called in Lahart and his detail from the top. Back downstairs, I beckoned to the little prohibition man, still standing motionless and white faced beside the truck with which we had crashed through the doors.

'Keep your gun on these birds. And if they move a finger, don't hesitate to let them have it. They're rough and they play for keeps, so you'd better be prepared to do the same thing.'

He gulped and moved a few feet closer to the prisoners. Actually, I didn't expect any trouble. They were unarmed and we were all around them as we set about the process of taking inventory and gathering evidence.

This brewery, I soon saw, was capable of turning out one hundred barrels of beer daily, a production quota which we were to discover later was the general rule in the Capone breweries.

Seven 320-gallon vats lined up in the room, which was cooled automatically so that beer fermented at a slow rate. The brewery was laid out so that each day 320 gallons of wort, or unfermented beer, were brought in by glass-lined tank truck. One hundred barrels would be filled with beer that had been fermented and spiked with carbonated gas.

Eliot Ness *The Untouchables*

Home Brew

'I reckon they got along. They were selling whiskey, using that old place for a headquarters, a blind. I don't reckon she knew that, about the whiskey. Leastways, folks don't know if she ever knew or not. They say that Christmas started it by himself three years ago, just selling to a few regular customers that didn't even know one another. But when he took Brown in with him, I reckon Brown wanted to spread out. Selling it by the half a pint out of his shirt bosom in any alley and to anybody. Selling what he never drunk, that is. And I reckon the way they got the whiskey they sold would not have stood much looking into. Because about two weeks after Brown quit out at the mill and taken to riding around in that new car for his steady work, he was down town drunk one Saturday night and bragging to a crowd in the barbershop something about him and Christmas in Memphis one night, or on a road close to Memphis. Something about them and that new car hid in the bushes and Christmas with a pistol, and a lot more about a truck and a hundred gallons of something, until Christmas come in quick and walked up to him and jerked him out of the chair. And Christmas saying in that quiet voice of his, that ain't pleasant and ain't mad either: "You ought to be careful about drinking so much of this Jefferson hair tonic. It's gone to your head. First thing you know you'll have a hare-lip." '

William Faulkner *Light in August*

Jake

Probably the worst drink that appeared during prohibition was fluid extract of Jamaica ginger, popularly known as Jake, which was almost 90 per cent alcohol. During the final years of the dry era large quantities were consumed in the Middle West, the South, and some parts of the East. Jake was occasionally used medicinally for stomach disorders, and could legally be sold at retail only on prescription. Drugstores and wholesale houses could obtain it only on federal permits issued by the Prohibition Bureau in Washington, but nobody seemed to have any trouble getting it; in 1928, for example, the government released two hundred barrels to a druggist in a small Texas town. This was enough to last him, if disposed of legitimately, for at least a hundred years. In many states drugstores sold Jake to all comers for thirty to fifty cents for a two-ounce bottle, and bootleggers peddled it at about the same prices. The principal buyers were poor people, and boys and girls, who couldn't afford more than one drink at a time and wanted something that would start them off with a bang. Since it was much too strong to be guzzled straight, Jake was usually mixed with ginger ale, soda pop, or a fountain drink. As far as is known, nobody died from drinking it, but even small quantities nearly always caused a terrible form of paralysis. It was described by William G. Shepherd in *Collier's Weekly* for 26 July 1930:

> The victim of 'jake paralysis' practically loses control of his fingers. . . . The feet of the paralyzed ones drop forward from the ankle so that the toes point downward. The victim has no control over the muscles that normally point the toes upward. When he tries to walk his dangling feet touch the pavement first at the toes, then his heels settle down jarringly. Toe first, heel next. That's how he moves. 'Tap-click, tap-click, tap-click, tap-click,' is how his footsteps sound. . . . The calves of his legs, after two or three weeks, begin to soften and hang down; the muscles between thumbs and index fingers shrivel away. . . .

Although a few cases were reported in 1928 and 1929, the use of Jake on a large scale apparently began in Kansas early in 1930. The first victims were looked upon as comical figures. They were called 'jake trotters', and were said to be 'jake jazzed', or to have 'jake feet'. Their peculiar locomotion was laughed at as the 'jake dance' or the 'jake step'. The merriment subsided, however, when health authorities discovered that in the city of Wichita alone there were more than five hundred cases of Jake paralysis, and many more in other parts of Kansas. In the summer of 1930 the Prohibition Bureau estimated that the number of victims throughout the county exceeded fifteen thousand, including eight thousand in Mississippi, one thousand in Louisiana, eight hundred in southern Tennessee, about four hundred in Georgia, and several hundred in Rhode Island, Connecticut, and Massachusetts. Many of them ultimately regained partial use of their hands and feet, but as far as the record shows, none completely recovered.

John Asbury *The Great Illusion*

Good Time Charley's

Of course I never buy any drinks in Good Time Charley's for hostesses, or anybody else, and especially for myself, because I am a personal friend of Good Time Charley's, and he will not sell me any drinks even if I wish to buy any, which is unlikely, as Good Time Charley figures that anybody who buys drinks in his place is apt to drink these drinks, and Charley does not care to see any of his personal friends drinking drinks at his place. If one of his personal friends wishes to buy a drink, Charley always sends him to Jack Fogarty's little speak down the street, and in fact Charley will generally go with him.

Damon Runyon *The Lily of St Pierre*

Abe North

'I don't believe his first stuff holds up,' he said. 'Even barring the Europeans there are a dozen Americans can do what North did.'

It was the first indication Dick had had that they were talking about Abe North.

'The only difference is that Abe did it first,' said Tommy.

'I don't agree,' persisted Hannan. 'He got the reputation for being a good musician because he drank so much that his friends had to explain him away somehow—'

'What's this about Abe North? What about him? Is he in a jam?'

'Didn't you read the *Herald* this morning?'

'No.'

'He's dead. He was beaten to death in a speak-easy in New York. He just managed to crawl home to the Racquet Club to die—'

'*Abe North?*'

'Yes, sure, they—'

'*Abe North?*' Dick stood up. 'Are you sure he's dead?'

Hannan turned around to McKibben: 'It wasn't the Racquet Club he crawled to – it was the Harvard Club. I'm sure he didn't belong to the Racquet.'

'The paper said so,' McKibben insisted.

'It must have been a mistake. I'm quite sure.'

'*Beaten to death in a speak-easy.*'

'But I happen to know most of the members of the Racquet Club,' said Hannan. 'It *must* have been the Harvard Club.'

F. Scott Fitzgerald *Tender Is the Night*

Moonshine

In Helena and Great Falls, we stayed at hotels, ordering gin from the bellboy to drink in our rooms. I liked the gin quite well, mixed with lemon soda and ice. Nothing to write home about, either, though on the drive up to Helena I had had an odd experience. As usual, we had a bottle of moonshine with us when we started out and we passed it back and forth, as usual, while we drove along. The road was rough and once, when it was my turn, I spilled a few drops on my silk stockings. That night when we were changing for dinner I found little holes in my stockings everywhere the liquor had spattered. I showed them to the girls, who positively could not understand it. The liquor, they pointed out, had been analysed by Bob in the drugstore.

We made jokes about it and kept the stockings for a trophy; yet the incident, so to speak, burned a hole in our minds. In Great Falls, Ruth suddenly decided that she did not like the looks of the bellboy who had brought us the gin. It tasted all right; it smelled all right; but Ruth remained suspicious, her dark brows drawn together, as we had one drink and started on a second. About half-way through the second, with one accord we set down our glasses. Ruth packed the bottle to take back to Medicine Springs for analysis. It was wood alcohol, sure enough, Bob Berdan told us a few days later. If so, we should have been dead, since we had each had two or three ounces of it. In fact, we felt no ill effects; perhaps the local moonshine had developed a tolerance in us – a tolerance not shared by my stockings. But the two incidents made us warier and tamer.

Mary McCarthy *Memories of a Catholic Girlhood*

No Good Liquor

Yes, the town is dreary. On August afternoons the road is empty, white with dust, and the sky above is bright as glass. Nothing moves – there are no children's voices, only the hum of the mill. The peach trees seem to grow more crooked every summer, and the leaves are dull grey and of a sickly delicacy. The house of Miss Amelia leans so much to the right that it is now only a question of time when it will collapse completely, and people are careful not to walk around the yard. There is no good liquor to be bought in the town; the nearest still is eight miles away, and the liquor is such that those who drink it grow warts on their livers the size of goobers, and dream themselves into a dangerous inward world. There is absolutely nothing to do in the town. Walk around the millpond, stand kicking at a rotten stump, figure out what you can do with the old wagon wheel by the side of the road near the church. The soul rots with boredom. You might as well go down to the Forks Fall highway and listen to the chain-gang.

Carson McCullers *The Ballad of the Sad Café*

LAST ORDERS

Kerouac

Kerouac died the classic drunkard's death, from cirrhosis of the liver. At the end of 1968, he had moved his wife and mother to St Petersburg, hoping the Florida sun would speed Gabrielle's recovery. Although Jack sometimes typed all night, he spent most of his time watching television, alternating beers with sips of whiskey. His mother lay bedridden in the back room, tended by Stella. On 20 October, after a sleepless night, he was watching *The Galloping Gourmet* on TV when his liver finally collapsed. He dragged himself to the bathroom, where Stella found him vomiting blood. He was given emergency surgery but never regained consciousness.

Barry Miles *Ginsberg*

Sonnet for Dick

My friend looked very beautiful propped on his pillows.
Gently downward tended his dreaming head,
His lean face washed as by underlight of willows
And everything right as rain except he was dead.
So brave in his dying, my friend both kind and clever,
And a useful Number Six who could whack it about.
I have described the man to whomsoever
The hell I've encountered, wandering in and out
Of gaps in the traffic and Hammersmith Irish boozers,
Crying, where and why did Dick Johnson go?
And none of the carloads and none of the boozer users,
Though full up with love and with camaraderie, know
More than us all-of-his-others, assembled to grieve
Dick who, brave as he lived things, took his leave.

Kit Wright

Last Orders

Squeeze the buzzer on the steel mesh gate like a trigger, but
It's someone else who has you in their sights. Click. It opens.
  Like electronic
Russian roulette, since you never know for sure who's who, or
  what
You're walking into. I, for instance, could be anybody. Though
  I'm told
Taig's written on my face. See me, would *I* trust appearances?

Inside a sudden lull. The barman lolls his head at us. We order
  Harp –
Seems safe enough, everybody drinks it. As someone looks
  daggers at us
From the *Bushmills* mirror, a penny drops: how simple it would
  be for someone
Like ourselves to walk in and blow the whole place, and
  ourselves, to Kingdom Come.

Ciaran Carson

Flood

He was always ashamed when he had to drive after he had been drinking, always apologetic to the horse. His apologetic frame made him facetious. He was aware of his inability to walk quite straight. Nevertheless his will kept stiff and attentive, in all his fuddledness.

He mounted and bowled off through the gates of the inn-yard. The mare went well, he sat fixed, the rain beating on his face. His heavy body rode motionless in a kind of sleep, one centre of attention was kept fitfully burning, the rest was dark. He concentrated his last attention on the fact of driving along the road he knew so well. He knew it so well, he watched for it attentively, with an effort of will.

He talked aloud to himself, sententious in his anxiety, as if he were perfectly sober, whilst the mare bowled along and the rain beat on him. He watched the rain before the gig-lamps, the faint gleaming of the shadowy horse's body, the passing of the dark hedges.

'It's not a fit night to turn a dog out,' he said to himself, aloud. 'It's high time as it did a bit of clearing up, I'll be damned if it isn't. It was a lot of use putting those ten loads of cinders on th'road. They'll be washed to kingdom-come if it doesn't alter. Well, it's our Fred's look-out, if they are. He's top-sawyer as far as those things go. I don't see why I should concern myself. They can wash to kingdom-come and back again for what I care. I suppose they would be washed back again some day. That's how things are. Th' rain tumbles down just to mount up in clouds again. So they say. There's no more water on the earth than there was in the year naught. That's the story, my boy, if you understand it. There's no more today than there was a thousand years ago – but no less either. You can't wear water out. No, my boy: it'll give you the go-by. Try to wear it out, and it takes its hook into vapour, it has its fingers at its nose to you. It turns into cloud and falleth as rain on the just and unjust. I wonder if I'm the just or the unjust.'

He started awake as the trap lurched deep into a rut. And he wakened to the point of his journey. He had travelled some distance since he was last conscious.

But at length he reached the gate, and stumbled heavily down, reeling, gripping fast to the trap. He descended into several inches of water.

'Be damned!' he said angrily. 'Be damned to the miserable slop.'

And he led the horse washing through the gate. He was quite drunk now, moving blindly, in habit. Everywhere there was water underfoot.

The raised causeway of the house and the farm stead was dry, however. But there was a curious roar in the night which seemed to be made in the darkness of his own intoxication. Reeling, blinded, almost without consciousness he carried his parcels and the rug and cushions into the house, dropped them, and went out to put up the horse.

Now he was at home, he was a sleep-walker, waiting only for the moment of activity to stop. Very deliberately and carefully, he led the horse down the slope to the cart-shed. She shied and backed.

'Why wha's amiss?' he hiccupped, plodding steadily on. And he was again in a wash of water, the horse splashed up water as she went. It was thickly dark, save for the gig-lamps, and they lit on a rippling surface of water.

'Well that's a knock-out,' he said, as he came to the cart-shed, and was wading in six inches of water. But everything seemed to him amusing. He laughed to think of six inches of water being in the cart-shed.

He backed in the mare. She was restive. He laughed at the fun of untackling the mare with a lot of water washing round his feet. He laughed because it upset her. 'What's amiss, what's amiss, a drop o' water won't hurt you!' As soon as he had undone the traces, she walked quickly away.

He hung up the shafts and took the gig-lamp. As he came out of the familiar jumble of shafts and wheels in the shed, the water, in little waves, came washing strongly against his leg. He staggered and almost fell.

'Well what the deuce!' he said, staring round at the running water in the black, watery night.

He went to meet the running flood, sinking deeper and deeper. His soul was full of great astonishment. He *had* to go and look where it came from, though the ground was going from under his feet. He went on, down towards the pond, shakily. He rather enjoyed it. He was knee-deep, and the water was pulling heavily. He stumbled, reeled sickeningly.

Fear took hold of him. Gripping tightly to the lamp, he reeled, and looked round. The water was carrying his feet away, he was dizzy. He did not know which way to turn. The water was whirling, whirling, the whole black night was swooping in rings. He swayed uncertainly at the centre of all attack, reeling in dismay. In his soul, he knew he would fall.

As he staggered something in the water struck his legs, and he fell. Instantly he was in the turmoil of suffocation. He fought in a black horror of suffocation, fighting, wrestling, but always borne down, borne inevitably down. Still he wrestled and fought to get himself free, in the unutterable struggle of suffocation, but he always fell again deeper. Something stuck his head, a great wonder of anguish went over him, then the blackness covered him entirely.

In the utter darkness, the unconscious, drowning body was rolled along, the waters pouring, washing, filling in the place. The cattle woke up and rose to their feet, the dog began to yelp. And the unconscious, drowning body was washed along in the black, swirling darkness, passively.

D. H. Lawrence *The Rainbow*

One Drunkard the Less

'Sir, Sir, he's dead!'

But the young man was watching those feet, and he shook his head. The bare feet sticking out at the end of the mattress were still dancing – they were none too clean, and the nails needed cutting. Hours went by. Suddenly they stiffened and stopped. Then the young doctor turned to Gervaise and said:

'That's it.'

Only death had stopped those feet.

Back in the tenement building, Gervaise found a whole gaggle of women in the Boches' lodge, gossiping excitedly. She thought they were waiting for her news as on the other days.

'He's kicked the bucket,' she said as she pushed the door to behind her. She was quite calm, but her face looked worn and bewildered.

But nobody was interested. The whole building was in an uproar. Oh, a marvellous story! Poisson had nabbed his wife with Lantier. The details were not quite clear because they all told the story in their own way. Anyhow, he had pounced on them just when they were least expecting him. Details were added that the ladies passed on with scandalized expressions. Such a sight, of course, had shocked Poisson out of his usual composure. Just like a tiger! That man, usually so taciturn, and who walked so stiffly that you'd say he had a truncheon up his backside, had roared and leaped about. But nothing had been heard since. Lantier must have explained things away to the husband. Anyway, it couldn't go on much longer. Thereupon Boche announced that the daughter at the restaurant next door was definitely going to take on the place and open it up as a tripe-shop. That artful dodger Lantier loved tripe.

Seeing Madame Lorilleux come in with Madame Lerat, Gervaise once again said in lifeless tones:

'He's gone . . . God, after four whole days of jigging and yelling.'

The two sisters could hardly do otherwise than take out their handkerchiefs. Their brother had had many faults, but still he was their brother. Boche shrugged his shoulders, saying loud enough for everybody to hear:

'Well, that's one drunkard the less!'

Emile Zola *L'Assommoir*, trans. L. W. Tancock

Over and Out

He had a drink. He had another and he got up and took off his coat and vest and tie. He had another and he brought the Scotch over and stood the bottle on the floor, and he got out his favourite records, which were in three albums. He put the albums on the floor. When he got drunk enough he would want to play them, but he wanted to have them near now. He lay down and then got up and brought the seltzer and the ice-bucket and stood them beside the Scotch. He examined the Scotch-bottle and saw there was not much more than a pint left, so he went to the dining-room and got another and opened it, then put the cork back. He drank while walking and this demonstrated the inadequacy of the glass. He had a smart idea. He took the flowers out of a vase and poured the water out, and made himself the biggest highball he ever had seen. It did not last very long. He got up again and got a plate of hors d'œuvres from the kitchen. They made him thirsty. He lowered his braces and felt much better.

'I think, if you don't mind, I think we shall play a little tune,' he said aloud. He played Paul Whiteman's record of 'Stairway to Paradise', and when the record came to the 'patter' he was screaming with jazz. The phonograph stopped itself but he was up and changing it to a much later record, Jean Goldkette's band playing 'Sunny Disposish'. He laid a lot of records out on the floor without looking at their titles. He spun a spoon around, and when it stopped he would play the record to which it pointed. He played only three records in this way, because he was pounding his feet, keeping time, and he broke one of his most favourites, Whiteman's 'Lady of the Evening', valuable because it has the fanciest trick ending ever put on a record. He wanted to cry but he could not. He wanted to pick up the pieces. He reached over to pick them up, and lost his balance and sat down on another record, crushing it unmusically. He did not want to see what it was. All he knew was that it was a Brunswick, which meant it was one of the oldest and best. He had a drink out of the glass. He used the vase for resting-drinking, and the glass for moving-drinking. That way he did not disturb the main drink while moving around, and could fill the glass while getting up and sitting down. Unintentionally he lay back. 'I am now', he said, 'drunk. Drunk. Dronk. Drongk.' He reached like a blind man for the fresh bottle and with eyes that he knew were sober he watched himself pour himself a drink. 'No ice I get drunk kicker. Quicker,' he said that aloud. To himself he said: 'I bet I look like something nice now.' He found he had two cigarettes burning, one in the ash-tray on the floor and the other getting stuck in the varnish on the edge of the phonograph. He half planned a lie to explain how the burn got there and then, for the first time, he knew it would not make any difference.

He got to his feet and went to the stairs. 'Anybody in this house?' he called.

'Anybody in this house.

'Any, body, in, this, *house*!'

He shook his head. 'Nope. Nobody in this house. You could wake the dead with that noise,' he said.

He got a package of cigarettes from the table and took the new bottle of Scotch. He wished he had time to look around the room to see if everything was all right, no more cigarettes burning or anything like that, but there wasn't time. There wasn't time to put out the lights or pick up anything or straighten the rugs. Not even time to put on a coat, pull up his braces or anything. He went out on the porch and down the steps and opened the garage door and closed it behind him. He shivered a little from the bit of cold, and it was cold in the garage, so he hurried. He had to see about the windows. They had to be closed. The ventilator in the roof was closed for the winter.

He climbed into the front seat and started the car. It started with a merry, powerful hum, ready to go. 'There, the bastards,' said Julian, and smashed the clock with the bottom of the bottle, to give them an approximate time. It was 10.41.

There was nothing to do now but wait. He smoked a little, hummed for a minute or two, and had three quick drinks and was on his fourth when he lay back and slumped down in the seat. At 10.50, by the clock in the rear seat, he tried to get up. He had not the strength to help himself, and at ten minutes past eleven no one could have helped him, no one in the world.

John O'Hara *Appointment in Samarra*

Sonnet: The Last Things

Of course there's always a last everything.
The last meal, the last drink, the last sex.
The last meeting with a friend. The last
stroking of the last cat, the last
sight of a son or daughter. Some would be more
charged with emotion than others – if one knew.
It's not knowing that makes it all so piquant.
A good many lasts have taken place already.

Then there are last words, variously reported,
such as: Let not poor Nelly starve. Or:
I think I could eat one of Bellamy's veal pies.
If there were time I'd incline to a summary:
Alcohol made my life shorter but more interesting.
My father said (not last perhaps): Say goodbye to Gavin.

Gavin Ewart

End of the Road

'Alice wasn't perfect,' Joe Lampton said. 'But who is? She was a jolly good sort, and I'm going to miss her very much.' He shook his handsome dignified head slowly. That meant that a moral exordium was on the way. 'I enjoy a drink myself, but no one in charge of a car should be allowed into a pub. It's lucky she killed only herself. My God, only yesterday she was alive and cheerful, and then, all in a second–

'A second?' Teddy said. 'She was still alive when the ambulance came. She didn't die till eight o'clock.'

'Jesus Christ,' I said. 'Jesus Christ,' I turned on Teddy fiercely. 'Who told you? Who told you?'

'My cousin works at Warley Hospital,' he said. 'Turned me up a bit when I heard about it. She was crawling round the road when a farm-labourer found her. She was scalped and the steering-column –'

I half-ran out of the office and went into the lavatory. But the W.C. door was locked, and it was nearly ten minutes before it opened and one of the Health Department juniors came out looking sheepish and leaving the compartment full of tobacco smoke. I locked the door and sat on the W.C. seat with my head between my hands, those gentle loving hands that had so often caressed what was, because of the treachery in the brain in the head between the hands, a lump of raw meat with the bones sticking through.

John Braine *Room at the Top*

Epitaphs

FU I

Fu I loved the high cloud and the hill,
Alas, he died of alcohol.

LI PO

And Li Po also died drunk.
He tried to embrace a moon
In the Yellow River.

Ezra Pound

Finis

Behold, the Lord maketh the earth empty, and maketh it waste, and turneth it upside down, and scattereth abroad the inhabitants thereof.

And it shall be, as with the people, so with the priest; as with the servant, so with his master: as with the maid, so with her mistress; as with the buyer, so with the seller; as with the lender, so with the borrower; as with the taker of usury, so with the giver of usury to him.

The land shall be utterly emptied, and utterly spoiled, for the LORD hath spoken this word.

The earth mourneth and fadeth away; the world languisheth and fadeth away; the haughty people of the earth do languish.

The earth also is defiled under the inhabitants thereof; because they have transgressed the laws, changed the ordinance, broken the everlasting covenant.

Therefore hath the curse devoured the earth, and they that dwell therein are desolate: therefore the inhabitants of the earth are burned, and few men left.

The new wine mourneth, the vine languisheth, all the merry-hearted do sigh.

The mirth of tabrets ceaseth, the noise of them that rejoice endeth, the joy of the harp ceaseth.

They shall not drink wine with a song; strong drink shall be bitter to them that drink it.

The city of confusion is broken down; every house is shut up, that no man may come in.

There is a crying for wine in the streets; all joy is darkened, the mirth of the land is gone.

In the city is left desolation, and the gate is smitten with destruction.

Isaiah 24:1–12

Acknowledgements

For permission to reprint extracts from copyright material, the publishers gratefully acknowledge the following:

NELSON ALGREN: 'A Walk on the Wild Side', Farrar Straus and Cudahy, 1956, copyright © Nelson Algren, 1956, by permission of Rogers, Coleridge and White Ltd. KINGSLEY AMIS: 'The Drinking Song' from *Collected Poems of Kingsley Amis*, Hutchinson, 1979, by permission of Hutchinson Publishers Ltd.; *The Anti-Death League*, copyright © Kingsley Amis 1966, Penguin, 1968, *I Like It Here*, copyright © Kingsley Amis 1958, Penguin 1968, *Lucky Jim*, Penguin, 1970, copyright © Kingsley Amis, 1954, by permission of Victor Gollancz Ltd. MARTIN AMIS: *Money*, Jonathan Cape, 1984, and *Other People*, Jonathan Cape, 1981, by permission of Jonathan Cape Ltd; 'Your Good Elf', *The New Statesman & Society*, 12 September 1975, by permission of The New Statesman & Society. ARISTOPHANES: 'The Wasps' from *The Frogs and Other Plays*, trans. David Barrett, Penguin Classics, 1964, copyright © David Barrett, 1964, by permission of Penguin Books Ltd. DIANA ATHILL: *After a Funeral*, Jonathan Cape, 1986, by permission of Jonathan Cape Ltd. W. H. AUDEN: 'September 1, 1939' from *Another Time*, Faber, 1954, by permission of Faber and Faber Ltd. JULIAN BARNES: *A History of the World in 10½ Chapters*, Jonathan Cape 1989, by permission of Jonathan Cape Ltd. ROLAND BARTHES: 'Wine and Milk' from *Mythologies*, Jonathan Cape, 1972, by permission of Jonathan Cape Ltd. HILAIRE BELLOC: 'West Sussex Drinking Song' from *The Complete Verse of Hilaire Belloc*, Pimlico, 1991, by permission of the Peters Fraser & Dunlop Group Ltd. SAUL BELLOW: *Herzog*, Weidenfeld and Nicolson, 1964, by permission of George Weidenfeld and Nicolson Ltd. JOHN BERRYMAN: No. 351 from *His Toy, His Dream, His Rest*, Faber, 1973, 'Drunks' from *Love and Fame*, Faber, 1973, 'Sonnet No. 13' from *Berryman's Sonnets*, Faber, 1968, and *from Recovery*, Faber, 1973, by permission of Faber and Faber Ltd. JOHN BETJEMAN: 'The Village Inn' from *Collected Poems*, fourth edition, John Murray, 1979, copyright © John Betjeman 1979, by permission of John Murray (Publishers) Ltd. RICHARD BOSTON: 'Pub Games' from *Beer and Skittles*, Collins, 1976, by permission of the author and HarperCollins Publishers. JAMES BOSWELL: *Boswell in Extremes*, Edinburgh University Press, by permission of the Yale Editions of the Private Papers of James Boswell and Edinburgh University Press. JOHN BRAINE: *Room at the Top*, Methuen, 1975, by permission of Methuen London. BERTOLT BRECHT: 'Little Song', trans. John Willett, and 'On the Pleasures of Drink', trans. H. B. Mallalieu, from *Poems 1913–1956*, Methuen, 1987, by permission of Methuen London. TRUMAN CAPOTE: 'A Capote Reader' from *Portrait of Elizabeth Taylor*, Hamish Hamilton, 1987, copyright © Truman Capote 1988, by permission of Hamish Hamilton Ltd. CIARAN CARSON: 'Last Orders' from *Belfast Confetti*, The Gallery Press, 1989, by permission of The Gallery Press. RAYMOND CARVER: 'Wine',

RAYMOND CARVER: 'Wine', 'Suspenders' and 'Miracle' from *A New Path to the Waterfall*, Collins Harvill, 1990, and 'Errand' from *Elephant and Other Stories*, Collins Harvill, 1988, by permission of Collins Harvill/ HarperCollins Publishers. C. P. CAVAFY: 'Two Young Men 23 to 24 Years Old' from *Collected Poems*, Hogarth, 1984, by permission of The Estate of C. P. Cavafy and The Hogarth Press. BRUCE CHATWIN: 'The Pub in Katherine' from *The Songlines*, Jonathan Cape, 1987, by permission of Jonathan Cape Ltd. ANTON CHEKHOV: *The Island of Sakhalin*, trans. Luba & Michael Terpak, Hutchinson, 1987, by permission of Hutchinson Publishers Ltd. T. E. B. CLARKE: *What's Yours*, Heinemann, 1938, copyright © T. E. B. Clarke, by permission of William Heinemann Ltd. WENDY COPE: *from* 'Strugnell's Sonnets' (i) from *Making Cocoa for Kingsley Amis*, Faber, 1986, by permission of Faber and Faber Ltd; 'A Green Song', by permission of the author. TOM DARDIS: *The Thirsty Muse*, Abacus, 1990, by permission of Macdonald & Co. (Publishers) Ltd. J. P. DONLEAVY: *The Ginger Man*, Penguin, 1968, by permission of the author. FYODOR DOSTOEVSKY: *Crime and Punishment*, trans. Constance Garnett, Heinemann, 1979, by permission of William Heinemann Ltd. SERGEI ESENIN: 'The Black Man' from *Confessions of a Hooligan*, trans. Geoffrey Thurley, Carcanet Press, 1973, by permission of Carcanet Press Ltd. GAVIN EWART: 'The Select Party' and 'Sonnet: The Last Things' from *The Collected Ewart 1980–1990*, Hutchinson, 1991, by permission of Hutchinson Books Ltd. WILLIAM FAULKNER: *Light in August*, Penguin, 1960, copyright © William Faulkner, by permission of Curtis Brown Ltd, London. JAMES FENTON: 'The Skip' from *The Memory of War and Children in Exile*, Penguin, 1983, by permission of the Peters Fraser & Dunlop Group Ltd. F. SCOTT FITZGERALD: *The Letters of F. Scott Fitzgerald*, ed. Andrew Turnbull, Charles Scribner's Sons, 1963, copyright © 1963 by Frances Scott Fitzgerald Lanahan, renewed 1991, by permission of Harold Ober Associates Incorporated; *The Crack Up*, The Bodley Head, by permission of The Estate of F. Scott Fitzgerald and The Bodley Head Publishing Company Ltd. PENELOPE FITZGERALD: *The Beginning of Spring*, HarperCollins, 1989, by permission of HarperCollins Publishers Ltd. SIGMUND FREUD: 'Civilisation and Its Discontents' from *The Standard Edition of the Complete Psychological Works of Sigmund Freud*, trans. and ed. James Strachey, Hogarth Press 1975, by permission of Sigmund Freud, copyrights © The Institute of Psycho-Analyses and The Hogarth Press. ALLEN GINSBERG: 'Uptown' from *Allen Ginsberg: Collected Poems 1947–1980*, Viking, 1985, copyright © Allen Ginsberg, 1968, by permission of Penguin Books Ltd. WILLIAM GOLDING: *The Inheritors*, Faber, 1955, by permission of Faber and Faber Ltd. GRAHAM GREENE: *The Power and the Glory*, Heinemann & The Bodley Head, 1971, by permission of William Heinemann Ltd, The Bodley Head Ltd and The Estate of Graham Greene. THE GUARDIAN: 'Trappist Monk item', 7 November 1990, © The *Guardian*, by permission the *Guardian* News Service Ltd. PATRICK HAMILTON: *Hangover Square*, Penguin, 1956, by permission of of A. M. Heath & Company Ltd. JOHN HEALY: *The Grass Arena*, Faber, 1990, by permission of Faber and Faber Ltd. SEAMUS HEANEY: 'Casualty' from *Field Work*, Faber, 1979, by permission of Faber and Faber Ltd. HEDYLOS: 'Epigram 91', trans. Adrian

Wright, from *The Greek Anthology*, ed. Peter Jay, Penguin Classics, Revised Edition, 1981, copyright © Peter Jay, 1973, 1981, by permission of Penguin Books Ltd. ERNEST HEMINGWAY: *For Whom The Bell Tolls*, Jonathan Cape, 1941, by permission of The Estate of Ernest Hemingway and Jonathan Cape Ltd. ADRIAN HENRI: 'Drinking Song' from *Collected Poems*, Allison and Busby, 1986, copyright © 1986 Adrian Henri, by permission of Rogers, Coleridge & White Ltd. HORACE: 'Book I, Epistle 5' and 'Book I, Epistle 19' from *Horace: Satires and Epistles*, trans. Niall Rudd, Penguin Classics, 1979, copyright © Niall Rudd, 1979, by permission of Penguin Books Ltd. TED HUGHES: 'Dick Straightup' from *Lupercal*, Faber, 1960, by permission of Faber and Faber Ltd. PEARSE HUTCHINSON: 'Fleadh Cheoil' from *Selected Poems*, The Gallery Press, 1982, by permission of The Gallery Press. JORIS-KARL HUYSMANS: *Against Nature*, trans. Robert Baldrick, Penguin Classics, 1959, pp. 58–9, copyright © The Estate of Robert Baldrick, 1959, by permission of Penguin Books Ltd. MICK IMLAH: 'Hall of Fame' from *Birthmarks*, Chatto & Windus, 1988, by permission of Chatto & Windus Ltd. CHARLES JACKSON: *The Lost Weekend*, Penguin, 1989, copyright © Charles Jackson, 1944, by permission of Penguin Books Ltd. ALAN JENKINS: 'Nineties' from *Greenheart*, Chatto & Windus, 1990, by permission of Chatto & Windus Ltd. JAMES JOYCE: *The Dubliners*, Jonathan Cape, 1967, by permission of the Estate of James Joyce and Jonathan Cape Ltd; *Ulysses*, Bodley Head, 1986, by permission of the Estate of James Joyce and The Bodley Head Ltd. GARRISON KEILLOR: 'A Glass of Wendy' from *Leaving Home*, Faber, 1988, by permission of Faber and Faber Ltd. PHILIP LARKIN: *All What Jazz*, Faber, 1970, 'Party Politics' from *Collected Poems 1938–1983*, ed. Anthony Thwaite, Faber, 1988, and 'Vers de Societé', 'Livings III' and 'The Card-Players' from *High Windows*, Faber, 1979, by permission of Faber and Faber Ltd. LIZ LOCHHEAD: 'Franglais' from *True Confessions and New Clichés*, Polygon, 1985, by permission of Polygon. CHRISTOPHER LOGUE: *War Music*, Faber, 1988, by permission of Faber and Faber Ltd. ROBERT LOWELL: 'The Drinker' from *For The Union Dead*, Faber, 1965, and 'To Delmore Schwartz' and 'To Speak of the Woe That Is in Marriage' from *Life Studies*, Faber, 1969, by permission of Faber and Faber Ltd. MALCOLM LOWRY: *Under the Volcano*, Jonathan Cape, 1967, by permission of Jonathan Cape Ltd. NORMAN MacCAIG: 'Walking to Inveruplan' and 'Hogmanay' from *Collected Poems*, Chatto & Windus, 1990, by permission of Chatto & Windus Ltd. MARY McCARTHY: *Memories of a Catholic Girlhood*, William Heinemann, 1957, by permission of the Estate of the late Mary McCarthy and William Heinemann Ltd. CARSON McCULLERS: *The Ballad of the Sad Café*, Cresset, 1953, by permission of Cresset Press. HUGH MACDIARMID: *from A Drunk Man*, Scottish Academic Press, 1988, copyright © Michael Grieve, 1988, by permission of Michael Grieve. LOUIS MacNEICE: 'The Brandy Glass' and 'Night Club' from *The Collected Poems*, Faber, 1986, by permission of Faber and Faber Ltd; *from The Strings are False*, Faber, 1982, by permission of David Higham Associates Ltd. DEREK MAHON: 'The Terminal Bar' from *The Hunt by Night*, OUP, 1982, and 'Homecoming' from *Poems 1962–1978*, OUP, 1979, by permission of Oxford University Press. OSIP MANDELSTAM: 'The thread of gold cordial flowed from the bottle' from *Osip*

Mandelstam: Selected Poems, trans. Clarence Brown and W. S. Merwin, OUP, 1973, by permission of Oxford University Press. DON MARQUIS: 'A Roach of Taverns' from *Archy and Mehitabel*, Faber, 1934, by permission of Faber and Faber Ltd. THOMAS MANN: *Confessions of Felix Krull*, Martin Secker & Warburg, 1955, copyright © Thomas Mann 1954, by permission of Martin Secker & Warburg Ltd. GEORGE MELLY: 'Breathing Space' by Pamela Nowicka, *The Times* 10 May 1990, by permission of George Melly, *The Times* and Pamela Nowicka. BARRY MILES: *Ginsberg: A Biography*, Viking, 1990, copyright © Barry Miles, 1989, by permission of Penguin Books Ltd. HENRY MILLER: *The Colossus of Maroussi*, William Heinemann, copyright © Henry Miller, 1941, by permission of William Heinemann Ltd. SPIKE MILLIGAN: *Puckoon*, Penguin, 1969, by permission of Spike Milligan Productions Ltd. BLAKE MORRISON: 'Pomagne' from *The Ballad of the Yorkshire Ripper*, Chatto & Windus, 1987, by permission of Chatto & Windus Ltd. OGDEN NASH: 'A Drink With Something In It', from *I Wouldn't Have Missed It*, André Deutsch, 1983, by permission of André Deutsch Ltd. ELIOT NESS: *The Untouchables*, Bailey Bros & Swinfen Ltd, 1967, by permission of A. M. Heath & Co. Ltd. JOSEPH NIGHTINGALE: *Memoirs of Queen Caroline*, edited and introduced by Christopher Hibbert, The Folio Society, 1978, by permission of The Folio Society. JOHN O'HARA: *Appointment in Samarra*, Faber, 1935, by permission of Faber and Faber Ltd. P. J. O'ROURKE: *Holidays In Hell*, Pan/Picador, 1989, by permission of Pan Macmillan Ltd. GEORGE ORWELL: 'The Pub and the People by Mass Observation' and 'The Moon Under the Water' from *Vol III Collected Essays, Journalism and Letters of George Orwell*, Martin Secker & Warburg, 1949, and *Nineteen Eighty-Four*, Martin Secker & Warburg, 1968, by permission of the Estate of the late Sonia Brownell Orwell and Martin Secker & Warburg Ltd. DOROTHY PARKER: 'You Were Perfectly Fine' and 'The Flaw in Paganism' from *The Collected Dorothy Parker*, Duckworth, 1973, by permission of Duckworth. PETRONIUS: *The Satyricon*, trans. J. P. Sullivan, Penguin Classics, revised edition, 1986, copyright © J. P. Sullivan, 1965, 1969, 1974, 1986, by permission of Penguin Books Ltd. FERGUS PICKERING: 'From the Convivial Epigrams in the Greek Anthology' and 'Imitation of Horace: Odes 1.27', by permission of John Whitworth. MARCO POLO: *The Travels*, trans. Ronald Latham, Penguin Classics, 1958, copyright © Ronald Latham, 1958, by permission of Penguin Books Ltd. STEPHEN POTTER: *One Upmanship*, by permission of Peter Fraser Dunlop Group Ltd. EZRA POUND: 'Epitaphs' from *Lustra*, Faber, and 'Canto II' and 'Canto XII' from *The Cantos*, Faber, 1954, by permission of Faber and Faber Ltd. PROSPER MONTAGNE with the collaboration of Dr Gottschalk: *Larousse Gastronomique*, ed. Nina Froud and Phileas Gilbert, Paul Hamlyn, 1961, by permission of Paul Hamlyn Publishers, part of Reed International Ltd. THOMAS PYNCHON: *V*, Pan/Picador, 1975, by permission of Pan Books Ltd. CRAIG RAINE: *The Electrification of the Soviet Union*, Faber, 1986, by permission of Faber and Faber Ltd. IRINA RATUSHINSKAYA: *Grey Is the Colour of Hope*, trans. Alyona Kojevnikov, Hodder & Stoughton, 1988, by permission of Hodder & Stoughton Ltd. PETER READING: *Perduta Gente*, Martin Secker & Warburg, 1989, copyright © Peter Reading 1989, by permission of Martin Secker & Warburg Ltd. JEAN *rhys*: *Good Morning Midnight*, André Deutsch, 1967, by permission of André Deutsch Ltd. THEODORE ROETHKE: 'My Papa's Waltz' from *Collected Poems*, Faber, 1968, by permission of Faber and Faber Ltd. DAMON RUNYON: 'The Lily of St. Pierre' from *On Broadway*, Constable, 1950, by permission of Constable & Company Ltd. SIEGFRIED SASSOON: 'Atrocities' from *The War Poems*, Faber, 1983, by permission of George Sassoon. DIMITRI SHOSTAKOVICH: *Memoirs of Dimitri Shostakovich*, edited by Solomon Volkov, Hamish Hamilton, 1979, copyright © Solomon Volkov 1979, by permission of Hamish Hamilton Ltd. ALAN SILLITOE: *Saturday Night and Sunday Morning*, W. H. Allen, 1958, © Alan Sillitoe, 1958, by permission of Rosica Colin Ltd. JAMES SIMMONS: 'Stephano Remembers' from *Poems 1956–1986*, The Gallery Press, by permission of The Gallery Press. JOHN STEINBECK: *Cannery Row*, Heinemann, 1939, by permission of William Heinemann Ltd. GRAHAM SWIFT: 'About Coronation Ale' from *Waterland*, Heinemann, 1983, by permission of A. P. Watt Ltd on behalf of Graham Swift. DYLAN THOMAS: 'Letter to Oscar Williams June 22nd 1953' from *The Collected Letters of Dylan Thomas*, Dent, 1957, copyright © the Trustees for the Copyrights of Dylan Thomas, 1957 and 'A Story' from *A Prospect of the Sea*, Dent, 1955, copyright © the Trustees for the Copyrights of Dylan Thomas, 1955, by permission of David Higham Associates Ltd. PROFESSOR JERRY THOMAS: *The Bon Vivant's Companion or How to Mix Drinks*, ed. Herbert Asbury, Alfred A. Knopf, 1928, © Professor Jerry Thomas, 1928, by permission of Random House, Inc. JAMES THURBER: 'If Grant Had Been Drinking at Appomattor' from *Vintage Thurber Vol. II*, Penguin, 1983, by permission of Hamish Hamilton Ltd. JOHN UPDIKE: *Couples*, Penguin, 1970, by permission of André Deutsch Ltd. WANG CHI: 'Passing the wine-seller's, II' from *The Penguin Book of Chinese Verse*, trans. Robert Kotewall and Norman L. Smith, Penguin, 1962, copyright © N. L. Smith and R. H. Kotewall, 1962, by permission of Penguin Books Ltd. EVELYN WAUGH: *Brideshead Revisited*, Chapman & Hall Ltd, 1945, 'Port' from *Wine in Peace and War*, Saccone & Speed Ltd, 1949, and *The Diaries of Evelyn Waugh*, ed. Michael Davie, Weidenfeld & Nicolson Ltd, 1980, by permission of the Peters Fraser & Dunlop Group Ltd. H. G. WELLS: 'The Potwell Inn' from *The History of Mr Polly*, Pan, 1963, by permission of A. P. Watt Ltd on behalf of The Literary Executors of the Estate of H. G. Wells. EDMUND WHITE: *States of Desire*, Pan, 1986, by permission of André Deutsch Ltd. JOHN WHITWORTH: 'Under Age Drinking at the Adelphi Hotel in Edinburgh 1963' from *Unhistorical Fragments*, Martin Secker & Warburg, by permission of Martin Secker & Warburg Ltd. P. G. WODEHOUSE: *The Code of the Woosters*, Vintage, 1990, and *Right Ho, Jeeves*, Arrow, 1990, by permission of Barrie & Jenkins. KIT WRIGHT: 'Sonnet for Dick' from *Short Afternoons*, Hutchinson, 1989, by permission of Hutchinson Books Ltd. EMILE ZOLA: *L'Assommoir*, trans. L. W. Tancock, Penguin Classics, 1970, copyright © L. W. Tancock, 1970, by permission of Penguin Books Ltd.

Faber and Faber Limited apologizes for any errors or omissions in the above list and would be grateful to be notified of any corrections that should be incorporated into the next edition of this volume.

Index

absinthe, 33–4, 136
After a Funeral (Athill), 367–71
Against Nature (Huysmans), 28–30
alcoholism, 76–7, 97, 488
ale, 21, 52, 53, 66, 67, 68, 84, 85, 194, 210, 299–303, 372, 373, 390, 478, 483, 491, 497
Algren, Nelson, 87–91, 443–4
All What Jazz (Larkin), 362
Amis, Kingsley, 5, 10–11, 20, 68–9, 95–8, 326–8, 390, 413–18, 423–5
Amis, Martin, 86–7, 108, 355–6, 394–5, 448, 488
Amis on Drink (K. Amis), 5, 10–11, 413–18
Anacreon, 50
anisette, 29
Anti-Death League, The (K. Amis), 95–8
Appointment in Samarra (O'Hara), 536–8
arak, 29
Aristophanes, 251–3
Aristotle, 314–15, 326
arrack-punch, 130
Arnold, Matthew, 185–6
Asbury, Herbert, 32
Asbury, John, 512–18, 523–4
Assomoir, L' (Zola), 535–6
At Swim-Two-Birds (O'Brien), 75–9, 363–4
Athill, Diana, 367–71
Atrocities (Sassoon), 145–6
Auden, W. H., 225–8
aversion therapy, 177–8

Ballad of the Sad Café, The (McCullers), 527
barmaids, 195, 197, 200
Barnaby Rudge (Dickens), 213–17, 305–9
Barnes, Julian, 43–4
bars, 221–31, 286–90, 464, 515
Barthes, Roland, 6–9
Bartholomew Fair (Jonson), 84–5
Baudelaire, Charles, 65
Beaujolais, 67, 354
beer, 52, 67, 85, 107, 108, 142, 143, 202, 206, 231, 261, 266, 289, 290, 299, 301, 326, 408, 448, 462, 482, 497
  bottled, 193
  consumption statistics, 193, 488
  drinking vessels, 195
  English, 20
  German, 124–7
  near, 514
  and Prohibition, 513, 514, 522
  Real Beer Movement, 208
  reasons for drinking, 193–4
  Saint Wendell's, 21–3
  sour, 196
  strong, 325
Beginning of Spring, The (P. Fitzgerald), 283–5
Belloc, Hilaire, 65–6
Bellow, Saul, 519–21
benders, 93–4
Benedictine, 29, 418
Bernard, Jeffrey, 71
Berryman, John, 150–1, 230, 413, 460
Betjeman, John, 202–4
bitter, 29
Black Man, The (Essenin), 455–9
blackcurrant liqueur, 30
Bloody Mary, 131, 417
Blotner, Joseph, 328, 462
Blue Blazer, 32
Bob Polter (Gilbert), 481–5
Bon Vivant's Guide, or How to Mix Drinks, The (Thomas), 32
bootlegging, 510–11, 513, 517–20, 523
Bordeaux, 359
Borough Inns, The (Crabbe), 199–201

Boston, Richard, xx, 197–8, 206–9
Boswell, James, 31, 109–10, 315, 392–3, 443, 449–51, 479–81, 491
Boulton, Agnes, 464–8
bourbon, 139, 515
Braine, John, 539
brandy, 3, 28, 29, 31, 92, 93, 109, 130, 177, 178, 224, 237, 286, 358, 359, 393, 395, 396, 397, 507, 509, 510
Brandy Glass, The (MacNeice), 99
Brecht, Bertholt, 70–1, 487
brewers, 299–305, 513, 522
Brideshead Revisited (Waugh), 9–10, 361–2
Brontë, Anne, 177–8
Brontë, Patrick Branwell, 28
Browning, Robert, 63–4
'Brugglesmith' (Kipling), 381–6
Burgundy, 4, 20, 79, 82, 113
Burns, Robert, 21, 134–5, 313, 435
Byron, Lord George Gordon, 49, 105–6, 113, 255–6, 358

cafés, 224–5, 242–4
Calvados, 354
Cannery Row (Steinbeck), 290–9
Cantos, The (Pound), 37–41, 389–90
Capote, Truman, 15–16
Card-Players, The (Larkin), 131–2
Carson, Ciaran, 532
Carver, Raymond, 16–19, 162–3, 428–9, 431–4
Casualty (Heaney), 146–9
Cavafy, C. P., 224–5
champagne, 4, 13–14, 15–19, 79, 80, 108, 238, 359, 514, 516
Chartreuse, 29
Chatwin, Bruce, 143–4
Chaucer, Geoffrey, 371–7
Chekhov, Anton, 510–11
cherry brandy, 190
cherry cider, 191
Chesterton, G.K., 48–9
Church-Porch, The (Herbert), 442
cider, 24, 196, 259, 326
Civilization and Its Discontents (Freud), 313
Civilized Drinking, Civilized Chat (Pickering), 136–7
Clare, John, 67–8
claret, 4, 31, 59, 108, 113, 129, 206, 360, 450
Clarke, T. E. B., 191–2
Clough, Arthur Hugh, 58
cocktails, 223–4, 516
Code of the Woosters, The (Wodehouse), 418–19
Coleridge, Samuel Taylor, 124, 140–1, 328–31
Colossus of Maroussi, The (Miller), 11–12
Come Home, Father (Work), 178–9
communion wine, 91–3, 235
Comus (Milton), 41–2, 275–6, 486–7
Condition of the Working Classes in England, The (Engels), 430–1
Confessions of Felix Krull, Confidence Man (Mann), 13–14
Cope, Wendy, 66–7, 469
Cotton, Charles, 50, 390
Counterparts (Joyce) 179–81
Couples (Updike), 262–71
Cowper, William, 485–6, 491
Crabbe, George, 199–201
Crack-Up, The (F. Scott Fitzgerald), 461
Credo (Baudelaire), 65
crème de menthe, 29
Crime and Punishment (Dostoevsky), 468–9
curaçao, 29
Currie, Dr James, 110–12
Cyder (Philips), 24

Daily Telegraph, 437
Dalrymple, William, 108–9
Dardis, Tom, 137
darts, 197–9
'Darts Night' (Rae), 198–9
David Copperfield (Dickens), 331–3
delirium tremens, 460–1, 463
Diaries (Waugh), 359
Diary (Pepys), 100–103
Dickens, Charles, 82–3, 213–17, 305–9, 331–3, 341–7, 495–501

Dipsychus (Clough), 58
Distracted Preacher, The (Hardy), 505–9
Do You Want to Live for Ever, Pig? (Pickering), 51
Don Jaun (Byron), 49
Donald Watt's Jolt, 417–18
Donleavy, J. P., 286–9
Dostoevsky, Fyodor, 468–9
double vision, 326
Drinker, The (Lowell), 139–40
Drinking Song (K. Amis), 68–9
Drinking Song (Henri), 353
Drinking Song, A (Yeats), 47
Drunk Man Looks at the Thistle, A (MacDiarmid), 115–18
Drunken Man's Praise of Sobriety, A (Yeats), 56–7
Drunken Swine, The (Cotton), 390
Drunks (Berryman), 150–1
drying out, 15–16
Duranty, Walter, 242–4
Dutch courage, 334–41

Ecclesiasticus, 441
Electrification of the Soviet Union, The (Raine), 356–8
Engels, Friedrich, 430–1
Ennis (Hutchinson), 239–42
Epistle to Bathhurst (Pope), 201
Epitaphs (Pound), 540
'Errand' Elephant and other Stories, (Carver), 16–19
Esenin, Sergei, 455–9
Ewart, Gavin, 271, 538

Faulkner, William, 328, 462, 522–3
Fenton, James, 407–9
Fermor, Patrick Leigh, 124–8, 256–8
Fernet Branca, 417
Fielding, Henry, 129–30, 316, 351–3
1 September 1939 (Auden), 225–8
Fitzgerald, Edward, 60–63
Fitzgerald, Francis Scott, 461, 462, 525–6
Fitzgerald, Penelope, 283–5
Flaw in Paganism, The (Parker), 65
For Whom The Bell Tolls (Hemingway), 33–4
Franglais (Lochhead), 353–5
Frayn, Michael, 395–403
Freud, Sigmund, 313
Friedman, Thomas, 221–3
From Beirut to Jerusalem (Friedman), 221–3
Fuel (Reading), 473

Gargantua and Pantagruel (Rabelais), 42, 58–60, 244–5
Gelb, Arthur, 464
Gelb, Barbara, 464
Genesis, 42–3
Gibbon, Edward, 123, 325
Gilbert, W. S., 481–5
gin, 4, 20, 26–9, 67, 107, 109, 136, 152, 177, 224, 288, 335, 359, 483, 498, 507, 526
  Hollands, 358
Ginger Man, The (Donleavy), 286–9
Ginsberg (Miles), 531
Ginsberg, Allen, 145
'Glass of Wendy, A' (Keillor), 21–3
Golding, William, 321–5, 391–2
Good Morning, Midnight (Rhys), 119–21, 455
gout, 4
Grand Marnier, 418
Grass Arena, The (Healy), 470, 471–2
Great Illusion, The (Asbury), 512–18, 523–4
Great Things (Hardy), 24–5
Greek Anthology, The (trans. Pickering), 51
Green Song, A (Cope), 469
Greene, Graham, 91–3
Grey is the Colour of Hope (Ratushinskaya), 511–12
Guardian, 427–8
Guid Ale Keeps the Heart Aboon (Burns), 21
Guthrie, Dr, 30

Haffenden, John, 462–4

Hall of Fame (Imlah), 152–4
hallucinations, 175–6, 455–9, 461, 462
Hangover Square (Hamilton), 69–70
hangovers, 44, 49, 70, 101, 367, 390–95, 404–7, 413–19, 428, 448, 460–1
Hardy, Thomas, 24–5, 186–9, 259, 505–9
Haven (Reading), 471
Head and Bottle (Thomas), 50–1
Headlong Hall (Peacock), 113–15
Healy, John, 470, 471–2
Heaney, Seamus, 146–9
Hedylos, 351
Hemingway, Ernest, 33–4
Henri, Adrian, 353
Henry IV Part I (Shakespeare), 138–9
Henry IV Part II (Shakespeare), 12–13
Herbert, George, 442
Herrick, Robert, 492–3
Herzog (Bellow), 519–21
Hibbert, Christopher, 236–8
highballs, 516, 536
His Fare-well to sack (Herrick), 492–3
History of the Decline and Fall of the Roman Empire, The (Gibbon), 123, 325
History of the World in 10½ Chapters, A (Barnes), 43–4
hock, 4, 49, 136
Hogmanay (MacCaig), 118–19
Holidays in Hell (O'Rorke), 223–4
Homecoming (Mahon), 132–3
Homer, 313, 403–4, 425–7
Horace, 242, 326
Housman, A. E., 52–4
Hughes, Ted, 141–3
Hugo, Victor, 334
Hunt By Night, The (Mahon), 230–1
Hutchinson, Pearse, 239–42
Huysmans, J. K., 28–30

I Like It Here (K. Amis), 20
I Write as I Please (Duranty), 242–4
'If Grant Had Been Drinking at Appomattox' (Thurber), 410–12
Imlah, Mick, 152–4
In Xanadu (Dalrymple), 108–9
indigestion, 358, 430, 431
Inheritors, The (Golding), 321–5, 391–2
inns, 186, 187, 190, 191, 199–203, 212–15
Isaiah, 430, 540–41
Island of Sakhalin, The (Chekhov), 510–11

Jackson, Charles, 460–61
Jenkins, Alan, 136
John Barleycorn (London), 93, 171–7
John Wilmot Earl of Rochester, His Life and Writing (Prinz), 212–13
Jonson, Ben, 84–5, 204–6
Journal (Byron), 358
Joyce, James, 179–81, 377–81

Keats, John, 54–6
Keillor, Garrison, 21–3
Kipling, Rudyard, 381, 509–10
kirsch, 29
Kümmel, 29

lager, 153
landlords, 58, 204–9, 212–13, 300, 408
Larkin, Philip, 131–2, 149–50, 261–2, 272, 362
Larousse Gastronomique, 3
Last Orders (Carson), 532
Lawrence, D. H., 157–61, 532–5
Letters and Journals (Byron), 105–6
Life of Burns (Currie), 110–12
Life of John Berryman, The (Haffenden), 462–4
Life of Johnson (Boswell), 31, 315, 443, 479–81, 491
Light in August (Faulkner), 522–3
Lily of St Pierre, The (Runyon), 525
liqueurs, 28–30
Little Song (Brecht), 487
Lochhead, Liz, 353–5
Logue, Christopher, 235
London, Jack, 93, 171–7
Looking for a Bluebird (Wechsberg), 238–9

Lost Weekend, The (Jackson), 460–61
lovemaking, 351–3, 370–1
Lowell, Robert, 139–40, 151–2, 154
Lowry, Malcolm, 32–3, 447–8
Lucky Jim (K. Amis), 326–8, 390, 423–5

Macbeth (Shakespeare), 314
MacCaig, Norman, 118–19, 135
McCarthy, Mary, 526–7
McCullers, Carson, 527
MacDiarmid, Hugh, 115–18
MacNeice, Louis, 99, 286, 477
Mahon, Derek, 132–3, 230–31
Making Cocoa for Kingsley Amis (Cope), 66–7
Mendelstam, Osip, 5
Mann, Thomas, 13–14
marc-brandy, 29
Marquis, Don, 209–12
Martin Chuzzlewit (Dickens), 82–3, 341–7
Martini, 26
mastic, 29
mavrodaphne, 11
mead, 122, 259
Melly, George, 109
Melville, Herman, 28
Memories of a Catholic Girlhood (McCarthy), 526–7
Memoirs of Queen Caroline (Hibbert) 236–8
memory blackouts, 470
'Merrymaking in Question, A' (Hardy), 259
'mild', 192, 208
Miles, Barry, 531
Miller, Henry, 11–12, 93–4, 333–4, 364–6
Milligan, Spike, 246–8
Milton, John, 41–2, 275–6, 428, 486–7
Miracle (Carver), 431–4
Misérables, Les (Hugo), 334
Misfortunes of Elphin, The (Peacock), 58
Money (M. Amis), 86–7, 355–6, 394–5, 448
moonshine, 517, 526–7
Morrison, Blake, 19–20
My Papa's Waltz (Roethke), 157
Mythologies (Barthes), 6–9

Ness, Eliot, 521–2
New Inn, The (Jonson), 204–6
New Statesman, 488
Night Club (MacNeice), 286
Nineteen Eighty-Four (Orwell), 3–4
Nineties (Jenkins), 136
Nuits-St-Georges, 10

O'Brien, Flann, 75–9, 363–4
Odoreida Iceberg, 26n
Odyssey, The (Homer), 313, 403–4, 425–7
O'Hara, John, 536–8
On the Need of Drinking (Anacreon paraphrased by Cotton), 50
'On the Pleasures of Drink' (Brecht), 70–1
One-Upmanship (Potter), 25–6
O'Neill (Gelb), 464
orgies, 259
O'Rorke, P. J., 223–4
Orwell, George, 3–4, 192–7
Othello (Shakespeare), 102–4, 435–6
Other People (M, Amis), 108
Outing: A Story, The (Thomas), 163–71

paralysis, 524
Parker, Dorothy, 65, 404–7
Part of a Long Story (Boulton), 464–8
parties, 105, 251–72, 291–9
Party Politics (Larkin), 272
Passing the Wine Seller's (Wang Chi), 75
Peacock, Thomas Love, 58, 113–15
Pepys, Samuel, 100–102, 449
Pernod, 119, 120
Petronius, 57–8, 253–5
Philips, John, 24
Pickering, Fergus, 51, 136–7
Pickwick Papers, The (Dickens), 359–61, 495–501

Pierpoint, Rev. John, 494–5
piot, 42
plonk, 7
Polish Bison, 417
Polo, Marco, 122
pomagne, 19–20
Pop-skull, 26
Pope, Alexander, 104–5, 201
port, 4, 200, 326, 359, 360, 448, 450, 491
porter, 75–8, 240, 497
Portrait of Elizabeth Taylor (Capote), 15–16
Pound, Ezra, 37–41, 389–90, 540
Power and the Glory, The (Greene), 91–3
Prinz, Johannes, 212–13
Problems (Aristotle), 314–15, 326
Prohibition, 22, 512–18, 523, 524
Proverbs, 441
Pslams, 428
Pub and the People, The (Mass Observation), 192–4
pubs, 191–2, 192–4, 194–7
Puckoon (Milligan), 246–8
punch, 3, 130, 328, 341
Punch, 27
Pynchon, Thomas, 289–90

Queen Victoria's Tipple, 5

Rabbi Ben Ezra (Browning), 63–4
Rabelais, François, 42, 58–60, 244–5
Rae, Simon, 198–9
Rainbow, The (Lawrence), 532–5
Raine, Craig, 356–8
Ratushinskaya, Irina, 511–12
Reading, Peter, 471, 473
Recovery (Berryman), 460
Reeve's Tale, The (Chaucer), 371–7
Rhys, Jean, 119–21, 455
Right Ho, Jeeves (Wodehouse), 334–41
Roach of the Taverns, A (Marquis), 209–12
Roethke, Theodore, 157
Rolling English Road, The (Chesterton), 48–9
Room at the Top (Braine), 539
Rubáiyát, The (E. Fitzgerald), 60–3
rum, 26, 29, 67, 109, 130, 146, 257, 258, 259, 269, 278, 279, 280, 282, 358, 518, 519
Runyon, Damon, 525

sack, 101, 138, 206, 318
St John's Gospel, 236
Samson Agonistes (Milton), 428
Sassoon, Siegfried, 145–6
Saturday Night and Sunday Morning (Sillitoe), 366–7
Satyricon, The (Petronius), 57–8, 253–5
School for Scandal, The (Sheridan), 79–82
'Scholar-Gipsy, The' (Arnold), 185–6
schnapps, 70
Schopenauer, Artur, 154
Scotch *see* whisky
Select Party, The (Ewart), 271
Shakespeare, William, 12–13, 99–100, 102–4, 138–9, 314, 316–20, 435–6, 477–8
Sheridan, Richard Brinsley, 79–82
sherris-sack, 12–13
sherry, 26, 109, 206, 261, 326, 448
Shostakovitch, Dmitri, 133–4
Sillitoe, Alan, 366–7
Simmons, James, 129
Skip, The (Fenton), 407–9
Smuggler's Song, A (Kipling), 509–10
smuggling, 506–12
sociability, 479–81
Song Lines, The (Chatwin), 143–4
Sonnet: The Last Things (Ewart), 538
Sonnet for Dick (Wright), 531
Sons and Lovers (Lawrence), 157–61
Spectator, 71
States of Desire: Travels in Gay America (White), 229–30
Steinbeck, John, 290–99
Stephano Remembers (Simmons), 129
Sterne, Laurence, 123
stingo, 68
stout, 67, 78, 195, 196, 197, 288, 355, 363, 497

Strings Are False, The (MacNeice), 477
Suspenders (Carver), 162–3
'Sussex Drinking Song, A' (Belloc), 65–6
Swift, Graham, 299–305

talkativeness, 328–35
Task, The (Cowper), 485–6, 491
teetotalism, 5
temperance, 491–501
Temperance Handbook, The, 30, 94–5, 106–7, 493–5
Tempest, The (Shakespeare), 316–20
Tenant of Wildfell Hall, The (A. Brontë), 177–8
Tender is the Night (F. Scott Fitzgerald), 525–6
'Terence, This is Stupid Stuff' (Housman), 52–4
Thirsty Muse, The (Dardis), xix, 137
Thomas, Dylan, 163–71, 260–61
Thomas, Edward, 50–51, 191
Thomas, Jerry, 32
Thread of Gold Cordial Flowed from the Bottle, The (Mandelstam), 5
Thurber, James, 410–12
Time of Gifts, A (Fermor), 124–8
Times, The, 109
tiplage, 42
TLS (Berryman) 413
To a Nightingale (Keats), 54–6
To Delmore Schwartz (Lowell), 151–2
'To Speak of Woe, That Is in Marriage' (Lowell), 154
Tolstoy, Leo, 277–82
Tom Jones (Fielding), 316, 351–3
Tom Thumb (Fielding), 129–30
Tour of the Western Isles and Hebrides, A (Boswell), 109–10, 392–3
Towards the End of the Morning (Frayn), 395–403
Trampwoman's Tragedy, A (Hardy), 186–9
'Trappist Silence Broken in Shoot-Out as Monks Defend Monastery Wine' (*Guardian*), 427–8
Travels, The (Polo), 122
Tristram Shandy (Sterne), 123
Tropic of Cancer (Miller), 93–4, 333–4, 364–6
Twelfth Night (Shakespeare), 99–100, 477–8
Two Young Men, 23 to 24 Years Old (Cavafy), 224–5

Ulysses (Joyce), 377–81
Under-Age Drinking at the Adelphi Hotel in Edinburgh – 1963 (Whitworth), 131
Under the Volcano (Lowry), 32–3, 447–8
Underburg, 417
Untouchables, The (Ness), 521–2
Updike, John, 262–71
Upon his Drinking a Bowl (Wilmot), 47–8

vermouth, 23, 26
Vers de Société (Larkin), 261–2
vespetro, 29
'Village Inn, The' (Betjeman), 202–4
Violins of Saint-Jacques, The (Fermor), 256–8
vodka, 284, 417, 511

Waggoner, The (Wordsworth), 491–2
wakes, 246–8
Walk on the Wild Side, A (Algren), 87–91, 443–4
Walking to Inveruplan (MacCaig), 135
Wang Chi, 75
War and Peace (Tolstoy), 277–82
War Music (Logue), 235
Wasps, The (Aristophanes), 251–3
Waterland (Swift), 299–305
Waugh, Evelyn, 4, 9–10, 259, 359, 361–2
Wechsberg, Joseph, 238–9
weddings, 236–8
Wells, H. G., 190
What's Yours? (Clarke), 191–2
whisky, 29, 97, 118, 135, 136, 153, 154, 157, 192, 247, 286–8, 291–4, 296, 297, 340, 354, 412, 432, 433,

443, 447, 463, 464, 470, 536, 537
  and alcoholism, 488
  in Blue Blazer, 32
  and dehydration, 162
  lethal effect of, 30, 51
  for preserving bodies, 30
  price of, 488, 516–17
  and Prohibition, 513, 515, 516–17, 520, 522, 523
  and soda, 337
  taste of, 336
  and vermouth, 23
White, Edmund, 229–30
Whitworth, John, 131
Willie Brew'd a Peck O'Maut (Burns), 134–5
Wilmot, John, Earl of Rochester, 47–8
wine, 3–4, 41, 42–3, 80, 114, 315, 325, 326, 334, 428–9, 430, 441, 479–80
  black, 11
  Bordeaux, 359
  communion, 91–3, 235
  Falernian, 57
  Florence, 31
  mythology of, 6–9
  Pramnian, 403
  red, 3, 5, 171, 173
  spirits of, 107
  tasting, 9–10
  white, 266
Wine (Carver), 428–9
Wine in Peace and War (Waugh), 4
winos/alcoholics, 470–3
Wodehouse, P. G., 334–41, 418–19
Wordsworth, William, 491–2
Work, Henry Clay, 178–9
'World's Temperance Reciter, The' (*Punch*), 27
Wright, Kirk, 531

Yeats, William Butler, 47, 56–7

Zola, Emile, 535–6